Published in 1988 by
The Hamlyn Publishing Group Limited
Michelin House, 81 Fulham Road, London SW3 6RB

ISBN 0 600 55759 6

Typeset by Vision Typesetting, Manchester
Printed in Yugoslavia

Material in this book previously appeared in 1000 *Great Events*
published by The Hamlyn Publishing Group Limited.

1,000 GREAT EVENTS

Through the Ages

Brenda Ralph Lewis

Philip Steele

Lynne Williams

HAMLYN

Introduction

This book describes one thousand of the greatest events that have occurred in the history of civilization. Some of them are great advances in the history of man – great medical or scientific discoveries for example. Others are disasters caused by man's inhumanity to man – such as the Thirty Years' War, or the dropping of the atom bomb – not 'great' but unfortunately important historical events.

Many of the events in this book are cultural milestones, famous books or paintings. And many events may not seem important to you at all: popular music or social customs may not seem as significant as revolutions and wars, but they nevertheless affect everyday life.

This book covers the last seven thousand years of the world's history. This seems like a long time, but it is quite brief compared with the four million years or so that man has walked the earth. Yet man himself is a real newcomer on the earth, although he has had more impact on his surroundings than any other creature.

The origins of the earth

It is estimated that our planet was born as much as *4,500 million* years ago. It has often been stated in the past that the world began as a hot, fiery ball. This is no longer thought to be true. A modern idea suggests that the earth and its satellite, the moon, were formed by the cold accumulation and compaction of gas and dust particles in space. As the earth compacted, enough heat was generated to start certain materials breaking down. These materials, known as radioactive elements, released even more heat. The earth now seems to be cooling down again but at the centre of the planet today the temperature is still estimated to be as much as $2,700°C$. You can get some idea of just how hot this is by remembering that water boils at a mere $100°C$.

Life begins on earth

It is all too easy to take for granted the variety of living creatures, including ourselves, that the earth supports. We should remember, however, that so far as is known at present, earth is the only planet in the solar system to support such a complicated living web of animals and plants and that it took a very long time for the first primitive life to develop.

In fact, it was about 1,300 million years after the birth of the earth before the first, tiny, simple, algae-like plants evolved. Before this time, there existed complicated chemical substances and it was not until these were able to reproduce themselves that they could be considered as living things. Traces of these first living forms can be found fossilized in rocks 3,200 million years old in southern Africa.

It was not until 600 million years ago, at the beginning of a period in the earth's long history that we call the Cambrian, that there seems to have been a sudden upsurge in the variety and numbers of animals and plants, although life was still mainly represented by two groups of sea animals – trilobites and brachiopods. Trilobites are now extinct but they were related to insects and spiders. Brachiopods are similar in appearance to cockles, although they are not related, and there are still members of this group alive today.

There were no vertebrates (animals with backbones) alive at this time. It took yet another 100 million years before the first fishes appeared in Ordovician times, and a further 100 million years before they became well established in the Devonian period. At this time too the land began to be colonized by the first primitive pond plants, which could in turn support animals similar to our modern spiders, centipedes and snails.

From water to land

There were two types of Devonian bony fishes, characterized by having either *ray fins* or *lobe fins*. Those with lobe fins, the lung fishes, were able to support their body weight on land and breathe air, so that they were able to withstand periods when the lakes dried out during the desert conditions of the Devonian. These became the amphibians. There are amphibians alive today, such as frogs. Amphibians have never been common and they are perhaps more important as the first stage of a line of evolution which ends in the world's most advanced creature – man.

The age of the dinosaurs

You will have realized that the last 600 million years are divided into periods which are characterized by the appearance of certain life forms; we have already looked at the first few. From the amphibians, reptiles evolved in Carboniferous times some 300 million years ago; in the next period, Permian, they became very important.

Then, between 230 and 180 million years ago a group of creatures evolved to dominate the earth, the dinosaurs, including some of the most formidable flesh-eating creatures the world has known, such as the terrible *Tyrannosaurus rex*.

Evolutionary changes in time led to the development of the warm-blooded birds from reptiles with the appearance of *Archaeopteryx* in late Jurassic times, about 150 million years ago, although the first mammals had already evolved by then. Mammals did not begin to occupy the important place they now hold until the extinction of the dinosaurs made room for them.

The origins of man

The early mammals evolved to more advanced forms. Most remarkable of all the mammals were the primates. One branch of primates, the ancestors of modern apes such as the chimpanzee, took to the trees. The other, living in open country, took to the ground and evolved human characteristics – they walked upright, could use their hands with precision, and they developed their brains.

The earliest member of the human family, *Ramapithecus*, lived some fourteen million years ago, but not until five to two million years ago did a more humanlike primate appear – *Australopithecus*. *Homo erectus*, who lived in China and Java about one to half a million years ago, mastered the use of fire: humans had emerged as unique creatures. Gradually man's tools and weapons became more sophisticated, as his brain became superior. Neanderthal man, a direct ancestor of modern man, lived in Europe about 70,000 to 40,000 years ago. The first modern human, known as Cro-Magnon man, made his appearance in Europe some 35,000 years ago.

Subsequently, human beings migrated all over the earth's surface, even to the frozen regions of the North near the Arctic Circle. Wherever they went, they found different types of climate and different terrain. Over many centuries, people adapted and changed to suit their surroundings so that different races of humans arose. Where the sun shone fiercely, as in Africa or India, their skins became black or brown to protect them from the harmful rays. In lands like central Asia or China, where icy winds may blow in winter, people gradually acquired protection for their eyes in the form of an extra fold of skin on their eyelids.

The birth of civilization

From about 1 million to 10,000 years ago, large parts of the earth were periodically covered with ice. When these Ice Ages were finally over, and the Northern Hemisphere became warmer, people began to settle down and live as farmers. This was in about 7000 BC. The agricultural societies that grew up in the fertile valleys of the Middle East about 4000 BC formed the basis of modern civilization. However, we shall commence our look at the events that have shaped human history some 14,000 years before the birth of civilization.

Early cave paintings tell us much about primitive man.

c. 18000 BC
From Asia into America

About 20,000 years ago, Asians from China and Siberia began to move eastwards across the Bering Strait, and so entered another continent: America. The Bering Strait is now a waterway, but two hundred centuries ago, a land bridge existed there. America, as far as anyone knows, had no original human inhabitants. Gradually, over many thousands of years, the newcomers from Asia spread all over North, Central and South America and became the bronzed or 'red'-skinned people we know as American Indians.

c. 8000 BC
The Aborigines reach Australia

Until 1788, when the first fleet of British ships arrived bringing convicts to settle in Australia, this huge island continent was inhabited only by Aborigines. The Aborigines, it is believed, had been in Australia for many thousands of years. The first arrivals probably reached Australia in about 8000 BC, either by way of the Sahul shelf, a part of the Malay archipelago which is now submerged, or by sea in primitive skin canoes or on rafts.

c. 5000 BC
The Melanesians in Malaya

Whilst civilization as we know it was being born in the Nile Valley and the Middle East, the rest of the world was peopled by more primitive tribes. It was around 5000 BC that the people of Australia, Polynesia and New Guinea, of the Australo-Melanesoid racial type, moved westward into Malaysia, where small groups of this origin are still to be found.

c. 4000 BC
Civilization in Sumer

In prehistoric times, people followed herds of animals and hunted them for food, and also gathered fruits, berries and other plants from the lands through which they passed. They had no permanent homes. Settling down and living in one place became possible only with farming and keeping animals, like cattle and sheep. When this happened, settled 'civilizations' arose. Almost always, they were near rivers which could provide the water which all life needs. Probably the first civilization was at Sumer, which lay in a broad, fertile valley between the Rivers Tigris and Euphrates. The area on which it was built was later given the name of Mesopotamia, 'the land between the two rivers' (now Iraq). The name in time applied to the whole length of the valley in which other early civilizations were also destined to settle.

The Sumerians built huts, clustered together to form villages, domesticated animals to give milk and meat and skins for clothing, and grew wheat, barley and other crops. They still hunted, but now, for the first time, they no longer relied on hunting to keep alive. So they were able to live in one place without being forced into a nomadic life, like all others before them.

The Sumerians invented the first written language: a form of abbreviated picture language called cuneiform (or wedge-shaped), written with reed pens on soft clay which was later baked. The invention of the wheel is also attributed to the Sumerians who must have been a most industrious and inventive people.

The Sumerians worked hard farming their land and building villages.

c. 3500 BC
The discovery of copper and bronze

The first important material which people used for tools, weapons and other implements was stone, which is why the earlier prehistory of human beings is known as the Stone Age. Then, in about 3500 BC, people discovered how to use metals. They did not discard stone, of course, however, metals enabled them to make better, sharper implements and also beautiful objects and adornments.

The first metal people used was copper. This was purified by smelting lumps of the copper ore (rock containing copper) on the hot stones that were used for cooking.

In many places, copper ore and tin occur in the same veins and it is believed that, through accident, the early smelters discovered the harder, better metal created by mixing or alloying copper and tin: this alloy was bronze. In bronze, nine parts of copper are normally used to one part of tin.

Weapons and implements of bronze have been found in Ancient Egyptian tombs of 2500 BC but it is also known that bronze was used by prehistoric people at least 1,000 years before that. The discovery of bronze marked a great step forward in human progress.

The first objects made from this alloy were cast in open moulds. The shape of the object was chipped from the surface of the flat stone, then the heated metal was poured into it and covered with a clay cap to slow down cooling.

c. 3100 BC
The gift of the Nile

Egypt is the 'gift of the Nile' wrote Herodotus, an ancient Greek historian, for without this river the country would not have come into being. Then, as now, the plains on either side of the Nile were flooded each year and the black, fertile soil that was left was ideal for crops that quickly ripened beneath the blazing sun.

The first people to settle in the Nile Valley were primitive people who, in time, learned how to build huts, grow crops and domesticate cattle. Their settlements stretched along the Nile's banks for some 1,200 kilometres, yet were rarely found more than fifty kilometres from the water's edge. The rest of the country was then, as now, a desert of sand and stone.

From the earliest times, the land was divided into two parts – Lower Egypt (the Delta area) and Upper Egypt (between the Delta and the Cataracts). About 3200 BC these were united and ruled by Pharaohs, to become a brilliant civilization that lasted until the death of Cleopatra in 30 BC, when Egypt became a Roman province.

The Egyptians were a nation of artists. They made jars of clay, decorating them with beautiful, brightly coloured designs; they created fine sculpture from stone but, above all, they knew how to *build*. It is from the massive remains of their temples and their tombs, the walls of which are still decorated with scenes of their everyday life, that we are able to know how they lived, worshipped and died.

From the annual rising of the waters of the Nile evolved the first 'calendar' of 365 days, which consisted of twelve months of thirty days with five holidays over.

c. 3000-2000 BC
The rise of Minoan civilization

In prehistoric times, people sailed across the Aegean Sea in primitive craft and settled along its shores. In time, they spread southwards through Greece into Macedonia. Their chief settlement was on the Greek island of Crete.

At first they lived in caves but soon found out how to build, first huts and then rectangular buildings with flat roofs and with doorways that always faced east so that the inhabitants woke up to the first rays of the sun. These were the early Cretans, and they were fine craftsmen, for remains of their pottery, sculpture, metalwork and jewellery prove them to be far superior to other nations of the time. This was mainly due to the fact that, for centuries, they were secure from invasion thanks to a powerful fleet, and their artists and artisans were left free to develop all the arts and amenities of life.

Their king was called Minos – as the kings of Egypt were always called Pharaoh – and in time the people of the island became known as Minoans. The supremacy of their sea power dates from 2000 BC when they began to open up the trade route from Crete to the Middle East (*see c. 1700–1400 BC The building of Knossos*).

An archaeologist working on the site of ancient Troy.

c. 2870 BC
The settlement of Troy

For centuries, Homer's *Iliad* (written about 850 BC) was believed to be merely an imaginative poem. Even Troy, and its ten-year siege by the Greeks, was thought to be legendary.

One man who believed the story implicitly, however, was a German, Heinrich Schliemann (1822–90), who spent the latter part of his life and much of his considerable fortune, in seeking the site of Homer's Troy. He began his work at Hissarlik, at the southern end of the Dardanelles, where an old mound looked very promising. Almost immediately he found pottery, weapons and other articles and then went on to uncover temples and palaces.

Altogether he found *nine* cities, one on top of the next, the earliest, at the bottom of course, dating from about 2870 BC and marking the site of the first neolithic settlers.

c. 2700-2600 BC
The building of the Pyramids

Standing like great sentinels in the desert, the three great pyramids of Gizeh are among the very few relics of ancient times which we can still see today. The Gizeh pyramids, like others elsewhere in Ancient Egypt, were the tombs of Pharoahs and their wives and other important people. The largest pyramid at Gizeh is the Great Pyramid, built to house the mummy (embalmed body) of the Pharoah Khufu, better known as Cheops. It is the only one of the original seven wonders of the world that still exists. It was

built of limestone and granite, more than two million blocks of stone being used, some of which weigh fifteen tonnes.

Each side of its base is 230 metres long, its height 138 metres. It is said that one hundred thousand slaves toiled for twenty years to build this mighty monument to a dead king, but they only worked for three months at a time, the annual three-month period when the Nile flooded its banks.

The granite was brought from Aswan, being floated about 900 kilometres down-river to a specially built wharf at Gizeh. It was then dragged up giant causeways, and fitted into place. The other two pyramids, those of Chephren and Mycerinus, like Khufu, kings of the 4th Dynasty, whilst not so large, were built in a similar fashion.

c. 2500 BC
The building of Mohenjo-daro

As with the Sumerian nation which developed between the Tigris and the Euphrates, and Egypt which originated in the Nile valley, the third oldest civilization also developed beside a river. This was the great state which grew up in the Indus river basin. Its capital, built about 2500 BC, was the amazing Indian city of Mohenjo-daro, constructed almost entirely of bricks made from sun-dried mud and clay, held together by mortar.

For its time it was far in advance of any other city. It was built to a plan obviously drawn up at

A bearded god from Mohenjo-daro.

its foundation, for the streets, laid out in rectangular blocks, were similar to those of a modern American city. It covered an area of some ten square kilometres and housed up to 50,000 people, a vast number for those days.

Indeed, the more one examines Mohenjo-daro, the more modern it appears; a sophisticated drainage and sewerage system existed beneath the streets and in many houses, revealing a high standard of private and public sanitation.

c. 2400 BC
The Aryan migrations

It is believed that in the Neolithic age, northern Europe had one original language from which most of the modern European languages have derived, and that between Central Europe and Western Asia were tribes which used only one. For convenience they have been named the Aryan peoples and their language, the Aryan tongue. These tribes originally came from the region of the Danube and South Russia and slowly spread southwards to warmer climes.

Originally, most of the countries of Europe had been peopled by a race known as the Iberians which had spread from the Mediterranean. They were dark and rather short and were soon pushed back by the advancing waves of the tall and fair Aryans who moved through central and southern Europe and thence into India leaving many settlements in their wake.

c. 2400-2183 BC
Sargon destroys Sumer

When the palaces and temples of Sumer rose from the flat but fertile Euphrates–Tigris valley, it was inevitable that many of her neighbours looked with envy at the riches of the country. Over the years, in consequence, border raids became commonplace.

To the west of Sumer lived several tribes of Semitic nomads and about the middle of the third millennium BC, these fierce tribes united under a great leader, Sargon. His first achievement was to crush the Sumerians. He then went on to conquer all the lands 'from the rising to the setting of the sun', thus creating the first empire in history. His people were known as Akkadians,

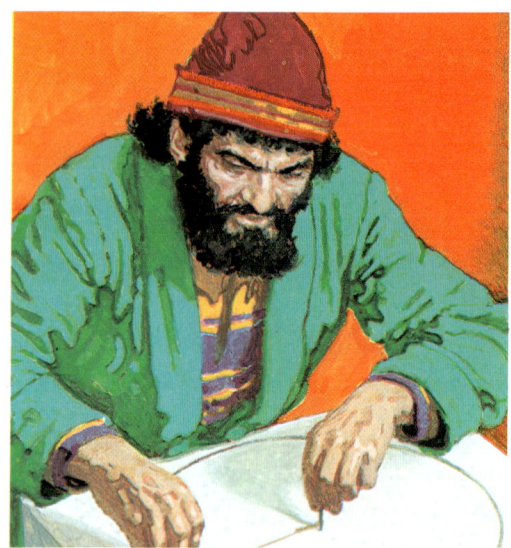

The Babylonians used their knowledge of mathematics and geometry in their study of the stars.

a name they took from the district of Akkad (or Agade) in the northern part of the Plain of Shinar, which in time was to include the cities of Babylon, Kish, Sippar and others.

c. 2350 BC
The first astronomical observatories

The ancient peoples – the Babylonians, Egyptians and Chinese, all believed that the heavenly bodies influenced the lives of men. The Babylonians, particularly, thought that the position of the stars represented messages from the gods and their priests spent much of their lives studying the firmament with great care. They divided the heavens into regions and the various groups of stars into constellations, naming them after gods or objects. These were later renamed by the ancient Greeks, to give us the twelve signs of the Zodiac.

In time they became very familiar with everything that was visible in the night sky, predicting what was to happen in the future. From this science came astrology, and the priest-diviners, after carefully observing the stars, would perform religious rites to ward off evil influences. To enable them to do this work, observatories were built upon the flat roofs of their temples.

c. 2205-1122 BC

The start of Chinese civilization

Civilization came to China when a number of Stone Age villages were built along the banks of the Hwang Ho. Little is known about these primitive people.

The first great dynasty in China is known as the Hsai dynasty and was created by the legendary Emperor Yü in the twenty-third century BC. Like the Pharaohs of ancient Egypt, he and the monarchs that followed were considered divine, and were given the title, 'Sons of Heaven'.

The Hsai dynasty gave way to that of the Shang which was led by their Bronze Age King T'ang, usually regarded as the first emperor of all China, who raised an army to overthrow the last of the Hsai kings, a tyrant. T'ang's dynasty began the Middle Kingdom era which lasted from about 1500 BC for some five hundred years. During this period, the country enjoyed organized government, the arts and trade flourished, and China was at peace.

During the Shang dynasty, bronze utensils were made which are considered to be amongst the finest the world has ever seen. Writing, based on pictures, also appeared in China at this time. Silk made from the world's first domesticated silkworms was to give China the monopoly of growth and manufacture which it held for thousands of years. Lacquer was also discovered during this rewarding period. The Chinese used it for the preservation and decoration of articles of wood and leather, whilst their carving of jade, known as early as 2000 BC, was the envy of the world.

A Chinese nobleman is escorted home while farmers work his fields.

c. 2200 BC
Indonesians in Malaya

The many islands of Indonesia were originally colonized by primitive peoples who came from the mainland of south-east Asia. In time, some of them decided to move on, and paddling their double-hulled canoes, they reached Malaya to become the ancestors of the Orang Malayu, the dominant race peopling the Malayan peninsula today.

c. 2100 BC
The building of Ur

At that point where the Tigris came closest to the Euphrates, a city was built called Ur, which became the capital of the Sumerians. Although the original people of Ur had been farmers, a

The head-dress of a Sumerian queen and the sculpture of a ram in a thicket, both discovered at Ur.

new generation of builders, artists, priests and scribes arose who brought true civilization to the city.

The Sumerians used the cuneiform system of writing and were skilled mathematicians. They counted in tens and, curiously, also in sixties; a fact which has resulted in a circle having 360 degrees, the hour sixty minutes and the minute sixty seconds.

A magnificent ziggurat (literally translated as 'mountain top') was discovered at Ur. This building had 'stepped' sides, like a series of blocks placed one upon the other and joined by stairs. Originally the temple of the moon-god, Su'en, it measured more than 200 metres at the base.

c. 2000-1200 BC
The first use of iron

What is now called the Iron Age began at the time of the Hittites, a fierce nation of Aryans who had conquered the Anatolian peninsula. United under their king, Labarnas, the Hittites began to extend their frontiers in all directions – to the Aegean Sea in the west, and eastwards and southwards to the plains of Syria, south of the Taurus Mountains.

They proved invincible because, before any other nation, they had discovered the art of refining iron ore. They first heated the ore until it became a paste-like mass then, as it cooled, they hammered it into the desired shape, whether weapon or implement. Their method was crude and the iron far from pure, but it was infinitely superior to bronze which was far 'softer' and had a tendency to bend.

The power of the Hittites grew, but was disturbed by internal troubles until King Telepinus (c. 1525–1500 BC) made the succession to the crown hereditary and founded what was, in fact, the true Hittite empire. The Hittites defeated a strong Egyptian army under their hero King Rameses II (reigned 1292–1225 BC) in 1286 BC, and although their own empire was to disappear some fifty years later, in the Syrian provinces their culture persisted for another five hundred years.

c. 2000 BC
The rise of Babylon

For centuries the fertile valley between the

The power of the Hittites grew as they developed the art of refining iron ore.

Tigris and the Euphrates had been under the control of the Sumerians. They finally grew weak with time, however, and were defeated by invading Semites who founded a nation of city-states. These city-states were constantly at war with each other until a king ascended the throne of a hitherto unimportant city called Babylon.

This new king, Hammurabi, was determined to bring the land back to the peace it had originally enjoyed under the Sumerians. He raised a standing army – the world's first – and proceeded to attack and destroy the other rival cities one by one. In time he had made himself master of the whole of Mesopotamia and of Assyria, an area which, taking its name from his own city, was then known as Babylonia.

With peace restored, Hammurabi began to build new temples, strengthen city walls and construct vast irrigation works. It is as a law-giver that he is most remembered, however, and for centuries other nations used the Law Code he developed. Also, copies of many of his letters (written on tablets of baked clay) have been found in the ruins of vast libraries which he had built.

c. 2000 BC

The Bronze Age reaches Europe

Round about 2000 BC Britain and her near European neighbours were subjected to an invasion that was to change their whole way of life. It came from the strange tribes known to anthropologists as the 'Beaker' folk, early metal-smiths who knew how to produce weapons and implements in copper – and the metal drinking vessels after which they have been named. As they moved, so they took the secret of this new craft with them. By 1800 BC they had spread across Europe and with their superior weapons easily overcame the primitive peoples of the Stone Age whom they met. They then began to intermarry with those they had conquered and a new form of civilization came to Europe.

Almost all southern Britain was taken over by them and the unique monuments that they erected such as Stonehenge, Silbury and Maiden Castle, date from this time. The most imposing is Stonehenge, described as 'northern Europe's first architecture', which stands today as a unique monument to the industrious builders of some four thousand years ago. Its most remarkable feature concerns the transport involved in getting the great stones to their final resting place. As the wheel had not then come to Britain, rollers, sledges – and a great deal of man-power – must have been used.

c. 2000 BC
The Jomons settle Japan

The first truly civilized people of Japan were the Jomons, originally a group of hunters who invaded the country and settled in the hinterland. Later Jomons, coming from China and Korea, settled in the lowland areas where they developed into a nation of farmers. They were also skilled potters, many fine examples of their work having been found.

c. 1900 BC
Abraham leaves Ur

Mentioned in the Bible as Ur of the Chaldees (*Genesis 11, v. 31*), this city had been home of the great Hebrew leader Abraham before he and his family left the city on the long journey to Canaan.

Patient excavation of Ur, begun in 1923, revealed that it had been a city of large, two-storied villas, many with up to fourteen rooms, including lavatories, with the walls plastered and white-washed.

Such discoveries made many people change their minds about Abraham's boyhood – there was no rough living in tents for *him*, at least, not until he was an adult and wandering in the desert.

Abraham and his followers eventually settled in Hebron, a part of Lower Canaan, mixing with earlier Semitic settlers from Mesopotamia. Abraham became regarded as the first Patriarch, the father of the Jewish people.

c. 1750-1560 BC
The Hyksos invade Egypt

After nearly one and a half thousand years, Egypt was facing a grave threat to its existence. The power of the Pharaohs had diminished and the whole country was in a state of chaos. The Nubians, the Thebans and the Libyans had all attempted to invade but, with difficulty, had been driven off. Then, at the close of what is called the Fourteenth Dynasty, a fresh invasion completely overwhelmed the people of Egypt.

The newcomers were the Hyksos, or 'Shepherd Kings', fierce nomads who came raging out of the desert to carry fire and pillage through a helpless land. They brought with them a 'secret weapon' against which the Egyptians were

By about 2000 BC Bronze Age people had reached Europe, bringing with them their bronze tools and weapons.

The Hyksos armed with bows of horn and leather, invaded Egypt in horse-drawn chariots.

powerless – the horse-drawn chariot. They also brought a new weapon, the composite bow made of horn and leather and which had a far greater range than any known before.

During the period the Hyksos ruled Egypt, the children of Israel settled in the land, Joseph and other Semites attaining high position during this period of alien control. The Hyksos were expelled by the Pharaoh Ahmose whose reign began the New Kingdom, in 1560 BC.

_c._ 1700-1400 BC
The building of Knossos

Heinrich Schliemann, who discovered Troy, had hoped to search for the palace of King Minos which, according to ancient Greek writers, had been built on the island of Crete. He died before he was able to do so and the archaeologist who was responsible for unearthing this legendary building was an Englishman, Sir Arthur Evans (1851–1941).

He began to dig in 1900 and continued, almost without pause, until his death. By then his discoveries had amazed the world, for he unearthed Knossos, 'the oldest civilization in Europe'. The 'palace' of King Minos was actually a mass of buildings set around a square court-yard, but to no apparent plan, for there was sometimes a difference of several storeys between the ground-floors in one building, with its roof serving as a terrace to the house behind it.

This seemingly haphazard building resulted in a great warren of twisting passageways which may well have given rise to the legend of the Minotaur, a creature half-man, half-bull which, according to the legend, lived in a labyrinth in Crete. This bull formed an important part of Cretan worship and was symbolized by an axe with two blades (a _labrys_). From this word most probably came the word 'labyrinth' to describe the maze-like world of Knossos.

Young Cretans – girls as well as boys – performed a sport called bull-leaping, in which the performer grabbed hold of a charging bull's horns and somersaulted over its back. Many paintings at Knossos depict this danger-ous sport. Life at Knossos was civilized, and full of revelry and pleasure: Cretan art is lively and urbane.

Eventually the whole Minoan civilization was wiped out by a wave of barbarian invaders called Dorians, who burned the palace, as deep layers of ash and scorch marks on columns clearly show, although its final destruction may well have coincided with an earthquake which com-pleted its ruin.

c. 1500 BC
The Book of the Dead

The ancient Egyptians believed that when they died they had to appear before Osiris, god of the dead, to be judged, before being given the blessing of eternal happiness if they were worthy. To save having to learn the necessary formulae, the spells and texts were inscribed on papyrus. The Book of the Dead, as it was called, was buried with the mummy.

A ritual vessel (right) carved in the shape of the Minotaur, dated about 1500 BC, and (below) young Cretans bull-leaping.

c. 1500 BC
The *Rig-Veda*

The hymns of the *Rig-Veda*, the literature of ancient India, are purely religious in character but give a great deal of information about the life of the country during the second millennium BC.

There are 1,028 psalms addressed to various gods in the *Rig-Veda*, and as the first book of the Hindu scriptures, it is the oldest sacred scripture of a living religion.

c. 1500 BC
Rise of the Ganges civilization

During the second millennium BC, the Aryans had advanced as far as the Indian frontier. Faced with primitive, aboriginal inhabitants, they moved across the frontier and the struggle for possession of India began. The rudimentary civilizations soon gave way before the more advanced and vigorous Aryans, who moved onwards, reaching the Ganges and the Jumna rivers. This migration ended about 1500 BC.

During the next five hundred years these Aryan invaders developed strong monarchs who ruled over great tribes and vast kingdoms. This was not done without continual fighting, especially with the uncivilized aborigines who lived in the great Punjab plain, but also with the civilized and well organized Dravidians of India. Realizing that they were faced with an entirely different opposition, the Aryans changed their policy of usurpation to one of amalgamation.

c. 1500-1200 BC
The building of Mycenae

Mycenae was described by Homer as 'a strong-founded citadel rich in gold'. Knossos apart, it was the finest capital city of its time and truly 'golden'. It was built, in the first instance, as a small but heavily fortified citadel on the east coast of the Peloponnese, some six kilometres from the harbour of Nauplia.

A later dynasty enlarged the citadel, enclosing it within a strong fortress-wall. This wall contained the imposing Lion Gate, a magnificent gateway adorned above the lintel with a carving of heraldic lions flanking a sacred pillar.

Life in this Mycenean palace in the fifteenth and fourteenth centuries BC was an odd mixture of primitive simplicity and a luxury that was almost modern. Everything – buildings, furniture and clothing – was lavishly decorated in a riot of flowing forms; a design which also spilt on to the palace frescoes, where hunting, dancing and feasting scenes bring back the gay and active life of the times. These pictures show, however, that the men of Mycenae were quite different from those of Crete, being tall, bearded warriors whilst the Cretans were shorter, clean-shaven and far less aggressive.

The industrious Schliemann (see 2870 BC The settlement of Troy) excavated the royal tombs at Mycenae to find death-masks, vessels, rings, wine-cups, and necklaces, all elaborately worked in gold. It is believed that these treasures were actually the work of Minoan craftsmen who had settled in Mycenae.

The tombs were known as tholos or 'beehive' tombs because of their strange shape. Most of them had been shattered by time and raided by despoilers, although the largest, known as the Treasury of Atreus, still reveals something of its former splendour. It is a cupola of heavy masonry, some fifteen metres in diameter and with a door lintel that weighs more than forty tonnes.

c. 1362-1356 BC
The reign of Tutankhamun

A Pharaoh of Egypt, Amenhotep IV, was a great religious reformer and not only tried to stop the worship of the old gods of his country but moved the capital from Thebes to Tell el-Amarna. This naturally upset the priests and civil war seemed inevitable when, in 1362 BC he suddenly died. His young son-in-law Tutankhamun moved the royal residence back to Thebes and restored the old religion. Although not an important prince – he was only eighteen years old when he died – the grateful priests enriched his tomb with priceless treasures. His

tomb remained hidden for three thousand years (see 1922 Tutankhamun's tomb is discovered).

c. 1230 BC
The Exodus from Egypt

About 1750 BC many Hebrews settled in Egypt and were well treated, but when the Hyksos were driven out and Egyptian Pharaohs again ruled the country, they were forced into labour. As the Bible says: 'they made their lives bitter with hard bondage in mortar and in bricks'. As they toiled for their Egyptian masters their one thought was of escape, but they needed a leader.

In time the ideal man appeared – Moses, a desert-toughened young man. He led out a great army of Hebrew men, women and children and evading the Egyptian troops who were ordered to bring them back by, it is believed, Rameses III, took them to the land 'flowing with milk and honey' that their god, Jahweh (Jehovah) had promised them. It was a long migration, taking some forty years, but at last they reached the river Jordan.

During their wandering they became a tough, independent people who lived by the Torah, the Mosaic law. Led by Moses' successor Joshua, they crossed the Jordan and entered the land of Canaan where, for the most part, they were content to let their neighbours live in peace in the cities whilst they preferred the freedom of an agricultural, tribal life.

c. 1200 BC
The rise of Phoenician seapower

For centuries the Phoenicians had lived in towns along the Mediterranean seaboard although, for much of that time, they were ruled by the Pharaohs of Egypt. Round about 1200 BC, however, the Phoenician princes saw an opportunity to throw off this yoke and become fully independent, although they had to fight to remain so. The principal cities on the coast were Tyre and Sidon which became the home of the greatest seamen of antiquity.

They were far ahead of their time, building ships that sailed across the Mediterranean and through the Straits of Gibraltar. They navigated their ships by the Pole Star and the positions of the sun at dawn and sunset. Indeed, the continent of Europe gets its name from the Phoenician word for 'sunset'. They were business men also, and invented a time-saving style of writing. This travelled to Greece, then Rome and thence to the rest of Europe.

---

*c.*1200BC

Ancient American civilizations

For a very long time, the peoples who migrated into America from Asia lived by hunting and gathering food. Some went on doing so and were still hunter-gatherers as recently as the 19th century. Other tribes, however, created civilizations in America. The first, in about 1200 BC, was the Olmec civilization in Mexico, which is chiefly known for the massive head carvings of Olmec rulers which can still be seen today. Later, civilizations were founded by the Zapotecs, the Mayas, the Toltecs and the Aztecs (Mexica) in Mexico. In western South America, too, great civilizations arose in the Andes Mountains region. These included the Empires of Chavin, Tihuanaco and Chimu, and the most powerful of them all, the Inca Empire of Tahuan-tinsuyu which stretched nearly 5,000 kilometres from present-day Ecuador down to central Chile.

People living in these civilizations were mostly sun-worshippers and many of them, particularly the Aztecs of Mexico, used to sacrifice humans to the sun as part of their religion. However, the Aztecs, Mayas and Incas in particular were brilliant mathematicians and astronomers, as well as skilled craftsmen in gold and silver and the builders of magnificent cities.

---

c. 1193 BC
The destruction of Troy

Situated at the north-east corner of the Aegean Sea, stood the powerful city of Troy. It was very rich, for it levied a toll on all merchants travelling between Europe and Asia who preferred – as most of them did – to use the narrow sea-crossing near Troy itself (*see 2870 BC The settlement of Troy*).

Immensely thick walls surrounded the city, in some cases as much as six metres high and five metres thick: these, together with the bravery of the Trojan warriors, successfully resisted the

According to the Bible, Moses presented the Hebrews with the Ten Commandments which God had dictated to him. During their long migration, the Hebrews learned to live by the Mosaic law, the *Torah.*

---

armed forces of the entire Greek nation for many years.

How, then, had it fallen? Schliemann, digging patiently through the debris of ages to find nine towns, could only guess that on the lowest level was but a village, but each successive town became larger until a considerable city with a great gated wall and fine houses was unveiled. It had obviously suffered terribly from an earthquake but had been rebuilt in an even more ornate style. This was the city that had been destroyed by the Greeks, and although it was rebuilt on a far smaller scale, it disappeared about the fifth century BC.

---

c. 1122-249 BC
The Chou dynasty

The five-hundred-year-old Shang dynasty ended when the country was overrun by the fierce Chou people from the west. They inter-married with the former inhabitants of China and began a settled dynasty of another five centuries.

During that period they made several great advances in science.

The prototype of the astronomical observatory was erected by Wen Wang, founder of the Chou dynasty. Constant observation by his wise men led to the creation of the almanac and the establishment of the date of the New Year. They also kept careful records of eclipses of the sun and moon. During this period also, great advances were made in medicine, especially in the study of healing drugs, and in acupuncture.

The Chinese at this time were magnificent artists and the maps they produced for the captains of their sea-going junks were highly decorative as well as very practical. A number of excellent pieces of literature were also written during the Chou dynasty. Taoism came into being and a dictionary, regarded as the world's first, was also produced during this period of great scientific and cultural progress.

c. 1100 BC

Founding of the Assyrian empire

At the time when the kings of Ur ruled the 'land between the two rivers', one of its cities was Assur, home of a Semitic people called Assyrians. They spoke a dialect of the Akkadian language which was quite different from that of their Babylonian cousins of the south.

They were mainly merchants, trading in textiles and metals, sending great caravans of camels and asses across Mesopotamia until they reached their trading colony at Kanesh, hundreds of kilometres from Assur.

As the Assyrians relied for survival upon these trade routes, they always sent strong companies of armed soldiers on horseback to defend them against attack by desert tribesmen.

Sometimes these skirmishes developed into small-scale battles but, for the most part, the Assyrians were always victorious.

For a time their nation was governed by Hammurabi, King of Babylon and then by the powerful Hittites. When this empire collapsed about 1200 BC, the Assyrians resolved to make themselves independent. With their superior iron weapons and skill acquired from centuries of desert fighting, they soon proved themselves invincible. Led by their king, Tiglath-Pileser I, they stormed and captured Babylon and by 1100 BC controlled a vast empire.

c. 965 BC
The temple built at Jerusalem

Abraham left Ur about 1900 BC as one of a small group of Hebrews. Nine hundred years later, under King David, the Israelites had become rich and powerful, with an empire that stretched from the Euphrates to the frontiers of Egypt and down to the Red Sea. Its capital was at Jerusalem.

Preparations for the building of a temple were made by David and his son Solomon, and on the former's death, the building began. It was designed to house the Ark of the Covenant and other sacred objects which had been carried during the forty years of the Exodus. The Phoenician Hiram, King of Tyre, provided cedars of Lebanon for the building of the temple which in plan and adornment resembled those of Babylon. The Ark was brought into the inner chamber and placed between two great winged figures of gilded olivewood.

c. 813 BC
The founding of Carthage

With the passing years, the fame and riches of the Phoenicians grew (*see 1200 BC The rise of Phoenician seapower*). Their settlements, the largest of which were Tyre, Tripoli and Arvad on offshore islets, and Sidon on the mainland itself, hummed with continual activity. Their ships

A bust of Homer, the great Greek poet.

c. 850 BC
The works of Homer

Homer, an Asiatic Greek, is traditionally pictured as a blind old man, wandering from village to village, reciting his poems which were later written down. The two major works credited to him are the *Iliad*, which tells of the siege of Troy, and the *Odyssey* which relates the many adventures of Odysseus (Ulysses) on his voyage home from the Greek wars.

The ancient city of Carthage, near modern Tunis in North Africa, the centre of Phoenician trade and maritime power.

waited in these harbours whilst desert caravans arrived from Egypt, Babylon, Arabia and even China, bringing precious burdens of spices, incense, ivory and ebony, ready for shipment to almost every part of the known world, including West Africa and Britain.

In 813 BC the Phoenicians founded Carthage in North Africa, building it in a bay not far from modern Tunis. Legend tells of Queen Dido arriving at the site and being allowed by the local inhabitants to have as much land as could be covered by the hide of a bull. She cunningly ordered the hide to be cut into very small strips which surrounded a very large area on which she built the city. Its citadel was called Byrsa (from the Greek for 'bull's hide') and the city grew up around it.

In time Carthage, with its advantageous situation, became one of the largest and most powerful cities of the ancient world.

c. 776 BC
The first Olympic Games

The Olympic Games, which today are held every four years, were revived after a very long interval in 1896, more than two and a half millennia after the first. The original Games were held amid the mountains in the sacred city of Olympia in Greece, taking place every fifth year at the first full moon after the summer solstice. During the festival month of the Games, a truce was in operation throughout all Greece and no one, going as a competitor or spectator, was allowed to bear arms.

Olympia lay beneath the conical height of Kronos where the holy grove, or *altis*, soon became surrounded with temples, many containing exquisite works of art including Pheidias' statue of Zeus, which was to become one of the seven wonders of the ancient world. Near the *altis* was the stadium or foot race course, where 45,000 spectators could watch the events.

c. 753 BC

Rome is founded

About 1000 BC, a wave of invaders of Indo-European stock moved through the Alpine passes and occupied parts of central and southern Italy. They were mainly of four tribes — Sabines, Samnites, Umbrians and Latins.

The Latins settled in central Italy and built small villages for themselves. By 800 BC, when forty such villages existed, they resolved to build a city. They chose a site beside the river Tiber, a dismal, malaria-ridden swamp for the most part, and began to clear the area and drain the marshes.

As they worked they were under constant threat from their neighbours the Etruscans who were on the north side of the Tiber. Realizing that their enemies could cross the river only at one point, and that the gentle slope of the Palatine Hill overlooked this ford, they chose that as the site for their new city.

Two legends tell of its founding. One legend credits Aeneas, the Trojan warrior. The other and more popular one gives the credit to his descendants, twin brothers Romulus and Remus who were raised by a she-wolf.

The date fixed for the founding, the legend goes, was in April 753 BC and according to custom, brushwood fires were lit and every man leaped through the fire to cleanse himself of evil. Then, having harnessed a snow-white cow and bull, Romulus ploughed a furrow along the lines of the future walls. In those days such lines were held to be sacred and it was desecration to enter other than at the place left for the gates. But Remus, jealous of his brother, leaped over the furrow exclaiming, 'Shall such defences as these keep your city?' For his impiety he was struck down and Romulus commented, 'So let it happen to all who pass over my walls.'

Seven kings were to rule Rome until 509 BC when it became a republic.

c. 621 BC

The laws of Athens

During the seventh century BC Greece was going through a period of great unrest. A situation had arisen where the aristocracy treated the freemen as slaves. A kind of ruler called a 'tyrant' had also appeared and the freemen were even more oppressed.

To avoid civil war, it was decided to give the freemen of Athens a voice in the government similar to that which they had enjoyed in the days of their Achaean ancestors. A noble called Draco was asked to provide a set of laws that would protect the poor against the rich. He began work in 621 BC but when completed his Draconian Laws, although impartial, contained such harsh penalties that they were impossible to enforce.

Twenty-five years later a more humane man called Solon was appointed chief magistrate in Athens in the hope that he might be able to resolve the situation. He did this by a number of reforms which were to improve the lot of the freemen and peasants without affecting the prosperity of the nobles. In effect, by his treatment of the common people (the *demos*) he may claim to have introduced 'democracy' (rule by the people).

Everyday life in the streets of Athens.

c. 620 BC

Aesop writes the *Fables*

The Greek writer Aesop is said to have been a Phrygian slave owned by Iadmon of Aamos who, recognizing his genius, freed him. Aesop is remembered for his fables, although he never wrote them down in his lifetime. In them the

Aesop's fable *The Tortoise and the Hare.*

characters are nearly always animals. Stories such as *The Wolf in Sheep's Clothing* and *The Frogs Asking for a King* are all witty illustrations of a moral point.

c. 604 BC
Birth of Lao-Tse

The Chinese philosopher Lao-Tse was the first of the three great religious leaders of the East, the others being Confucius and Buddha. He taught that life had to be spent in searching for *Tao* (or 'the Way') which was the virtue of individuality, offering eternal life through the understanding of the secret processes of nature. His treatise the *Tao Teh King* was later to form the basis of the Taoist religion.

c. 600 BC
The teachings of Zoroaster

Zoroaster (or Zarathustra) was a great legislator and prophet of ancient Persia. We know little about his life. He saw life as a battle in which good and evil constantly struggle for mastery. Fire, the symbol of cleanliness, was an important part of the Zoroastrian form of worship which, however, received its death blow in the middle of the seventh century AD with the Moslem invasion.

c. 600 BC
The Celtic migrations

The Celts, whose name derives from the Greek term for all who lived in Northern Europe – *keltoi*, or savages – were a warlike Indo-European people who had settled in Western and Central Europe during the New Stone and Bronze Ages. Their civilization gradually developed, centred upon north-east France, south-west Germany and Bohemia.

Aggression from northern Germanic tribes forced them to migrate southward to Greece and Italy, and westward to western France and Spain. Successive waves of Celtic tribes brought the Iron Age to Britain, where their power was supreme until the Roman conquest in AD 43.

Celtic civilization in the British Isles, pushed ever westward by Anglo-Saxon and Norman invasions, survives today in Wales, Scotland, Ireland and the Isle of Man, and also in France, in Brittany. The modern Celtic languages fall into two main groups: 'Goidelic', including the Scots Gaelic and the Irish language, as well as Manx (the former language of the Isle of Man); and 'Brythonic', which includes Breton, Welsh and the now extinct Cornish language.

Although warlike and quarrelsome, the Celtic tribesmen were successful farmers and outstanding craftsmen, producing ornaments of rare beauty and intricate design. Their priests, or druids, engaged in philosophy and poetry, but also practised human sacrifice. The Celtic migrations were to change the face of Europe and introduce a unique civilization.

586 BC
Nebuchadnezzar burns Jerusalem

Nebuchadnezzar (*d.* 562 BC), a Chaldean, had already gained much fame as a warrior before he succeeded his father, Nabopolasser, to the throne of Babylon in 605 BC. A rebellion in Tyre caused him to lead an army against the Phoenicians' stronghold which he was forced to besiege for thirteen years.

When he had captured the city he went on to deal with another revolt, this time in Jerusalem, led by King Jehoiakim of Judah. In 597 BC he captured the city and placed a new king on its throne – Zedekiah. But he also rebelled against his overlord and a furious Nebuchadnezzar returned to assault it once again. This time, however, it held out against him for eighteen months. Life for the besieged became very hard, for the food stocks ran low and famine broke out in the city.

At last in 586 BC the walls were breached and the Chaldeans swept in. Zedekiah's sons were killed while he was taken in chains to Babylon where he died in prison. Jerusalem's stout walls were pulled down, the temple, palace and homes of the nobility were looted and then burned and many of the Hebrews taken off to captivity in Babylon. (*see* c. 965 BC *The temple built at Jerusalem*).

c. 560 BC
Birth of Buddha

Gautama Buddha (c. 560–483 BC) was born Sīddhartha, the son of a nobleman who lived in Northern India. He was the pampered son of a very rich man. As he grew older, however, he saw three moving sights which, it is said, were to change his life. They were a man enfeebled by age, another crippled with leprosy, and a corpse. These brought home to him the realities of life

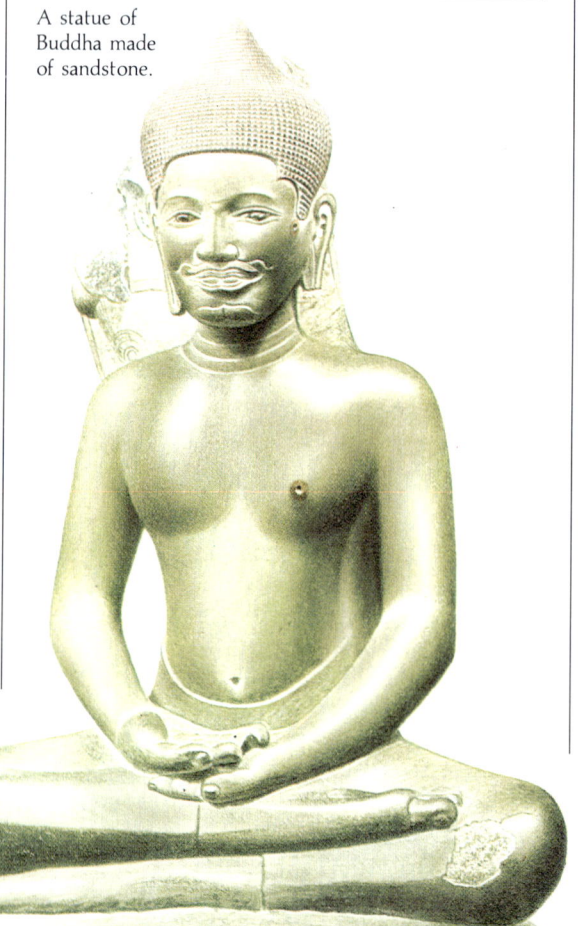

A statue of Buddha made of sandstone.

Confucius teaching his disciples.

and he decided to find a way to help his fellow men.

He turned his back on his home, his wife and young son, and set out on his search.

At first he tried to live as a strict Brahman who believed that a man could only reach a state of perfection if he neglected his body and fasted continuously, but Buddha nearly died from the results of such self-denial. He went on to develop a religion which was contrary to the prevailing Brahmanism. It was pure, moral and humane in its origin although it subsequently became mixed with the idolatrous worship of other deities. As it included a protest against the caste system, it was eagerly adopted by the non-Aryan inhabitants of India.

c. 553 BC
The work of Pythagoras

Pythagoras was a Greek who settled in Crotona in southern Italy and founded the school of 'Pythagoreans'. He is regarded as one of the greatest of early Greek philosophers although much of his early work was based on the vast accumulated knowledge of the ancient world,

upon all who practised Confucianism to culti-
vate all the virtues that seemed worthy —
industry, modesty, sobriety, gravity and
thoughtfulness towards others. He attracted a
great number of disciples who, when he died,
buried him with great pomp. On his death, c.479
BC, Confucianism rapidly became the state religion of China.

538 BC
Cyrus takes Babylon

Cyrus the Persian (d. 529 BC), later to be known
as 'the Great', was one of the greatest warriors of
the ancient world. He was destined to forge a
band of ill-equipped men into a great army
which was to establish the first truly great
empire in history. The *Book of Ezra* quotes Cyrus
as saying, 'The Lord God hath given me *all the
kingdoms of the earth.*'

He first led his men against Astyages of
Media (551 BC) and then against Lydia (546 BC),
the city of King Croesus whose name, even
today, is synonymous with great wealth. He
then moved to attack Babylon, then ruled by
Nabonidus who had offended the priesthood of
the god Bel Narduk by bringing in other gods.

Cyrus appeared before the mighty walls of
the great city (538 BC), there was a brief skirmish
and then, with the help of the priests, he and his
men entered the city without fighting.

He proved to be a very humane ruler,
respecting local customs and religions, even
allowing the long-exiled Jews to leave Babylon
and return to Jerusalem.

reintroducing astronomical facts to his own time
that had been known to the ancient Egyptians
and Babylonians.

His great discovery was in music. He was the
first to determine that an octave has eight notes.

His famous theory of the 'square on the
hypotenuse' came from a study of ancient
Egyptian engineers who constructed a triangle
with sides in the ratio of 3:4:5 in order to make a
right-angle. By mathematics he proved that the
earth was a sphere; previously it had always
been thought flat. He also believed that the souls
of dead people returned to earth, sometimes in
animals.

c. 550 BC
Birth of Confucius

The third great religious movement of the East
was Confucianism, named after its Chinese
founder, Kung-fu-tse, or Confucius (c.550–
c.479 BC). Whilst still a young man he established a school of learning and the principles he
taught appealed to 'practical' men. It was basically
a system of morality and as it did not involve
worship of a god, cannot really be called a
'religion' in the accepted sense of the word today.

It praised the present world, was inclined to
doubt the existence of a future one, and called

c. 520 BC
Shwe Dagon Pagoda, Burma

It is said that two rich Burmese merchants had
occasion to pass through Buddha's village. They
offered him a gift and, in return, the prophet
gave them eight hairs from his head. They
decided to build a temple to house them and the
result was the Shwe Dagon Pagada, the most
revered shrine in Indo-China and the most
beautiful in the world.

c. 517 BC

Hecataeus' map of the world

Hecataeus was an early Greek historian who travelled widely and then decided to write a book about his experiences. Giving it the grand sounding title of *A Tour of the World*, it was fascinating because he illustrated it with a map. This showed the world as a disc divided into two equal parts, Europe and Asia.

509 BC

Founding of the Roman Republic

In 509 BC Tarquin the Proud, last of the Roman kings who reigned 534–510 BC, was expelled from the city for a disgraceful deed. The rising against him had been led by the heads of the Roman family clans and as the very name 'king' had become a hated word, a republic was formed, the leaders being formed into a Senate with two of their number appointed as consuls.

The consuls were the virtual rulers of Rome, but so that they did not assume too much power, they had to vacate their office after one year.

Thus, the Republic was ruled by the consuls and Senate and also by the people (*senatus populusque romanus*). The citizens of Rome were divided into the *patricians* (or aristocracy) who assumed public office automatically, and the *plebians* who formed the majority of the free citizens who elected their own representatives.

About 506 BC the people of republican Rome began work on the Capitol, building a temple to Jupiter on the Capitoline Hill to house their Senate. This led to the great architectural glories of later Rome when the great temples, baths, circuses and triumphal arches were built.

c. 500 BC

Building of the theatre at Delphi

The first 'man of the theatre' was a Greek called Thespis who lived about 500 BC. He was said to have travelled round Greece with a group of

Two officials of the Roman Republic: the praetor (left) and the lictor (right), who carried the *fasces*.

strolling players and a wagon used as a stage. He was also the first to introduce actors (instead of just using the traditional chorus) so it was in ancient Greece that the modern theatre was founded.

Plays were first performed as part of the religious festivals in honour of the god Dionysus (Bacchus) and they often lasted for several days.

Greek theatres such as the famous one at Delphi were built on hillsides in the open air. The theatre at Epidaurus (built *c.* 340 BC) is a perfect example and is still used for performances of ancient Greek masterpieces. These include *Antigone* by Sophocles (486–406 BC), the *Oresteia* by Aeschylus (525–456 BC) and the *Bacchae* by Euripides (480–406 BC).

490 BC

The Battle of Marathon

Cyrus the Great (*see 538 BC Cyrus takes Babylon*) was followed by Cambyses (*d.* 522 BC) who added Egypt to the already vast Persian empire. Darius I (*c.* 549–486 BC), the Mede, and third of the Persian rulers was, almost literally, the monarch of the world. The Greek colonies along the Aegean which paid a yearly tribute, began a revolt against their Persian overlords and Darius decided to subjugate not only the colonial Greeks but also the European Greeks as well.

In 490 BC his troops landed at Marathon to the north of Athens, where they were totally defeated by an Athenian army which sent the remnants of the once great Persian army scrambling back into their boats. Heartbroken, Darius died soon afterwards and his son and successor, Xerxes (c. 519–465 BC), resolved to avenge this defeat. When it was heard that the Persian emperor was assembling the greatest army the world had ever seen, the kingdoms of Greece forgot their rivalries and joined together to meet the threat to their homeland.

A number of battles was fought, including the battle of the Pass of Thermopylae and Salamis, both in 480 BC. Salamis was the first recorded sea battle, in which the Persian fleet was trapped by the Greeks. Then, at Plataea in 479 BC the Persians were finally defeated. The end of the war was marked in 478 BC by a confederation of Greek states known as the Delian League.

490-429 BC
The age of Pericles

The Delian League marked the beginning of the Golden Age of Greece which for thirty years was dominated by one of the most outstanding men in history – Pericles (490–429 BC). He was the son of noble parents who provided him,

The Parthenon was built on the Acropolis in Athens under the administration of Pericles.

when a youth, with the finest and most advanced teachers of the day.

By 461 BC he had become one of the leaders of the democratic party, assuming control when its leader, Ephialtes, was assassinated. He carried the democratic system further, insisting that every officer of state, except the generals and judges, were to be chosen by lot. Also, any person carrying out such civic duties was to be paid accordingly, thus allowing even the poorest citizen to become an office-holder.

His work was interrupted by war with Athens' great rival, Sparta, which broke out in 456 BC, Pericles becoming one of the Athenian generals. War ended in 451 BC and Pericles was able to devote himself to the rebuilding of his capital city. Much of it had been burned by the enemy during the Persian wars and Pericles resolved to make Athens the most beautiful city in the world. He engaged the greatest architects (Ictinus and Callicrates) and sculptor (Pheidias) and these men produced the magnificent Parthenon, high on the Acropolis.

He did more than rebuild Athens architecturally, he also did much to rebuild men's minds. In addition to the architects and sculptors he gathered together a number of men whose influence has lasted to the present day – Sophocles and Euripides, the great dramatists, Anaxagoras who spoke about the solar system and Herodotus, the greatest historian of the ancient world, who gave lectures on his travels.

He again led his country to war against the Spartans in 431 BC, the time of the Great Peloponnesian War during which he was deposed by the Council, dissatisfied with his strategy, but reinstated before his death two years later.

399 BC
Death of Socrates

Socrates (*c.* 469–399 BC), a controversial figure in Athenian society, was to become one of the greatest philosophers the world has ever known. He was continually surrounded by men of all ages who wished to learn from him. His own particular style of teaching was by 'question-and-answer', whereby wisdom could be learned by recognizing one's own ignorance.

With 'Socratic irony' he often exposed the pompous and pretentious as shallow and stupid and although, through this, he gained a great following amongst the young, he also acquired a number of enemies from those whose bubble of self-importance he had pricked.

In 399 BC he was brought to trial, charged that he did not worship the state gods and that he corrupted the young men of the city with his lectures. He was condemned to death and died by drinking a draught of poison called hemlock. His teachings were preserved by Plato, Xenophon and Aristotle.

Socrates drinks poison.

387 BC
Plato founds the Academy

Plato (*c.* 427–347 BC) was a noble Athenian who, not wishing to attain high office like others of his family, chose to become a disciple of Socrates. On his master's death he assumed leadership of Socrates' followers and founded a philosophical school in Athens known as the 'Academy'.

He intended that this should produce philosopher-statesmen, for he criticized the Athenian form of government whereby men with no special training were allowed to fill important political posts.

He dealt with this in one of his early works – *The Republic*, in which he outlined his ideal – an aristocratic elite. His message was simple – all can live in another and wiser fashion if they choose to think and work everything out for themselves, and become fully aware of their own potential. He was working on an important work called *Laws* when he died in 347 BC.

Plato addresses pupils from his Academy.

338 BC
Philip of Macedonia invades Greece

Lying between Thrace and Thessaly was the small kingdom of Macedonia. It was peopled by tough mountaineers who were very independent but, as a nation, Macedonia was little regarded by its neighbours, the more powerful Greek states.

Philip II, King of Macedonia (382–336 BC),

however, was to make them change their minds. He was a brilliant diplomat and strategist and managed to weld his independent warriors into a disciplined army. In a style new to warfare, he armed them with four-metre-long pikes and drilled them in an equally new tactic of warfare – the *phalanx*. His foot soldiers held the enemy at bay with their long pikes, leaving the Macedonian cavalry free to charge at the enemy's weakest point.

The Greek states of Athens and Thebes joined together to fight him, meeting the at Battle of Chaeronea in 338 BC where Philip scored a great victory, which opened the frontiers of Greece to his army.

336 BC
Alexander the Great becomes king

After the battle of Chaeronea (*see 338 BC Philip of Macedonia invades Greece*) Philip II was preparing to lead a Greek and Macedonian army into Persia and put an end to their empire. Before he could do so he was murdered by one of his nobles, and his son, Alexander (356–323 BC) took over the command.

A mosaic portrait of Alexander the Great, conqueror of a vast empire.

He was only twenty-two when he set out with his army, and was never to see his homeland again. Indeed, he was destined to make himself master of the world during the next eleven years and to earn himself the title of 'the Great'.

He marched into Syria and defeated King Darius III of Persia (reigned 336–330 BC) at the battle of Issus (333 BC) then swept on to capture Tyre after a siege of seven months, before invading and conquering Egypt. He next led his army into Mesopotamia to defeat Darius III yet again at the battle of Arbela (331 BC) then pushed on, despite grumblings from his weary army, until he reached northern India. He finally made his way down to the Indus and then, satisfied at last, he agreed to lead his world-conquering warriors home again. He reached Mesopotamia once more but became stricken with fever and died in Babylon at the early age of thirty-three.

335 BC
Aristotle founds School

One of Plato's finest pupils at his Academy was the Greek philosopher Aristotle (c. 384–322 BC). He left Athens when Plato died in 347 BC, to wander the world, teaching as he went. One of his pupils was the future Alexander the Great, whom Aristotle educated for three years.

The Colossus of Rhodes.

Returning to Athens he founded the Lyceum school. His followers were known as Peripatetics, because his school had a garden in which he would walk about with his pupils, engaging in philosophical dialogue – 'peripatetic' means 'walking about'.

Aristotle remains one of the most influential philosophers of all time. His work forms the basis of modern deductive logic, and his work on ethics and aesthetics has had an incalculable influence on western civilization.

For political reasons Aristotle had to escape from Athens and he died in Chalcis in Euboea in 322 BC.

c. 300 BC
Euclid, Alexandria's great mathematician

In 332 BC, Alexander founded the great city which was named after him – Alexandria at the mouth of the Nile. He built a great library within the city and this, a centre of learning known as the Museum, attracted scholars from every part of the ancient world.

One of these was Euclid, probably the most famous mathematician of all time. The dates of his birth and death are unknown but he had studied under Plato in Athens before going to Alexandria where he founded a school during the reign of Pharaoh Ptolemy I (306–283 BC).

His great work was the *Elements*, contained in thirteen books, in which he drew upon the work of his predecessors, but of which much was entirely original; he opened up a new world of geometry and of mathematics. This work is the oldest scientific text-book in the world, having been in use, almost unchanged, for more than two thousand years.

c. 300–280 BC
The Colossus of Rhodes

One of the seven wonders of the ancient world was an immense statue placed at the entrance to the harbour of Rhodes. Formed in the likeness of Helios (Apollo), the sun god, it was designed by Chares. It was in position for little more than fifty years when in 224 BC an earthquake brought it toppling down to crash in pieces.

279 BC

Completion of the Pharos Lighthouse

Another of the seven wonders was a huge lighthouse erected at Alexandria. Built of white marble to the design of Sostratus of Cnidus, it stood some 180 metres high. Its beacon was constantly burning and the light was increased in range by a clever system of mirrors. It stood until the fourteenth century AD.

*c.*279 BC

Aristarchus' Theory of the Universe

Aristarchus of Samos, a Greek astronomer who was active between 280 and 264 BC, was the first to maintain that the Earth, instead of being the centre of the universe as formerly believed, was actually one of several planets which revolved around the Sun. Some of his theories anticipated the findings of later astronomers, such as Copernicus, who lived in the fifteenth century AD.

275 BC

Pyrrhus fights the Romans

King Pyrrhus (*c.*318–272 BC) proved to be a fighting man from a very early age. He occupied much of Macedonia but was defeated at Edessa and forced to return to his own kingdom of Epirus. In 281 BC he fought against Rome, leading an army of twenty-five thousand men; had he received support from other Greek cities Rome's history might have been vastly different.

Pyrrhus relied upon his cavalry and elephants to defeat the Roman army at Heraclea but the slaughter on both sides was so severe that, in reality neither side was the winner. From this battle has come the phrase 'a Pyrrhic victory' meaning a victory which costs the victor so much that it was not worth winning. Finally, at Beneventum in 275 BC, he was defeated by a combined army of Romans and Carthaginians. He returned to Epirus and continued to fight until his death. He wrote a history of the art of war which became a classic of the ancient world.

c. 264 BC

Asoka becomes Emperor of India

According to one story, Asoka, ruler of a vast empire in India from *c.*264–224 BC, was a cruel monster, coming to the throne after the massacre of all his brothers. As he later became a devout Buddhist, it is believed that he was himself responsible for this story as he wished to show the beneficial effect his religion had upon his original blood-thirsty nature.

Indeed, his nature had changed so much that he suppressed all hunting and sent a number of Buddhist priests around his kingdom to teach the sanctity of life, even of animals, birds and insects. He also sent missionary priests to the farthest parts of his vast empire and to countries beyond, telling them of the blessings of Buddhism. One such country which accepted his religion was Sri Lanka.

Asoka was also one of India's greatest rulers, expanding trade, encouraging the arts, and stabilizing his empire.

264 BC

The beginning of the Punic Wars

With Carthage becoming the richest and largest trading nation of her time (*see 813 BC The founding of Carthage*), and Rome becoming master of Italy (*see 509 BC Founding of the Roman Republic*), it was inevitable that the two nations should come into conflict. In 260 BC a long series of wars began which were to become known as the Punic, or Carthaginian, Wars. The name 'Punic' came from the Latin for Phoenician, the people who originally founded Carthage.

The first (264–241 BC) was fought over the possession of Sicily, and ended in a Roman victory. Hannibal, a Carthaginian general (247–*c.*183 BC), swore to take revenge.

This began the Second Punic War (218–201 BC). Hannibal invaded Italy from Spain, crossing the Alps in extreme hardship with soldiers and elephants. Although he scored outstanding victories in Italy, culminating in the Battles of Lake Trasimene and Cannae, he had to leave eventually when he learned that a Roman army under Scipio Africanus (237–183 BC) was attacking Carthage. This war ended with the defeat of Hannibal at Zama. Carthage was

In 280 BC Pyrrhus defeated the Romans at Heraclea, terrifying his enemies with elephants that thundered against the Roman flanks.

compelled to withdraw her army from Spain and surrender her great navy.

Yet Carthage became powerful again, causing Cato, the Roman senator (234–149 BC) to warn the Senate with the words, *'Delenda est Carthago'* ('Carthage must be destroyed'). At the end of the Third Punic War (149–146 BC) Carthage was conquered and the Romans ploughed up the ground on which Carthage had stood.

c. 255 BC
The Septuagint

Alexandria in the third century BC was a great centre of learning. Ptolemy Philadelphus (*d.* 247 BC) arranged the translation of the Old Testament from Hebrew to Greek. The High Priest Eleazar sent seventy learned Jews to Alexandria to start the long task – hence the title, from the Latin word for seventy (*septuaginta*). This work was to have great influence on Jewish and, later, Christian scholarship.

c. 250 BC
Archimedes' Principle

One of the many scientists who studied at the Museum of Alexandria was Archimedes (*c.* 287–212 BC), a Greek from Syracuse.

It is said that the King of Syracuse suspected that a jeweller had cheated him and asked Archimedes to determine whether his purchase was of pure gold. Later, whilst in his bath, Archimedes noticed that his body displaced some of the water and at once realized a way of solving the king's problem. Thrilled with the discovery he is said to have run home without bothering to dress shouting *'Eureka!'* ('I have found it!') His principle, in simple terms, was that when a solid is weighed in air and then in liquid, the apparent loss in weight in the liquid is equal to the weight of the liquid displaced.

Archimedes researched in the fields of geometry, mechanics and hydrostatics, and his theories were to prove of great help to Galileo, Newton and other scientists who followed.

c. 215 BC
The Great Wall of China

It has been said, with considerable justification, that the Great Wall of China is the most stupendous example of human endeavour. Known in China as the *Wan-Lich'ang Ch'en*, the Wall of Ten Thousand Miles, it formed the northern boundary of the Chinese Empire and was actually some 2,400 kilometres long, varying in height from four-and-a-half metres to nine metres.

It was built at the command of Shih Huang Ti, of the Ch'in dynasty (221–206 BC) who wanted to keep the barbarian Tartars from invading China. Shih Huang Ti commanded every third able-bodied man in his kingdom to build the wall. The result was truly the eighth wonder of the world. It was built across northern China, over high mountains and through very difficult country. In terms of human suffering and futility a writer once said, 'The Chinese never got over it . . . but the Tartars did!'

Shih Huang Ti was a brutal ruler who cared little for art and learning, and who ordered that every book in China should be burned with the exception of religious, medical and agricultural

The Great Wall of China built to keep the Tartars from invading China.

works. In 206 BC, Liu Pang led a revolt against the Ch'in and, changing his name to Kao Tsu, became the first ruler of the Han dynasty.

c. 200 BC
The Rosetta Stone

For centuries men had puzzled over Egyptian hieroglyphs. Then in 1798, a black slab of inscribed stone was unearthed in Egypt. It had fifty-four lines in Greek, thirty-two in demotic Egyptian, whilst the rest was in hieroglyphs. It dated from 200 BC. A Frenchman, Jean François Champollion began work on the inscription and by 1822 had discovered how to decipher hieroglyphs.

c. 200 BC
The *Mahabharata*

One of the great epic poems of the Indian nation is called the *Mahabharata* meaning 'the great poem of the Bharates'. Actually it is not a single work but a collection of poems which tell of the heroes of two great houses of ancient India and of their deadly rivalry. The *Mahabharata* is divided into eighteen separate books.

167 BC
The Maccabean Revolt

Antiochus IV of Syria (*d.* 163 BC), sometimes called Epiphanes the 'Madman', had crushed a rising by the Jews of Jerusalem. He allowed his troops to plunder the Temple and had all the copies of the Law of Moses burned, while altars to Greek gods were erected throughout the country.

A Syrian officer, sent to the city of Modin, ordered Mattathias, the city headman (*d.* 166 BC), to worship at a hastily erected altar and for the rest of the Jews to follow. When Mattathias refused, the officer called to some of his guard to punish him, but Mattathias summoned his five stalwart sons to support him and within minutes the Syrian and his men were dead.

This incident provoked a great revolt against the armies of Antiochus. The leadership passed to Mattathias' son Judas Maccabeus (the 'Hammer') and ended in the defeat of Antiochus in 167 BC and independence from Syria.

c. 140 BC
Venus de Milo

Venus (Aphrodite) was an important Greek goddess and a continual source of inspiration to Greek sculptors. Indeed, perhaps the most famous piece of sculpture in the world depicts Venus de Milo (or Aphrodite de Melos). Although her arms were broken off when found, it is believed that one held an apple, symbol of the island of Melos where the statue was found.

133 BC
The reforms of Gracchi

Two Roman brothers, Tiberius and Gaius Gracchus, were to become known to history as political reformers. When their father died, their mother, the noble Cornelia, devoted her life to their education.

Tiberius Gracchus (168–133 BC) saw service in Spain then, on his return, pressed for the re-establishment of ancient laws which forbade the rich to possess great estates. This roused the anger of the wealthy and Tiberius and many of his supporters were assassinated.

The Gracchi brothers, Tiberius and Gaius.

Gaius (*c.* 159–121 BC) who was in Spain at the time of the murder, returned to Rome and continued his brother's social reforms. The rich senators and others were alarmed and, once again, a Gracchus and his supporters were murdered. As a token of the people's love and appreciation, however, in later years a statue was erected in the Roman forum which bore the simple words, 'To Cornelia, the Mother of the Gracchi.'

106 BC
Marius elected consul

The death of the Gracchi marked the beginning of a century of civil war in Rome. From that day in 121 BC when Gaius died, armies, not votes, were to determine events.

Two powerful men succeeded the Gracchi, Gaius Marius (*c.* 156–86 BC) and Lucius Sulla (138–78 BC). Marius, who had gained popularity when he defeated Jugurtha, King of Numidia, took advantage of Sulla's absence to march on Rome with his army – an unprecedented happening.

Sulla returned and began a reign of terror, slaughtering some eight thousand of Marius' followers. By his orders lists of people to be executed were published and often the lists exceeded two hundred names.

Many Romans, including a young Julius Caesar, had to flee for their lives, until Sulla, who made himself dictator of Rome, was dead.

73 BC
The Slaves' Revolt

During the Jugurthine War (111–106 BC) slaves owned by Roman masters broke into revolt. This was the second so-called Servile War in Rome's history and like the first was quelled with very little trouble.

The slaves, for the most part, were incapable of standing up to the men of a Roman legion. However, the third Servile War, in 73 BC, was quite different. It began when two hundred trained gladiators in Capua killed their guards and escaped.

They were joined by others and put themselves under the command of a young gladiator, Spartacus. They defeated a strong Roman force and the rebel army grew daily until it reached a hundred thousand desperate men.

Spartacus led his force towards the Alpine passes in 71 BC but was met by the praetor Marcus Lucinius Crassus (c. 115–53 BC), leading a large Roman army, at the Battle of Lucania. After a terrific struggle, Spartacus was killed and Crassus took six thousand of the survivors to crucify them along the road between Rome and Capua.

63 BC
Cicero and the Catiline conspiracy

Marcus Tullius Cicero (106–43 BC) was educated in Athens and Rome and soon became recognized as the greatest orator of his time, although he was looked on as a 'new man' because none of his ancestors had reached high office.

In 63 BC an impoverished aristocrat named Lucius Catiline (c. 108–62 BC) planned to seize power in Rome and free himself from the burden of his debts. His plans were disclosed and Cicero, one of the consuls for the year, acted with urgency. He attacked Catiline in the Senate in a speech so vigorous that his opponent was forced to flee from Rome. The next day Cicero made an even more forceful oration in the Forum and in consequence Catiline was declared an outlaw

and an army sent to deal with him. Catiline was killed and, mainly thanks to Cicero's silver tongue, the threat to Rome was over.

60 BC
The First Triumvirate

The rivalries and bloodshed of Marius and the Third Servile War left Rome in a state of collapse, its people anxious for a settled peace. It finally came when the three most powerful men in Rome formed the First Triumvirate (or three-man rule). They were Crassus (c.112–53 BC) an immensely rich man and the general who had

Gnaeus Pompeius Magnus, known as Pompey.

defeated Spartacus, Pompey (106–48 BC) a very popular general who had crushed the slave rebellion in the Second Servile War, and Julius Caesar (102–44 BC) a man destined for greatness. Pompey married Julia, Caesar's daughter, and the pair seemed very united.

In 58 BC Caesar was elected consul and proposed some very popular laws. The next year he was appointed governor of Transalpine Gaul (or Gaul beyond the Alps) to command three legions. With this small army, about 18,000 men, he began a series of conquests that astonished everyone in Rome. Pompey was made governor of Spain and Crassus sailed for Asia and war with

Parthia but was soon to die in battle. Pompey, on the other hand, remained in Rome and then, becoming jealous of Caesar's continual triumphs, began to plot against him.

58-51 BC
The conquest of Gaul

Soon after Julius Caesar arrived in Gaul as governor, the Helvetii, a Celtic people, decided to migrate and pass across Roman territory. Although greatly outnumbered, Caesar brought them to battle and defeated them utterly. Realizing Caesar's mettle, some Gallic chieftains appealed to him to aid them against the Germanic King Ariovistus and he fought and destroyed that king's army also.

He then went on to crush other tribes, soon becoming master of almost the whole of Gaul.

Julius Caesar's second invasion fleet approaches the coast of Britain in 54 BC.

His last great battle before returning to Rome was against the Arverni. In 51 BC Vercingetorix, their leader, surrendered, riding into Caesar's camp to announce that he was prepared to surrender himself if his followers were allowed to disperse. This showed unusual courage – and optimism. Vercingetorix was thrown into prison and a million Gauls were deported to Rome as slaves. Caesar's brilliant campaign in Gaul was over.

55 BC
Caesar's expedition to Britain

Late in the summer of 55 BC, a fleet of eighty ships commanded by Julius Caesar arrived off Dover. His men struggled ashore, and after a brief clash with British tribesmen, established a camp. But an unusually high tide wrecked many of his ships and after a few more skirmishes, Caesar was glad to return to Gaul.

He returned in July of the following year, in command of eight hundred ships bearing five legions and two thousand cavalry. This large force was landed somewhere near Sandwich and soon began to move inland. A brisk action was fought near Canterbury and another against the British leader Cassivelaunus, in which the Roman legionaries had to contend with the fast-moving British chariots.

Caesar moved north, crossing the Thames somewhere near Brentford and then, re-crossing the river, returned to the coast and sailed away leaving an unconquered country behind him.

49 BC
Caesar crosses the Rubicon

As Caesar was finishing his ten years' campaign in Gaul, the Senate, urged by Pompey, sent a messenger ordering him to give up his command. Knowing that this would mean his political ruin he refused and led his army to the banks of the river Rubicon. It was a grave offence to cross into Roman territory with an army, as it was considered an invasion; but with the words 'The die is cast', Caesar led his troops onward. Hence the saying 'to cross the Rubicon' meaning to take an irrevocable step.

As Caesar advanced, so Pompey retired, finally sailing for Greece. On June 6, 48 BC, the two armies met at Pharsalia in a battle to decide the fate of the Roman world. Pompey rode from the field a defeated man and made for Egypt. As he landed he was seized and beheaded. And that irrevocably ended the First Triumvirate.

44 BC
The murder of Caesar

The Battle of Pharsalia made Caesar lord of Rome. He then had to deal with a revolt in Africa. A short campaign ended in the victory being

Julius Caesar is murdered by conspirators led by Brutus and Cassius.

announced in the Senate as *Veni, vidi, vici* (I came, I saw, I conquered). He returned to Rome and took supreme command; the Republic was at an end. Now the head of the army controlled the empire.

Unlike Marius and Sulla, Caesar proclaimed a general pardon for all his former opponents and not one was put to death. He then instituted a number of popular reforms, but some jealous men who wished to restore the Republic waited for him in the Forum and stabbed him to death.

A Second Triumvirate was formed consisting of Marcus Antonius (Mark Antony), Lepidus and Octavian, Caesar's nephew and heir.

43 BC
Cleopatra, Queen of Egypt

Regarded as the most famous woman in history, Cleopatra (*c.* 68–30 BC) was the daughter of Ptolemy V although, like her father, she was entirely Greek, not Egyptian. In 51 BC she became joint ruler of Egypt with her young brother but they quarrelled and she was forced to leave and go into Syria. At this time Julius Caesar arrived in Alexandria and Cleopatra, using her charms, persuaded him to make war on her behalf. Her brother was killed and she become Queen of Egypt once more.

Caesar took her to Rome with him, but following his assassination she returned to Egypt. She then became the mistress of Marcus Antonius (Mark Antony, *c.* 83–30 BC) and added her fleet to his at the Battle of Actium (31 BC), where she fought against Octavian (later to become Caesar Augustus). Realizing all was lost, she poisoned herself with an asp; the line of Ptolemies ended with her death and Egypt became a Roman province.

c. 38 BC
The Laocoön sculpture

Laocoön, according to Greek legend, was a priest who tried to warn the Trojans of the Greek wooden horse. An angry Apollo destroyed him and his two sons with serpents. This legend was a popular one in ancient times and in 38 BC Agesander, a Rhodian sculptor, produced a wonderful group showing the three victims in agony as the serpents tightened about them.

37 BC
Herod captures Jerusalem

The Jewish King Herod the Great (*c.* 73–4 BC) had a stormy early life, being constantly at war with the various factions fighting in Palestine and Syria after the assassination of Caesar.

In 39 BC Mark Antony put the Roman troops in Palestine at his disposal and with them he laid siege to Jerusalem. The Holy City was taken by storm, although Herod did his best to restrain the butchery of his people and the plunder of the temple. He later rebuilt much of the city, including the temple, and went on to build other great cities and fortresses.

On Antony's fall Herod allied with Augustus. His reign as King of Judaea was marked by suspicion, intrigue and cruelty. He ordered the death of his wife Mariamne and his two sons by her, and is said to have ordered the massacre of the innocents referred to in the Bible. He was succeeded by his son Herod Antipas, who died sometime after AD 40.

c. 20 BC
Virgil completes *Aeneid*

Publius Virgil (70–19 BC) is considered the greatest poet of ancient Rome. He was born near Mantua which earned him his title of 'The Mantuan Swan'. He was a master of epic, didactic and idyllic poetry, his finest work being the *Aeneid*, an epic poem which tells of the wanderings of Aeneas and of the fall of Troy.

c. 14 BC
Agrippa builds the Pont du Gard

Marcus Agrippa (*c.* 63–12 BC), was a great general yet is best remembered for his building works. The Pantheon, for example, begun by him in 27 BC is still the chief Roman building more or less intact. His greatest work (*c.* 14 BC) was the Pont du Gard in Nîmes, France, an aqueduct which is still impressive today.

THE ROMAN EMPIRE

The Romans began to build their empire after 149 BC, when they finally defeated their old rivals, the Carthaginians, in the Punic Wars. With that, they took over the territories of Carthage and in time these became the basis of an Empire stretching from Britain in the north, across most of southern and western Europe to North Africa in the south.

The Romans were well suited to control such vast possessions. They had a well-founded and efficient system of government and law and they were already experienced in dealing with conquered peoples. By 275 BC, the Romans had vanquished other tribes in their homeland of Italy, and had usually turned them into allies, sharing many benefits of the Roman way of life.

The Romans were also expert at using the ideas and skills of others and gave great opportunities to architects, craftsmen, writers and artists which they would never have otherwise enjoyed. The Romans knew, too, the wisdom of granting some freedom to subject peoples which did not endanger their overall power, but still gave these peoples a certain satisfaction. For example, temples were dedicated in Rome to foreign religions and devotees of those religions were allowed to worship as long as they recognized the Roman Emperor as a god.

The Romans, in other words, gave the peoples of the Empire some persuasive reasons for accepting their rule and did not rely solely on their military might to keep control.

Nevertheless, Roman military might was very considerable. Theirs was the best, most disciplined and most successful army in the ancient world. Without it, the Empire could never have survived, for Roman soldiers guarded the Empire's borders and defended it against the 'barbarian' tribes outside.

Within the Empire, life could be comfortable and safe in ways quite impossible beyond its frontiers. This was described as Pax Romana (Roman peace) and was another good reason for welcoming Roman power. People could travel without the fear of being waylaid and robbed by brigands. This was especially beneficial for merchants who carried large amounts of valuable goods for trade. The Roman road system, which at its greatest extent included 80,000 kilometres of major roads and 322,000 kilometres of secondary roads, was the only one of its kind in the world, and Roman roads were so well built and sited that they lasted for hundreds of years. Many roads in Britain and other parts of Europe still follow routes worked out by the Romans. Because of the roads, communications within the Empire were extremely • good and travel was relatively easy as well as safe.

The Romans also built aqueducts to carry fresh water to towns where life, at its best, could be pleasant and even luxurious. The better houses were well-built, with proper drainage and 'central heating' provided by hypocausts which warmed the walls and floors. There were public baths, schools, theatres, public meeting places (forum) and even a police force and fire brigade. Shops were full of fine foods and delicacies from all over the Empire, as well as clothes, furniture, utensils and ornaments.

Not everyone, of course, enjoyed such good living. There was great poverty, bad and unsafe housing and much cruelty and oppression as well. And not everyone considered Pax Romana worth exchanging for independence. There were rebellions, and the Romans did not hesitate to put them down with maximum force and to punish the ringleaders with great severity. Many rebels were enslaved and so added to the vast numbers of slaves in Rome and other parts of the Empire. In the 1st century AD, there were 20,382,000 slaves in Italy alone. The more fortunate might be purchased in the slave markets as tutors to the children of rich Roman households or as personal servants, but the majority were doomed to back-breaking labour. Countless thousands of men, women and children were literally worked to death. Some toiled in the mines. Others were put in the galleys of Roman ships where they were chained to the rowing benches. Others became gladiators and fought, often to the death, to entertain crowds at the Games. Or they drove in the highly dangerous, frequently fatal, chariot races at the Circus, again for public entertainment. Other, equally brutal, 'shows' were put on by wild animals which tore each other to pieces while the crowds roared in delight.

Life within the Empire, whether good or bad, remained the only way of life for several generations, for the Empire lasted in all over 1,600 years. No Empire in Europe has ever continued so long, or covered such a vast area. By AD 293, it had become too large for a single Emperor to control, so it was divided in two, one half, the Western Empire, centred on Rome and the other, the Eastern, centred on Byzantium (now in Turkey). In AD 313, Emperor Constantine who later built a great new capital city of Constantinople at Byzantium, was converted to Christianity, which then became the official religion of the Roman Empire. The Eastern

'Byzantine' Empire continued until 1453, when the Ottoman Turks, who were Moslems, captured Constantinople, overthrew the Christian Emperor and renamed the city Istanbul. In Christian Europe this was regarded as a terrible disaster and in many ways it was. The Byzantine Empire had been the most dazzling and important Christian state, its art, culture and architecture had been unsurpassed, its trade was rich and its army as powerful and successful, until 1453, as its predecessor in ancient Rome.

By the time Constantinople fell, the Western Empire centred on Rome had long ago disintegrated. Among the chief reasons were the weak, often corrupt, rule of the later Emperors in Rome, and also the growing inability of the Roman Army to stop invasions by barbarian tribes. The last truly strong, just Emperor had been Marcus Aurelius, who died in AD 180. After Marcus, no Emperor was able to rule satisfactorily for any length of time. Some were actually mad, like Marcus' son Commodus. Others, like Septimus Severus, who became Emperor in AD 193, were military dictators. Others were degenerate, like Didius Julianus (AD 193) who won the imperial throne by gambling for it. Many of these later Emperors were murdered, often by the army which was more interested in political power struggles than in defending the Empire.

Meanwhile the barbarian tribes outside the borders were demanding more strongly than ever to be allowed into the Empire's territories. The Roman Army was too weak to keep them out and in the 5th century AD, barbarians made several raids within the Empire and even attacked Rome. In three successive years – AD 408, 409 and 410, the Visigoths swooped on Rome, and pillaged, murdered and destroyed as they pleased. Meanwhile, other barbarians, such as the Vandals and Alani terrorized the Roman province of Gaul (France) and invaded Spain. In AD 455, the Vandals ravaged Rome yet again and soon afterwards barbarian tribes swarmed over the Empire's borders. Finally, in AD 476, a German called Odoacer, made himself King of Italy and dethroned the last Roman Emperor, a boy of about 15. With that, the Western Roman Empire ceased to exist.

The influence of the Roman Empire, however, continues to this day – in the 'romance' languages like French and Spanish, in 'classical' styles of architecture, in legal and governmental systems, and also in the Catholic Church which is still centred on the city of Rome.

The Roman Empire at the beginning of the 2nd century AD, the period of its greatest extent.

9 BC

Livy writes *History of Rome*

Titus Livius, or Livy (59 BC–AD 17) was a Roman historian born in Padua. He went to Rome when still a young man and gained the favour of Caesar Augustus and his successor, Tiberius. Although he wrote books on several subjects, his favourite was history, his masterpiece being the *History of Rome* in one hundred and forty-two books, of which only thirty-five have survived.

c. 6 BC

The birth of Jesus Christ

The actual year of the birth of Christ is still in doubt. The main indication of the year is contained in St Luke's Gospel, which states that Caesar Augustus issued an order that the people of his empire should return to their own city to be counted. St Matthew also states that Christ was born in the reign of Herod the Great (*see 37 BC Herod captures Jerusalem*), who at some period not more than two years afterwards ordered a massacre of all infants at Bethlehem.

The Bible story is well-known: amongst the thousands who travelled for the census was Joseph, a carpenter of Nazareth, who returned to his family home in Bethlehem. By the time he arrived in the small city he found that all the accommodation had gone, but through the good services of an innkeeper, he and his wife Mary were allowed to stay in an outhouse. Here, in humble surroundings, Jesus Christ was born.

c. 2 BC

Ovid writes *Ars amatoria*

Publius Ovid (43 BC–AD 17) was a fashionable poet and one of the leading figures in Roman society. In AD 8 he offended Augustus Caesar and was banished to Tomis (Costanza) a dismal frontier town on the Black Sea. The reason given was that his book *Ars amatoria* ('Art of Love'), offended public morality.

AD 9

Arminius defeats Varus

During the early part of the first century AD, three Roman legions were stationed on the German frontier. Lulled into security by the local chief Arminius (18 BC–AD 19), P Quintilius Varus (*d.* AD 9), the Roman general, did not heed the massing of the Germanic tribes all about him.

Arminius, who had been educated in Rome and well understood the working of the Roman military mind, arranged for a local rising that would tempt Varus to move from the safety of the camp and into the neighbouring thick forests. The ruse was successful and the legion began to march. As they did so Arminius summoned all the Germanic tribesmen for miles around and in September AD 9 the legions were ambushed in the Teutoburger Wald.

Although they fought bravely and desperately, the legionaries were hopelessly out of formation and were slaughtered where they stood. Varus, realizing the inevitable, fell on his sword. This battle was a great turning point in history for it proved that Rome's dreaded legions were not invincible.

AD 28

Execution of John the Baptist

In the fifteenth year of the reign of Tiberius Caesar, John, son of Zacharias, began to preach 'in all the country about Jordan', baptizing and announcing the coming of the Messiah. He baptized Jesus Christ, recognizing his identity. John was later imprisoned by Herod Antipas whose wife, Herodias, persuaded the king to have the prophet beheaded.

c. AD 29

Crucifixion of Jesus Christ

When Jesus Christ was about thirty years old he was baptized by John, and then entered upon his life's work. After forty days' meditation in the wilderness, he walked along the shores of Galilee until he had gathered twelve disciples around him.

With them as companions he spent the next

The crucifixion of Jesus Christ.

three years teaching and giving sermons, wandering from place to place, and healing the sick. The New Testament tells of many miracles he performed. Although he was careful not to offend Jewish religious laws, speaking mainly of the love of God and of man's duty to his neighbour, he was continually harassed by the Scribes and Pharisees.

The officials finally decided to stop his activities, the religious authorities being jealous of his growing following, and the political authorities wary of more unrest in Judaea. He was seized and brought before Pontius Pilate, Roman Procurator from AD 26 to 36, who sentenced him to death. He was taken to a hill outside Jerusalem called Calvary and crucified between two thieves. Christians believe he later rose from the dead and ascended into heaven.

In the years after the death of Jesus Christ, his teachings spread rapidly; within three hundred years Christianity was the state religion of the Roman Empire.

AD 32
Conversion of Saul of Tarsus

Saul was born at Tarsus in Asia Minor but was trained as a rabbi in Jerusalem. As a young Pharisee he energetically persecuted Christ's followers but when on his way to Damascus he saw a vision and was converted to the new faith. It is due to the intense missionary activity of Paul — as he became known — that Christianity established such a firm foothold, first throughout the Roman Empire and subsequently throughout the world.

His journeyings took him to Ephesus, Philippi, Corinth and the cities of Galatea, and his letters to the converts in these places form a large part of the books of the New Testament. He was tried at Caesarea for causing a disturbance and, as a Roman citizen, appealed to Caesar. He was sent to Rome and after two years' captivity, was executed in AD 64.

AD 41
Assassination of Caligula

Caligula's real name was Gaius Caesar (12 BC–AD 41) and when as a small boy he accompanied his father Germanicus on a Syrian campaign, he wore a specially made legionary's uniform. With it he wore soldiers' boots (caligae) to earn him the nickname of Caligula.

He was adopted by Tiberius as his co-heir and succeeded him in AD 36. He then had a terrible illness and when he recovered, his character had changed completely. He became a monster of cruelty and vice, confessing that he hated the people of Rome so much that he wished they all had but one head so that he could chop it off with a single blow.

He managed to rule for four years until an officer of the guard named Chearea, whom he had insulted in public, struck him down when he was on his way to the Games, and all Rome rejoiced.

AD43
The Romans invade Britain

Julius Caesar had come and gone (*see 55 BC Caesar's expedition to Britain*) and it was to be nearly a century before Roman soldiers came to Britain again. The second invasion came in AD 43 when the Emperor Claudius sent four legions to Britain, this time to conquer and to stay. Britain was a country of small kingdoms, a confederation of which, paying allegiance to King Cunobelinus (Cymbeline, *d. c.* AD 43), were to meet the first attack.

It was delivered by the legions of General Aulus Plautius, who defeated the British and then marched northwards, crushing all who opposed them.

In AD 50 Caractacus (Caradoc, *d.* AD 54), chief of the Silures, led his tribe against the Romans but was defeated and taken to Rome. Here his manly bearing and an inspired speech caused Claudius to pardon him and his family and allow them to live on in Italy.

Roman rule in Britain lasted for nearly 400 years and during that time, the country was known as 'Britannia', and was part of the vast Roman Empire.

AD61
Revolt of Boudicca

Boudicca (sometimes known as Boadicea) was the Celtic Queen of the Iceni, a tribe living in what is now Norfolk. For some reason her elderly husband, Prasutagus, had willed half his kingdom to the Emperor Nero and half to his two daughters. On his death in about AD 60 the Romans moved in and began to loot the palace. When Boudicca objected, she and her daughters were roughly handled.

She swore revenge and soon, not only her own Iceni were in arms, but many tough warriors of other tribes. Erupting into sudden revolt, the blood-crazed tribes swept southwards descending upon Colchester, London and Verulamium (St Albans) to leave ruin and corpses behind them.

Only Suetonius Paulinus, with two under-strength legions, stood against the British army

(Left) Coin of Claudius, who sent Aulus Plautius to conquer Britain in AD 43. (Right) Boudicca, Queen of the Iceni, leads the revolt against the Romans.

of 100,000 men. The Romans, however, were the most successful soldiers in the ancient world, and though outnumbered, they won a hard-fought victory and so preserved Roman rule in Britain.

AD 64
The burning of Rome

The Roman emperor Nero (AD 37–68), like his predecessor Caligula, became completely mad. His reign began with much promise, but he was weak and too easily influenced by his mother and he soon plunged into tyranny and debauchery. It is possible that the great fire that almost demolished Rome was begun on his orders even if he did not, as legend would have it, stand watching the holocaust whilst plucking at a lyre.

The fire broke out in a number of shops and was soon blazing with great fury. Tacitus, the historian (see AD 120 Tacitus writes the Annales) has described how the fire raged throughout the city and how nearly everyone was involved in the conflagration. The fire continued for six days and when it was finally quenched, only four of the fourteen quarters of the city remained. Nero, seizing the opportunity, began a building scheme which was to result in a far more beautiful and stately city than the Rome which

had vanished in smoke and ashes. He did not live long to enjoy it, however, for four years later he committed suicide during a revolt.

AD 78
Agricola becomes governor of Britain

Gnaeus Agricola (c. AD 37–93) arrived in AD 78 to become governor of Britain. He was to prove himself the greatest of them all. One of his first tasks was to conquer Scotland and he met and defeated the Highland tribes at the battle of Mons Graupius in AD 84.

When it came to controlling the Britons under his rule, Agricola used a very clever method. He introduced them to the very comfortable, even luxurious Roman way of life. Many Britons began to live in Roman-style towns or villas, wore Roman clothes and sent their children to Roman schools. After the end of Roman rule in the fifth century AD, the Britons would not know such comfort again until the nineteenth century.

AD 79
The destruction of Pompeii

The little town of Pompeii, facing the beautiful Bay of Naples, was a popular holiday resort in ancient times, yet otherwise was of little importance. It has since attained immortality.

One pleasant morning in August, AD 79, the volcano Vesuvius, which had been showing signs of activity for some days, suddenly erupted and began to bury the town with fine volcanic ash. The eruption lasted for forty-eight hours, and when it was over no trace of Pompeii was left; it was buried beneath seven metres of ash and lava. The survivors tried to recover their buried treasures but had little success. They drifted away and the world forgot the place.

In 1710, Pompeii was again located, and after 1748, archaeologists were at work, retrieving the town from its deep covering of ashes. The excavations at Pompeii saw the start of modern archaeology, though few places are so well preserved. Though there is still more of Pompeii

News of the burning of Rome is brought to the capricious and tyrannical emperor, Nero.

to be uncovered, even today, people can now walk through its streets and see an ancient city which seems frozen in time.

AD 114
Trajan's Column

A magnificent column, nearly forty metres high, still stands in Rome and marks the many victories of the Emperor Trajan (AD 53–117). During his reign the empire reached its greatest extent, for he made Armenia, Assyria, Dacia and Mesopotamia Roman provinces. More than a victorious general, however, he built roads, bridges and libraries and the magnificent Forum Trajanum.

c. AD 120
Kanishka, King of Afghanistan

The country now known as Afghanistan was ruled by the Parthians for some three hundred years until they, in turn, were expelled by the Yue-chi, an Asiatic tribe. At first the Yue-chi had been a loose-knit federation of five tribes, but in about AD 80 they were formed into one powerful nation which went on to conquer the Kabul valley and remove the remains of Greek domination.

It was ruled by Kanishka who became famous as a patron of Buddhism. He convened a great Buddhist council and established that religion throughout his empire, which eventually included the whole of northern India and considerable stretches of central Asia.

c.AD120
Ptolemy's experiments

Ptolemy (Claudius Ptolemaeus) of Alexandria (c. AD 90–168) was one of the cleverest men of antiquity – mathematician, astronomer, and geographer. One of his interesting discoveries was his theory of refraction of light. In pure mathematics he was outstanding, especially in his exposition of trigonometry. He also wrote several books on music, including *Harmonica*. In his book *The Almagest* Ptolemy set down the ancient Greek view, which placed the Earth at the centre of the universe, with the Moon, the Sun and the planets revolving around it, followed by a sphere containing the fixed stars – a theory accepted for more than 1,300 years.

He is perhaps best remembered for his cartography. His great work was the construction of a series of twenty-six maps and a general map of the then known world.

c.AD120
Tacitus writes the *Annales*

Tacitus was born about AD 55 and lived through the reigns of ten emperors before dying some three years after Trajan. He became a first-class historian, his two most important works being the *Historiae* and the *Annales*. Through Tacitus we have been provided with knowledge of some eighty years of important Roman history.

AD 122
Hadrian builds wall

Southern Britain became settled and prosperous under Roman rule, and the Romans built mighty fortresses to guard the area they controlled. Nevertheless, the northern frontier of Roman Britannia was continually ravaged by tribesmen

Hadrian's Wall, northern outpost of the Roman empire.

from Caledonia (Scotland) called Picts, and the tribe of Brigantes occupying what is now Yorkshire. Consequently, in AD 122, the Emperor Hadrian (AD 76–138) ordered a barrier to be built to keep out the Pict raiders, a wall to stretch some 110 kilometres, with detached forts every six kilometres, from the Tyne to the Solway. It served its purpose well, although the legionaries guarding it could never relax.

In AD 197 the Governor of Britain withdrew the legions in an unsuccessful attempt to gain the empire. The northern tribes immediately swarmed over the wall until the new emperor, Septimus Severus, bought them off. In AD 367 the northern tribes again crossed the wall, aided by Saxons, and order was restored only when legions were brought in from the Continent.

AD 164
Galen at work in Rome

Galen (c. AD 130–200) was a Greek physician who arrived in Rome about AD 164. His skill in healing brought him imperial favour and he was made personal physician to the emperors Marcus Aurelius and Commodus. He wrote of his work, and those of his writings that survived were studied by other physicians for centuries.

AD 212
New citizens of Rome

When the Emperor Caracalla (AD 188–217) succeeded Severus his great sprawling empire was running short of cash. One great burden was the vast sums paid to keep barbarian chieftains at peace. In AD 212, therefore, he decided to grant citizenship to every free man in his empire to increase his tax revenue. His decree was called the *Constitutio Antoniniana*. For the first time in history men from Asia to Spain could proudly claim 'I am a citizen of Rome'.

AD 220
End of the Han dynasty in China

It has been said that more inventions occurred during the Han dynasty (202 BC–AD 220) than at any time in the history of the world.

One of these was the compass, the Chinese realizing that magnetized strips of iron would always settle along a north–south line when hung from a cord. They also discovered an explosive powder made from potassium nitrate, charcoal and sulphur (gunpowder) but used it only to make fireworks for celebrations.

Ink and paper also made their first appearance during the Han dynasty, the latter being used in the first century AD as a substitute for silk cloth.

Astronomical instruments were greatly improved; an astronomer of the time first used water power to run an 'orrery', from which has grown the modern clock.

All these inventions were set against a period of great expansion. A steady trade was carried on with the Roman Orient, both by land and sea. At this time also, Buddhism was introduced into China to become the state religion.

AD 224
The Sassanid dynasty founded in Persia

The Sassanid (or Sassanian) dynasty was founded by Ardashir I (d. 241), a ruler of one of the small kingdoms into which Persia had been divided. Its name came from Sassan, an ancestor of the founder.

Ardashir had to fight hard for his new country. It was ruled by the Parthian King Artabanus, but when he died Ardashir marched at the head of a large army and slowly began to overrun Mesopotamia, to form a national Persian empire once more.

The Romans felt threatened by Ardashir's activities. The Roman legions invaded, and retrieved many of the newly-conquered territories. Roman power, however, was soon on the wane. In AD 251, the Emperor Decius was defeated and killed in battle by the barbarian Goths. After this, the Roman legions were in a continual state of mutiny, several of Decius' successors were weak rulers and many of them were murdered.

Ardashir's son Shapur (d. AD 272) decided to exploit the weakness of the Romans and continued the war, plundering Antioch and conquering Armenia. The Roman Emperor Publius Valerian (AD 193–260) marched against Shapur, but was heavily defeated at Edessa (AD 260). He was taken prisoner and tortured to death. The Sassanid dynasty was to continue for four centuries until it was destroyed by the Arabs in AD 637.

AD 320
Gupta empire founded in India

The classical age of Indian civilization began with the Gupta dynasty, and with Chandragupta I who founded it in AD 320 after a series of foreign invasions. His son, Samudragupta (c.. AD 340–80) enlarged his father's empire whilst *his* son, Chandragupta II Vikramaditya proved to be a most energetic soldier, extending the empire until it was one of the largest of the ancient world, leading his armies far to the south in search of fresh kingdoms. It eventually included Nepal, Assam and the kingdom of the Punjab.

The Gupta empire was to last for about one hundred and fifty years although members of the family still ruled areas long after this. The whole era is remarkable for the advances made in art, science, medicine, mathematics and Sanskrit literature.

AD 330
Constantinople becomes the new capital

During the early part of the fourth century AD, Rome was continually under attack from barbarian tribes striking from the east. It had also become an old and inconvenient city in which to live. These factors encouraged the Roman Emperor Constantine (c. AD 280–337) to move his capital to the city of Byzantium which in AD 330 was nearly one thousand years old, having been founded about 657 BC by Byzas the Greek.

Constantine chose Byzantium because he was attracted by the city's position – with any attack coming only from the west as the other three sides were protected by the sea. He was baptized as a Christian in AD 337 by which time his architects and engineers had transformed the old city into a new and magnificent fortress (*see* AD 532 *Building of St Sophia*).

AD 410
Sack of Rome by Visigoths

In AD 410 a host of fierce barbarians, followed by their women, children and cattle, poured across Europe in a great, all-engulfing flood. The barriers of the Roman empire were down and the savage tribesmen of the northern forests joined up with Visigoth warriors; led by an able commander, Alaric (c. AD 370–410), they first poured into Greece, Athens, Sparta and Corinth. All fell and were thoroughly pillaged, and the inhabitants carried off into slavery.

With Greece and then the Balkans thoroughly devastated, Alaric began the march upon Rome and soon appeared at the foot of the Julian Alps, the first invader to threaten the city since the days of Hannibal, five hundred years earlier. Stilicho, a gallant Roman general, did his best to stem the relentless tide, but to no avail. In August AD 410 the hordes assembled before the city of Rome and were soon inside the walls of the doomed city. After three days of looting, Alaric gathered his men together and faced with a food shortage, led them off again, leaving behind a city in ruins. He took them south but died shortly after in Sicily.

AD 413
St Augustine writes *The City of God*

Augustine (AD 354–430) was born of Roman parents in Tunis. Although they were Christian he did not profess any faith during his early

Constantinople, eastern capital founded by Constantine on the site of Byzantium (now Istanbul).

years. When thirty-four, however, he accepted Christianity, was baptized and studied to become a priest. Amongst his greatest works were *Confessions* (AD 397) and *De Civitate Dei* ('The City of God', AD 413–26).

AD 428
Foundation of the Merovingian dynasty in France

One Frankish tribe was the Salians who occupied a region near the Meuse river. In the fifth century when Roman legions were withdrawn to fight the barbarian invasion, the Frankish Salians became an independent people, giving their name to France. An early Salian king was Merovech, founder of the Merovingian dynasty, the first to rule over France; his son was Childeric I (AD 457–81) and his grandson was Clovis.

AD 432
St Patrick's mission to Ireland

St Patrick (c. AD 385–461), the patron saint of Ireland, was born in Britain near the River Severn. He was educated as a Christian but when he was sixteen years old he was carried off by a band of Irish pirates, sold, and forced to become a shepherd until he managed to escape in a ship which landed him in Gaul.

After religious training he returned home to Britain for a while, then had a vision in which he was asked to return to Ireland and carry the Gospel to that mainly pagan land. In order that he might prepare for his work, he returned to Gaul to study at Tours, and was later consecrated as a bishop by Pope Constantine I in AD 432. The same year he took a ship for Ireland to begin his missionary work and despite early opposition, he persevered, bringing Christianity to the island.

c. AD 435

Britain invaded by Jutes, Angles and Saxons

For centuries Britain had been a settled land, backed by the power of Rome, but early in the fifth century AD, the city of Rome, heart of the Empire, was under serious threats from barbarian attacks. Legions were withdrawn from Britain to help defend Rome and in AD 410 the Roman Emperor told the Britons they would have to be responsible for their own defence. By 426 AD, the last of the Roman legions had left, never to return. This left Britain wide open to invasions from barbarian tribes from Germany and Denmark. These tribes, the Angles, Jutes and Saxons had already attacked Britain while the Romans were still in charge, so the Britons knew what they were in for.

The first invaders were a pagan Teutonic tribe known as the Angles, coming from north-west Denmark. They first came to pillage and then to stay, giving their name to East Anglia.

Their neighbours were also a Teutonic tribe, the Saxons, and like the Angles their influence on the development of early England was very great. Yet another Teutonic tribe descended on Britain's coasts. These were the Jutes, but the other two tribes seem to have been the more dominant. The Anglo-Saxons gradually conquered the Britons, pushing Romano-Celtic civilization to the west (*see c. AD 500 The Battle of Mount Badon*).

AD 451

Attila the Hun invades Gaul

Attila the Hun (*c.* AD 406–53), was a man whose very name brought a sudden chill to thousands of people during the fifth century, being aptly named 'The Scourge of God'. He was born about

AD 406 and on the death of his uncle, became the ruler of the race that came from the easternmost edges of the great plains of Europe – the Huns.

In AD 447 he led them across the Danube and was soon compelling tribes living on the fringes of the Roman empire to flee. Pillaging, burning and killing as they went, the Huns swept across Germany and in AD 451 crossed into Gaul.

Aetius, a Roman, and Theodoric, a Vandal, combined to stop them and a battle fought near Châlons-sur-Marne ended in the complete rout of the Huns. Forced to retreat, their battered army invaded and devastated Italy. Attila died in AD 453 and without his guiding hand, the Hun hordes began to drift apart.

c. AD 500
Clovis and the Franks accept Christianity

The Merovingian dynasty, founded in AD 428, steadily became more and more powerful, advancing across France to establish their capital at Tournai. In AD 481 they had a new king, a young warrior named Clovis (*c.* AD 466–511). One of his first actions was to fight a battle with Syagrius, a Roman general who had created a kingdom for himself nearby, and heavily defeated him.

Clovis then led his Salian Franks to a new capital he built in Soissons and slowly extended his kingdom until it was almost an empire. In AD 493 he married Clotilda, a Burgundian princess and a Christian. He allowed his children to be baptized but continued as a pagan until, in battle against the Alemanni, he swore to become a Christian if victory were his. He triumphed and he was accordingly baptized in AD 496 in Rheims, with three thousand of his fellow Franks.

c. AD 500
The Battle of Mount Badon

The Anglo-Saxon invaders of Britain eventually conquered most of Britain except Scotland, Wales and Western Cornwall, yet they often found very stiff opposition. Although the Romans had gone, many retired legionaries were left behind, and a blend of Roman-Christian and Celtic civilization lingered on in the villas of important Britons.

These families maintained the Roman knowledge of warfare, and resisted the Saxons. These troubled times are described in Gildas's *De Excicio et Conquestu Britanniae* ('On the Destruction and Conquest of Britain', AD 518).

One hero from this period is a British general, Arthur, who seems to have collected a band of warriors about him, and fought at least twelve battles against the Saxons, the last and greatest being at Mount Badon, probably near Swindon, *c.*AD 500.

Arthur soon became a legendary figure in Celtic folklore, and one of the favourite subjects of later medieval literature, in which he is transformed into a great king at the head of a chivalrous court.

*c.*AD 500
Chichén Itzá flourishes

One great civilization occupying Central America was that of the Mayas who, about AD 300, began to migrate northwards to search for a more suitable place in which to build again. Such migrations were frequent in olden times because they had not learned how to enrich the soil and were forced to move on when crops failed.

One of the eighteen Mayan clans chose a site in Mexico called Chichén Itzá which, unlike most cities, was not founded on or near a river. They obviously knew what they were doing, however, for their city was built upon limestone through which the annual rains percolated to collect in pools beneath. The Mayans built large reservoirs, called 'cenotes', assuring themselves of cool sweet water throughout the year.

The city was very large with several massive buildings of white gleaming sandstone and, towering above all a huge pyramid topped with a temple, twenty-six metres high. All these buildings were covered with rich carvings. There was also a sacred well used for the sacrifice of maidens. In its heyday Chichén Itzá was regarded as a holy city.

The 'Church' at Chichén Itzá. It is decorated with large masks of the rain god Chac with his long nose and in the frieze are four deities which support the sky; they are disguised as a snail, a turtle, a crab and an armadillo.

AD 523

Boethius: *On the Consolation of Philosophy*

Anicius Boethius (AD 480–524) has been described as 'the last of the Romans and the first of the Scholastics'. In AD 500 he was made a consul and soon proved himself a fair but determined man. Without justification he was accused of treason and sent to prison where he wrote his great work, *De Consolatione Philisophiae* ('On the Consolation of Philosophy', AD 523).

AD 532

Building of St Sophia

The ancient name of Byzantium (*see AD 330 Constantinople becomes the new capital*) was changed in honour of the emperor to Constantinople. After the Emperor Diocletian divided the Roman Empire into two in AD 293, the Western part, based on Rome, declined, but the Eastern, with Constantinople as its capital, became very powerful. It also became very beautiful, for it developed into a fortress-city of palaces and theatres, circuses and churches, the whole of Rome's great empire being ransacked for treasure with which to decorate the capital. Within six years of Constantine founding the city the work was completed and Constantinople dedicated to Christianity.

It reached the zenith of its glory during the reign of the Emperor Justinian (AD 483–565) who had two main aims. One was to win back the Western Empire from the barbarians (in which he was only partially successful), and the other was to give his empire a new code of laws. His *Codex constitutionum* was produced in AD 529 to clarify and bring up to date all previous Roman laws.

Amongst the fine buildings erected during his reign, the most beautiful was (and is) the Church of St Sophia, a masterpiece of beauty and grandeur, where the sweep of curve upon curve rises to a height of fifty-three metres at the apex of its great dome. It is now an Islamic mosque.

Justinian and his court. Mosaic from Ravenna, *c.* AD 540.

AD 540

The first Welsh poets

As the Anglo-Saxons pushed the Celtic peoples westward, we see the flowering of poetry in the region of Wales, much of which found inspiration in Irish myths and legend. The songs of bards such as Taliessin (*c.* AD 540), Aneirin (sixth to seventh century AD), and Llywarch Hên (*c.* AD 700) were later written down in the middle ages. Aneirin's main work, the *Gododin* laments British heroes killed in battle with the Saxons.

AD 563

St Columba founds Iona

One of the Hebrides is the small island of Iona. It is remarkable as the cradle of Christianity in Scotland. After St Columba landed on the island to found a monastery, it became one of the most famous in the country and a centre of Christianity in the north. Iona itself also became the see of a bishop.

AD 602

St Augustine founds Canterbury Cathedral

The second St Augustine (*see AD 413 St Augustine writes The City of God*) was originally the prior of a Roman monastery. In AD 597 he was sent to England by Pope Gregory I with about forty monks. King Aethelbert of Kent allowed them to settle in Canterbury, and was later baptized by Augustine. In AD 602 work began on the magnificent Cathedral. Augustine died in AD 604.

AD 618

Foundation of the T'ang dynasty

When the great Han dynasty, which had ruled China for more than four centuries, collapsed in AD 220, nomads invaded from the north and for another four centuries China was without a stable government.

In AD 618 the T'ang dynasty came to power. From that date the country was to become large and prosperous, T'ang armies extending the frontiers of China to make it the greatest empire in the world. The next three centuries of T'ang rule are today regarded as China's golden age.

The greatest of all T'ang emperors was Li Lung-chi who proved to be well worthy of his title 'Son of Heaven', for his reign was one of

Glazed earthenware horse and rider, T'ang dynasty.

great artistic achievement. He founded academies of music, dancing and poetry and also took a great interest in scientific problems, even ordering the building of history's first iron suspension bridge.

AD 622

Mohammed's flight from Mecca

In 622 AD, Mohammed, founder of the Islamic religion, was forced to leave Mecca, where he was born, and escape to Medina to get away from his enemies. This escape, is known as the Hegira, and AD 622 is the date from which the Moslems, the followers of Islam, reckon their calendar.

Mohammed (AD 570–632) was the son of a poor tradesman and a member of the powerful Koreish tribe in Mecca. Mohammed became unhappy with the traditional pagan religion followed in Mecca and began to preach a new monotheistic faith in which there was only one invisible god, Allah. In this, he was commanded by the archangel Gabriel who, it is said, appeared to him in a vision.

The pagans in Mecca naturally became very hostile towards Mohammed, but once he had escaped to Medina, he found many people willing to follow him. Mohammed became increasingly influential in Medina. He declared a holy war, or 'jihad', on the Meccans and defeated them. Peace was made in AD 628 and his missionaries were allowed to travel throughout Arabia.

Mohammed made his last pilgrimage to Mecca in AD 632 and died shortly after. The new faith, Islam, and its holy book, the Koran, was carried by victorious armies throughout the Middle East to Africa, the Mediterranean and Spain.

AD 638

Jerusalem captured by Moslems

Within two centuries of Mohammed's death his followers conquered an empire which was larger than the former Roman empire. The first great warrior of Islam was Caliph Omar who came to power in AD 634 to continue Mohammed's original policy of 'conversion by force'. One of his first triumphs was the capture of Jerusalem, then a Christian city. The inhabitants resisted for four months and only surrendered when Omar promised that life and property would be spared on payment of tribute. A promise he kept.

Omar died in AD 644 but the Moslems swept on, besieging Constantinople (AD 673–8) and swarming into Carthage (AD 698) and Spain (AD 711) until stopped at Tours by Charles Martel (AD 732) in a battle which saved Christendom.

c. AD 650

Invention of wood printing blocks

The most important invention to come out of China at this time was that of printing, using simple wooden blocks, which was developed during the T'ang dynasty (AD 618–907). Wood around the design to be printed was carved away so that the design was in relief. The block was then inked and applied, under pressure, to the material and later, on to paper.

AD 664

The Synod of Whitby

From the year AD 597 when Augustine and his small band stepped ashore, England had steadily become converted to Christianity. Missionaries went out from Canterbury and St Columba's isle of Iona and the Gospel was taken throughout England. Within a century paganism had virtually disappeared, even though the fierce old Saxon gods took a long time to lose their influence.

Because the missionaries came from two different centres, however, a problem had arisen. Was England to adopt the Roman form of Christianity as preached by the followers of St Augustine, or the Celtic form as practised in Iona, Ireland and Northumbria?

Finally King Oswy called a great ecclesiastical council, or Synod, in the Yorkshire town of Whitby in AD 664. The outcome was a victory for those supporting Rome, the date of Easter was established, and the Celtic church agreed to accept the same doctrines and control as the Roman Church.

AD 700

Lindisfarne and its *Gospels*

Lindisfarne, a small island some three kilometres off the Northumberland coast, was the home of St Aidan, a monk who had sailed from Iona to build a monastery there in about AD 635. Aidan used the island as a base from which to reconvert Northumbria which had lapsed into paganism about AD 633 and, helped by King Oswald, the kingdom was soon Christian once more.

Aiden died in AD 651 and one of his successors was St Cuthbert who was bishop of the see until his death in AD 687, travelling constantly over all Northumbria, baptizing vast numbers of men and women. About AD 700 the artist-monks of the island's monastery produced what is now known as the *Lindisfarne Gospels*, one of Europe's finest illuminated manuscripts. When in AD 875 the island was attacked by Vikings, the monks fled, taking with them the body of St Cuthbert and their priceless possession – the *Lindisfarne Gospels*.

c. AD 715

Beowulf

Beowulf is the hero of the oldest epic poem in the English language, which tells the story of his fight with a grim monster and a dragon. The phrases and the style of writing used are identical with those of the monks of the seventh century and experts consider that the poem was first written down early in the eighth century, about AD 715.

AD 731

Bede writes his *History*

Bede (known as the Venerable) (c. AD 673–735) was the greatest of all early English historians. When a child he entered the monastery of Wearmouth, and then moved to the monastery of Jarrow. He was a brilliant scholar and his *Ecclesiastical History of the English Nation* has proved of inestimable value to subsequent historians. He died in AD 735.

AD 750
The *Book of Kells*

The eighth century produced several master-pieces of illuminated manuscript art such as the *Lindisfarne Gospels* and the Irish *Book of Durrow* of AD 750. Perhaps the finest early Christian art is contained in the magnificent Irish *Book of Kells*. This manuscript of the gospels in Latin is decorated with intricate design in the Celtic manner and fine illustrations.

AD 778
The death of Roland

The famous French epic poem about the warrior-knight Roland (*see 12th century The growth of medieval literature*) seems to have been based on historical fact. In about AD 820 the Frankish historian Einhard wrote a history of the life of his patron Charlemagne (*see AD 800 Charlemagne crowned Holy Roman Emperor*), in which he mentions the death of Roland, or Hruodland, the prefect of the Breton marches, at the Battle of Roncesvalles.

In AD 778 Charlemagne invaded Spain. He captured Pamplona, but failed to take Saragossa. News came to him of a Saxon revolt on the Rhine, and he was forced to return to France

through the Pyrenees. Charlemagne's rearguard was cut off from the main army by hostile Basques, who destroyed them.

The epic's dramatic tale of a great Saracen army, the blowing of the horn, and the friendship of Oliver and Roland, is purely part of the legend that grew up around the Battle of Roncesvalles.

AD 782
Offa's Dyke

Offa (*d.* AD 796) became King of Mercia in AD 757 and immediately set out to restore his kingdom to its former greatness. He finally controlled almost all of Britain south of the Humber. To protect his northern frontiers, in AD 782–3 he built a great earthwork, now known as Offa's Dyke, which ran from sea to sea between the Severn and the Dee.

AD 793
The first Viking raid on Britain

The Vikings who first attacked Britain in AD 793 earned themselves a reputation for bloodshed and destruction. They were tall, bearded warriors who swept in from the sea to murder and ravage and then disappear over the horizon

Offa's Dyke, the great defensive earthwork built by the King of Mercia, in AD 782.

bgeueramo

before reinforcements could be rushed to the spot. Despite this, they were far from being a barbaric people, their way of life and culture being as advanced as that of their victims.

At home, after a raid, they would return to being farmers, traders or craftsmen. They were great travellers, sailing southwards to Byzantium or northwards to Russia, which is called after them – 'men of Rus'.

They were particularly famous for their ships – long, beautifully designed craft which did not butt their way through the water but slid over it like a sea-bird. Fortunately several Viking boats have recently been unearthed in a remarkably good state of preservation.

AD 800

Charlemagne crowned Holy Roman Emperor

Christmas Day, AD 800, can be regarded as one of the most important dates in history, for it was on that day that Charles, King of the Franks, was crowned by Pope Leo III and was to become known as Charles the Great, or Charlemagne (c. AD 742–814). This date is often looked on as the beginning of the Middle Ages.

Charlemagne was the grandson of Charles Martel, who defeated the invading Saracens at the battle of Tours (AD 752), and his father was Pepin the Short who seized the Frankish kingdom from Childeric, the last of the Merovingian kings. On Pepin's death in AD 768 his kingdom was divided between his two sons, Charles and Carloman, but the latter died three years later and Charles became king of all France.

He faced a grim world. Europe was torn apart by dissension, ignorance, greed and superstition which surrounded him on all sides. With a cross in one hand and a sword in the other he began his great work. He conquered the Saxons and the Lombards, subdued the barbarian Avars on the Danube, fought in Spain against the Moslems and in Germany against the Magyars. By the time of his death he ruled an empire that stretched from the Baltic to the Spanish marches, from Brittany to the Lower Danube.

He was not only a soldier, however. He encouraged scholarship and music and also built many churches and palaces. At his death only one of his sons, Louis the 'Pious' (AD 778–840) was living. By the Treaty of Verdun (AD 843) the empire was divided amongst Louis' sons, and split into quarrelling fragments.

AD 828

Egbert recognized as Overlord of England

In AD 748 Cynewulf of Wessex died, and Egbert, son of a king of Kent, laid claim to the throne. His rival Bertic was elected, however, and fearing that his life might be in danger, Egbert took refuge first at the court of Offa, King of Mercia and then at the court of Charlemagne.

Here he was able to study the ways of the great king and when in AD 802 he became King of Wessex on Bertic's death, he was able to follow Charlemagne's example, deciding to win superiority over England as the other had over the continent of Europe.

England's southern kingdoms accepted his rule without question but he had to fight and defeat Mercia (AD 823) until, in AD 828, he was finally acknowledged Overlord of all England with the title of Bretwalda or 'Wealder of Britain'. He died in AD 839.

AD 844

Coronation of Kenneth I of Scotland

Kenneth, son (Mac) of Alpin is considered to be Scotland's first king. He had become King of the Scots in AD 832 and as his grandmother had been a Pictish princess, he considered that he should have the throne of the Picts as well, Scotland then being divided between Picts and Scots. War was declared between them and dragged on until AD 843 when a final battle brought death to the King of the Picts and most of his nobles.

Thus Kenneth MacAlpin became ruler of both nations and was the first to call his kingdom Scotland. He proved to be a good king, treating his subjects justly, and occasionally leading a combined army of Picts and Scots over the border into England. He invaded Northumbria on six occasions before his death in AD 860.

A page from the *Book of Kells*.

AD 850
Acropolis of Zimbabwe

In the thirteenth century Bantu tribes drove out the Bushmen from South-Central Africa and gave the area the name of Zimbabwe – or 'house of stones' – for there they found a number of large stone buildings.

The largest of these, a great fortified mound of stone and cement is about ninety metres high, and was probably built by eastern traders in about AD 850.

AD 868
The first printed book

The earliest printed book we know of is a copy of the Buddhist scripture the *Diamond Sutra*, found in a Turkestan cave in 1900. A five-metre scroll, it is made up of six pages of text printed from wood blocks and one page of woodcut illustrations glued together. Printed by one Wang Chieh in AD 868, it was distributed free in memory of his parents.

AD 871
Accession of Alfred the Great

Alfred (AD 849–99) was born at Wantage, the youngest son of Aethelwulf of Wessex. When still in his teens he helped his brother Aethelred fight an invading army of Danes, winning fame at the battle of Ashdown in AD 871. His brother died in the same year and Alfred became King of

Alfred the Great (*see* AD 871) built a fleet which for the first time managed to fight off Danish raiders from the English coast.

THE MOSLEM WORLD

The founder of Islam, which believes in one God, Allah, was Mohammed (AD 570–632) who was born in Mecca, Arabia. Not long after Mohammed's death, Moslems, the followers of Islam, began conquering and converting territories around Arabia until by 945 AD, a Moslem 'empire' stretched from Spain and North Africa in the west to Afghanistan in the east, and included parts of central Europe. Within this

'empire', great advances were made and high standards reached in art, architecture, medicine, poetry, music, navigation and map-making, astronomy, botany, mechanics and other sciences. Cities such as Damascus (Syria), Granada (Spain) and Baghdad (Iraq) where Haroun al-Raschid was ruler in the 9th century AD, became great centres of learning and culture. Haroun, whose court was the setting for the famous

The Thousand and One Nights had a library containing sixty thousand books at a time when most European kings were illiterate. Similarly, the Islamic world produced brilliant philosophers such as Maimonides (1135–1204) in Spain, doctors like Avicenna (980–1037) in Persia, and the splendid architecture of the Alhambra in Spain and the Taj Mahal in India, whose beauties can still be seen today.

Wessex in his stead. In time he was to be acknowledged as the Overlord of all England.

He was defeated by another Danish army and was forced to take refuge in Somerset, but it was not long before he had gathered an army to defeat the enemy at Edington in AD 878.

This was followed by a treaty in which it was agreed that Alfred and the Danish leader Guthrum should divide the country between them, Alfred taking the south and west. He had to fight further hordes of invaders in AD 884, but held his own. He died in AD 900 and was buried at Winchester.

c. AD 900
The building of Angkor Wat

The great city and temple complex of Angkor was little known to Western travellers until the present century. It lies buried deep in the jungle in the north of Cambodia. In spite of some thirteen centuries and the ravages of the encroaching forest, Angkor has changed very little, and even its earliest buildings are intact.

The city of Angkor became the capital of a nation known as the Khmers at the end of the ninth century AD. Its finest temple, still a place of pilgrimage, is the Angkor Wat, built for the worship of Buddha, a vast building some two and a half kilometres from the original royal city and surrounded by a moat measuring more than five thousand metres. The building is in the

shape of a pyramid, rising in three stages, with profusely decorated walls showing gods, men and animals.

AD 950
First reference to chess

The earliest written reference to chess is by Masudi, an Arabic author writing about AD 950. The word 'chess' is the modern English equivalent of the Persian *shah* or king and the term 'checkmate', used in the game, is from *shah mat* or 'the king is dead'.

AD 982
Erik the Red colonizes Greenland

The Viking settlement of Iceland, known as the 'Land-taking', had been colonized by farmers and fishermen from Norway and from Norse settlements in Britain. One of these was Erik the Red who, having killed two men in a quarrel, was outlawed for three years. He remembered the tale of a strange land some three hundred kilometres to the west which had been sighted by Vikings. He followed their route across the Atlantic and after some days saw a great land mass. He spent most of his exile exploring the coast and gave it the name of Greenland.

AD987
Founding of the Capetian dynasty

Since AD 814, the kingdom of the Franks had been ruled by the descendants of the house of Charlemagne (see AD 800 Charlemagne crowned Holy Roman Emperor) – the Carolingians – whose kings became steadily weaker whilst other men, rendering great service to their country, were coming steadily to the fore. One of these was Eudes, son of Robert the Strong, who was elected king because of his gallant defence of Paris against the Vikings, the Carolingian king, Charles 'the Fat', having been deposed. He headed a new dynasty known as the Robertians.

A long struggle began, the Carolingians and the Robertians seeming to alternate with each other on the throne. Finally, in AD 987, Hugh Capet (c. AD 938–96) came to the throne to found the celebrated Capetian dynasty to which, for nearly nine centuries, the kings of France (including the Valois and Bourbons), and many of their most powerful nobles belonged.

AD991
The Battle of Maldon

Edward, King of England, later known as 'the Martyr', (c. AD 963–78) was murdered at Corfe Castle by his step-mother Elfrida who wanted her son, Aethelred (AD 968–1016), to be king. Her plan succeeded and her ten-year-old son came to a throne he was to occupy for nearly forty years.

England was soon in great difficulties, for the Danes took advantage of the fact that the country was now ruled by a weak and cowardly young king. The beginning of his reign coincided with the third period of the Danish invasion, with the Danes determined to conquer England for their own.

In AD 991 they went plundering through Essex and were met at Maldon by Brihtnoth, alderman of the East Saxons, with a hastily gathered army. The English fought courageously but, terribly outnumbered, were finally defeated by the better armed and more battle-tried Danes.

AD1000
Leif Eriksson discovers North America

Leif, son of Erik the Red (see AD 982 Erik the Red colonizes Greenland) was living in the new colony when he heard a strange story from a Viking who had newly arrived in the island. The man, Bjarni Hergulfsson, had sailed from Iceland for Greenland, but missing his landfall, had sighted a range of low-lying islands. Not bothering to explore he turned his boat's bows around and headed eastwards.

In AD 1000 Leif hired Bjarni's boat, gathered thirty-five comrades and set off to find the unknown land. The first landfall was a low, barren coast with high mountains that shone like glass. His boat grounded on the stony shore and Leif jumped down, the first European to set foot on the shores of the New World. At the place where he landed, which was probably the island of Labrador, Leif founded his colony of Vinland, which lasted for three years.

1007
Aethelred pays Danegeld

Despite signs of his subjects' courage as revealed by the Battle of Maldon, Aethelred II, soon to become known as the 'Redeless" or 'Unready', began the shortsighted policy of trying to buy off the invaders, levying a new tax called Danegeld. This merely encouraged Danes to come and collect more 'easy' money.

In AD 994, Sweyn, King of Denmark and Olaf, King of Norway appeared together and harried Kent, Sussex and Hampshire. They, too, were bought off but others followed and the country was rarely free from the invaders.

In 1002, when the country was briefly at peace, the stupid Aethelred ordered all Norsemen and Danes who had settled in the country to be slaughtered. Furious, Sweyn returned to ravage and slay with hardly any resistance and Aethelred was forced to flee to Normandy. He returned on news of Sweyn's death but died himself soon afterwards, in 1016.

Canute is said to have publicly demonstrated that the power of kings is not divine by showing that he could not control the waves.

1014

The Battle of Clontarf

Brian Ború (*c.* AD 926–1014) was the son of one of the cheiftains of Munster, in Ireland, then a loose collection of tribes. He was a tough young man who lived for fighting and was soon kept fully occupied with the Danes who constantly tried to ravage his father's lands.

On his father's death his brother, Mathgamhain became chieftain, but was murdered. After avenging the deed, Brian became chieftain. Partly by force and partly by persuasion he forced the other tribes of Munster and Leinster to acknowledge him as overlord.

With a greatly enlarged army he attacked the Danes who were surrounding Dublin, defeated them, and overthrew the chief king of Ireland to become king himself.

He fought the Danes again, almost annihilating them at the Battle of Clontarf in 1014, but after the battle the old king, aged nearly ninety years, was assassinated.

1016

Accession of Canute

On the death of Aethelred (*see* AD 991 *The Battle of Maldon*) his son, Edmund Ironside

(*c.* AD 981–1016) who was quite the opposite of his cowardly father, was elected king by the citizens of London. But it was Canute, claiming what had been won by his father, Sweyn, who was supported by most of the leading men of the realm. Their two armies met several times in battle, the last being fought at Assandune in Essex, where Canute (*c.* AD 994–1035) won a crushing victory.

The two kings then met on the island of Olney where it was agreed that Edmund should be overlord and possess the southern shires whilst Canute should have Mercia and Northumberland. Edmund did not live to enjoy his new kingdom for he died seven months later.

Canute found a rival in Edwy, Edmund's brother, but the council (Witenagemot) decided that England should be united under one strong king. This made Canute king over all England as well as Denmark and, later Norway; he finally proclaimed himself overlord of Sweden. He put away his Danish wife to marry Emma, widow of Aethelred and daughter of Richard, Duke of Normandy, a union which was to cause much trouble later.

1040

Macbeth slays Duncan

Our view of eleventh-century Scotland has been coloured by Shakespeare's play *Macbeth*, which does not present an accurate picture. When Duncan came to the throne in 1034, he was to face a number of serious defeats by the Northumbrians and the Norsemen. In 1040 an unsuccessful raid into England sparked off a civil war at home. The Scottish general Macbeth, Mormaer of Moray, who had a claim to the throne, both in his own right and through his wife Gruoch, slew Duncan and became king in 1040.

Macbeth's rule was efficient and stable, helped by the support of Thorfinn, the Norwegian Earl of Caithness and Sutherland, a cousin of Duncan. Scotland was at this time an entirely Celtic society and culture, and Macbeth's accession marked a reaction against the influence of England and the south. Macbeth was killed in 1057 by Duncan's eldest son Malcolm Ceanmor, who became Malcolm III.

1050

The *Rubáiyát* of Omar Khayyám

Omar Khayyám was considered, in his time, as the greatest mathematician in the Middle East. His treatise on algebra made him famous even in the western world and he also reformed the Moslem calendar. He is, however, best remembered as a poet, his famous *Rubáiyát* being translated by Edward Fitzgerald to give delight to millions. He died in 1123.

1050

The *Mabinogion*

For a time the principal language in the north-western and south-western corners of Wales was Irish. This area became the centre for a number of poets (*see AD 540 The first Welsh poets*) and their influence was considerable. Eleven mythological Irish romances became popular with later Welsh poets, especially young bardic aspirants. They were later collected into one work to be called the *Mabinogion*.

c. 1063

The building of St Mark's, Venice

Dominating one end of the Piazza, Venice, is St Mark's Cathedral, begun about 1063 by Doge Contarini and consecrated about thirty years later. The wealth of the East was used to beautify it – columns from Byzantine basilicas, rare marbles from the Indies and four antique bronze horses brought from Constantinople in 1204.

1066

The Battle of Stamford Bridge

On the death of Edward the Confessor in January 1066, there emerged three main claimants for his throne – William, Duke of Normandy; Harald Hardrada, King of Norway, a son of Edmund Ironside; and Harold Godwinson, Earl of Wessex.

It was Harold that the Witan elected. He was soon aware that the two others were raising armies with which to claim their inheritance. In September it was learned that Harald Hardrada had landed and was advancing south, having joined forces with Tostig, Harold's own brother. The king set out to meet them and the two armies met at Stamford Bridge. By evening both Harald Hardrada and Tostig were dead and their armies utterly defeated. As Harold began to move south again his other rival, William of Normandy, had already set sail and was making for England.

1066

The Battle of Hastings

Learning that William of Normandy had already landed in Pevensey Bay, Harold led his tired army on the long march southwards. He reached a small hill called Senlac and waited for further troops from the southern shires to join him. Not all came and Harold was forced onto the defensive. His army consisted of housecarls (the king's personal bodyguards), magnificent troops, but the rest was composed of peasants equipped only with spears and farming implements.

The battle began and it was soon obvious that the Norman knights, despite their horses and armour, were being beaten, so William tried a ruse, ordering some of his men to pretend to retreat. Excited by this, some of the Saxons broke their ranks and followed, only to be cut down. Harold stood in the centre of his housecarls but their numbers were growing less, especially when William ordered his archers to fire into the air. Harold was shot in the eye and his two brothers were also killed and the Saxon army was thrust from the hill and slaughtered. This battle was later portrayed in the famous Bayeux Tapestry, the work of Matilda, wife of William, and her ladies.

1072

Defeat of Hereward the Wake

William I had been crowned in Westminster Abbey but resistance to his rule continued for many years. One Saxon rebel was Hereward the Wake, a Lincolnshire land-owner who made his headquarters on the Isle of Ely and gathered many supporters. In 1072 he was betrayed but it is not certain what became of him.

1077
The humiliation of Canossa

The Holy Roman Emperor was responsible for the worldly welfare of his subjects. The Pope, who was also the Bishop of Rome, looked after their spiritual welfare. Sometimes, however, they would clash, as in 1077.

The emperor was Henry IV (1050–1106), the Pope was Hildebrand (*c.* 1020–85), Pope Gregory VII, who, immediately upon his accession began to put in hand a number of urgent reforms, asserting his authority over mere temporal power. When, at the Diet of Worms (1076) Henry decreed that Gregory be deposed, he in turn was excommunicated. Henry was forced to yield in the end when his subjects began to throw off their allegiance to him, and he had to travel to Canossa in Calabria. Here he was forced to wait at the gates, dressed humbly as a penitent, craving the Pope's pardon. Gregory finally saw him and lifted the ban of excommunication.

1086
The *Domesday Book*

By order of William the Conqueror (*see 1066 The Battle of Hastings*) a survey was taken of all holdings throughout his new lands and this record is known today as the *Domesday Book*. It gives details of holdings in every shire, except those of the north, their value and the names of the holders, their possessions and other details.

1094
El Cid takes Valencia

Rodrigo Diaz de Vivar was born near Burgos in Spain about 1040. He was to become the hero of

El Cid before Valencia.

the struggle between Christian and Moslem in the eleventh century but his deeds are so obscured by legend it is difficult to tell fact from fable. He was born at a time when Christian and Moor were struggling for mastery of Spain. His deeds won him his Spanish title of *El Campeador* – 'the Champion' – when he defeated the enemy's champion in single combat. His enemies, who respected a hero, gave him the more familiar title of *El Cid*, the 'Lord'.

Whilst on one campaign, however, he was banished from the Spanish court, after which he hired himself out to fight for Christians and Moors. He captured the city of Valencia in 1094, reigning there until his death in 1099.

1095
Proclamation of the First Crusade

During the 11th century the Christian Byzantine empire, with its capital at Constantinople, came under great pressure from the Seljuk Turks, the dominant Moslem power in the region. In 1071 the Seljuk victory at Manzikert left the Byzantine empire with little besides the city itself, and the emperor requested help from the West.

In 1095 Pope Urban II appealed to the rulers and nobility of Western Europe to wage a holy war against the Turks and, in particular, to recapture the Holy Land (Palestine) and Jerusalem, which had been in Moslem hands for over 400 years. Every man who took part would be pardoned from all his sins. The response was overwhelming. Spurred by the promise of absolution and the possibility of loot, volunteers assembled in every Christian country in Europe.

Because each man wore a cross as a badge, the enterprise was known as a crusade (from the Latin *crux*, or cross). After much fighting, which included a battle at Antioch lasting for seven months, the Crusaders finally reached Jerusalem which they captured in 1099.

1100
Death of William Rufus

William I died in 1087 and his second son, also a William, succeeded him. The Conqueror chose him as his successor rather than his heir, Robert of Normandy, who was too weak to be king of a still-troubled land. William II (reigned 1087–1100) became more familiarly known as William Rufus, or the Red King, because of his red hair and violent and cruel temper.

He was determined to crush remnants of Saxon resistance that still persisted and to bring peace to the land, for many of the nobles, in support of Robert of Normandy, were also up in arms. Rufus soon dealt with them, arming his Saxon subjects to aid him when necessary. He made many enemies and no one was very surprised when in 1100 he was found dead in the New Forest with an assassin's arrow in his breast. He was succeeded by his brother, Henry.

c. 1100
The *Samurai* are formed in Japan

The Heian dynasty of Japan lasted for nearly four centuries. At first it was an era of gentleness, with great store being placed upon good manners, art, poetry and calligraphy. The new capital was at Heian-kyo (on the site of present day Kyoto) but as the years passed, so the power of the provincial barons grew.

Soon these nobles began to assume power, forming themselves into groups of fighting men which, in turn, offered their services to the great lords. Thus a form of feudal system was born. These freelance warriors became known as the *Samurai*. They had a strict code of honour and in many ways resembled the mediaeval knights of Europe. In time they were to bring down the Heian dynasty, in 1160.

1121
Turlough O'Connor becomes Ireland's High King

For many years Ireland had consisted of a number of independent kingdoms, the last great king who had exercised some control over them all being Brian Ború (*see 1014 The Battle of Clontarf*). He was followed by a number of kings, many of whom claimed to be king of all Ireland – or *Ard Ri* – but with little justification.

During the early part of the eleventh century,

Japan's warrior knights, the *Samurai*.

Turlough O'Connor, who was King of Connaught, one of the four kingdoms of Ireland, put forward his own claim when the King of Ulster, Domhnall O'Lochlainn died in 1121. He gave a vast amount to the church at Armagh to support his claim but despite this, he had to spend the rest of his long reign (he was seventy-seven when he died) fighting for supremacy. He was, as it happened, Ireland's last great king.

1138
Civil War in England

Henry I of England died in 1135, having nominated his daughter, Matilda, as his successor. Her husband was Geoffrey, nicknamed 'Plantagenet' from a sprig of broom (*planta genista*) he wore in his helmet.

The Council, however, put aside the dead king's wishes and chose Stephen, Henry's nephew. Furious at the decision, Matilda began a civil war which was to last for eight weary years. The war gave the great barons an opportunity to wage war on their own account, first on one side, then on the other. Soon conditions in England were so terrible that a chronicler of the time wrote 'Men said that Christ and His Saints slept.'

The war ended tamely, Matilda agreeing that Stephen should reign until his death and then be succeeded by her son, Henry Plantagenet. A year later Stephen was dead and Henry II reigned over England.

1140
The Council of Sens

Few religious teachers have had such an enthusiastic following of young people as the French scholastic, Pierre Abélard (1079–1142). Although Abélard greatly influenced the minds of his contemporaries and the course of medieval thought, he is better known in modern times for his tragic love affair with Héloïse. The two lovers were married in secret, but Héloïse, fearing that she would hinder Abélard's career, ran away to a convent. Her furious uncle broke into Abélard's home, attacked him savagely and castrated him. Abélard become a monk.

For many years Abélard had been the opponent of Bernard of Claivaux (1090–1153). Bernard's eloquence and studious life made him the oracle of Christendom, but he rejected Abélard's teachings; he upheld the principle of unhesitating faith and Abélard's rational inquiry seemed to him sheer revolt.

In 1140 the two men met at the Council of Sens, in northern France. The meeting was concerned with matters of religious doctrine and Abélard pleaded his cause on a charge of heresy. He appealed to Rome but he was condemned and died two years later.

1145

Proclamation of the Second Crusade

When Jerusalem fell during the First Crusade (*see 1095 Proclamation of the First Crusade*) the Latin Kingdom of Jerusalem was established, a kingdom that was to last for many years. Nevertheless, the Moslems began to win back much of the territory they had lost and the fall of Edessa on Christmas Day, 1144, sparked off the Second Crusade.

It was begun, as before, by the urging of a Pope, this time Eugenius III, and was immediately supported by King Louis VIII of France and the Emperor Conrad III of Germany. But there was little unity between the Crusaders themselves and, indeed, Conrad's men of northern Germany never reached the Holy Land at all, stopping on the way to attack southern Germany, whilst Crusaders from England and the Low Countries plundered Lisbon on the way. They began a siege of Damascus which was unsuccessful and soon afterwards the whole crusade collapsed, the two kings returning home separately.

1152

Frederick Barbarossa becomes emperor

Frederick (c. 1123–90) was born into the powerful Hohenstaufen family about 1124 and in 1147 became Duke of Swabia. Soon afterwards he accompanied his uncle, Conrad III, on the disastrous Second Crusade. Conrad was so impressed with him that he urged that he should be Germany's next king.

Frederick was accordingly crowned at Aix-la-Chapelle in 1152 as Frederick I, but was commonly known as 'Barbarossa' or 'Red-beard'. As Holy Roman Emperor he set to work to create unity and order in the Empire. He led six campaigns into Italy in the hope of restoring the Empire's power, but he was opposed both by the rich Italian cities and the Pope.

Frederick had a magnetic personality and his reign both as king of the German people and Holy Roman Emperor marks one of the most brilliant periods in the Empire's history. At the height of his power, he was one of three leaders of the Third Crusade against the Moslem general Saladin, but he was drowned on his way to the Holy Land.

Frederick Barbarossa drowns whilst on his way to the Third Crusade.

1154

Accession of Henry II

Henry II (1133–89) who gained the throne of England through his mother (*see 1138 Civil War in England*) was, at the time of his coronation, by far the richest prince in Europe. From his mother he gained the throne of England, through his father the Duchy of Anjou. Two years before he came to the throne he married Eleanor of Aquitaine who brought with her as dowry the whole of south-western France.

Henry began his reign by restoring order from the chaos left by years of civil war. In 1155 he prepared to invade Ireland, but his scheme was not carried through. However, Malcolm of Scotland was forced to restore the northern counties of England, and Wales was finally conquered. He also began to reform the English system of law, founding a tribunal of the *Curia Regis* which grew into the courts of King's Bench and Common Pleas.

c. 1155
Foundation of the University of Paris

Europe's oldest university is the University of Paris. It is the most famous of all medieval seats of learning and one on which most others have been modelled. The original name for a university was *studium* (place of study) but was later changed to university because it was controlled in Paris by the guild (*universitas*) of teachers and the name survived.

This guild became very powerful and was the first to free itself from the control of the Church, especially from the Chancellor of Notre Dame Cathedral. It also gave teachers the right to grant licences, *Licentia docendi* (the right to teach), to their pupils which would enable them to be teachers also.

The University of Paris was probably founded about 1155, the actual date being unknown, but it is recorded that King Philip II granted it certain privileges in 1200 and Pope Innocent III in 1215.

1163
Foundation of Oxford University

Oxford University began in a very modest way. About 1120, Theobald of Etampes, under the patronage of Henry I, was teaching 'sixty to one hundred clerks' outside the city, but it was not until 1163 that a university (*studium generale*) came into being. It began to attract many pupils and soon its teachers were claiming it as second only to Paris. The first colleges to be founded were University College (1249) and Balliol (c. 1263).

Cambridge University was founded a little later. In 1209 a body of students moved to Cambridge from Oxford where they had been expelled. In 1214 they were allowed to return but some stayed to begin the foundation of the University. Its earliest colleges were Merton (1274) and Peterhouse (1284).

The college system in both universities was originated by the friars, who influenced their future in the thirteenth century.

1170
The murder of Becket

Thomas Becket first joined the household of Theobald, Archbishop of Canterbury, becoming archdeacon and then Chancellor of the Cathedral. He was powerful and ambitious. He also became a close friend of Henry II, hunting and feasting with him. When Theobald died in 1162, it was inevitable that Becket was made Archbishop in his stead.

By this act, Henry hoped to bring the church under his control and he was surprised and angry when he realized that his *protégé* had changed, becoming withdrawn and austere. Becket also proved determined to uphold the rights of the Church against Henry.

The two men, no longer friends, became bitter opponents until, in 1170, Henry is said to have asked in a fit of anger if there was no one 'that will free me from this quarrelsome priest?'

Four knights heard the remark, rode straightaway to Canterbury and on December 29 they murdered Becket within his own Cathedral. The murder shocked the Christian world and two years later Becket became a saint. The Pope ordered Henry to make a public penance at the altar of Canterbury Cathedral, where he was scourged by the monks, and Canterbury became a place of pilgrimage.

1189
The Third Crusade launched

After the fiasco of the Second Crusade a new and more powerful Moslem army had come into being. Led by Saladin it captured one Crusader stronghold after another and in 1187 Jerusalem itself.

Consequently the Third Crusade was launched. This was formed by three armies led by three kings – Richard I of England, Frederick Barbarossa of Germany and Philip II of France. They set out separately for the Holy Land. Barbarossa died before he reached Palestine, Philip became ill and returned to France, and Richard of England was left in command. His victory over Saladin at Arnif earned him the title of 'Lion Heart' (*Coeur de Lion*). He captured Acre and Jaffa but not Jerusalem.

Richard I of England was victorious over Saladin at Arnif and captured Acre for the Crusaders. He abandoned plans to capture Jerusalem.

In 1192, on his way home, he was taken prisoner in Germany and held captive for two years until a large ransom was paid for his release. He died in battle in 1199.

1194
Building of Chartres Cathedral

'Gothic' architecture began during the middle of the twelfth century. It was a slender and graceful style and its finest example is Chartres Cathedral, southwest of Paris. It was begun in 1194 and compared with the dim interiors of former churches, it was ablaze with many-tinted lights from its stained glass windows, regarded as the world's finest.

12th century
The growth of medieval literature

In the early Middle Ages, Latin was the literary and ecclesiastical language used throughout Europe. The twelfth century saw the birth of modern European literature, as courts developed a taste for spoken or sung poetry in the language of the country.

Troubadours

Written in about 1100 the French epic the *Chanson de Roland* presents a legendary version of Roland's death in AD 778. The medieval epics were stories of heroic battle and feudal bonds, often revealing glimpses of an older epic tradition, as in the German *Nibelungenlied* (c. 1200), which has elements inherited from old Scandinavian sagas.

Singers and poets travelled the rough roads of Europe at the time of the crusades, seeking patronage at castles. In Provence a new convention developed among these *troubadours*: the idea of 'courtly love'. For the first time woman was exalted and ideal love pursued. This new verse spread with the *trouvères* of northern France and the German *Minnesänger*. Notable troubadours included Bertrand de Born (c. 1140–c. 1215); the greatest *Minnesänger* was Walther von der Vogelweide (c. 1170–1230).

Much of the best literature concerns tales of Arthur and his knights, and associated legends originating from Brittany. Authors of Arthurian romance include Thomas, Chrétien de Troyes and Marie de France in the twelfth century, and Wolfram von Eschenbach and Gottfried von Strassburg in the thirteenth.

c. 1200
The first known Inca

The beginnings of what was to become the great Incan empire are related in legends. According to them, a small band of migrants calling themselves the Children of the Sun were looking for a suitable place in which to settle. They were led by Manco Capac and finally chose the fertile Valley of Cuzco. A later leader of the band, Sinchi Roca was either the son or descendant of Manco Capac. In any case, he was the first to call himself *Sapa Inca* (the Only Inca) and was to found a long line of kings who ruled the golden land until their unique civilization was destroyed by Spaniards in the sixteenth century.

By then the empire of the Incas had grown to more than half a million people living in what is now Peru, Ecuador, Bolivia and northern Chile. This vast territory was ruled by the Inca aided by thousands of officials who looked after people's welfare and collected the taxes. The Incan people were clever farmers, engineers and wonderful craftsmen, their work in gold and silver being magnificent.

1204
The Fourth Crusade

Innocent III, who became Pope in 1198, decided that the best way to revitalize religion would be to begin a new Crusade in the traditional medieval manner. He hoped to lead it himself, but the actual leader was Boniface, Marquess of Montferrat, whose aims had little to do with religion, but with loot.

Montferrat's army never reached the Holy Land. He made an agreement with the Venetians to help them capture and loot the Christian city of Constantinople.

The Fourth Crusade turns against Constantinople.

They then proceeded to alter the map of Europe. Count Baldwin of Flanders was made the first 'Latin Emperor of the East' whilst Venice took over a quarter of Constantinople and captured most of the trade that had formerly gone through that city.

1206
Temujin proclaimed Ghengis Khan

For centuries the people of China had tried to keep out the fierce tribes of barbarians that threatened the borders of their sacred soil. The wildest of these tribes was the Mongols who, although utterly ruthless and completely savage,

St Francis renouncing his inheritance – a fresco from the school of Giotto.

continually fought amongst themselves and thus presented little danger.

Then in 1162 a Mongolian was born called Temujin. He succeeded his chieftain father and began to fight the neighbouring tribes. Finally, after many years of struggle, he brought every Mongolian tribe under his control to earn himself the name of Genghis Khan ('Very Mighty Ruler'). Within five years he had assembled an enormous army of 200,000 horsemen which easily burst through the Great Wall to conquer the whole of northern China, then went on to overrun the Turks of Asia Minor and the small kingdoms of Russia. When the Khan died in 1227 he had carved out the largest empire then known to history.

1208
The Albigensian Crusade

During the twelfth century, a new sect began in Southern France. Its followers were known as the Albigenses after the town of Albi, not far from Toulouse. Its members were considered heretics although they lived austere lives which contrasted with the laxity of most of the clergy.

They grew in numbers until Pope Innocent III was forced to send missionaries amongst them to 'bring them back to the accepted Church', but when in 1208 his legate was murdered whilst in their country, he declared a Crusade against them.

His call was eagerly answered by many northern barons who saw an opportunity of plunder and they were led by Simon de Montfort whose son (see 1265 De Montfort's Parliament) of the same name, was to play a large part in English history.

The Albigenes were exterminated after the capture of their fortress of Montsegur in 1244, and their sect disappeared.

1210
Francis of Assisi founds the Franciscans

Born in 1181, Francis was the son of a cloth merchant of Assisi in central Italy. When he was young he wished to become like the heroes of chivalry in the *chansons de gests*, but experience of fighting soon changed his mind.

Later he felt the urge to wander about the world doing good and, travelling to Rome, received the Pope's blessing on his idea. By 1223 he had gathered an army of several thousand disciples and his converts became known as Franciscan friars.

They did not live in monasteries like other monks but spent their lives travelling from country to country working and preaching and, when necessary, begging for food. They practised total poverty and were the poorest of the poor. Their leader (later to become Saint Francis) died on October 3, 1226 in the 'Chapel of the Little Portion' which still stands outside Assisi.

1215
Magna Carta

King John (1167–1216) came to the throne on May 27, 1199 following the death of his brother, Richard I. Even during Richard's absence at the Crusades, John had proved himself wicked and tyrannical. On ascending the throne he seemed to become worse. He lost a great part of the English lands in France, became involved in a struggle with the Pope over the appointment of Stephen Langton to the see of Canterbury and then in a series of quarrels with his barons.

Finally England had had enough. He was not deposed, as one would have expected, but at Runnymede in June 1215 he was forced to sign *Magna Carta* ('The Great Charter') which stated, amongst other important principles, that the king was subject to the law. The spirit of *Magna Carta*, with its sixty-three sections, has influenced the law of England ever since.

1240

Alexander of Novgorod is called 'Nevsky'

In 1224 the Tartar Mongols appeared in the southern steppes of Russia and were soon ravaging central Russia itself, laying waste to the south and sacking Kiev. Their domination of Russia was to last for over two centuries.

One part of Russia which had suffered less than other cities was Novgorod which, however, had other enemies – the Swedes and the German Knights of the Teutonic Order.

In 1240, under Prince Alexander (1220–63) the men of Novgorod attacked the Swedes in the Neva region and defeated them, giving their leader the title of Alexander Nevsky (of the Neva). Two years later he smashed the German knights in a battle fought on the frozen surface of Lake Peipus.

He was realistic enough to know that his army could never defeat the seemingly limitless Mongol hordes and after he paid tribute and homage to the Great Khan, his country was left unmolested.

1254

End of the Hohenstaufen dynasty

The Hohenstaufen were a princely family whose members were emperors or German kings from 1138–1254. The empire became particularly powerful when Frederick Barbarossa (1123–90) became Holy Roman Emperor in 1152. The last emperor was Frederick II (1212–50) and the last king was Conrad IV (1250–54). The execution of Conrad's son in 1268 brought an end to the male line of the Hohenstaufen.

1257

Llywellyn becomes Prince of Wales

During the 1250s, a Welsh battle of power was won by Llywellyn ap Gruffydd (d. 1282) who soon made himself lord of north and south Wales. At the time of his accession his country was overrun by English barons and his first

The barons force King John to sign Magna Carta.

task was to rid Wales of the foreign invaders. In this he was successful and in 1257 Henry III (1207–72) of England acknowledged him as Prince of Wales and Overlord of his country.

Henry's successor, however, was Edward I (1239–1307) who was determined to rule over an undivided kingdom. In 1277 he led a powerful army into Wales, forcing Llywellyn to come to terms. In a further rising the prince was killed in a skirmish near Builth Wells in 1282. Two years later, at Caernarvon Castle, Edward offered his own son, a baby, as the first English Prince of Wales.

1260

Kublai Khan becomes the Great Khan

The great Genghis Khan left an empire that stretched from the Yellow Sea to the Persian Gulf and the Black Sea. His son Ogdai sent armies into most of the northern countries and it was only his death, which recalled the Mongol leaders to dispute the succession, that saved Europe.

The new leader was Kublai, a grandson of Genghis who took the title Great Khan. He completed the conquest of China and founded the Yuen dynasty, becoming the ruler of more subjects than any man in history.

Kublai Khan, ruler of the immense Mongol empire, presided over a magnificent court whose fame spread to Europe.

Yet he was a far more civilized person than the earlier Mongols and it was during his reign that reports of 'far Cathay' were received in Europe, finally resulting in the appearance of Marco Polo at his court (*see 1271 Marco Polo's journey*).

On Kublai's death his empire fell apart, although his successors continued to rule over many conquered territories.

1265
De Montfort's Parliament

Before the Norman Conquest the Saxons had no parliament but a Witanagemot (Assembly of the Wise). In Norman times there was a Great Council but this did very little and kings did as they pleased until King John was checked by his barons and forced to sign the Magna Carta (*see 1215 Magna Carta*).

John's son, Henry III (1207–72) was little better, with a great idea of his own importance, but little ability. Within four years he had bankrupted his kingdom and finally his powers were wrested from him by the nobles who were tired of helping finance his foreign wars. In 1258, led by the idealistic Simon de Montfort, Earl of Leicester, the barons governed the country by committee.

In 1265 de Montfort formed England's first Parliament with nobles and commoners. He was killed at the Battle of Evesham later that year. The first true or 'Model' Parliament was called together in 1295 by Edward I and was the pattern for later legislatures.

1271
Marco Polo's journey

In 1260, Nicolo and Maffeo Polo, two Venetian merchants, left Constantinople to travel towards the east, hoping to find new areas in which to trade. They finally reached the court of Kublai Khan, the great Tartar emperor, who treated them most kindly. They set out for the east again in 1271, this time accompanied by Marco, Nicolo's fifteen-year-old son.

After a long and arduous journey, they arrived at Kublai Khan's court at Peking where the Khan took young Marco into his service, showing him many favours. The Polos were to stay at the court for some twenty years until 1292. Finally they sailed to Persia by Sumatra and southern India, the first Europeans to take this route.

They reached Venice in 1295 but not long afterwards Marco was captured in a sea battle and imprisoned for a while. He used the time to good advantage, getting a fellow prisoner to write the stories of his many adventures, although many did not believe them, they were so incredible. He died in about 1324.

1291
The Everlasting League of Uri

For centuries there was no such country as Switzerland. As early as the first century BC, the territory of two tribes, the Helvetii and the Rhaetii were conquered by Julius Caesar and taken into the Roman Empire.

When that crumbled they were overrun by Germanic tribes from the north. The eighth century saw the territory as part of Charlemagne's Holy Roman Empire and it later came under the rule of the Hapsburgs.

This royal family of Austria was headed by Rudolph of Hapsburg and on his death the inhabitants of the valleys of Uri, Schwyz and Nidwalden, determined to be an independent people, banded together and on August 1, 1291 formed the 'Everlasting League' for mutual defence. From this, the Swiss nation slowly and painfully achieved complete independence by 1848.

1298
The defeat of Wallace

Scotland was facing dark days indeed. Edward I of England had stripped John Baliol, the Scottish king, of all his powers, and he and his nobles were forced to pay homage. Edward also carried off the sacred Stone of Scone to place it in Westminster Abbey. Then, when the country's fortunes seemed at their very lowest, a patriot came forward – Sir William Wallace.

He quickly gathered an army of the people about him and after turning them into a reliable fighting force, stormed and captured stronghold after stronghold.

He fought a pitched battle at Stirling Bridge in 1297, utterly routed the English and for a year reigned in Scotland as Baliol's deputy.

Edward was forced to lead another army to Scotland. He met Wallace at Falkirk on July 22, 1298 and defeated him. Wallace escaped but was treacherously handed over to Edward who had him executed in 1305.

1306
Robert Bruce crowned at Scone

Six months after Wallace's death, Robert Bruce and John (the 'Red') Comyn met to decide who should assume leadership of Scotland. There was a quarrel and Bruce stabbed his rival in an outburst of anger. Assembling his vassals Bruce now asserted his rights, and in 1306 was crowned at Scone.

Fully committed now, Bruce began to gather an army to combat the English remaining in Scotland after Falkirk but in March 1306 he was decisively beaten at Methven. By the spring of 1307 he had raised another army and Edward was again forced to march north, but died on the way, his son, Edward II (1284–1327) taking command.

The two armies met on June 24, 1314 at Bannockburn and the English were completely defeated. The treaty of Northampton recognized Scotland as an independent country in 1328, but Bruce died in the following year.

1309
The Papacy moves to Avignon

The fine city of Avignon in France, standing high above the river Rhone, is dominated by a great palace which, for many years, was occupied by the Popes rather than Rome, their home for centuries. This came about when a new king Philip IV (1285–1314) known as 'The Fair' and the founder of modern France, sought to bring the Papacy under his control, the Pope of the time being Boniface VIII.

Agents of the king seized Boniface who died soon afterwards and from 1309 Avignon became the home of the Popes until 1378, a period sometimes called the 'Babylonian Captivity'.

After this Pope Urban VI and his successors ruled from Rome whilst an 'anti-pope', Clement VII, set up his court at Avignon. Called the Great Schism, this situation lasted until 1417.

1310
Giotto's *The Ascension*

Giotto di Bondone was an Italian artist born near Florence about 1266. Cimabue, a great artist of the time, quickly recognized the young Giotto's skill and made him his pupil. Much of Giotto's work is lost but his campanile at Florence, his frescoes at Assisi and Padua and his magnificent painting of Christ's Ascension reveal his genius.

1314
Dante writes *La Divina Commedia*

Dante Alighieri was born in Florence in 1265 and eighteen years of his later life were occupied in writing his immortal work *La Divina Commedia* ('The Divine Comedy') which tells of a soul's pilgrimage, guided by Virgil representing philosophy and Beatrice (Dante's ideal love) representing religion. Dante died in 1321.

c. 1327
The Aztecs found Tenochtitlán

The great nation that was to become that of the Aztecs, came originally from somewhere in North America. From similarities of language with the Piman, a Red Indian tribe, it may well have been from what is now Arizona. Several tribes linked together to begin a great migration southwards about 1100 and reaching the kingdom of the Toltecs, settled there.

The Aztecs became fishermen and farmers, and also hired themselves as soldiers to fight for other tribes. As soldiers, the Aztecs were known for their extreme savagery. Ultimately, they became so hated for their brutality and for their custom of sacrificing humans to their sun-god that they were driven out of every territory, until they reached a land that no one else wanted: the unhealthy marshes round Lake Texcoco in the Valley of Mexico.

An Aztec legend had foretold that the tribe would found a great city at a place where they saw an eagle, perched on a cactus, devouring a snake. This, apparently, was seen at Lake Texcoco where the Aztecs founded their lake city of Tenochtitlán in 1325. Tenochtitlán later became the present-day Mexico City.

From this first settlement grew the great and powerful nation of the Aztecs. Within fifty years they had elected their own king, although their greatest was to be Itzcoatl (c. 1430) who made them the premier nation of Mexico with boundaries that extended over most of southern Mexico as far south as the isthmus of Tehuantepec.

They were conquered by Cortés (see 1521 Conquest of the Aztecs in Mexico) and their existence as a great empire was over.

1338
Start of the Hundred Years' War

Known to history as the Hundred Years' War, the long struggle between England and France started in 1338 and, with brief truces, was not to end until 1453.

The Kings of England were also hereditary Dukes of Aquitaine and for two centuries had paid homage to the King of France for this duchy, an act they resented. Things came to a head when Philip VI of France took over Edward III's land in France and war began.

The first major encounter was a naval battle in 1340 when two hundred and fifty English ships fought a French fleet at the mouth of the River Sluys and at the end of the day only twenty-four French ships escaped.

Edward III (1312–77) later won the famous victory of Crécy, fought on August 23, 1346. Masses of heavily armed French cavalry attacked the lines of English archers only to fall to their deadly arrows, some 60,000 French troops being annihilated. The supremacy of long bow over heavy armour was decisively proved.

At Crécy, Edward, Prince of Wales, the Black Prince who was only sixteen, fought very bravely. After the battle, he toured the battlefield and from the dead King of Bohemia who was killed there, took the three plumed feathers

and the motto *Ich Dien* ('I serve') which have been the badge and motto of Princes of Wales ever since.

Robert the Bruce defeats the English at Bannockburn in 1314.

1348

Black Death reaches Europe from the East

Since the early part of the fourteenth century, a terrible disease had been ravaging Egypt, China and India. Today it is realized that it was bubonic and pneumonic plague.

This dreadful infection was carried by fleas living in the fur of black rats, though this was not known until many centuries afterwards, in 1894. In the fourteenth century, no one knew the cause, though some came to see the Plague as the judgment of God on a wicked world.

The Plague moved towards Europe and England with the caravans that carried silks and spices from the bazaars of the Orient. Then, in January 1348, three galleys docked at Genoa, in Italy, and so brought the Plague to Europe with its infected cargo. From then on, the Plague raged all over Europe, killing about one third of the inhabitants. From the swellings that were the symptoms of the Plague, the epidemic became known as the Black Death.

Once a victim had contracted the disease he died soon afterwards, usually after a few hours of terrible pain. No one knows how many victims the Black Death claimed although a conservative estimate gives the number of deaths in England alone at half a million, a large percentage of the population.

The pestilence reached its peak in the spring of 1349 and died out during the autumn, having ravaged Europe, dislocating society and ruining trade.

c. 1350
Sir Gawain and the Green Knight

This long alliterative poem was written by an anonymous English poet of the fourteenth century who used the language of northwest England. It describes the exploits of Gawain, a knight of Arthur, who undergoes a series of temptations in his quest for vengeance on a giant knight dressed in green.

1353
Boccaccio writes the Decameron

The *Decameron* (Greek for 'ten days') was written by an Italian, Giovanni Boccaccio (1313–75). It is a collection of one hundred short stories related over ten days by a party of young people who have left Florence for the hills during the plague. The *Decameron*, which includes tales that are both bawdy and full of pathos, greatly influenced European literature.

1356
The expansion of the Hanseatic league

During the twelfth century a number of important towns in northern Europe, especially those on the Baltic Sea and along the Rhine, found themselves coming into conflict with one another over trade.

Some of these towns soon realized that, by forming themselves into some kind of union, they could secure main trading privileges when developing commerce with foreign countries. The members became known as *Hansa*.

In 1356 the various *Hansa* united for even greater strength and led by the maritime towns of Lübeck, Hamburg and Bremen, the great Hanseatic League was created which became richer and more powerful than many important European states.

Hanseatic merchants settled in England and soon became the most important group of foreign merchants in the country. They had special privileges which were later confirmed by Richard III, after some difficulty had been experienced with jealous English merchants.

c. 1362
Langland writes *Piers Plowman*

One of the most important books to come from late medieval England is *The Vision of William concerning Piers Plowman*. An allegory, written by a priest named William Langland, the story is centred around the Malvern Hills and provides invaluable glimpses of rural life in fourteenth-century England.

1366
Petrarch writes the Canzoniere

Francesco Petrarca, known as Petrarch (1304–74) went to live in Avignon where in 1327 he began to write prolifically in verse and prose, especially in the type of sonnet to which he gave his name. He became infatuated with a girl named Laura and wrote about her in a series of poems called *Canzoniere* (1366).

1368
Foundation of the Ming dynasty

Following the return of the Polo family from the court of the Great Khan (*see 1271 Marco Polo's journey*) the news of 'far Cathay' compelled others to follow, especially merchants and missionaries. When the great Mongol Empire collapsed, however, the trade routes became dangerous and when an anti-foreigner campaign began in China, few Europeans dared make the journey.

After the Mongols a wholly Chinese dynasty came into being in 1368 – the Ming. The first emperor was Hung Wu and his dynasty was to last until 1644. The country became settled and prosperous, the capital being established at Nanking.

The third emperor, Yung Lo, was one of

Bronze vessel of the Ming dynasty.

Chu Yuen-Chang seizes Peking to become Hung Wu, first of the Ming emperors.

China's greatest builders and many of the palaces, temples and pagodas that exist in China today were built during his reign and those of his Ming successors.

A new kind of blue-and-white porcelain ware was developed during this dynasty which also saw a very high standard of textiles, brocades and embroideries and especially beautiful Chinese rugs and carpets. Realizing the settled nature of the Ming dynasty, Europeans began to return to China, some Portuguese being the first, reaching the country in 1514.

1377

Wycliffe and the Lollards

John Wycliffe (c. 1324–84) was an English religious reformer who was born near Hipswell in Yorkshire about 1324. He became Master of Balliol College, Oxford about 1360 and in 1374 became a priest in the rectory of Lutterworth where he was to stay until his death in 1384.

He spent the latter part of his life attacking the worldly power and evil lives of the clergy and soon collected a large number of followers who became known as Lollards (from the Dutch *lollen* 'to sing in a low voice'). The first complete translation of the Bible is credited to him and he did much to influence the Protestant Reformation.

The leadership of the Lollards was taken over by Sir John Oldcastle, originally a soldier and friend of Henry, Prince of Wales, afterwards Henry V.

Oldcastle was imprisoned for heresy in 1413, escaped from the Tower but was later recaptured and burned to death.

1381

The Peasants' Revolt

It is said that Wycliffe's Lollards did much to increase discontent amongst English peasants and artisans by their teaching. They had fertile ground, certainly, for the peasants were still little more than serfs whilst the labourers were forced by law to work for near starvation wages.

In 1381 this discontent reached a climax when the government passed a poll-tax (so much tax per head) to pay for the French war (*see 1338 Start of the Hundred Years' War*) and a leader appeared.

He was Wat Tyler, a tiler from Kent, who had killed a tax collector and then gathered an army of ill-armed peasants to march on London. They burned the houses of officials and grasping landlords as they went. One priest took as his text the rhyme:

'When Adam delved and Eve span,
Who was then the gentleman?'

Others joined them on their way and by the time they had reached Smithfield, where they were met by young King Richard II (1367–1400) they had grown into a force of thousands.

John Wycliffe, English religious reformer.

Richard granted them everything they asked and they then dispersed quietly. Tyler, however, stayed until the following day for another interview at which he was stabbed by the Lord Mayor because, he said, Tyler had insulted the king.

c. 1383

Chaucer writes *Canterbury Tales*

The *Canterbury Tales* was the last, longest and most famous work by the English poet, Geoffrey Chaucer (c. 1340–1400). The *Prologue* to the tales describes thirty pilgrims who agree to tell each other stories on their way from London to Canterbury and is particularly noteworthy. The tales range from the romantic *Knight's Tale* to the bawdy *Miller's Tale*.

Geoffrey Chaucer

1397

Scandinavian Union of Kalmar

King Haakon VI of Norway (1355–80) married Princess Margaret of Denmark. Their son, Olaf V, who had become King of Denmark in 1375, became King of Norway in 1381, but died seven years later aged eighteen.

His widowed mother, Margaret, then became the 'right sovereign' of all three Scandinavian kingdoms although, for a time, the real power lay in the hands of the nobles. By 1396, however, she had forced them to destroy their strongholds and renounced their newly acquired privileges, including freedom from taxation.

Margaret's triumph was to present her great-nephew Erik of Pomerania (1389–1440) as her successor and ruler of the three kingdoms by the important Union of Kalmar of 1397. Nevertheless she remained Regent of Norway, Sweden and Denmark until her death in 1412.

However, in 1436 Erik III was deposed and Norwegian nobles made his nephew Christopher of Bavaria their king in 1442.

1398

Timur conquers North India

Timur of Samarkand (1336–1405) had the nickname of *Timur i Leng*, 'the lame Timur', from which has come his more familiar name of Tamberlaine or Tamerlane. Lame or not, he soon proved himself to be a doughty warrior and the greatest world conqueror since Alexander the Great. Son of a tribal chieftain, he fought some khans and supported others until his army had occupied Moscow and conquered a huge territory.

The following year (1381) he took an army into Persia and smashed aside all opposition. In 1398 he invaded India, crossed the Indus and attacked Delhi which he left in ruins.

1399

Henry of Lancaster seizes the throne

Throughout the thirteen and fourteenth centuries in England, kings had been succeeded by their rightful heirs. However, the boy King Richard II, who succeeded his grandfather in 1377, proved to be a weak yet despotic monarch. He made the great mistake of wronging one of his most powerful subjects, Henry Bolingbroke, Earl of Lancaster. Bolingbroke and another nobleman, the Duke of Norfolk were mortal enemies. King Richard ordered them to settle their differences in combat, but at the last moment, he stopped the fight, and exiled Norfolk for life and Bolingbroke for ten years. Shortly afterwards, when Bolingbroke's father, John of Gaunt, died, the king illegally seized his lands. Henry, now Duke of Lancaster, returned to England to claim his stolen inheritance. Other nobles came to his support and in 1399, King Richard was forced to abdicate (resign the crown). Henry afterwards became King Henry IV. King Richard was imprisoned in Pontefract Castle where he died in 1400, it is believed as the result of starvation.

Lancaster's claim to the throne was through his father, John of Gaunt, third son of Edward III which, although somewhat slight, at least showed he had royal blood in his veins. His reign began the rule of the House of Lancaster.

1400

Welsh War of Independence

Owen Glendower was born to a noble Welsh family about 1359. He studied law at Westminster and then in 1385 fought for Richard II against the Scots. It was partly his association with the deposed king that encouraged him to fly the banners of revolt soon after Henry IV came to the throne. Claiming descent from the old Welsh princes, he gathered an army.

The invincible Timur defeated the Ottoman sultan Bayazid II at Ankara in 1402.

Henry, in turn, led an army against him on several occasions but with little success. Soon Owen was intriguing with another rebel, Henry Hotspur (*see 1403 The Battle of Shrewsbury*) and hoping that a simultaneous rising would topple the new English king. But it was not to be, and both were defeated. Glendower retired to Wales to carry on the fight for another ten years, dying a natural death in 1415. He was the last independent Prince of Wales.

1401

De Haeretico Comburendo

On becoming king, Henry IV sought the support of the Church to regularize his claim to the throne. Knowing that the Lollards were violently opposed to the Church he had Parliament bring in a law – *De Haeretico Comburendo* – which allowed civilian authorities to burn heretics, even priests, who held views 'contrary to the truth of Holy Church' and had been condemned in a spiritual court.

1403
The Battle of Shrewsbury

The most powerful noble in England during Henry IV's reign was Henry Percy, nicknamed 'Hotspur' (1364–1403). He had played an important part in the rebellion that had deposed King Richard II and had made himself a hero by defeating the Scots at Homildon Hill in Northumberland. But he and the king quarrelled and Hotspur, aided by his father the Earl of Northumberland, rose in rebellion, calling the king a usurper and hinting that Richard II had been taken from Pontefract Castle and was still alive. Hotspur gathered his own large army and made a pact with Owen Glendower (see 1400 Welsh War of Independence) to bring another against the king and to join forces. But before the junction had been made, Henry's own army arrived and the Battle of Shrewsbury was fought on July 21, 1403.

The armies were well matched but by nightfall Hotspur lay dead on the field of battle and his army was routed.

1415
The Battle of Agincourt

When Henry V (1387–1422) came to the English throne in 1413 his country was still suffering from the troubled years of his father's (Henry IV) reign. To distract his subjects from problems at home he decided to revive an old claim which the kings of England had to the throne of France and sailed for France to lay siege to Harfleur. Then, with an army weakened by sickness, he marched for Calais, but his passage was blocked by a French army which outnumbered his by four to one.

On the morning of October 25, 1415 the two armies faced each other and when the heavily armed French knights began their lumbering advance, the air was suddenly filled with the deadly hiss of English arrows. As at Crécy (1346) and Poitiers (1356) the English archers proved their supremacy and the chivalry of France lay dead or was driven from the field.

By the Treaty of Troyes (1420) Henry was made Regent of France and married Catherine, the French king's daughter.

1419
Hussites rise in Bohemia

John Huss, born about 1370, was a Bohemian reformer. He became a priest and then, in 1402, Rector of Prague University. He began to preach similar doctrines to Wycliffe and was charged with heresy. By then he had collected a large following and despite excommunication he continued to preach.

In 1412 he retired from active work to write his opus, De Ecclesia, and three years later, despite a promise of safe conduct, was arrested when attending a Council and was burned as a heretic.

His martyrdom made his followers more fanatical and for several years they made war on the Emperor Sigismund (1368–1437) who had been responsible for Huss's death, winning several battles including Aussis and Tachau, in Germany. Peace was made in 1431 by one of the two Hussite parties but it was to be several years before the other party followed suit.

1431
The burning of Joan of Arc

The Hundred Years' War, begun in 1338, was ending at last. Henry V, England's great warrior king, had died in 1422 and a few months later France's Charles VI followed him. Charles's successor, King Charles VII, did not have power over the whole of France, due to the civil war that was raging at the time. In addition, English armies were controlling large parts of the country.

Then, with dramatic suddenness, a young peasant girl, Joan of Arc, arrived at the royal court. She had heard voices, she claimed, which told her to free the town of Orleans from the English army. God, Joan believed, desired that Charles VII should be crowned king of all France at Rheims. Although most of the nobles mocked her, the army, inspired by her courage, followed her into battle. She drove the English from Orleans and stood at his side whilst the king was crowned Charles VII in Rheims Cathedral.

Although she was later betrayed, sold to the English and, found guilty of sorcery and heresy, burned at the stake, she had helped unify France – leaving behind a symbol of hope and of courage.

Joan of Arc is burned at the stake, accused of heresy.

1434

Van Eyck: *Giovanni Arnolfini and his wife*

It was in the fifteenth century, through the work of Jan van Eyck (c. 1385–1441) that Flemish painting developed a deliberately new, realistic style. The portrait *Giovanni Arnolfini and his wife* illustrates van Eyck's attention to detail and his psychological observation. Other paintings by van Eyck include the *Adoration of the Lamb*, a masterpiece in Flemish art, and the *Annunciation*.

1434

The rise of the Medicis

The name 'Medici' first appeared in a Florentine chronicle of the twelfth century, but it was to be Giovanni dei Medici (1360–1429) who should be considered the founder of the family's vast fortunes. He was basically a trader and created his family's fortune with a number of banks he opened in Italy and elsewhere.

On his death his business was shared between his two sons, Lorenzo and Cosimo (1389–1464). When Cosimo's political rivals were exiled, he became in fact, though not in name, ruler of Florence in 1434. He was not only a brilliant businessman but a most astute politician. He insisted on being regarded as a private citizen and refused to accept any public office, yet with his wealth, influence and connections, was the absolute ruler of a very republican country.

Cosimo was a great patron of the arts and a great builder and many of his palaces, churches and villas were truly magnificent. He saved priceless Greek and Latin manuscripts for posterity and opened public libraries where students and others could study them.

He died in 1469 leaving his two sons, Lorenzo and Giuliano to continue the fortunes of the Medici family.

1436

Henry the Navigator founds Institute

Prince Henry (1394–1460), a younger son of King John of Portugal, was fascinated by the idea of ocean exploration. After fighting with an expedition against the Moslems in North Africa in 1415, he determined to promote the exploration of the coast of Africa in order to find a way

Prince Henry the Navigator.

round it and so reach the Orient and its great riches by sea. This was imperative, because the land route from Europe to the Orient was blocked by the deadly enemies of Christian Europe, the Moslems. After 1418, Henry sent several expeditions to explore further and further down the African coast, and in 1436 founded his Colonial and Naval Institute at Sagres, where sailors could learn navigation, mathematics and map-making.

Mehmet II having taken Constantinople.

The explorations by sea continued and in the next years, Portuguese navigators explored further and further southwards. By 1444 they had reached Cape Verde, and in 1460, the year Henry died, they reached Sierra Leone in West Africa. Ultimately, it took almost thirty more years before the Cape of Good Hope, at the extreme south of Africa, was rounded (1488) and Vasco da Gama finally sailed the sea route to Asia, to land in western India in 1498.

1438
Albert becomes Holy Roman Emperor

The Hapsburgs were an Austrian imperial family who took their family name from the castle in which they lived near the junction of the Rhine and the Aar rivers. The founder of the family was Albert, Count of Hapsburg, who together with his son, made his family the most powerful in Swabia.

In 1273 Rudolph of Hapsburg became not only King of Germany but also Holy Roman Emperor, having wrested Upper and Lower Austria, Styria and Carniola from Ottokar of Bohemia. This greatly increased the power of his family.

In 1356 the Golden Bull issued by Emperor Charles IV made the imperial throne elective; emperors were to be chosen by a majority vote of seven German electors. However, in 1438, Albert, Archduke of Austria, another Hapsburg, became emperor and although the imperial power remained elective it passed permanently to the Hapsburgs. It remained with their family until the end of the empire in 1806.

1448
Fra Angelico paints the Vatican frescoes

Guido da Fiesole (1387–1455) entered a monastery and was called Fra (frater or brother) and Angelico because of his lovable and humble nature. A brilliant artist, he did much work in Rome and in the Vatican, in the Chapels of Nicholas V (SS. Stephen and Lawrence) and also frescoes in Florence, Orvieto and elsewhere.

1453

The Turks capture Constantinople

In 1451 a new Sultan, Mehmet II, came to the Turkish throne and swore to capture Constantinople. He trained an army of fighters called 'janissaries' and engaged a Hungarian engineer to cast guns which proved to be the world's largest; one was nearly eight metres long and fired a 545 kilogram ball. By April 1453 his army was ready to attack.

Within the great walls the garrison, weakened and impoverished, could only muster seven thousand men, whereas Mahomet II had an army of over eighty thousand.

The big Turkish guns began a bombardment which was to continue, without pause, for six weeks. The garrison fought bravely, filling up breaches in the walls, fighting off attack after attack. But the end was inevitable. On May 29 the final assault began. Wave after wave of Turks poured into the city, the Emperor Constantine XI died a hero's death and by nightfall the city had fallen. Its conquest was to alter history, for its scholars had already fled, taking their manuscripts and documents with them to spread a new interest in learning throughout Western Europe.

1454

Gutenberg sets up his printing press

Johann Gutenberg (c. 1398–c. 1468) was born in the German city of Mainz but lived for part of his early life in Strasbourg. Here he worked as an artisan but spent all his free time working on an idea that had come to him . . . printing.

He returned to Mainz and in partnership with a Johann Fust, from whom he borrowed money to continue, began work on a large Latin Bible. It was similar to the work of the monks, for the wooden printing type was large whilst spaces were left at the beginning of some lines in order that a hand-illuminated letter might be inserted. This work was finished about 1456 with some smaller books and folios.

Gutenberg soon realized that due to the difficulty of carving, wooden type was inef-ficient, so he developed a technique of casting type from metal.

In 1462 Mainz was stormed and sacked and a number of printers fled to other cities. Within fifty years, printing was going on in more than two hundred places in Europe and books and leaflets were becoming available to far more people than before.

A page from Gutenberg's Bible.

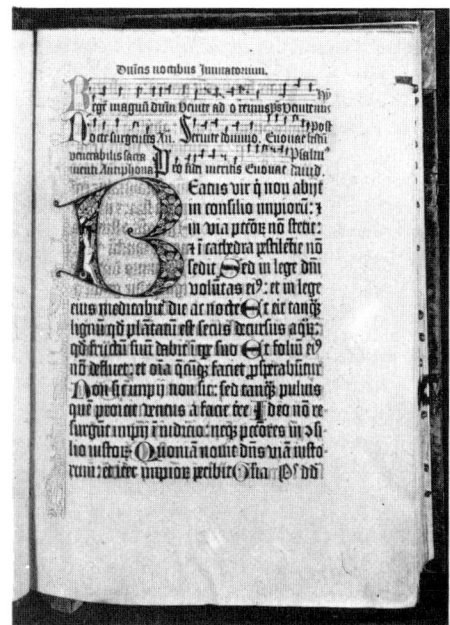

1455

Alfonso becomes Pope Calixtus III

Borgia (the Italian form of Borja) was the name of an ancient noble family who came originally from the Spanish province of Valencia. The family (who came to Italy in 1443) achieved great prominence, power and notoriety in the fifteenth century.

In 1455 Alfonso de Borja (1378–1458) who was a bishop, became Pope as Calixtus III. He made his nephew, Rodrigo (1451–1503) a cardinal and he also ascended the papal throne, in 1492, as Alexander VI.

The most powerful of them all, however, was Cesare Borgia (1476–1507), son of Alexander, who exercised royal power and steered the fortunes of his country at that time. Another member of the family was Lucrezia (1480–1519), Cesare's sister, who was later accused of all manner of evil things including assassination, but who in later life, became a patron of art and learning and a supporter of charitable works.

1455
The Wars of the Roses

The Wars of the Roses, England's first full-scale civil war, began in 1455 and did not end until thirty years later in 1485. The war got its name because the two rival parties each chose a rose as a symbol: York (white) and Lancaster (red). It began when Henry VI (1421–71) became insane and Richard, Duke of York claimed the throne.

A number of battles followed (beginning with that of St Albans in 1455) with periods of truce between them. At the battle of Northampton (1460) Henry was captured and at Wakefield (1461) York was killed. The Lancastrians were defeated at Towton in the same year and their position seemed hopeless until the powerful Earl of Warwick, the 'King-maker', and hitherto a Yorkist supporter, changed sides.

Henry was released from prison and again made king, but the Lancastrians were defeated at Barnet (1471) where Warwick was killed and the Battle of Tewkesbury placed York's son Edward IV (1442–83) firmly on the throne. He was succeeded by his brother Richard III (his own son Edward V dying mysteriously in the Tower) who reigned for two years until he died on Bosworth Field fighting the Tudor prince who was to become Henry VII (1457–1509).

---

c. 1460
Development of Japanese Nō theatre

About the middle of the fifteenth century, a new style of acting and music was created in Japan which, quite unchanged, is still to be seen in Japanese theatres today. From about 1460 the language, costumes and setting have been exactly as they were at the outset and the drama and music combine to form Nō theatre.

The plays are performed on a square stage, the audience sitting on three sides whilst the fourth leads to the dressing rooms. The players are all male, the principal actor wearing a succession of masks to mark his changing moods, which are also reflected by traditional movements of a fan. The orchestra is usually composed of three drums and a flute. A small chorus, housed in a balcony, comments on the events of the play, while the actors dance and chant in a formal, traditional style.

1469
Malory writes *Morte d'Arthur*

The shadowy world of the historical Arthur bore little resemblance to the many fine chivalrous epics of the Middle Ages (*see 12th century The growth of medieval literature*). Malory's classic presents the complete legends of King Arthur and the Knights of the Round Table, Merlin, Lancelot and Guinevere. Sir Thomas Malory died in 1471, and *Morte d'Arthur* (The Death of Arthur) was published by Caxton, in twenty-one books, in 1485.

1469
Lorenzo the Magnificent rules Florence

Cosimo dei Medici (*see 1434 The rise of the Medicis*) was succeeded by his two sons, Lorenzo and Giuliano. It was soon obvious that the stronger character was Lorenzo who fell out with another powerful family, the Pazzi. When the two brothers were at mass in Florence cathedral, they were attacked by assassins and Giuliano, stabbed in the back, fell dying. Lorenzo was able to escape, gather his men and storm the palace of the Pazzi. Some of his enemies were cut down, others hanged from the palace windows, others sent into exile.

The Pazzi family disposed of, Lorenzo became the most powerful man in Florence which although technically a republic, was ruled by him until his death in 1492. His rule proved beneficial, commerce and art flourishing equally. Lorenzo himself was a brilliant writer and poet.

1476
Caxton sets up his printing press

Kentish-born William Caxton was originally apprenticed to a London mercer but in 1441 went to Europe to study the new craft of

THE GREAT EMPIRES OF PORTUGAL AND SPAIN

The Portuguese Empire

The Portuguese were the first to start building an overseas empire in modern times. Their territories were mostly the result of their explorations to find a sea route from Europe to Asia, and the consequent setting up of trading stations along that route. The territories the Portuguese acquired in this way included: Madeira (1420), the Azores (1427), Cape Verde Islands (1460), Cochin (India) (1502), Goa, Daman and Diu (India) (1510), St Thomas and Prince (1495), Portuguese Guinea (1588) and the larger territories of Mozambique (1505) and Angola (1574). Brazil, in South America, was discovered by Pedro Alvarez Cabral after he was blown off course while heading down the African coast. First

Portuguese settlements in Brazil c.1537. Macau (China) leased from China 1557, recognized as Portuguese territory 1887.

Independence: Brazil 1822; Angola and Mozambique 1975; Portugal's Indian territories were taken over by India in 1961. Macau: 1986: start of negotiations between Portugal and China for eventual return of Macau to China.

The Spanish Empire

The Spanish Empire in America followed the explorations of Christopher Columbus (1492–1504). The first settlement was Santo Domingo on the island of Hispaniola (1493), followed by Puerto Rico (1511),

Panama (1513) and Cuba (1515). The first major Spanish colonies on the mainland of America were in Mexico (after 1521) and Peru (after 1532). By 1600, Spain ruled over the whole of Central and South America, except for Brazil (see Portuguese Empire, above). Other Spanish possesssions were the Philippines (1565), Spanish Sahara (1885), Spanish Guinea (1885) and Spanish Morocco (1912).

Independence: South and Central (Latin) America 1811–25; Philippines: ceded to USA 1898, independent 1946; Cuba: occupied by USA 1898, independent 1902; Spanish Sahara: ceded to Morocco 1958; Spanish Guinea 1968 (now Equatorial Guinea); Spanish Morocco 1956.

---

printing. In 1476 he set up a printing press at Westminster – the first in Britain – where he was to print ninety-six books including *The Canterbury Tales* and *Le Morte d'Arthur*.

1479

Aragon unites with Castile

In AD 711, Moslem Moors from North Africa invaded Spain, and while their main power lay in the south, they threatened for a long time to overrun the whole country. Their opponents, the Christians of Spain had one important weakness: Spain was not a united country, but was divided up into small kingdoms. These kingdoms managed to remain independent in northern Spain but for centuries were unable to make any real progress against the Moors in the south. The main Spanish kingdoms were Navarre, Castile, Leon and Galicia.

Towards the middle of the thirteenth century, Castile and Leon were united, whilst eastern Spain formed the kingdom of Aragon. In 1469 Isabella, the heiress of Castile married Ferdinand,

son of the King of Aragon and on his father's death in 1479 Aragon and Castile became one powerful kingdom under united sovereigns; Spain was now to be reckoned as a major political force in Europe. In 1492, after nearly eight hundred years, the Moors were finally overcome, and Spain became a Christian realm.

c. 1480

Inquisition becomes active in Spain

The Inquisition was founded as early as the thirteenth century by Pope Gregory IX in France in order to stamp out heresy, and was initially under the control of members of the order of St Dominic. The first court of inquisition (or tribunal) was set up at Toulouse. In 1252 Innocent IV introduced torture and those who were guilty, or pleaded guilty to stop the pain, were then handed over to the secular laws of the land, usually to be burned.

From France the system spread to Italy, Spain,

A navigator on Columbus's first voyage.

the Netherlands, Portugal and later to the Catholic countries of the New World. It reached its peak of infamy during the fifteenth century in Spain where the court was presided over by an Inquisitor-General, the most notorious of whom was Torquemada (1420–98).

The accused was heard in secret session and often had no knowledge of his accuser; such tortures as the rack and an ingeniously horrific device known as the Iron Maiden were used to extract the 'truth'.

1484

Botticelli's *Birth of Venus*

Sandro Botticelli (1448–1510), the son of a tanner, was born in Florence and obtained a position in the studio of Fra Filippo Lippi, proving himself better than his famous artist teacher. His paintings are ranked amongst the world's finest and include, *The Birth of Venus*, *Adoration of the Magi*, and *Virgin with the Pomegranate*.

1487

Pretenders to the English throne

Henry VII (1457–1509) came to the throne after the Battle of Bosworth Field (1485) and was to reign over England for fourteen years. He was a Lancastrian. His claim to the throne was a vague one, based on the fact that his mother was a descendant of John of Gaunt. Inevitably there were a number of pretenders to the throne, the two greatest being Lambert Simnel (*c.*1477–*c.*1534) and Perkin Warbeck (*c.*1474–99).

Simnel claimed to be the Earl of Warwick, son of the 'Kingmaker' at the time in the Tower. He was crowned in Dublin as Edward VI (1487) but Henry soon dealt with him and, to show his contempt, made him a scullion in the royal kitchen. Warbeck (1492) was a more dangerous pretender. He was treated well at first but when he made a further attempt in 1499 Henry had him executed.

1492

Columbus discovers the West Indies

In 1492 Christopher Columbus (*c.* 1451–1506), an Italian captain in the service of Spain, sailed across the Atlantic Ocean in a ship not much bigger than a modern racing yacht. Sailors then never willingly sailed out of sight of land so, in setting out across the Atlantic Ocean, Columbus was taking a dangerous gamble.

Unlike many people at that time, Columbus knew that the world was round, and he calculated that by sailing toward the west he would find a valuable new trade route to the riches of the Far East. It was a good plan, except for two details.

First, Columbus believed that the world was much smaller than it really is. Second, he did not – and could not – know that the two great continents of North and South America lay in his way. So when he sighted land after a ten-weeks'

Columbus sets foot in the New World.

voyage he believed he had reached the outlying parts of Asia, and he called the islands he had discovered the Indies.

Columbus made three more voyages to the West Indies, still hoping they were part of Asia. He died in 1506, not knowing that the Spaniards who followed him to the New World would soon discover riches greater than those he had ever hoped to find in Asia.

1497

John Cabot discovers Newfoundland

Like Columbus, Cabot was an Italian sailor in foreign service, and while Columbus was trying to get support for his voyage of discovery in Spain, Cabot was doing the same thing in England. The news of Columbus's successful voyage must have been a heavy blow to him. But in 1497 he gained the support of King Henry VII and sailed from Bristol in the *Matthew*. He took with him his son Sebastian, later a great explorer himself.

Following a more northerly route than Columbus, Cabot had a rougher voyage, but when the water was running low and the food beginning to stink, land was sighted. Cabot called it the 'New Found Land' and it has kept the name to this day.

The English were disappointed by Cabot's discovery. Although the fishing was good, there were no gold, silks or spices. Unlike the Spaniards, who were building an empire in Central and South America, the English waited over one hundred years before they began colonies in North America.

Girolamo Savonarola

even the ordinary people, for whom Savonarola had fought many battles, turned against him. He was thrown into prison, tortured, and hanged from a burning cross in the market place.

1498

Savonarola burned in Florence

Girolamo Savonarola (1452–98) was an Italian monk who tried to reform politics and religion in Florence. A spell-binding preacher, he attacked the vices of the ruling class and fiercely denounced opponents as powerful as the Pope and the Medici princes who ruled Florence. He feared nobody, and never minded making himself unpopular. When the French king Charles VIII (1470–98) invaded Italy, Savonarola boldly hailed him as the instrument of God sent to punish the Italians for their sins.

The invasion caused a revolt against the Medici in Florence and Savonarola became the real ruler of the city. He made fun-loving Florence a solemn city with psalm-singing instead of drunken feasts; but he gave it many wise laws. Savonarola's rule was severe and his tongue was bitter. Believing himself inspired by God, he would tolerate no criticism, and at last

1498

Erasmus visits Oxford

Like Savonarola, the Dutch scholar Desiderius Erasmus (1466–1536) was a severe critic of the Roman Catholic Church. He attacked the ignorance, superstition and greed of the clergy, and his writings, especially his translation of the New Testament, prepared the way for the Reformation of Luther and others.

Erasmus himself never became a Protestant, although he lived nearly twenty years after Luther had nailed his paper to the church door at Wittenburg. He accused the Reformers of being as rigid and narrow-minded as the Church they attacked.

Erasmus travelled to many centres of learning throughout Western Europe. A wise and kind man, he had many friends among the scholars of all countries. In 1498 he visited England, but refused an offer to teach at Oxford. On a later visit he stayed in the house of his friend Thomas More, and it was there that he wrote his most famous book, *Praise of Folly* (1509).

1498

Dürer: *The Apocalypse*

Albrecht Dürer (1471–1528) was perhaps the greatest artist of the Renaissance in northern Europe. His greatest gift lay in drawing, rather than painting, and he is most admired for his engravings, and the fifteen large woodcuts of *The Apocalypse*, published as a book in 1498. They show the strong influence of the Gothic style of his native Germany. Dürer's later work was influenced by the ideas of the Italian Renaissance.

Dürer: *Self Portrait.*

1498

Vasco da Gama reaches India

Vasco da Gama, the Portuguese navigator who crowned nearly eighty years of exploration by sailing the sea route to Asia, left Lisbon, the Portuguese capital, with four ships in July, 1497. He sailed south through the Atlantic, saving time by not following the coast. After rounding the Cape, he sailed up the east coast of Africa and visited the rich cities of the Arab merchants from Moçambique to Mombassa. From the coast of Kenya he crossed the Indian Ocean, and in spring, 1498, he landed in India at the trading port of Calicut.

Although it was so long a voyage, many Portuguese ships soon followed the route that Vasco da Gama had pioneered. Portuguese trading posts, and later colonies, were founded in East Africa and on the western coast of India. Goa became Portugal's chief colony, and it remained in Portuguese control until the Indian government took it in 1961.

1499
Amerigo Vespucci's voyage to America

After Columbus, other captains sailed across the Atlantic on voyages of discovery. One of the most important was the voyage of Amerigo Vespucci (1454–1512) and Alonso Ojeda in 1499, who sailed in the service of Spain.

Vespucci was an Italian merchant, who settled in the Spanish inland port of Seville in 1492 and probably invested money in Columbus's second voyage (1493). He was a member of an expedition that discovered the coast of Central America in 1497, and in 1499–1500 he and Ojeda explored hundreds of miles of the northern coasts of South America. On a later voyage in 1503, Vespucci sailed farther south along the coast of Brazil.

Amerigo Vespucci was one of the first to realize that Columbus had discovered a huge 'New World', between Europe and Asia, quite separate from any known continent. His name will never be forgotten, because it was after him that the New World was called 'America'.

1502
Safawid dynasty established

The Safawid, or Sufi, dynasty, founded by Shah Ismail, ruled Persia (Iran) from the beginning of the 16th century to the middle of the 18th. The Safawids were the first true Persian rulers of Persia for nearly nine hundred years.

The most able of the Safawid dynasty was Abbas the Great (1586–1628), who fought several successful wars. He added Iraq to his empire, and with British help took the island of Ormuz from the Portuguese. Abbas raised splendid buildings and encouraged trade and the arts, especially the art of carpet-making. But he had his children blinded, because he feared them as rivals.

However, later rulers were less successful than Abbas, and the attacks of Afghans, Turks, Russians and other old enemies brought chaos to Persia. The last Safawid shah, a little child, died in 1736.

1503
Leonardo da Vinci: *Mona Lisa*

The most famous painting in the world now hangs in the Louvre in Paris. It is a portrait of a young woman, faintly smiling, by Leonardo da Vinci (1452–1519). At first sight it appears a rather simple painting, but, looking harder, the subtle mystery of the woman's expression seems more extraordinary. It is hard to imagine how Leonardo could make such an effect with paint on a flat surface. Unfortunately, few of Leonardo's paintings have survived, partly because he was always experimenting with new materials, which did not last, and partly because he left so much work unfinished.

A true 'Renaissance man', Leonardo was interested in everything. Once he made a mechanical lion for a play – and designed the actors' costumes as well. His mind was full of ideas and his notebooks full of drawings and plans of machines and engines of war, even a submarine and a flying machine. Few of them were built, and they might not have worked anyway, but certainly Leonardo was an inventive genius far ahead of his time.

Leonardo spent his early life in Florence, later moving to Milan where there were few rival artists and good opportunities to study mathematics. He spent his last years in France.

1504
Raphael: *Marriage of the Virgin*

Raphael (1483–1520) was one of the greatest painters of the Italian Renaissance. He completed *The Marriage of the Virgin* in 1504, and it marks a turning point in his life. In that year he went to Florence, where he came under the influence of Leonardo and Michelangelo. Four years later he went to Rome, where he stayed until he died, producing, with the help of assistants, an enormous amount of work for Pope Julius II.

Leonardo da Vinci: impressions of this great artist's sketchbooks reveal a mind fascinated by anatomy, mechanics, and technological inventions.

1504
Giorgione: *Madonna*

With Bellini and Titian, Giorgione (c.1478–1511) was one of the greatest painters of the Renaissance in Venice. He was partly responsible for the rich colours of Venetian painting and its free choice of subjects. But very little is known of his life except that he died of plague in his early thirties. Only five or six pictures are definitely known to be his; many of the paintings he began were finished by others. His *Madonna* was painted in 1504.

1508
Michelangelo paints the Sistine Chapel

While Raphael was painting his great frescoes in the Pope's apartments, not far away Michelagniolo Buonarroti – Michelangelo (1475–1564) – was standing on a high platform painting Bible scenes on the vault (ceiling) of the Sistine Chapel. This tremendous work, the most beautiful of religious paintings, covered an area of 1,500 square metres. Michelangelo began painting the ceiling frescoes in 1508 and did not finish until 1512.

Michelangelo suffered pain in his neck, from bending his head back, for years after he had finished it. Much later, from 1535–41, he also painted *The Last Judgment*, a grimmer masterpiece, on the wall behind the altar of the Sistine Chapel.

The greatest artist of his time, Michelangelo was not only a painter but also an architect, a poet and, above all, a sculptor. One of his most beautiful marble sculptures, of the Virgin Mary holding the body of Jesus, stands in the church of St Peter's, Rome, the great dome of which was also designed by Michelangelo.

The genius of Michelangelo, whose long life spanned the greatest years of the Renaissance in Florence and Rome, sprang from marvellous natural ability combined with a superhuman drive towards perfection. When he was at work, not even the Pope could get a polite word out of him. Yet his greatest work was a failure. He spent forty years on the tomb of his patron, Pope Julius II, and never finished it to his satisfaction. Michelangelo considered that he 'wasted the whole of my youth on this tomb.'

EXPLORATIONS ON EARTH

c. AD 725   Irish monks believed to have discovered and settled in the Faeroe Islands.

AD 790   Irish monks reach Iceland.

AD 874   Vikings reach Iceland.

AD 981   Iceland Vikings discover Greenland

AD 986   Viking Bjarni Hergulfsson discovers the coast of North America.

1270   Portuguese navigators start exploring the west coast of Africa.

1271–95   Travels of the Venetian Marco Polo in central Asia, China, India and Persia.

1420   Portuguese reach Madeira.

1427   Portuguese Diogo de Silvo discovers the Azores islands (Atlantic Ocean).

1492   Christopher Columbus reaches America.

1493–96   Columbus discovered the Caribbean islands.

1497   John Cabot sails to Newfoundland.

1497–98   Vasco da Gama sails round Africa from Portugal to India.

1498   John and Sebastian Cabot explore the North American coast. Columbus reaches the South American coast.

1499–1502   Voyages of Amerigo Vespucci to South America convince him that America is a previously unknown 'new' continent.

1502–04   Columbus explores the Central American coast from Honduras to Panama.

1513   Portuguese Jorge Alvarez in Canton, China. Spaniard Vasco Nunez de Balboa crosses the isthmus of Panama to discover the Pacific Ocean.

1517–19   Spanish explorations of the Mexican coast (Gulf of Mexico).

1519–22   Ferdinand Magellan's fleet is first to sail round the world. Magellan Strait between the Atlantic and Pacific Oceans, and the Philippine Islands are discovered.

1521 on   Spanish conquest and exploration of Mexico.

1521   Spaniard Juan Ponce de Leon explores Florida.

1532 on   Spanish conquest of Peru and exploration of South America.

1534   Frenchman Jacques Cartier explores Canadian coast and discovers the St Lawrence River.

1536   Spaniard Alvar Nunez Cabeza de Vaca crosses Texas and northern Mexico.

1540–42   Spaniards explore Kansas, Texas and Oklahoma, and discover the Grand Canyon.

1541   Spaniard Hernando de Soto discovers the Mississippi River.

1542   Portuguese reach Japan.

1567   Spaniards discover Solomon, Marshall and Ellice islands (Pacific Ocean).

1576   English explorer Sir Martin Frobisher seeks the North West Passage (the sea route from the northern Atlantic to China). He discovers Baffin Land (see 1903–06).

1591   Spanish and Portuguese cross the Sahara Desert.

1595   Spaniards discover the Marquesas and Santa Cruz Islands (Pacific Ocean).

1598–1608   Spanish explorations in the Gulf of California.

1509

Accession of Henry VIII

As a young king, Henry VIII (1491–1547) was well-educated, good looking and adored by his people. He left the management of his kingdom in the hands of Wolsey (see 1530 Death of Wolsey) but when Henry wanted to divorce his queen, Catherine of Aragon, Wolsey failed to get permission from the Pope. This marked the beginning of the Church of England which was independent of the Pope's control.

Thomas Cranmer (1489–1556), Archbishop of Canterbury, annulled Henry's marriage and allowed him to marry Anne Boleyn. The Pope immediately excommunicated Henry who declared himself Supreme Head of the English Church; the king now had absolute authority both in spiritual and temporal matters.

Henry was ruthless not only to his wives, but also to his nobles. (He had six wives in all. They were Catherine of Aragon, Anne Boleyn, Jane Seymour, Anne of Cleves, Catherine Howard and Catherine Parr.) He had his second and fifth wives beheaded for infidelity and mercilessly hounded his first wife, Catherine of Aragon, and her daughter Mary. At the start of his reign, his people had looked on him as a brilliant, enlightened monarch but by the time he died in 1547, he was regarded as a cruel tyrant.

1606 Spaniards discover Tahiti (Pacific Ocean).

1610 English navigator Henry Hudson discovers Hudson's Bay (northern Canada).

1616 Dutchman Dirk Hartog lands on an island off the west Australian coast.

1642–44 Abel Tasman (Dutch) discovers Tasmania, Tonga and Fiji and sails round Australia, though without sighting it.

1679–83 Robert de la Salle (French) explores Lake Michigan and the Mississippi region.

1722 Dutch discover Easter Island and Samoa.

1732–43 Survey of the Siberian coast of Russia, carried out by the Russian government.

1750 Discovery of the Cumberland Gap which leads westwards into the interior of America.

1768–73 James Bruce (English) explores Ethiopia.

1768–71 Captain James Cook sails round New Zealand and discovers the east coast of Australia (1770).

1772–75 Captain Cook explores New Hebrides, New Caledonia, Norfolk Island and circumnavigates Antarctica.

1774–76 Spaniards explore the west coast of North America and discover the mouth of the Columbia River.

1776–79 Captain Cook discovers Christmas Island and Hawaii, and explores the coasts of Asia and North America near the Arctic.

1795–1805 African explorations of Scottish explorer Mungo Park in the Gambia and Nigeria.

1802–11 Portuguese explorers cross the African continent from Angola to the Zambesi River.

1804–06 Meriwether Lewis and William Clarke cross the United States and reach the Californian coast overland.

1817–18 John Oxley begins the exploration of the Australian interior.

1845–48 Sir John Franklin's expedition discovers the course of the North West Passage, but ice prevents them from traversing it.

1849 David Livingstone crosses the Kalahari Desert.

1853–56 Livingstone discovers the Victoria Falls after crossing the African continent.

1858–59 Richard Burton and John Speke discover Lake Tanganyika and Lake Victoria Nyanza which they conclude is the long-sought source of the River Nile.

1860 First overland crossing of Australia by Robert O'Hara Burke and William John Wills.

1898 Fridtjof Nansen (Norwegian) makes the first crossing of Greenland.

1903–06 Roald Amundsen (Norwegian) navigates the North West Passage for the first time.

1909 Charles H. Peary (United States) reaches the North Pole.

1911 Roald Amundsen (Norwegian) reaches the South Pole.

1912 Robert Falcon Scott (British) reaches the South Pole five weeks after Amundsen.

1957 Sir Vivian Ernest Fuchs (British) makes the first land crossing of Antarctica.

1513
Machiavelli: *Il Principe*

Niccolo Machiavelli (1469–1527), a civil servant in Florence, wrote his book *Il Principe* ('The Prince') as a guide to rulers of his time. It was a practical handbook, not concerned with ideas, nor questions of right and wrong, only with methods that governments use to make themselves strong. Machiavelli discussed politics as they really are, not as they should be, and although his book contained much good sense, many were shocked by its advice that rulers should tell lies and use violence if necessary.

1516
Thomas More writes *Utopia*

The Greek word *utopia* means 'nowhere', and *Utopia* by Sir Thomas More (1478–1535) was a description of an ideal state, where life is based on reason and tolerance. It caused great argument, and it is still studied today. But it did not make life in sixteenth century England less unreasonable or intolerant.

By the time *Utopia* was published, More was well-known as a brilliant humanist scholar (the humanists were interested in the study of humanity – mankind and all his works). He conducted wars of words with reformers like Tyndale, and held posts in Henry VIII's government.

When Cardinal Wolsey fell from power in 1529, More became Lord Chancellor. While sympathizing with some of the ideas of the Reformation, he remained a Roman Catholic and refused to recognize the king as head of the English Church. For that he was condemned as a traitor and executed in 1535. He was canonized as a saint by Pope Pius XI four hundred years later.

1516

Ariosto writes *Orlando Furioso*

The Italian poet Ludovico Ariosto (1474–1533) spent most of his life in the service of the d'Este family, rulers of Ferrara. His fame rests on this one long poem, which he expanded in later editions. It is an epic of chivalry and romance, love and adventure – one of the great poems of the world.

1517

Luther's *Theses* at Wittenberg

When a thick-necked Saxon monk named Martin Luther (1483–1546) angrily posted his

Ninety-five Theses (arguments) on the church door at Wittenberg, it was not the first time that the Church and the Pope had been criticized. Others had condemned the practice of 'indulgences' – offering forgiveness of sins in return for cash – and some had been burned as heretics.

But Luther's action proved decisive in starting the events that led to the Reformation, when half Europe broke away from the Roman Catholic Church and set up separate Protestant Churches.

Earlier critics had attacked the behaviour of the Roman Church, but Luther attacked its beliefs. A man, said Luther, is saved by his religious faith, not by indulgences. He condemned the power and wealth of the Pope and the influence of priests over the people.

Luther was condemned by the Pope, and when he refused to renounce his beliefs at the Diet (parliament) of Worms in 1521 he risked death as a heretic. But he was saved by politics. Powerful princes protected him, partly because they agreed with his ideas, partly because they wished to increase their own power by reducing the power of the Church.

Many of Luther's supporters wanted to go much farther than he, and in later years he spent much of his time restraining their zeal. Meanwhile, he helped to bring God nearer the people by translating the whole of the Bible into German.

1518
Titian paints *The Assumption*

This is one of the finest religious paintings of Titian (c. 1490–1576), the greatest master of the school of Venice, who became court painter to

the Emperor Charles V and Philip II of Spain. Titian lived to a great age but never stopped developing his technique. He achieved rich and brilliant effects by applying many, thin, transparent layers of colour.

1521
Conquest of the Aztecs in Mexico

After Columbus's discovery in 1492, many Spanish adventurers travelled to the West Indies seeking their fortunes. One of them was Hernán Cortés (1485–1547), who in 1518 was given command of an expedition to Mexico.

The rulers of Mexico were the Aztecs, a race of warriors who controlled the longer standing inhabitants of the region by force. Aztec society was a strange mixture: they made beautiful fabrics and pottery, but had few metal tools; they built grand cities with huge palaces and temples, but the highlight of their religious ceremonies was the bloody sacrifice of hundreds of human beings.

When Cortés landed at San Juan de Ulua in 1519, Aztec power was not fully established, and Cortés gained support from some of their rebellious subjects. Cortés had other advantages

Montezuma welcoming Cortés to Tenochtitlán.

unknown in Mexico, like guns and horses. His small force captured the capital, Tenochtitlán (Mexico City), and took the Aztec king, Montezuma II, prisoner. Later, while Cortés was absent, a rising took place in the city. Returning, the Spaniards were allowed to enter, but fighting began again. Montezuma was killed and Cortés's small band narrowly fought their way out to safety. They raised a new army among the native people and in April, 1521, renewed the attack on the Aztec capital. After a four-month siege in which the splendid city was ruined, the Aztec empire was destroyed. Another twenty-five years passed before the whole of Mexico came under Spanish rule. Though Cortés received rich lands in Oaxaca, in southern Mexico, as his reward, jealous rivals at the court of the King in Spain prevented him being proclaimed Governor of New Spain, as he thought he deserved.

Magellan's *Victoria*: the first ship to sail around the world.

1522

Magellan's voyage around the world

The search for a new trade route to the east continued after the discovery that America blocked the way (*see 1499 Amerigo Vespucci's voyage to America*). Ferdinand Magellan (*c.*1480–1521), a Portuguese veteran who had fallen out of favour in Portugal, volunteered to find a route for the Spanish government.

He sailed with five worm-eaten ships, and crews from many countries, in August, 1519. By the end of the year he was off South America, where his men mutinied on learning of his plan to look for a strait in the far south of the continent. Magellan crushed the mutiny, and in October–November, 1520, he sailed through the strait now named after him, into the Pacific.

After a terrible voyage across the Pacific with no fresh supplies, Magellan reached the Philippines. There he was killed in a local war by a local chieftain whom he was attempting to convert to

Prima ego velivolis ambivi Curfibus Orbem
Magellane novo te duce ducta freto.
Ambivi. meritoq́ɜ vocor VICTORIA: sunt mî
Vela, alæ, precivꝭ gloria, pugna, mare.

VICTORIA.

Conveniunt rebus nomina fepe suis.

Christianity. Under Sebastian del Cano, Magellan's one remaining ship, the *Victoria*, returned safely to Portugal in September, 1522, the first ship to sail around the world.

1525
Zwingli's reformation in Switzerland

Ulrich Zwingli (1484–1531), a priest at Zurich cathedral, was the leader of the Reformation in German-speaking Switzerland. Influenced by Erasmus and Luther, Zwingli in turn influenced the English Reformation. His success sprang from his willingness to co-operate with the local government, as long as it recognized the need for reform in the Church and the authority of the Bible. He is thought by many to have been the most open-minded and liberal of the reformers.

1525
Tyndale's Bible

Protestant reformers upheld the authority of scripture against the rules and rituals of Rome. Luther made scripture available to ordinary people, who could not read Latin, by translating the Bible into German, and William Tyndale produced his English New Testament in exile in 1525. Later he translated part of the Old Testament also. He was executed as a heretic in Germany in 1536.

1527
Baber and the Moghul Empire

During the thirteenth century, Afghanistan was invaded by the Mongols (*see 1206 Temujin proclaimed Genghis Khan*) and much of the country was later to become part of the vast empire of Timur (*see 1398 Timur conquers North India*).

In 1504 Baber (1483–1530) a descendant of both Timur and Genghis Khan was expelled from his small country in Afghanistan by more powerful neighbours and was forced to seek refuge in the mountains. He had one great ambition – to regain Timur's empire and to seat himself on the golden throne of Samarkand.

He had many setbacks but at last, in 1526, he led an army through the Khyber Pass and his cavalry made a great victory possible. At a subsequent battle near Patna the other Afghan chiefs were completely crushed. With all opposition overcome he attempted to create a Moghul Empire but only lived two more years, thus being unable to consolidate it.

1530
Death of Wolsey

Henry VIII (*see 1509 Accession of Henry VIII*) was greatly assisted by Thomas Wolsey (c. 1471–1530) in the early part of his reign. Wolsey became a royal chaplain in 1506 and his rise under the king was so rapid that he became Archbishop of York and then, in 1515, both Cardinal and Lord Chancellor.

Wolsey was a brilliant administrator and one of Europe's leading diplomats, carefully balancing the rival powers of France and Spain. He gathered a large personal fortune, some of which he used to found Christchurch College, Oxford, and also to build Hampton Court. His downfall began when he failed to obtain a divorce for his royal master from Catherine of Aragon. In 1529 he was deprived of his offices and then arrested for treason. He died whilst on his way to trial.

1531
Pizarro's expedition to Peru

In 1531, Francisco Pizarro (1475–1541) set out from Panama to conquer the Inca Empire, in the Andes Mountains of South America. The Inca Empire, Tahuantinsuyu, was larger than present-day Peru and included parts of Bolivia, Ecuador and Chile. With only 168 men, Pizarro crossed the Andes, and at Cajamarca captured the Inca king, Atahualpa. Atahualpa offered to pay the Spaniards a roomful of gold and two roomsful of silver for his freedom. It was the greatest ransom ever paid. All the same, Pizarro executed Atahualpa and in the next few years conquered his empire. Pizarro founded Lima, the present Peruvian capital, in 1535. He was murdered there six years later by rival Spanish captains.

1532

Calvin becomes a Protestant

John Calvin (c. 1509–64) was a theologian who was born in Noyon, France. He first studied for the priesthood but about 1532 became a Protestant and lived in Geneva, where he became a very active social reformer.

In 1538 he was banished by the city authorities and went to Strasbourg, but being recalled to Geneva in 1541, lived and preached there. He was determined to make the city a place of complete righteousness, and all who transgressed were punished, one man being burned after Calvin had denounced him.

He nevertheless greatly improved the city, education being encouraged whilst trade flourished and increased. His great work was The Institute of Christian Religion which he wrote in Latin in 1536 and which, translated into English, became the second 'Bible' of the Protestants in Britain, especially Scotland.

1533

Accession of Ivan the Terrible

Ivan III (1440–1505) started the growth of Muscovy, the small principality around Moscow which developed into Russia, when he expanded his territory northwards and eastwards as far as the Arctic Ocean and the Ural Mountains. He even started to build the Kremlin, which has housed Russia's government for centuries.

In 1533 Ivan's grandson Ivan IV (1530–84) became Grand Duke of Muscovy and in 1547 he was crowned first emperor (Czar) of Russia. For years Ivan was dominated by the powerful nobles or 'boyars', but he soon took over the

Ivan the Terrible besieges a fortress.

government and made himself head of the Eastern Orthodox Church.

Ivan determined to bring as much European influence to his lands as possible. When an expedition from England, led by Richard Chancellor, arrived in Russia in 1553, Ivan welcomed the opportunity for trade which this brought. However, Ivan's cruel and barbarous treatment of his people which earned him the name 'Ivan the Terrible' made him greatly feared outside his country. When the tyrannical czar died, Russia fell into chaos.

1534
Cartier explores Canada

The first explorer to attempt to settle in Canada was a Frenchman from Brittany, Jacques Cartier (1491–1557). In 1534 he set off on a voyage of exploration, hoping to find a North-West passage to India.

Cartier sailed along the north shore of Newfoundland and entered what is now the Gulf of St Lawrence, taking possession of the country in the name of Francis I of France. Having spent five months away from France he then returned to Brittany.

The following year Cartier set out again to explore the St Lawrence river, sailing up it as far as an Indian village on a hill which he named *Mont Réal* (Mount Royal). In 1541 Francis I decided to colonize New France, as he called Canada, so Cartier set off on a third expedition. But no colonists would settle there for they disliked the winter cold and the wilderness. Fifty years later another French expedition was sent to colonize New France.

1534
Rabelais writes *Gargantua*

François Rabelais (c.1494–c.1553) was born in Chinon, France, and became a monk, a teacher, a professor of anatomy and finally a priest. His lively imagination is shown in his two books written between 1532 and 1564 – *Gargantua* and *Pantagruel* which reveal a love of humanity and culture. Both these bawdy and witty books show Rabelais to be one of the world's great satirists.

1534
Loyola founds the Jesuits

Ignatius Loyola (1491–1556) was a Spanish nobleman who spent his youth at the court of Ferdinand and Isabella. He became a great soldier until the siege of Pampeluna (1521) where his leg was shattered by a cannon ball.

Whilst recovering from his wound, he began to read the lives of the saints and when he was well enough began to devote his life to the service of Christ.

Despite many hardships, including imprisonment by the Inquisition, he persevered and finally in 1534 he and six companions took vows in a church in Montmartre to found a 'Society of Jesus' (Jesuits).

Six years later his Society received the blessing of the Pope who appointed Loyola its first 'general', or commanding officer. He spent the rest of his life in Rome organizing his Society which, within a few years, was to become very influential. He died in 1556 and was canonized in 1622.

1537

Vesalius becomes professor of surgery at Padua

Galen, the great pioneer of medicine (*see AD 164 Galen at work in Rome*) set standards that were unequalled for thirteen hundred years. During the Middle Ages, so-called doctors had little knowledge and much of their art of healing depended on Galen, leeches and even magic.

The father of modern medicine was a Belgian, Andreas Vesalius (1514–64). His research was greatly assisted by the epidemics of the time, which afforded him a number of corpses upon which to work. He was appointed professor of surgery at Padua and began to write his major work: *De humani corporis fabrica* ('On the fabric of the human body'). It turned anatomy into an exact science and his enthusiasm attracted others to Padua which was to become the centre of medical research in Europe.

A diagram from Copernicus's treatise clearly shows his belief that the sun was at the centre of our solar system, and not the earth.

1540

Copernicus publishes treatise

Nicolaus Copernicus (1473–1543) was one of the most original thinkers of his time. Born at Thorn, Poland, he studied mathematics, optics and perspective at Cracow, astronomy and law at Bologna and medicine at Padua.

From 1507 until 1513 he worked on his treatise *De Revolutionibus Orbium Coelestium* ('Concerning the Revolutions of the Heavenly Spheres') which showed the relationship of the earth to the sun and the planets. At first he was reluctant to publish his theories but the summary aroused such interest that in 1540 he agreed to the publication of the whole work.

Copernicus's theory contradicted the Ptolemaic theory adopted by the Church (*see c. AD 120 Ptolemy's experiments*). Ptolemy believed that the earth was the centre of the universe, but in his treatise Copernicus suggested that the sun is a star, that the planets revolve around it and that the earth is simply one of these planets.

1540

Execution of Thomas Cromwell

The fallen Wolsey (*see 1530 Death of Wolsey*) was replaced by Thomas Cromwell (*c.* 1485–1540) who had been Wolsey's secretary. He was admitted to the Privy Council and soon became Henry VIII's principal adviser.

Cromwell was to be the architect of the English Reformation, supporting the king in his break with Rome, helping to arrange Catherine of Aragon's divorce and the dissolution of the English monasteries. He was so active in this latter work that he earned himself the name of *malleus monachorum* ('hammer of the monks').

He also played a large part in Protestantism by encouraging the translation and printing of the Bible and, by his Act of Supremacy (1534), confirmed the king as head of the English church.

He arranged Henry's marriage with Anne of Cleves (1540) but when the king recoiled from his choice, Cromwell's days were numbered. He was arrested on June 10, 1540 and charged with high treason, quite without cause. Found guilty, he was beheaded six weeks later. Henry soon realized his mistake and until his own death in 1547 spoke of the loss of 'the best servant I ever had'.

1549

Edward VI's Book of Common Prayer

An important step taken during the Reformation was the provision of a book for services held in the new Church of England. It was printed in English (earlier books being in Latin) and was condensed and simplified. Much of the preparatory work was done by Archbishop Cranmer (executed by Mary Tudor in 1556) and it was issued in January 1549, an Act of Uniformity making its use compulsory in all churches on and after the following Whit-Sunday.

It was produced during the reign of the young Edward VI (1537–53) and three years after its publication another edition was introduced. This edition lasted for only eight months for Mary Tudor came to the throne (1553) and reintroduced the old Latin services. She died in 1558 and by another Act of Conformity, Elizabeth reverted to the second Prayer Book.

1551

Suleiman the Magnificent campaigns in Persia

The Turk Suleiman I (1494–1566) proved a prince of good fortune from childhood. From his

Suleiman the Magnificent.

father, whom he succeeded in 1520, he inherited a well-trained and disciplined army, a full treasury and a prosperous and contented country. He was also surrounded by wise councillors and good generals. His campaigns, thirteen of which he led in person, ravaged Persia and East Europe – up to Vienna. The Holy Roman Emperor was forced to pay tribute to him.

In turn he was to conquer Belgrade, Rhodes, Budapest, Baghdad, Aden and Algiers and soon his Ottoman empire was extremely powerful. Although regarded as a great warrior, he was also a very just man, organizing a new set of laws that gave him his Turkish name of *Kanuni* ('Lawgiver'). To the rest of the world, and to history, however, he is known as Suleiman . . . the Magnificent.

1553

Lady Jane Grey's brief rule

Lady Jane Grey was born in 1537 and by the will of Henry VIII, her great-uncle, had been placed next in succession after his children, Edward, Mary and Elizabeth. Her unscrupulous uncle, Duke of Northumberland, caused her to be married to his son, Lord Guildford Dudley, hoping that he himself could continue in power after the death of the ailing Edward VI.

The king died on July 6, 1553 and Lady Jane was proclaimed Queen of England. The supporters of Mary Tudor, however, proved too strong and by July 19 Lady Jane was in the Tower after the shortest and most pathetic reign in English history. She was later tried and sentenced to death for high treason and, preceded by her young husband, the unfortunate 'queen' was beheaded on Tower Hill (1554).

1554

Cellini: *Perseus with the head of Medusa*

Benevenuto Cellini (1500–71) is regarded as the world's finest goldsmith. He studied in Rome and Paris then moved to Florence. His works include the bronze statue of *Perseus with the head* of *Medusa* (1554). His *Autobiography* is a very candid book, revealing him as a brawling soldier of fortune and a braggart, but nothing can dim his exquisite craftsmanship.

1555
Nostradamus writes *Centuries*

Nostradamus (1503–66) was the assumed name of Michel de Notredame, a French astrologer. In 1555 he wrote a book entitled *Centuries* which brought his name to the notice of the powerful Catherine de'Medici. He attended her court and for a time was employed in casting horoscopes. He also became physician to Catherine's son, Charles IX.

1555
Burning of Latimer and Ridley

When Mary I (1516–58), daughter of Henry VIII, came to the throne in 1553 a major question was that of the queen's marriage. In spite of the protests from the nation she obstinately set her heart on Philip of Spain. Their marriage in 1554 caused the Protestants to turn from Mary and to regard her sister, Elizabeth, as their champion.

Mary altered much of what had been done in her father's time, especially doing her best to

Mary Tudor married Philip of Spain in 1554.

stamp out the new Protestantism and to bring back the Roman Catholic Church. She then began to persecute the Reformed Clergy; married clergy were ordered to abandon their wives and those who would not conform she expelled, putting Catholic priests in their pulpits.

Mary sent two leaders of the English Church – Bishops Latimer and Ridley – to the Tower and in April 1554 they were taken before a court and offered their freedom if they would recant. Both refused and on October 16, 1555, they were burned together.

1555
Tintoretto paints *St George and the Dragon*

Born in Venice in 1518, Jacopo Robusti studied under the great artist Titian. He then changed his name to 'Tintoretto' (or 'Little Dyer') a popular name from his father's trade, and began to produce a number of masterpieces. These include *St George and the Dragon*, *Belshazzar's Feast* and *The Last Supper*. He died in 1594.

1555
Formation of *La Pléiade*

Pierre de Ronsard (1524–85) spent his youth at the French court but later, becoming deaf, he turned to writing, especially poetry. He formed a group with du Bellay (1522–60) and other poets which endeavoured to improve French verse. The group was called *La Pléiade* and was directly responsible for the increase in classical influence in their country's poetry.

1556
Akhbar the Great creates an empire

When Baber died in 1530 (*see 1527 Baber and the Moghul Empire*) he had tried, but failed, to establish an empire, an achievement to be left to his descendant Akhbar (1542–1605).

Akhbar was the son of Humayun, King of Delhi, a minor kingdom, and on becoming king himself he determined to complete what Baber had begun and create a great Moghul empire.

He led an army against his neighbours in 1556 and within six years his kingdom consisted of the Punjab and other large areas of India together with Kabul in Afghanistan.

He had created his empire but was not satisfied. Another fourteen years of constant warfare followed until he was ruler of the whole of northern India. He then marched into the Deccan and added further vast territories to his already huge empire which was to consist of fifteen great provinces.

He was more than a warrior, however. He was a great and just ruler who attempted to create a united India out of its jumble of warring races and religions. As the 'Great Moghul' he corresponded with England's Queen Elizabeth I.

1558
Accession of Elizabeth I

It is incredible that Elizabeth I (1533–1603) ever reached England's throne at all. Soon after she was born her father, Henry VIII, executed her mother, Anne Boleyn, and declared his daughter illegitimate. Later, as a young princess, many people tried to draw her into plots against her

Mary's reign saw the Roman Catholic church briefly re-established in England.

half-sister Mary (*see 1555 Burning of Latimer and Ridley*) and during the nine days' reign of Lady Jane Grey (*see 1553 Lady Jane Grey's brief rule*) she pretended to be ill until the luckless Jane was imprisoned.

With Mary on the throne, Elizabeth was constantly the hope of the Protestants, especially when it was learned that Mary intended to marry the Catholic Philip of Spain. Although she had no part in the uprising that followed this news, Elizabeth was thrown into the Tower and her later release was due to her keeping a cool head.

Back at court she was always conscious that a moment's indiscretion might see her back in the Tower, perhaps kneeling in the same place where her mother had died under the headsman's axe. Then a great cloud seemed lifted from her mind when she learned that Mary had died on November 17, 1558, and that she, at twenty-five, was the new and undoubted Queen of England.

Elizabeth I

1561

Mary, Queen of Scots, returns from France

Mary Stuart (1542–87), the daughter of King James V of Scotland (1512–42) became that country's queen when only a week old, her father being killed at the Battle of Solway Moss (1542). She went to the French court when a girl and married Francis II, to become Queen of France as well. She was also heiress to the English throne as next of kin to Elizabeth.

On the early death of her husband she returned to Scotland as queen. Being a Catholic she was opposed by the Protestant Calvinist movement and especially their leader, John Knox. She married her cousin, Lord Darnley who, jealous of her Italian secretary Rizzio, had him murdered before her eyes in 1566. Darnley was himself murdered soon afterwards.

Mary then married Lord Bothwell; her nobles turned against her and she was forced to flee to England (*see 1587 Execution of Mary, Queen of Scots*).

1562

Hawkins commences the slave trade

Devon-born John Hawkins (1532–95) has the unenviable reputation of being the first Englishman to engage in the terrible slave traffic. In 1562 he took goods to the African coast where he bartered them for kidnapped negroes. These he carried to the Spanish settlements in America and exchanged them for pearls, sugar and ginger.

On a privateering voyage in 1567–8, Hawkins' fleet included two ships belonging to Queen Elizabeth. Hawkins, who was accompanied by Francis Drake, fell foul of the Spaniards in the Bay of San Juan de Ulua where he had sheltered for repairs to his vessels. After a fierce fight, all but two of the English ships were sunk and Hawkins barely escaped with his life. He afterwards rose to high rank in the navy but died at sea in November, 1595.

1564

Birth of Shakespeare

William Shakespeare (1564–1616) one of the world's greatest dramatists, was born in Stratford-upon-Avon, England, on or about April 23, 1564. When he was eighteen he married Anne Hathaway and had a family of three children.

In 1587, leaving his wife and family behind, he went to London and was immediately attracted to the theatre. At first he had quite

William Shakespeare.

A private performance of *A Midsummer Night's Dream* before the court of Elizabeth I.

menial jobs – small parts and, as a writer, a patcher of old scripts – but in time he became the head playwright and part-owner of the Globe Theatre, Bankside, in Southwark.

By the 1590s Shakespeare's reputation as a writer was growing steadily; he wrote some of the most beautiful sonnets in the English language and by the end of his life he had written thirty-seven plays, including histories, comedies, romances and tragedies. His drama appeals to all tastes, for it contains poetry, action, love, excitement and humour.

The rich poetry of Shakespeare's plays allows his characters to speak with a vividness and variety that have perhaps never been equalled. It reveals the innermost thoughts of his characters, creates atmosphere and sets scenes. Some of the most famous plays by him include *Macbeth, A Midsummer Night's Dream, Hamlet* and *As You Like It*.

1566

Breughel paints *The Wedding Dance*

Pieter Breughel (*c*. 1525–69) was the son of a Flemish peasant and although he was to travel in France and Italy, visiting Rome and Naples, he never forgot the scenes of his youth. His paintings, such as *The Wedding Dance* are full of humorous, high-spirited peasants, all obviously enjoying life. His two sons, Pieter and Jan also became outstanding artists.

1569

Mercator's world map

When European navigators began to sail out into the oceans during the fifteen century, the only maps they possessed were the charts long used in sailing round coasts or in the Mediterranean Sea.

These charts served well in those circumstances, but they were not suitable for ocean sailing, with its greater distances and long weeks spent out of sight of land.

Often, such charts used for ocean voyages showed bearings wrongly and put islands many kilometres away from their true position. This was because the charts took no account of the curves of the round earth.

In 1569, the Flemish geographer Gerhardus Mercator (1512–94) provided a special chart for ocean voyaging.

In Mercator's 'projection', which is still used on maps today, all the meridians and parallels (lines of longitude and latitude) are straight lines and they cross at right angles. A compass course between any two points is the straight line connecting them.

1570
Palladio's treatise on architecture

Italian-born Andrea Palladio (1518–80) was one of the outstanding architects of his time. He showed great promise as a child and his patron, Count Trissino, made it possible for him to study art and architecture in Rome. In 1547 he returned to Vicenza, his birthplace, where he was to design some very fine buildings, including several ornate palaces for Italian noblemen. He later built stately churches in Venice and some further palaces, this time on the Grand Canal.

He was a student and admirer of classical works and much of what he designed reflects that admiration, giving the name 'Palladian' to his grandiose style. His *I quattro libri dell'architettura* ('Four Books of Architecture') were translated into many languages, the English version being published by the great architect Inigo Jones, and his influence spread throughout Europe.

1571
The Battle of Lepanto

The Turks had been capturing many of the finest harbours in the Middle East, their fleets sailing from Constantinople which had become their capital. They were ruled over by Suleiman the Magnificent (1494–1566) and then by his son Selim II, who was most ambitious. For a time things went his way for the Christian powers were jealous of each other, but at last Pope Pius V called Venice and Spain together to form a Holy League to fight the Turks.

By the summer of 1571 a fleet of more than three hundred ships, commanded by Don John of Austria (1547–78), a young man of twenty-four, was ready. It sailed for the Greek harbour of Lepanto and on October 7, 1571 one of the world's greatest naval battles took place. The fighting ended at dusk when the Turkish fleet of two hundred and seventy-five galleys was

virtually destroyed and the naval power of the Sultan was ended. Lepanto was the last great sea battle in which galleys were used.

1572
The St Bartholomew's Day Massacre

For a considerable time there had been a great deal of friction between Catholics and Huguenots (Protestants) in France. Clashes were frequent but the bloodshed was not too severe. Then, overnight, things changed dramatically. In August 1572 Henry, King of Navarre, and Marguerite, sister of the French King Charles IX, were to be married and many nobles, Catholic and Huguenot, had gathered in Paris for the celebrations.

With so many of both factions gathered together it was not long before rioting began. Taking advantage of the situation, Catherine de' Medici, the queen mother, persuaded her son Charles IX to organize a massacre of the Huguenots. Some 30,000 were killed, mostly in cold blood, not only in Paris but in other cities throughout France. This terrible massacre took place on the feast of St Bartholomew, hence its name.

It was to affect Charles's brain and he died soon afterwards in his twenty-fourth year.

1576
Tycho Brahe builds Uraniborg observatory

Danish-born Tycho Brahe (1546–1601) specialized in astronomy and was invited by Frederick II of Denmark to build a magnificent observatory at Uraniborg. Although he was a brilliant astronomer (he discovered the constellation Cassiopeia) he disagreed with Copernicus, maintaining that the earth was the centre of the universe and remained still, though he did agree that the other planets revolved around the sun.

His chief astronomical work was concerned with improvements in the art of observation of the universe and also a catalogue of fixed stars which he assembled in 1576. He gave the position of 777 although this number was

The massacre of French Huguenots on St Bartholomew's Day.

increased by Kepler in 1605 to 1,627.

Brahe also published several books including *De Nova Stella* ('The New Star') in which he recorded his observations of the galactic supernova he had seen in 1573.

1577

Francis Drake sails round the world

On December 13, 1577, Francis Drake (*c.* 1540–96), a seaman from Devon, set sail in the *Pelican* with a fleet of five ships and a hundred and sixty-six men from Plymouth. He reached the Brazilian coast on April 6, 1577 and on August 21 entered the Straits of Magellan. His ships became separated in a storm and he carried on alone in his ship, now renamed *Golden Hind*, capturing many unsuspecting Spanish ships.

By July 1579 he was in the Moluccas and then eleven months later he was rounding the Cape of Good Hope, homeward bound. On September 26, 1580 he sailed triumphantly into Plymouth harbour, the first English captain to sail around the world, a journey which took some two years and ten months. Soon afterwards Queen Elizabeth went on board the *Golden Hind* and knighted him for his achievement.

1578

Hilliard paints *Queen Elizabeth I*

Nicholas Hilliard (*c.* 1537–1619) brilliantly portrayed the personalities who thronged the court of Queen Elizabeth. He was apprenticed to a London goldsmith and almost immediately began to produce beautiful miniature portraits. One of his earliest, dated 1578, is of the queen herself. During half a century he created some of the most exquisite works of art ever produced.

1579

The Union of Utrecht

During the Middle Ages, what are now Belgium and the Netherlands were small feudal counties and duchies. They gradually passed into the control of the Burgundian dukes, Charles the Bold (*d.* 1477) seeking to weld them into one country, but without success. His daughter Mary married Maximilian of Austria and the 'Low Countries' (or Netherlands) passed quietly into the realms of the Hapsburgs.

King Charles of Spain, who was also the Holy

Roman Emperor Charles V, inherited the provinces from his father, Philip the Fair of Hapsburg, and after Charles' abdication in 1556, they passed to his son, Philip II. Spain, however, was a Catholic country while the northern provinces were Protestant. Consequently, a revolt broke out and in 1579 the Protestant provinces formed the separate Union of Utrecht, sometimes called the Dutch Netherlands or United Provinces, controlled by William, Prince of Orange. By the League of Arras (1579) the ten southern provinces, which were Catholic, recognized Philip II as their sovereign but retained their independence.

1586

Creation of the *kabuki* theatre

The traditional Japanese, all-male theatre, *kabuki*, is said to have started in 1586 when a woman called O Kuni performed parodies of Buddhist prayers. With her troupe of men and women dancers it was the first theatrical presentation of any stature that had been specifically aimed at the masses. Previously such entertainments had been the prerogative of the rich with the *nō* dramas and *kyōgen* comedies.

In 1629 the *kabuki* was banned as it was said to be vulgar and frivolous but it managed to continue as *wakashū* in which young boys played all the roles, including those of the women. This, too, was frowned upon by the authorities and eventually outlawed. But this time the theatre, as *yarō kabuki*, continued to thrive with an all-male cast. It is this form of all-male, highly stylistic, and traditional theatre that remains popular to the present day.

1586

El Greco paints *The Burial of Count Orgaz*

The Greek-born painter, Domenico Theotocopuli (*c.* 1541–1616) is better known by his Spanish nickname 'El Greco'. It is thought that in

Kabuki, the popular theatre of Japan, with its stylized acting, music and dancing, has remained popular up to modern times.

1570 he went to Rome where he studied as a pupil of Titian, painting several religious subjects, but in 1577 El Greco settled in Spain. His works include *Assumption of the Virgin, Burial of Count Orgaz* and *Christ and the Money Changers*.

1587
Marlowe writes *Tamburlaine*

Christopher Marlowe (1564–93), a brilliant dramatist, has been called the father of English tragedy and the creator of dramatic blank verse. He was born in Canterbury but soon moved to London where he associated with Shakespeare, Ben Jonson and others of their brilliant circle.

Between 1587 and 1593 he wrote four plays: *Tamburlaine the Great, Dr Faustus, The Famous Tragedy of the Rich Jew of Malta* and *Edward the Second*. The first three are concerned with power and the effect it has on men; heroes of the plays are tragic figures, villains battling against their fate. His *Tamburlaine the Great* was the first poem to be written in English blank verse.

Little is known of Marlowe's life, but he was known as a free-thinker and suspected of atheism. In 1593 he was stabbed at Deptford in a tavern brawl, possibly in Queen Elizabeth's service as a secret agent.

1587
Execution of Mary, Queen of Scots

Queen Mary escaped to England (*see 1561 Mary, Queen of Scots, returns from France*) only to be imprisoned by Elizabeth for nineteen long years. For a time she kept quiet and then, encouraged by promises of support from outside, she allowed herself to be involved in a plot to rescue her, whilst soldiers from Spain and Catholic supporters in England would be ready to beat down any opposition and escort her to her coronation.

Called the Babington plot, after one of the conspirators, it was easily revealed by Walsingham, Elizabeth's minister. Mary Stuart stood trial and was condemned to death, Elizabeth signing the death warrant on February 1, 1587.

By then Mary had been moved to Fotheringay Castle and a high scaffold had been built in its great hall. Dressed in black, Mary knelt down

at the block and at the second blow her head was severed from her body.

Mary, Queen of Scots, prepares to meet the executioner at Fotheringay.

1588
Defeat of the Spanish Armada

In 1585 England was at war with Spain and Drake took a fleet to the Spanish Main where he sank a large number of Spanish ships and plundered several of their rich cities. Two years later he sailed into the Bay of Cadiz and sank a number of ships he found assembled there. He called this enterprise 'Singeing the King of Spain's beard'.

The following year Drake was at Plymouth when news was received by him and his fellow captains that a great Spanish fleet had been sighted in the Channel. Known as Spain's Invincible Armada, its lumbering galleons were chased by the lighter and more active ships of the English fleet along the Flanders coast and into the North Sea where they were left to the violence of a fierce storm. Few of that once great Armada returned to Spain.

The Armada Battle by an unknown contemporary
painter. *Ark Royal,* one of the finest ships built during
Queen Elizabeth I's reign, is on the extreme right.

1590

Spenser writes the *Faërie Queene*

Edmund Spenser (c. 1552–99) was born in London of humble parents and was educated as a 'poor scholar' at Merchant Taylors' School and then at Cambridge. He began to write, his first important poem being *The Shepheardes Calendar* (1579). He later took up a post in Ireland and continued to write, his best known work being *The Faërie Queene*, an allegorical poem which was to glorify his country and show the behaviour of the ideal courtier.

1590

Galileo publishes *De Motu*

Galileo Galilei (1564–1642) was born in Pisa, Italy, and when only nineteen discovered the isochronism (regularity) of the pendulum; in 1587 he formulated the law of falling bodies ($h = \frac{1}{2}gt^2$) proving his theory by dropping leaden and wooden balls of the same size and watching them hit the ground at the same time.

A swinging lamp in Pisa Cathedral is said to have inspired Galileo's observations on the pendulum.

His theories were published in *De Motu* in 1590.

In 1592 he became professor of mathematics at Padua where he conducted some important experiments and firmly stated that the Copernican theory of the planets moving round the sun was true. For this he was imprisoned by the church authorities but, being released by the Pope, continued laying the foundation of modern experimental science.

In 1609 he constructed the first astronomical telescope with which he discovered the valleys of the moon, the phases of Venus and the four satellites of Jupiter. Nevertheless, the church authorities kept him under house arrest until his death.

1590

Jansen invents the microscope

A Dutch spectacle maker, Zacharias Jansen, is credited with the invention of the microscope about 1590. It was a somewhat unwieldy piece of equipment, about the same size as a telescope. Nevertheless it worked, an observer of the time remarking, 'With this long cannon you can see flies which appear to be as big as sheep'.

1591

The death of Grenville

In 1591 a squadron of six English ships were watering in Flores Bay in the Azores when a pinnace raced in with the warning that a large Spanish fleet was approaching. The commander of the squadron, Sir Richard Grenville (c. 1542–91) ordered the rest of the ships to escape but stayed himself to pick up half of his crew who were lying ill ashore. By the time he had tacked out of the bay it was too late – he was surrounded by fifty-three tall Spanish galleons.

For the next fifteen hours, Grenville's flagship, the *Revenge*, kept them at bay until she was an absolute wreck, her masts shot away, her hull and upperworks riddled with the shot that kept crashing into her from at least six ships at a time. At last, with his ship sinking beneath him, Grenville was reluctantly forced to surrender, dying soon afterwards of his wounds.

1596

Caravaggio paints *Boy with a Fruit Basket*

Michelangelo Amerighi Caravaggio (1569–1609) was born in Lombardy and founded a revolutionary school of painting in Naples, teaching his students to paint subjects in a natural way and not idealistically as formerly. Most of his sitters were young boys and his masterpieces include *Boy with a Fruit Basket, Fortune Teller* and *A Music Party*.

1598

The Edict of Nantes

For many years France had been torn apart with religious and civil wars, the Catholics fighting the French Protestants (Huguenots), first one side and then the other gaining the advantage. Finally, in 1598, King Henry IV of France decided to end the useless, self-destroying struggle for ever. He passed a law, to become known as the Edict of Nantes, which gave virtual religious liberty to the Huguenots.

It offered them liberty of conscience throughout all France; the right to hold public worship where they had held it previously; the grand nobility could hold Protestant services in their *châteaux*, and lesser nobles could do the same, but the gathering was limited to thirty persons. Full civil rights were granted to Protestants, including access to all official positions. Many other concessions were granted, whilst a committee of ten Catholics and six Protestants was established to deal with any religious disputes.

1600

English East India Company founded

For some years the Dutch had maintained a monopoly of the spice trade with Indonesia and the Moluccas and as the prices soared, the merchants of London became very concerned. On the last day of the sixteenth century, Queen Elizabeth granted a Charter to a new company giving permission to trade in 'all parts and places in Asia, Africa and America between Cape Cod and the Strait of Magellan'.

Four ships of the company sailed from the Thames in 1601 bound for the East by way of the Cape of Good Hope. Soon other ships followed and in time the East India Company grew into an organization which rivalled the British navy for ships and men. It continued until 1874.

Inspired by the success of 'John Company', as it was called , other companies, both British and European, were formed to trade with North America and Canada.

1602

Monteverdi composes *Arianna*

Claudio Monteverdi (1567–1643) was an Italian composer whose patron was the Duke of Mantua. In 1613 he became *Maestro di capella* at St Mark's, Venice, where his religious compositions restored the musical reputation of the church. In 1602 he wrote his first opera *Arianna* in which he used unaccompanied madrigals. His next, *Orfeo*, made an even greater impact and established him as a great composer.

1603

A Scots king on the English throne

By the year 1603, Elizabeth had reigned for forty-five of her seventy years. Although she knew she could not live much longer, she refused to name her successor until, a few days before her death in March 1603, her chief minister Robert Cecil sent a messenger spurring northwards to inform James Stuart that he would be the next King of England.

He was already James VI of Scotland (1566–1625) having ascended the throne in 1567 at the age of one, on the abdication of his mother, the ill-fated Mary Stuart (*see 1561 Mary, Queen of Scots, returns from France*). His father was the unfortunate Lord Darnley, whilst he was Elizabeth's cousin twice removed.

He came to the English throne as first of the Stuart dynasty and to be known as James I of England, having descended from Margaret, eldest daughter of King Henry VII. He prided himself on his 'kingcraft' but actually was so inexperienced in diplomacy that a French statesman described him as 'the wisest fool in Christendom'. He left behind a poor country for a rich one and his extravagance upset many of his new subjects. Nevertheless, he was the first king to rule over both England and Scotland.

1604
Lope de Vega writes *Peregrino en su Patria*

During the sixteenth century, Spanish writers stopped imitating those of France and Italy and a new style of Spanish writing was developed. A great innovator of this style was Lope de Vega (1562–1635) who wrote about two thousand plays. *Peregrino en su Patria* ('A Pilgrim in his own Land') is a romance which illustrates de Vega's flowing, easy, musical verse.

1605
The Gunpowder Plot

Despite his mother's Catholicism, James I had been brought up as a strict Protestant and soon after his accession in 1603 a plot was laid by a group of fanatical Catholics to kill him.

Guy Fawkes

One of their number, Thomas Winter, persuaded Guy Fawkes (1570–1606), then fighting in Flanders, to join them. They evolved a plan: to blow up the king and his ministers when Parliament re-assembled on November 5, 1605, then take over control during the confusion which was bound to follow.

At the last moment, however, one of the plotters warned his brother-in-law of the plot; he in turn alerted the officials and the cellars were searched on November 4. Fawkes was discovered near some barrels of gunpowder with a slow fuse in his pocket. Fawkes and seven others were executed on January 31, 1606, but he has been remembered every year since on Guy Fawkes night, 5th November.

1608
The 'Plantation of Ulster'

The English conquest of Ireland began in 1169 during the reign of Henry II and had been carried on for more than four centuries. During the reigns of Elizabeth I and James I both monarchs believed that they could conquer the country, not only by armed forces, but also by more subtle means; the national costume was to be abolished together with the Catholic religion, whilst whole territories were to be cleared of the Irish natives and replaced by English and Scots settlers.

The turning point came when the great Irish chiefs were defeated at the battle of Kinsale (1602) and fled from the country. This 'Flight of the Earls' marked the end of the Irish chieftains and their vast estates. The confiscation of their lands began and the six northern counties were added to the English crown by the 'Plantation of Ulster' of 1608, only the three counties of Monaghan, Antrim and Down being excluded.

1608
Lippershey invents the telescope

The first telescope, it is believed, was made by another Dutch spectacle maker of Middleburg (*see 1590 Jansen invents the microscope*) called Hans Lippershey. Holding up a pair of spectacle lenses he directed them towards a steeple and found that it appeared nearer. Mounting them in a tube, some distance apart, he produced . . . the telescope. Galileo took the idea, improved upon it and used the telescope in his observation of the heavens.

1609

Kepler's *Planetary Movements*

Johann Kepler (1571–1630) was born in Weil, Germany, and succeeded Tycho Brahe as Professor of Mathematics and Astronomy at Prague University, previously having published his *Prodomus* in 1596 when he was only twenty-five.

At first he relied a great deal upon Brahe, his master, and his great and most significant discovery, published in 1609, was that every planet follows an elliptical rather than a circular orbit round the sun. He also stated that the line drawn from a planet's centre to the sun takes the same time to move over equal areas of the ellipse, and that the square of a planet's period of revolution is proportional to the cube of its mean distance from the sun. These laws are basic to modern astronomy. Because new ideas of astronomy were frowned on by the Church, Kepler wrote many of his theories and ideas in the form of science fiction.

1613

The first of the Romanovs

Poles invaded Russia in 1609 and in the following year Vladislav, son of the King of Poland, made himself Czar, whilst the Swedes seized several Russian cities. The people of Russia united to drive out the invaders and in October 1612 regained control of their country. Fifteen-year-old Michael Romanov was chosen to be Czar, thus founding a new Russian dynasty, which lasted until 1917 (*see 1917 Outbreak of the Russian Revolution*).

1615

Inigo Jones becomes surveyor general

Inigo Jones (1573–1651) was the son of a cloth-worker, yet was to become one of Britain's finest architects. His talent as an artist soon became apparent and he was sent by his patron, the Earl of Arundel, to study in Italy. He changed from landscape-painting to architecture and was particularly influenced by the work of Andrea Palladio (*see 1570 Palladio's treatise on architecture*).

Jones acquired such a reputation that he was invited to Denmark to design the two royal palaces of Rosenberg and Frederiksborg for King Christian IV.

In 1604 he was appointed architect to England's royal court where he also designed sets and costumes for the court masques. He was later appointed surveyor general and designed such magnificent works as the Banqueting Hall, Whitehall and Greenwich Hospital.

Under Cromwell he was forced to pay heavy fines for being a courtier of Charles I, and he died in poverty.

1615

Cervantes writes *Don Quixote*

Miguel de Cervantes (1547–1616) lived an adventurous life, being a soldier who was taken prisoner by Barbary pirates. Returning to Spain he began to write, and created his immortal 'hero', the Spanish knight, Don Quixote de la Mancha, whose mind was turned by tales of the medieval knights. In his book Cervantes was mocking both sixteenth century Spanish society and its romantic literature.

1617

Jonson becomes first poet laureate

In recognition of his services to poetry and drama, Ben Jonson (*c.* 1573–1637) was awarded in 1617 a royal pension by James I and thus became the first poet laureate, though not in name. His plays record contemporary scenes and are a shrewd criticism of mankind. Famous plays by Jonson include *The Alchemist* (1610) and *Bartholomew Fair* (1614).

1618
Outbreak of the Thirty Years' War

Since 1555 Germany had been divided into two religious camps – the Lutherans (Protestants) and Catholics, forming a Catholic 'League' and a Protestant 'Union'. Then, in Bohemia, an event occurred which was to begin the Thirty Years' War.

It began when the Czech leaders in Prague, protesting against the strict rule of the Catholic Hapsburgs, threw out their state officials and elected as king Frederick, the Elector Palatine, a Protestant prince. Soon afterwards, however, a battle was fought at White Mountain in 1620, Frederick was defeated and, it seemed, the revolt was over.

But the war that had begun in Bohemia soon became a European conflict. Christian of Denmark (1577–1648) led a Protestant Union against a powerful army of the Catholic League led by Count Tilly and the Imperial General Wallenstein. Christian was defeated to be replaced by Gustavus Adolphus of Sweden (1594–1632). They next met at Breidenfeld (1631) where Adolphus almost destroyed Tilly's forces and avenged his sacking of the city of Magdeburg four months earlier.

Wallenstein was beaten the following year at Lützen and after that the war lost its religious character to become a political struggle. Battle followed battle and much of Europe was plunged into chaos and brutal strife until the war was ended in 1648 by the Treaty of Westphalia.

The Battle of Lützen: Gustavus Adolphus (below) defeated the brilliant Wallenstein (above) but lost his life.

1618
Van Dyck becomes a guild member

Dutch-born Anthony Van Dyck (1599–1641) was only nineteen years of age when he became a full member of the Antwerp Guild of Painters. When he visited England he became court painter and was knighted by Charles I. His paintings include an equestrian portrait of Charles (*see page 128*) and another of the king, Queen Henrietta Maria and their children.

1618

Execution of Raleigh

Walter Raleigh was a Devon man, born near Sidmouth in 1552. He became a member of Elizabeth's court and, as legend says, came to her attention when he gallantly spread his cloak before her on the muddy ground.

He soon became her favourite courtier and in 1585 sent a fleet to America to found the colony of Virginia, named after the 'virgin queen'. He was supplanted by the Earl of Essex and for a time he went to Ireland, although he was later restored to the queen's favour.

On her death Raleigh realized that there was no place for him under a Stuart king. He was actually imprisoned in the Tower of London for twelve years on a charge of treason during which he wrote his *History of the World* and *A Discovery of War*.

He was allowed his freedom to sail for South America and search for El Dorado (the man of gold), but only on condition that he did not clash with the Spaniards who were in power there. A clash was, however, inevitable for the Spaniards objected strongly to the English entering their territory.

Finally, a fight broke out between Raleigh's men and the townsfolk of San Thome, Guiana. This sealed Raleigh's fate, and when he returned to England, having apparently defied his orders, he was condemned to death and executed, in 1618.

1620

The voyage of the *Mayflower*

After unsuccessful attempts to settle an English colony on the mainland of North America in the 1580s, success was at last achieved in 1607, with the foundation of Jamestown, Virginia. This success inspired others to cross the Atlantic Ocean and set up colonies in the New World. America was also a haven for those who suffered religious persecution in Europe and prominent among these were the extreme Protestant Puritans in England.

'Puritans' was a name given in Elizabethan England to those who wished to see practised simpler and more devout worship than that existing after the Reformation, where many of the old rituals of the Catholic church still remained.

The Established Church and James I were hostile towards them and following a number of persecutions, many were forced to leave England and settle in Leyden, Holland, in 1608. They soon found, however, that the industrial life they had to follow was not to their liking and decided to begin a new life – in the New World.

They finally obtained permission from the Virginia Company to settle in North America and eventually, on September 6, 1620, their ship, the *Mayflower*, sailed with one hundred and two men, women and children who looked forward to a new life, and freedom to worship as they wished in America.

It was a difficult and dangerous passage. The weather was rough and, soaked and miserable, the Pilgrims huddled together with only their faith to sustain them. During the storm one of the main beams cracked but it was repaired, and at last, on the evening of November 19 they anchored in the sheltered but bleak harbour of Cape Cod, Massachusetts.

1624

Richelieu becomes chief minister

Armand de Richelieu (1585–1642) became a cardinal in 1622 and chief minister to Louis XIII (1601–43) in 1624. His ambitions were clear: to quash the Huguenots (*see 1627 The siege of La Rochelle*); to increase France's greatness; and to secure all power in the hands of the king and himself. He achieved all this (although he oppressed the people, overwhelmed them with taxation and denied them many of their local liberties) and can be regarded as the founder of absolute monarchy that reached its height under Louis XIV.

Richelieu's first task was to curb the power of the nobles who enjoyed virtual independence from royal authority. Their conspiracies to depose Louis and kill Richelieu led him to destroy their castles and to forbid private warfare. In 1630 he foiled an attempt by the Queen Mother, Marie de Medici, and leading nobles to arrange his downfall; Marie de Medici fled to Brussels and several nobles were imprisoned or executed.

In his foreign policy Richelieu was equally aggressive, and determined to combat the threat of the Hapsburgs. By the Treaty of Westphalia in

Richelieu besieges La Rochelle.

1648 (see 1618 Outbreak of the Thirty Years' War) he had made France capable of dominating the peace negotiations.

1625
Rubens: *Adoration of the Magi*

Peter Paul Rubens (1577–1640) was perhaps the greatest of all Flemish painters. In 1600 he went to Italy where he studied the works of Titian and Veronese; it was here that the foundations of his style were laid. Amongst his most well-known paintings are the *Adoration of the Magi* and *The Assumption of the Virgin*.

1627
The siege of La Rochelle

During Richelieu's campaign against the Huguenots (see 1624 Richelieu becomes chief minister) he began a siege of La Rochelle, then a great maritime city and the centre of French Protestantism. As soon as his troops appeared the Huguenots appealed to England for help and the Duke of Buckingham arrived with a strong fleet of forty-two warships and seven thousand troops, both infantry and cavalry, to deal with the situation. When he arrived, however, the people of La Rochelle refused him permission to land, declaring that they did not want to show any hostility to their king.

Buckingham then turned his attention to the Isle of Ré but the French threw in a superior force and he was completely defeated, more than half of his men being slaughtered. He returned to England soon afterwards to face the contempt of the people.

1628
The Petition of Right

King Charles I of England (1600–49) believed that he ruled by Divine Right, that is he had been appointed by God Himself. Believing that Parliament had no right to 'interfere' with royal rule, he ordered a commission to raise taxes without waiting for Parliament's approval. The Commission, however, disliked bypassing Parliament and were unwilling to collect the money. King Charles then issued an order on February 28, 1628, putting a duty on various goods. This brought the merchants against him and the people of England sent as many strong men as possible to the next Parliament.

When the four hundred men of the Commons assembled they included such as Cromwell, Hampden and Pym, men who would stand against the king if he acted unconstitutionally.

Parliament drew up a limiting Petition of Right and forced the king to sign, but in 1634 and 1635 he broke this statute when he ordered other than maritime towns to pay 'ship money'. This act was to become a great issue between king and Parliament.

1628
Harvey discovers circulation of blood

In 1628 Englishman William Harvey (1578–1657) published an account of how the heart works as a pump, circulating blood to every part of the body. He deduced this by actually measuring the output of blood from the ventricle (a chamber of the heart) and inferring that it returned via the auricle (another chamber). From this has grown the whole science of physiology.

1628
Piet Heyn captures the silver fleet

During the early part of the seventeenth century, Holland became a powerful and prosperous nation, her great trading colonies in the West and East Indies bringing in huge revenues. There had been an uneasy truce with Spain who, for a time, had ruled Holland, and in 1621 war again broke out between the two countries.

Dutch fleets went into action, sinking every Spanish ship they met, their greatest success being in September 1628 when one of their admirals, Pieter ('Piet') Heyn, captured the entire Spanish fleet carrying bullion from the silver mines in America.

Another triumph of the Spanish–Dutch war was the Battle of the Downs in 1639 when a Dutch fleet under the great admiral Marten van Tromp (1597–1635) crushed the Spanish fleet to establish Dutch naval supremacy.

1632
Taj Mahal begun by Shah Jehan

The mausoleum of Taj Mahal standing by the Jumna River outside Agra in India is regarded as the finest example of Islamic architecture. Standing on a rectangular platform 580 metres by 304 metres, the highly decorated 'onion' shaped dome of the octagonal tomb in white marble is flanked by four smaller domes. At each corner is

The magnificence of the Moghul empire: Shah Jehan built the Taj Mahal as a mausoleum for his wife.

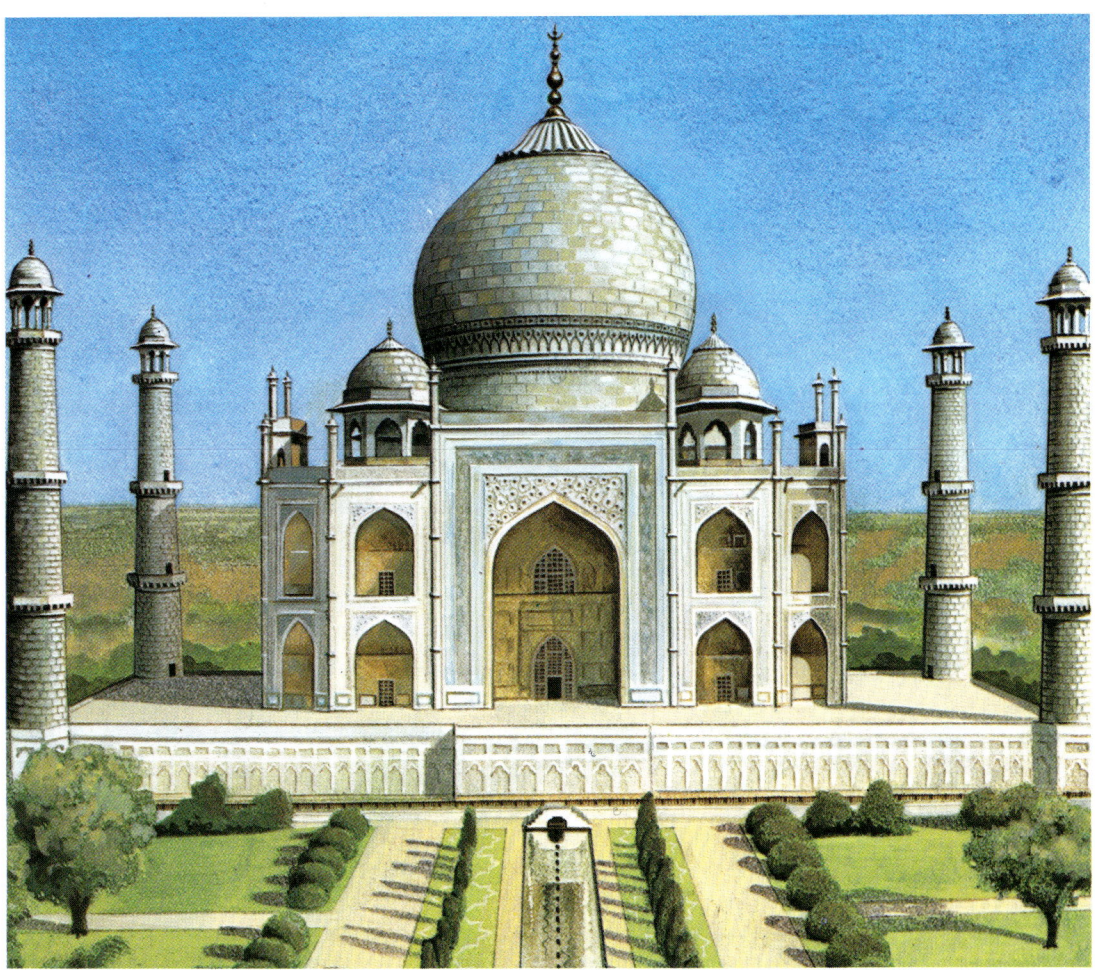

a slender minaret, and a pool lined with cypress trees reflects the whole edifice.

The mausoleum was commissioned by the Moghul emperor Shah Jehan in 1631 for his beloved wife who died in childbirth. The construction began the following year, took twenty-two years to complete and employed twenty thousand workers. The inside of the building is just as ornate as the exterior, with semi-precious jewels set into the marble. At the centre is an ornate cenotaph and in a vault below this lie Shah Jehan and his wife.

1633
Bernini: the Tomb of St Peter

Giovanni Bernini (1598–1660) was the last of the universal geniuses produced by the Italian Renaissance. Architect, painter and dramatist, he is most renowned for his exquisite sculptures and his work on St Peter's Basilica, Rome.

A church had existed in some form over St Peter's Tomb since Emperor Constantine's reign (*d.* AD 337), though this 1000 year-old edifice was demolished in 1506 for the construction of the present St Peter's. The cathedral was enlarged constantly and in 1624 the twenty-six-year-old Bernini designed the *baldachin*, an immense canopy in gilt-bronze over the Tomb of St Peter at the heart of the building.

This masterpiece, completed in 1633, consists of four twisted columns and a canopy richly decorated with carved cherubs, laurels, bees and papal insignia. Bernini was later to design the impressive 'key-hole' shaped colonnade surrounding the piazza in front of the cathedral, and to sculpt many famous pieces for the interior.

1635
Foundation of *L'Académie Française*

L'Académie Française (the French Academy) was established by order of King Louis XIII in 1635, the year Richelieu declared war on Spain. The Academy had begun several years earlier when a small group of writers and poets agreed to meet once a week to read and discuss their works.

Richelieu, who missed very little, soon heard of them and, convinced that they were strictly non-political, offered to form the group into a properly recognized society. He also informed the king and in consequence, letters patent were granted on January 29, 1635.

A committee was formed with a chancellor at its head, Richelieu himself being appointed its chief patron to secure freedom from interference by similar bodies. One of the great achievements of the new Academy was begun in 1639, a dictionary of the French language, the first edition appearing in 1694.

1636
Corneille's *Le Cid* is produced

The French dramatist Pierre Corneille (1616–84) was one of the 'Five Poets' employed by Cardinal Richelieu to write plays under his direction. His tragedy called *Le Cid* (first produced in 1636) marks an epoch in the history of French drama. It introduced a favourite theme of Corneille's, that of the conflict in a human soul between passion and honour.

1637
Descartes: *Discours de la Méthode*

The French philosopher René Descartes (1596–1650) said in his *Discours de la Méthode* that everything should be doubted in the quest for absolute certainty. He argued that the senses deceive us, but there was one thing of which he was certain: *Cogito, ergo sum* (I think, therefore I am). Methodical thought, wrote Descartes, was to be the foundation of all knowledge.

1638
Death of Jansen

Cornelius Jansen (1585–1638) was a Dutch clergyman and teacher of theology. After studying and then teaching at a number of universities he went to Louvain (Leuven, now in

Belgium) to take charge of a theological college. Although a Catholic, he was violently opposed to the Jesuits and did everything he could to discredit them.

He began work on *Augustinus*, a study of the theology of St Augustine, which was to occupy the rest of his life. In it he outlined his religious beliefs, putting forward a doctrine that would reform Catholicism. His principles were to become known as Jansenism and were to rend France during the rest of the seventeenth and early eighteenth centuries.

1642

Outbreak of Civil War in Britain

The struggle between King Charles I and his Parliament was reaching a climax, for he believed in the divine authority of kingship whilst his Parliament believed in the democratic right of Englishmen to be governed by their elected representatives. Charles's tax called Ship Money (*see 1628 The Petition of Right*) further widened the gulf between king and Parliament.

The near-penniless king was forced to recall Parliament but when he tried to arrest five members, England was thrust into a Civil War that was to last from 1642 until 1649. At first the victories were all Royalist ones, the dashing cavalry led by Charles's nephew Rupert, sweeping aside the poorly armed, mainly peasant soldiers. But his opponent, Cromwell, slowly developed a new breed of fighting men, a psalm-singing but tough and well-drilled 'New Model Army' and with them he won a series of important victories – Marston Moor (1644), Naseby (1645), Preston and Colchester (both 1648).

Charles sought refuge in Scotland but was handed over to his enemies (*see 1649 The execution of Charles I*).

1642

Tasman discovers Van Diemen's Land

In 1606 Willem Jans sailed along the coasts of northwest Australia and New Guinea, believing them to be the same stretch of land. In 1616, Luis de Torres sailed through the straits to which he has given his name, while part of southwest Australia was discovered by two more Dutchmen, Dirck Hartogszoon (1616) and Cornelis de Houtman (1619).

Then in 1642 came the greatest of them all – Abel Tasman (*c.* 1603–59). He sailed from the Dutch settlement of Batavia (now Jakarta) along the coast of New Guinea and onward, to discover both New Zealand and Tasmania. The latter island he named Van Diemen's Land after the governor of the Dutch East Indies, but in 1853 the British renamed it after its discoverer, calling it... Tasmania.

1642

Rembrandt paints *The Night Watch*

Rembrandt van Rijn (1606–69) is considered to be one of the world's greatest artists. He was born in Leyden, Holland, but settled in Amsterdam where he was greatly influenced by Italian art and more especially by the work of Caravaggio. His masterpieces include *The Night Watch* and *Pilgrims at Emmaus*.

1643

Mazarin becomes chief minister

When Louis XIII died in 1643 his son, Louis XIV was only five years old and his mother, Anne of Austria, became regent. A year earlier the great Richelieu had died and in almost his last breath begged the king to appoint Jules Mazarin as his successor. His wishes were carried out and it was not long before Mazarin was the real ruler of France, the regent wisely leaving the running of the country to him during her son's minority.

Mazarin (1602–61) was never a popular man; a Sicilian who had been entrusted with several delicate missions by Pope Urban VIII, he was mistrusted by the French. He became a naturalized Frenchman, however, and accepted Richelieu's suggestion that he join the French court.

His first important act on Richelieu's death was to bring the Thirty Years' War to an end with the Treaty of Westphalia in 1648 although war continued between France and Spain.

1644

The foundation of the Manchu dynasty

The great Ming dynasty came to an end when fierce invaders from the north called Manchus swept into China and drove the weakened dynasty before them. Originally they had been a loose collection of tribes but they were welded into one fighting force by Nurhachu.

Soon after Nurhachu's death in 1626 there were internal troubles in China when a usurper seized the throne and the last Ming emperor, Chung-Chang (1627–44) committed suicide. The Manchus joined forces with a Ming general to throw out the usurper and when this was done a Manchu prince was made emperor in his stead. A period of rebellion followed but by 1662 the Manchus had made themselves secure and were to rule China until 1912.

The most significant event during their dynasty was the increasing number of Europeans who visited China, although only one port, Canton, was open for foreign trade – silks, tea and pottery, mainly – the European traders being confined to 'factories' or trading centres.

1648

Outbreak of the Fronde

The name 'Fronde' comes from a game in which slings (frondes) were used by boys in their mock street 'battles' in Paris. The name was given to two uprisings in France which occurred after Mazarin (see 1643 Mazarin becomes chief minister) had imposed heavy taxes on the French at a time when his unpopularity was growing.

The Frondeurs, or rebels, had no united programme and their leaders were divided by rivalries. The First Fronde (1648) was an alliance of the middle class and the nobility led by the Parlement; when their leader was arrested, the mob rose in anger and set up barricades, but peace was restored in 1650.

The Second Fronde (1651–53) began when Mazarin imprisoned Condé, a rebel from the nobility. The intrigues of other nobles made Mazarin flee from Paris, but soon the nobles lost popularity and the movement came to an end.

The famous equestrian portrait of King Charles I painted by Anthony Van Dyck in 1636.

1649

The Execution of Charles I

When Charles I was returned to London it was decided to bring him before a Court of Commissioners. The trial opened on January 20, 1649, and when the king was brought in he was blamed for causing all the misfortunes that had befallen the nation since the beginning of the Civil War. For his part, the king claimed that the court was illegal, because the House of Commons was not a court of law.

Charles refused to plead 'not guilty' when brought before the court again on January 27 and was then declared guilty.

He was kept under close guard for three days although he was allowed to say goodbye to his children and then, on January 30, the king left

Charles I on the scaffold.

St James's Palace, walking on foot with a large escort. Taken to the Banqueting House in Whitehall, he stepped out onto a scaffold that had been erected in the street and after a brief speech he said, 'I shall say but very short prayers, and then thrust out my hands.' The king knelt with his head on the block and soon stretched out his hands. The axe fell and a groan rose from the thousands who thronged the street. Then, with many weeping, the crowd silently dispersed.

1652
Outbreak of the Anglo-Dutch War

Unlike so many other wars which had been fought for religious reasons, that between England and Holland which broke out in 1652 was purely commercial, each nation being jealous of the other's trading successes, particular in the North Sea and the East Indies.

The war began when a Dutch fleet in English

The Anglo-Dutch Wars: commercial rivalry led to a number of clashes between the English and Dutch navies.

waters refused to salute the English flag, and hostilities broke out soon afterwards. The first action was fought off Dover when Van Tromp (1629–91) attacked a fleet commanded by Admiral Blake (1599–1657) who captured two Dutch ships.

These wars were the First (1662–4) and the Second (1664–7) Dutch Wars which ended with the Treaty of Westminster and the Peace of Breda respectively. The Third War (1672–4) saw the Dutch actually sail into the Medway and tow away England's latest warship and ended when the Dutch leader, William of Orange, forced England to make peace.

1652
Cape Colony founded

The Portuguese navigator, Bartolomeu Diaz, (c. 1450–1500) returned from his voyage round the southern tip of Africa in 1488 and showed the King of Portugal a map with a headland marked, 'Cape of Storms'. However, the king changed it to *Cabo da Boa Esperance* ('Cape of Good Hope'). Cape Town was founded in 1652 by Dutch colonists, but was captured by the British in 1806.

1653
Caldéron's *Life is a Dream*

Pedro Caldéron (1600–81) was one of Spain's greatest dramatists, who after ten years' soldiering became superintendent of amusements to King Philip IV. Caldéron wrote with perfect fidelity to the Spanish thought and manners of his day. His most famous work is *La Vida es sueno* ('Life is a Dream').

1653
Cromwell becomes Lord Protector

Charles I was executed in January 1649 and in the following May Oliver Cromwell (1599–1658) established the Free Commonwealth of England with himself at its head. He next crushed rebellious Royalist and Irish forces, sending an army into Ireland with orders that 'no quarter' should be given.

In December 1653 Cromwell was formally installed as Lord Protector of England, Scotland and Ireland, taking the oath in Westminster Abbey. Then, almost immediately, he dissolved Parliament. For the next eighteen months the country was governed by his major-generals.

During Cromwell's period of power, England became a very gloomy place. Sunday sports,

Oliver Cromwell

horse-racing, even dancing round the maypole which had been enjoyed since medieval times, were all banned. Cromwell later assembled another Parliament which offered him the throne but his army objected so strongly that he did not even consider the idea. He proved to be an able ruler, with a great love of his country. His foreign policy especially was aimed at making Britain respected overseas.

Cromwell's health began to suffer and during the night of September 3, 1658, to the accompaniment of a great storm that was sweeping across England, he died.

1653
Izaak Walton's *The Compleat Angler*

Izaak Walton (1593–1683) was an accomplished writer of biographies and treatises on the monarchy. However, his fame rests on his modest little book, *The Compleat Angler*, in which he describes the sport of angling as a simple, gentle and contemplative rural pastime. Later republished as *The Universal Angler*, it was over one hundred years before it achieved the true recognition it enjoys today.

1655
Verbiest's steam carriage

The first steam powered vehicle is credited to Father Verbiest, a Jesuit missionary in China, in 1655. The motive power was an aeolipile, a primitive steam reaction turbine first described by Hero of Alexandria in 130 BC. It is said that Verbiest's vehicle could move at a 'good speed' for as long as the steam lasted.

1656
Velasquez paints *Las Meninas*

Court painter to the King of Spain, Diego de Silva y Velasquez (1599–1660) began painting in a naturalistic style but, greatly influenced by Titian, developed a flowing style demonstrating less awareness of form than of impressions. His painting is distinguished for its unflattering realism and his wide choice of human subjects including *Las Meninas* ('Maids of Honour', 1656) and *Las Hilanderas* ('The Spinners').

1659

Samuel Pepys's *Diary*

On January 1, 1659 Samuel Pepys (1633–1703) began his *Diary*. Written in his own shorthand, undeciphered until 1825, it proved an intimate picture of his character, official and social life of his time, with eye-witness accounts of the Plague and the Fire of London (*see 1666 The Great Fire of London*). On May 31, 1669, his sight failing, he discontinued the *Diary*.

1660

Restoration of the monarchy

After the death of Oliver Cromwell in 1658, his son Richard, who succeeded him as Lord Protec-

Louis XIV and the glories of Versailles.

future. A London wit wrote of him: 'We have a very pretty king, Whose word no man relies on; He never said a foolish thing, And never did a wise one', a sentiment with which the cynical Charles would have agreed.

1661
The building of Versailles

When Louis XIV (1638–1715) came to the throne in France, the government was largely in the hands of Mazarin (*see 1643 Mazarin becomes chief minister*). In 1661 Mazarin died and Louis took complete control declaring *'L'Etat, c'est moi'* (I am the state).

In the same year Louis decided to develop the small hunting lodge at Versailles. It was here that the glories of *le Roi Soleil* (the Sun King) were to be reflected and by 1682 the fantastic palace was completed and Louis moved in with his dazzling court. Everything there was grand (the symbol of *le Roi Soleil* was repeated in the decoration and furniture) and the nobility of every country in the world flocked to see Louis, who had made Versailles the symbol of his and France's power.

tor, proved a weak ruler. Anarchy threatened England and there was much relief when King Charles II (1630–85), son of the executed Charles I, was recalled from exile in Europe. Now, after the miserable days of Puritan rule, everyone, except the Puritans, looked forward to brighter, happier times. As the king rode through the streets of London on his thirtieth birthday, May 29, 1660, the whole city seemed to be caught up in a frenzy of wild enthusiasm.

Charles, too, was glad to be home. He had lived, surrounded by exiles, in the courts of France and the Netherlands, often hungry and always in need of money. Now that was all over and, from the faces of his people and his ministers, he would want for nothing in the

Although Versailles with its rituals, masques, ballets and fountains was the envy of every prince, the ordinary people of France were to suffer miserably from Louis' heavy expenditure and his aggressive foreign policy.

1661
The Clarendon Code

Charles II relied a great deal upon his ministers, encouraging them to govern the country on his behalf so that he had more time for his many amusements. His chief adviser was the Earl of Clarendon who had shared Charles's exile and, two years before the Restoration had been made Chancellor of the Exchequer. On their return in 1660 he became his principal minister but, forced to resign in 1667, went to France and stayed there until his death seven years later.

Whilst in power Clarendon forced four laws through Parliament (known as the Clarendon Code) which were intended to strengthen the position of the Church of England. They were the Corporation Act (1661), the Act of Uniformity (1662), the Conventicle Act (1664) and the Five Mile Act which forbade all expelled clergymen to live within that distance of a town unless they had taken an oath to be loyal to the established order.

1663
Milton writes *Paradise Lost*

John Milton (1608–74) revealed his genius very early, his *Lycidas* (1637) being one of the most moving elegies in the English language. For a while he was secretary to Cromwell but became blind about 1652 and retired from public life to write *Paradise Lost* and *Paradise Regained*. The former is one of the world's great poems and placed Milton second only to Shakespeare.

1665
The Great Plague

Plague had recurred frequently throughout Europe for many centuries but London had been unusually free of it during the years before the Great Plague. It really began in 1664, when a few isolated cases were observed but in 1665 sixty-eight thousand people died of it in London alone.

The situation in London grew so desperate that Parliament moved to Oxford and the Court to Salisbury. Meanwhile the capital had become a wilderness of closed doors as people tried to protect themselves and their families. Infected rats carried the disease from street to street; buildings were daubed with red crosses and the words 'Lord have Mercy on us' to show that they housed dying or dead; and ringing bells announced the arrival of carts to take away the corpses.

From London the terrible disease spread across the country, but by 1667 the epidemic had died out. The disappearance of the Great Plague in London has been attributed to the Great Fire but it died out in other cities without such a cause.

1666
The Great Fire of London

At 2 am on September 2 a fire was discovered in the house of John Farynor, the king's baker, in Pudding Lane, a narrow street east of London Bridge. Fanned by a strong east wind, the flames spread rapidly through the city. For four days the fire raged. Even the king, Charles II, and his brother turned out to fight it.

First it reached London Bridge, which had

The Great Fire.

wooden buildings upon it, and then it spread northward to Lombard Street and Cornhill. On the third day it destroyed Cheapside and Fleet Street before continuing on to the Inner Temple and Newgate.

Over 121 hectares, containing more than thirteen thousand houses, were destroyed. The fire was not, however, a complete disaster for it destroyed many of the main areas of infection remaining from the Plague and made it possible to create a new city with wider streets and brick buildings to replace the cramped medieval streets and wooden buildings.

1666
Stradivarius makes his first violin

Antonio Stradivarius (1644–1737) made stringed instruments from 1666 to 1737. Although best known for his violins, the best of which were made between 1700 and 1725, he also made violas and 'cellos. Stradivarius made more than a thousand instruments, many of which still exist – and are extremely valuable.

1667
The War of Devolution

Louis XIV of France instigated several wars in his efforts to become dictator of Europe. In 1667 he claimed Spain and her possessions through his Spanish-born wife, the Infanta Maria Theresa. The queen had renounced all rights to the Spanish throne in 1659 but this was conditional upon the payment of a marriage dowry. Eight years later Louis asserted his wife's claims on the grounds that the agreement was invalid because the dowry had never been paid.

Fifty thousand French troops marched into the Spanish Netherlands in May, 1667. In 1668 England, the United Provinces, and Sweden formed the Triple Alliance to prevent French expansion and Louis prudently made peace with Spain with the Treaty of Aix-la-Chapelle.

Louis never forgave the Dutch for checking his advance and in 1672 he invaded many areas of Franche-Comté and Belgium. Fighting continued until 1678 when Louis dictated the peace terms at Nijmegen.

1667
First public performance of *Tartuffe*

A three-act version of Molière's *Tartuffe* was performed before the king, Louis XIV, at Versailles on May 2, 1664 but it was not until August 5, 1667 that it received a public showing. It was immediately banned as it was felt that Molière was being irreligious and in 1669 a new five-act version was produced.

Jean Baptiste Poquelin Molière (1622–73) is regarded as the greatest of French comedy playwrights. Born in Paris, he studied law before joining his father as an apprentice upholsterer. In 1643 he was one of the founders of *L'Illustre Théâtre* and eventually became its leading actor. His first play, *L'Étourdi,* was written in 1655 and was followed by some forty comedies including *Les Précieuses ridicules* (1659), *L'Ecole des femmes* (1662), *Le Misanthrope* (1666), *Le Bourgeois gentilhomme* (1670), and *Le Malade imaginaire* (1673).

1670
Origins of Hudson's Bay Company

This famous trading company, the oldest chartered company in the world, began in 1670 when Charles II gave a charter to the 'Company of Adventurers of England trading into Hudson's Bay'. The bay is named after the explorer, Henry Hudson who, with his son, was turned adrift in the area by a mutinous crew in 1610.

The company traded in fur with the Indians but faced bitter rivalry from French traders until 1713 when, under the Treaty of Utrecht, France ceded Hudson's Bay to England.

In 1783 the North-West Company was formed, but in 1821 the two were amalgamated to form the Hudson's Bay Company. In 1869 the company surrendered a large portion of its land holdings to Canada to form three new provinces, but retained sufficient land for development and sale.

Even to this day the company operates as a fur trading company but is now better known for its large department stores in the principal towns and cities of Canada.

1670
Publication of Pascal's *Pensées*

Blaise Pascal (1623–62), the French philosopher and mathematician, was born at Clermont-Ferrand. Educated by his father he soon revealed a precocious genius for mathematics but later became more interested in religious philosophy. In 1670 he published his *Pensées* ('Thoughts') a fragmented apology for Christianity written in 1657, but not published until after his death.

1670
Vermeer paints *Artist in his studio*

Jan Vermeer (1632–75) was born in Delft, Holland. When he was thirty he became master of the Guild of Painters of Delft but on his death was 'forgotten'. He was 'rediscovered' in the 1860s and heralded as a true Dutch master. Amongst his fine works are *Street in Delft*, *The Lacemaker* and *Artist in his studio* (1670).

1674
Henry Morgan is appointed lieutenant-governor of Jamaica

During the seventeenth century many pirates operated in the Caribbean attacking and looting the ships of Spain, who then ruled the West Indies. One of the most notorious of these buccaneers was the Welshman Henry Morgan (c. 1635–88).

In 1668 Morgan commanded an expedition to capture Puerto Principe (now Camaguey) in Cuba and the following year he attacked Maracaibo in South America. In 1671 he captured Panama.

Eskimos trading skins with a ship of the Hudson's Bay Company.

As Spanish power declined the British, French, and the Dutch began to settle in the West Indies and in 1670 Spain acknowledged Jamaica as an English possession. At the same time many pirates were being captured and punished for their crimes. In 1672 Morgan was sent under arrest to England but he managed to gain the favour of Charles II who, in January 1674, awarded him a knighthood and the post of lieutenant-governor of Jamaica.

1675
Rebuilding of St Paul's

Within a week of the Fire of London (*see 1666 The Great Fire of London*) Christopher Wren (1632–1723), at that time assistant surveyor general, presented plans for rebuilding the entire city. The plans were approved by Charles II but the high cost led to their ultimate rejection. Included in the plans was a new design for St Paul's Cathedral which had been damaged in the

fire. Soon after receiving a knighthood in 1672 Wren presented a second plan for St Paul's but this, too, was turned down.

Several other designs were submitted, and eventually one received official blessing, so work began in 1675. Luckily Wren was allowed to make such alterations as he saw fit and so many of his original ideas were incorporated into the new building which was completed in 1716.

Wren also designed fifty-four other London churches but several were destroyed by bombing during the Second World War.

1675
Leeuwenhoek describes blood corpuscles

Anthony van Leeuwenhoek (1632–1723), the Dutch maker of microscopes, made several important scientific advances. These include the discovery of protozoa (1675), the first accurate description of red blood corpuscles (1675) in support of the theory of blood circulation, and the observation of spermatazoon from dogs and other animals (1677). A drawing by Leeuwenhoek published in 1683 shows the first representation of bacteria.

1678
Publication of *Pilgrim's Progress*

This famous book is a religious allegory that relates the adventures of Christian and Hopeful on their journey from the City of Destruction to the Celestial City. Written by John Bunyan (1622–88) whilst in Bedford gaol, the book was such an instant success that a second book describing the pilgrimage of Christina, Christian's wife, and Mercy was published in 1684.

1678
Titus Oates and the 'Popish Plot'

In September 1678 it was revealed that Roman Catholics in England were plotting to murder

Charles II and to set the Duke of York (later James II) on the throne. The informant was Titus Oates (1648–1705), a man whose activities had already caused him to be sent down from Cambridge, thrown out of the Royal Navy, and dismissed from two religious colleges.

In spite of the man's dubious background many people believed in the 'Popish Plot' and a wave of anti-Catholic hysteria resulted in the execution of thirty-five Catholics and the imprisonment of many more.

In 1685 Oates was found guilty of perjury; he was flogged, imprisoned for life and ordered to be exposed annually in the pillory. After William III (1650–1702) came to the throne Oates was released and granted a pension.

1682

Accession of Peter the Great

Peter the Great (1672–1725) acceded to the czardom of Russia jointly with his rather weak half brother Ivan in 1682, although neither was old enough to assume power.

In 1689 Peter ousted the regency of his sister Sophia and took control of the government. Following the death of Ivan in 1696 Peter ruled alone and started on his plans to extend the borders of Russia to the Baltic Sea in the north and the Black Sea in the south.

A campaign against Turkey won him the port of Azov on the Black Sea and the chance to build a Russian navy. To this end he visited Holland and England, working in the shipyards of both countries. On his return to Russia, with European engineers and scientists, he began to reorganize the country along western lines.

Peter immediately attacked all outward signs of oriental life. Russian nobles were made to wear European dress and to shave off their beards which were considered a barbarous eastern fashion. Anyone who refused received Peter's personal attention. He cut off their beards himself!

During a lull in the Great Northern War of 1700 Peter began building his new capital, his 'window on the west', at St Petersburg (now Leningrad) on the newly acquired Baltic coast.

1685

The Battle of Sedgemoor

On February 6, 1685 Charles II died and the throne of England passed to his brother the Duke of York (1633–1701) (James II). Four months later the Duke of Monmouth (the illegitimate son of Charles II) formed an army to assert his claim to the throne. He had himself proclaimed king at Taunton, Somerset and on July 6, 1685 he attacked the king's forces on the plain of Sedgemoor, near Bridgewater.

Monmouth decided upon a night attack but an accidental pistol shot alerted the king's men. Hopelessly outnumbered and inadequately armed, Monmouth's men were no match for the royalist troops.

Monmouth escaped from the battlefield but was later captured and beheaded at Tower Hill, London on July 15, 1685. His supporters were tried by the notoriously cruel Chief Justice Jeffreys and were hanged or deported. As a result of the harsh sentences the trial became known as the 'bloody assize'.

1687

Publication of Newton's *Principia*

With Cambridge University closed because of the plague, the young mathematician, Isaac Newton (1642–1727), was sent home to Lincolnshire where he could work at his leisure. His experiments in optics here, showing that white

Isaac Newton

light consists of many colours, are famous but his work into gravitation had a far deeper effect.

Newton's notion was that the force of gravity is not limited to terrestial objects but acts everywhere and can even be extended to heavenly bodies like the moon. It is said that this idea was suggested to Newton by the fall of an apple, but this story is probably a legend.

Newton used his invention the 'calculus', to show mathematically that the moon was held in its orbit by gravity; otherwise it would move in a straight line at a tangent to its orbit. He went on to describe mathematically the shape of the earth, the tides and even the motion of the whole universe, using his theory of universal gravitation which stated that every body attracts every other with a force that depends on their masses and the square of their distance apart.

Newton only disclosed these ideas much later in 1687 in his book – the *Principia* – probably one of the most influential scientific works ever written.

1688

The Glorious Revolution

James II, who acceded to the English throne on the death of Charles II, was so unpopular because of his strong Catholic beliefs that in 1688 he was forced to flee to France. The government had already invited the Dutch leader William of Orange (1650–1702) and his wife Mary (1662–94), James II's daughter, to take the throne and William landed in England from Holland on November 5, 1688. The strength of the government was such that William and Mary had to agree to the Declaration of Rights which effectively placed the monarchy within the control of parliament.

William and Mary were declared joint sovereigns on February 13, 1689. The ousting of James II became known as 'The Glorious Revolution' for it was achieved without bloodshed and because it had such a profound effect on the conduct of the monarchy in England.

The declaration prevented any Catholic or anyone married to a Catholic from reigning and ruled that the sovereign could no longer raise taxes or keep a private army. It formed the basis for the system of constitutional monarchy that applies in Britain to this day.

1689

Purcell writes *Dido and Aeneas*

Dido and Aeneas by Henry Purcell (1685–95), the great English-born composer, is one of the classics of musical drama. Written originally for a performance at a girls' school in Chelsea, London it is the first English opera entirely without spoken dialogue.

1689

Locke's *Treatises on Government*

In his two *Treatises on Government* the English philosopher John Locke (1632–1704) stated that all govenments ultimately derive their authority through the consent of the populace. He also claimed that any government that threatens the fundamental rights of the people is liable to be ousted from power. Such democratic principles have since formed the basis of the political ideals of many Englishmen.

Support for the Jacobite cause was strong in Scotland, and also in Ireland, where the former king, James II, was defeated by the Protestant forces of William III (below) at the Battle of the Boyne, in 1690.

A piper of the Grant clan. In the 18th century the English government outlawed the wearing of tartan.

1692
The Glencoe Massacre

Following the suppression of the Jacobite insurrection of 1689 the Scottish government declared an amnesty to everyone who swore an oath of allegiance by December 13, 1691. Lord Stair (1648–1707) made plans for severe military action in case of refusal.

When the time came all had sworn with the exception of the chief of the MacIans (a branch of the Macdonald clan) of Glencoe, an old enemy of Stair. The MacIans took the oath on January 6 but Stair concealed this fact from William III and obtained an order for the total destruction of the Macdonalds.

The Campbells, also old enemies of the Macdonalds, were instructed to carry out the order. First they feigned friendship with the Macdonalds, and accepted their hospitality. But during the early hours of February 13, 1692 the 120-strong Campbell force rose up and attacked their hosts, murdered most of them, seized their possessions, and burned their homes.

1700
Great Northern War

In 1697 Charles XII (1682–1718) acceded to the Swedish throne. He was only fifteen and this prompted Peter I of Russia to ally with Denmark and Poland to capture land from Sweden. Charles, however, a born soldier, reacted in 1700 by attacking the Danes and then dictating his terms in the Peace of Travendal.

During Sweden's war with Denmark, Russia was laying siege to Narva in Livonia. Charles turned to relieve Narva with only eight thousand men against Russia's sixty thousand and scored a resounding victory. Next he became concerned with Poland, thus giving Peter time to retrain his army and to begin building St Petersburg.

Charles's fortunes began to change in 1709 when, after a crushing defeat at Potlava, he took refuge in Turkey until 1714. Following his death in December 1718 whilst besieging Frederiksten, Norway, the Swedes were forced to accept the Peace of Nystadt in 1721.

1700
Leibnitz founds Prussian Academy of Sciences

Gottfried Wilhelm Leibnitz (1646–1716), the great German philosopher and mathematician, in 1700 persuaded Frederick I of Prussia to form the Prussian Academy of Sciences. Leibnitz, whose contributions to science, mathematics, philosophy, and law were of considerable importance, was elected perpetual president of the Academy.

1701
Execution of Captain Kidd

On May 23, 1701, the Scottish pirate William Kidd (b. 1650) was hanged at Execution Dock, London. It is said that his ship, the *Adventure*, engaged in piracy until 1699, when he was captured in Boston, Massachusetts, but there is now some doubt as to his guilt.

1701
Act of Settlement

Passed by parliament in June 1701 this Act ruled that should the reigning monarchs William and Mary fail to have children the crown would pass to Sophia of Hanover and her heirs. It was formulated so that the Stuarts could not again ascend the English throne and in order to prevent the creation of a Catholic monarch. The duchess and her children were, of course, Protestants and were descended from Elizabeth, the daughter of the first Stuart king, James I.

The Act, which contained eight clauses in addition to those concerning the succession, also applied to Ireland. Scotland accepted its provisions under the Act of Union (*see 1707 Union of England and Scotland*).

It stated that all future British sovereigns had to be members of the Church of England; wars entailing the defence of lands not owned by England could not be engaged upon without the consent of parliament; judges could not be dismissed from office except by parliament; and the sovereign could not prevent an impeachment.

1701
War of Spanish Succession

This war was fought by France, Spain, and Bavaria against Britain, Austria, the Netherlands, Denmark, and Portugal. It was caused by Louis XIV's acceptance of the Spanish throne on behalf of his grandson Philip of Anjou although he had renounced all such claims under the Partition Treaty of 1700. This treaty ruled that, upon the death of Charles II of Spain (1661–1700), the Spanish throne should pass to the Archduke Charles of Austria.

Although the French had the largest army in Europe their power was weakened by the fact that they had to fight on several fronts. In 1704 they attempted to march on Vienna but were cut short by a crushing defeat at Blenheim on August 2. The French retreated, followed by their adversaries under the command of the Duke of Marlborough (1650–1722) and Prince Eugene of Savoy (1663–1736).

Most of the war, however, was fought on Belgian soil where Marlborough scored decisive victories at Ramillies (May 23, 1706) and Oudenarde (July 11, 1708). It was not until the Treaties of Utrecht (1713) and Rastadt (1714) that the bitter, fierce fighting eventually ceased.

1707
Union of England and Scotland

At the end of the seventeenth century there was growing dissension, particularly in Scotland, regarding the relationship between Scotland and England. William III was more interested in England because of its value to him in his European affairs and so Scotland was relegated to second place in the affairs of the two countries.

Many people advocated that the two kingdoms should become separate states, but William and his advisers were more in favour of an incorporated union, although Scottish feeling was of the opinion that such a union would stifle Scotland even further.

In 1706 Queen Anne (1665–1714) set up a commission to draw up a treaty for union. The resultant Act guaranteed freedom of trade, religious practices, and law-making for Scotland and decreed that the two countries be united as Great Britain under one parliament and one flag. It became law in May 1707.

1714
Fahrenheit's mercury thermometer

Gabriel Daniel Fahrenheit (1686–1736), a German instrument maker, invented the mercury thermometer in 1714. At the same time he introduced a new temperature scale in which the zero is equal to a temperature thirty-two degrees below the freezing point of water (32°F) and the highest point (212°F) is the temperature of boiling water (see 1742 Introduction of the centigrade scale).

1715
The Jacobite Rebellion

The name 'Jacobites', from the Latin Jacobus for James, describes those people who continued to support James II after his dethronement in 1688 (see 1688 The Glorious Revolution).

After the accession of George I (1660–1727) in 1714, the Earl of Mar, a Scottish nobleman, proclaimed James Edward Stuart (1688–1766), the son of James II, as James III, the rightful king. On September 6, 1715 Mar (1675–1732) raised the flag of James III, 'the Old Pretender', at Braemar to mark the start of the rebellion. Many nobles joined the earl and within a month he controlled Perth and the ports on the east coast. But his attempts to gain Edinburgh, Dumfries, and Fort William resulted in failure.

At this point the earl, nicknamed 'Bobbing John' because of his hesitancy, could not make up his mind what to do next and the rebels became disunited. One group moved south to England and got as far as Preston before they were forced to surrender on November 13. On the very same day Mar was defeated at Sheriffmuir, near Stirling. In January 1716 James Edward arrived to support Mar but the rebellion, known as 'the fifteen', was already lost and he returned to France a month later.

1715

Handel composes the *Water Music*

In 1711 the opera *Rinaldo* by the German composer George Frederick Handel (1685–1759) was performed in London. Soon afterwards Handel decided to settle in England and in 1715 he composed his *Water Music* in honour of King George I for a royal procession on the Thames. Handel wrote all kinds of music including over forty operas and almost thirty oratorios.

George Frederick Handel

1717

First inoculations against smallpox

In the western world today not many people get smallpox, but until the eighteenth century it was extremely common. Many people caught it and many died as a result. Those that lived to tell the tale bore 'pock marks', unsightly holes in the skin where the smallpox scabs had been.

Smallpox, or variola, is a very infectious and contagious disease that starts as a rash which develops into blisters. Within a few days the blisters fester and then start to crack and dry up.

In 1717 Lady Mary Wortley (1689–1762) noticed that people in Turkey, where her husband was an ambassador, sometimes used the fluid from smallpox blisters to protect people who had not been infected. Four years later she introduced the practice, known as variolation, into Britain where it was quickly accepted. Although the inoculation itself killed some people, the overall death rate was dramatically reduced (*see 1796 The first cowpox inoculations*).

1719

Publication of *Robinson Crusoe*

On April 25, 1719 the English novelist Daniel Defoe (c. 1660–1731) published the first volume of *Robinson Crusoe*. A second volume was published later the same year and a sequel issued in 1720. Defoe based his tale on the adventures of Alexander Selkirk who lived alone for fifty-two months on the island of Más-a-Tierra, Juan Fernández Island, in the South Pacific.

1720

The South Sea Bubble

In 1720 The South Sea Company, formed in 1711 to trade with South America, offered to take over the national debt (money borrowed by the government). The company offered an advance of £7,567,000 to the government in return for certain commercial concessions.

Although, in fact, the trade with South America never materialized the public were given the impression that the company would make enormous profits and people from all walks of life rushed to buy shares.

In February 1720 the £100 shares were worth £130, but by June they were changing hands at £1,050.

Unscrupulous businessmen, anxious to cash in on the boom, sold shares in suspect companies. The directors of the South Sea Company called for the government to make eighty of these companies illegal (including one formed for the importation of jackasses from Spain) and in so doing burst the 'bubble'. People rushed to sell their shares, their values tumbled drastically, and thousands of people lost a great deal of money.

1720

Bach composes the *Brandenburg concertos*

Between 1720 and 1721 Johann Sebastian Bach (1685–1750) composed his famous *Brandenburg concertos*. Dedicated to Duke Christian Ludwig of Brandenburg, the six concertos are scored for a combination of strings with or without solo piano, woodwind, or brass. They are classified as *Concerti Grossi* (Great Concertos).

1721

Walpole becomes first prime minister

When the South Sea Bubble burst in 1720 the task of sorting out the financial tangles fell to Robert Walpole (1676–1745) who was appointed First Lord of the Treasury and Chancellor of the Exchequer in 1721.

Walpole held this post from April 3, 1721 to February 12, 1742 and is generally regarded as the first British prime minister although the post was not officially recognized until 1905. The office evolved as a result of George I's unwillingness to attend cabinet meetings because of his difficulties with the English language.

Walpole had entered Parliament in 1701 and very quickly became renowned for his wizardry with figures, his accurate judgement of people, and his shrewd capability. In 1708 he became secretary of war in the Whig administration but four years later was sent to the Tower on a charge of corruption. He returned to office in 1714 when George I came to the throne.

Walpole's premiership, the longest in British history, lasted until he was defeated in Parliament in 1742. He had been knighted in 1726 and after his defeat became Earl of Orford.

Sir Robert Walpole

1726

Publication of *Gulliver's Travels*

Gulliver's Travels was originally published as a satirical work highlighting some of the foolishness and pomposity of the day. However, it is also an exciting adventure story and is read by both adults and children. Its author, Jonathan Swift (1667–1745), is also well known for his *Battle of the Books* and *Tale of a Tub*.

Swift's hero Gulliver, meeting a Lilliputian.

1728

First performance of *The Beggar's Opera*

The first performance of this ballad opera was produced at Lincoln's Inn Fields, London on January 29, 1728. Based on popular tunes of the day, with music selected and arranged by John Pepusch (1667–1752) and with a libretto by John Gay (1685–1732), it is a lyrical drama of thieves and highwaymen.

1729

Founding of the Methodist Society

The Methodist Society was founded at Oxford in 1729 when a group of young men began to meet regularly for Bible readings and prayers. They became known as 'Bible Moths', the 'Holy Club', or, because they tried to live methodically in accordance with the tenets of the New Testament, 'Methodists'.

The founder of the movement was John Wesley (1703–91), a tutor at the University. He was educated at Christ Church, Oxford and ordained in the Church of England in 1728. In the following year he returned to Oxford to teach. His brother Charles (1707–88), also one of the original Methodists, was the principal preacher and theologian of the movement. He was also a prolific writer of hymns.

The precepts of the movement are John Wesley's four volumes of sermons and his notes on the New Testament. Originally formed within the Church of England the Methodists did not become a separate body until 1795.

John Wesley

1733

Jethro Tull's *Horse-hoeing Husbandry*

Early in the eighteenth century several land-owners realized that the growing population would necessitate higher crop yields and more efficient methods of farming.

Jethro Tull (1674–1741) introduced new methods of cultivation and, in 1701, devised a drill to furrow the soil and sow seeds mechanically. In 1733 he published his ideas in *Horse-hoeing Husbandry*. Charles Townshend (1674–1738), a member of the House of Lords, retired from politics in 1730 and devoted his life to agricultural improvements. He introduced a system of crop rotation and the use of cultivated grasses and clovers. He was the first English farmer to plant turnips as a field crop and so was nicknamed 'Turnip Townshend'.

These men, and others, were responsible for the rebirth of agriculture in Britain and started an Agricultural Revolution that was as important as the Industrial Revolution that was to follow.

1735

Publication of *The Rake's Progress*

The Rake's Progress is a set of eight pictures painted, then engraved, by the English artist William Hogarth (1697–1764). The set of engravings was published in 1735. It depicts the downfall of a young man of fashion who lives loosely, gambles, is gaoled for not paying his debts, and ends up in a lunatic asylum. It followed the success of the artist's previous series of satirical pictures *The Harlot's Progress* (1731).

1735

Canaletto paints *Regatta on the Grand Canal*

Giovanni Antonio Canaletto (1697–1768) painted many scenes of the life and architecture of Venice, his best known work being *Regatta on the Grand Canal* (1735). In 1746 he settled in London and his paintings of the Thames are remarkable for their use of colour and perspective.

1735

Linnaeus begins *Systema Naturae*

Linnaeus (Carl von Linné, 1707–78), the Swedish botanist, began in 1735 his new system for the classification of plants. He devised a method of grouping plants in orders and classes in accordance with the number of stamens and pistils in their flowers. This system formed the basis for modern plant classification.

1739

Execution of Dick Turpin

Dick Turpin (1706–39), the notorious highwayman, was born at Hempstead in Essex. He was apprenticed to a butcher but after he was discovered cattle stealing he joined a band of outlaws who, under his leadership, robbed farms in the area.

In 1735 Turpin joined forces with Tom King, a highwayman, but he shot his partner by accident and then fled to Yorkshire. There, under an assumed name, he started in business as a horse dealer, but in 1739 he was arrested for stealing a black mare and a foal. Found guilty of the crime he was hanged at York on April 7, 1739.

Many of the heroic tales about Dick Turpin's exploits, including his famous ride from London to York, are nothing but folk legends. In the main they were created by the author William Harrison Ainsworth (1805–82) in his novel *Rookwood*.

1739

The War of Jenkins' Ear

On April 9, 1731 Captain Robert Jenkins was returning home from Jamaica when his ship, the *Rebecca*, was boarded by the Spanish coastguard. The Spanish commander cut off one of Jenkins' ears instructing him to carry it to the king with the message that if the king had been present he would have received the same treatment.

Jenkins related his story at the bar of the House of Commons on March 16, 1738 and the event created so much hostility towards the Spanish that it ultimately led to the war that broke out in 1739. Naturally enough the war became known as 'The War of Jenkins' Ear'.

There is, however, considerable doubt as to the truth of Jenkins' story. It is almost certain that he had lost an ear, or at least part of one, but he probably received the injury in a brawl.

1740

Accession of Frederick the Great

When Frederick II (1712–86), known as Frederick the Great, became King of Prussia in 1740 the country was prosperous, efficiently organized, and had a large and powerful army. These he used effectively to make his power and that of Prussia a force to be reckoned with.

One of Frederick's first actions on his accession was to claim Silesia from Austria and he fought two wars to assert this claim (*see 1740 The War of Austrian Succession*).

In addition to great military power he also fostered the improvement of Prussia's industry and agriculture, established an educational system, encouraged religious tolerance, and reformed the country's judicial system. Although Frederick is regarded as one of the great soldiers of history he had a great passion for music and the arts, wrote prodigiously, and played the flute for relaxation.

In 1756 he attacked Saxony and in the Seven Years' War that followed suffered several defeats but eventually managed to retain his territories. He further enlarged Prussia in 1772 when, through a treaty with Russia, he forced Poland to give up some of its lands.

Although every inch a king, Frederick dressed sloppily and often wore a battered grey hat, a snuff-stained, once blue, uniform, and dirty boots.

1740

The War of Austrian Succession

Emperor Charles VI had no surviving son to succeed him, so in 1724 he issued a pragmatic sanction (a royal decree) stating that his possessions in Austria and its dependencies were to pass to his daughter Maria Theresa (1717–80) on his death. He succeeded in attaining the assent of other European rulers to his daughter's succession, but when he died in 1740 the agreements were ignored.

Frederick the Great invited the French philosopher Voltaire (left) to his court.

Frederick II of Prussia claimed Silesia; France claimed the Austrian Netherlands; and Charles Albert of Bavaria, supported by France and Spain, claimed the Hapsburg lands. As a result war raged across Europe for the next eight years. Britain was already at war with Spain (*see* 1739

Maria Theresa and her heir.

The War of Jenkins' Ear) and in 1742 began fighting in support of Maria Theresa.

In 1743 an army of British, Austrians, and Hanoverians under the command of George II (1683–1760) beat the French at Dettingen and the Austrians entered Bavaria. (This was the last battle in which a British sovereign was personally involved.) But the French, under Marshal Saxe, defeated the British, Dutch, and Austrian troops at Fontenoy (1745), and Lawfeldt (1747). In the naval encounters of the war British strength proved superior. The war ended with the Treaty of Aix-la-Chapelle on October 18, 1748.

1741

Garrick appears on the London stage

David Garrick's (1717–79) appearance in Shakespeare's *Richard III* at Goodman's Fields Theatre, London, created a great sensation. His style of acting was natural and in great contrast to the staid delivery of previous actors. From 1742 to 1745 he performed at Drury Lane and eventually became its principal proprietor. He is still regarded as an actor of outstanding genius.

1742

Introduction of the centigrade scale

The centigrade scale for thermometers was devised by the Swedish astronomer Anders Celsius (1701–44). The scale is divided into one hundred degrees, so 0°C is the freezing point and the upper fixed point of 100°C is the temperature of steam coming off boiling water (*see 1714 Fahrenheit's mercury thermometer*).

1745

Rebellion of the 'Young Pretender'

In July 1745 Charles Edward Stuart (1720–88), son of the 'Old Pretender' James Edward Stuart sailed for Scotland to promote the Jacobite cause (*see 1715 The Jacobite Rebellion*). He had been advised not to attempt a second rebellion but when, on August 19, he raised his father's standard at Glenfinnan, near Fort William, many Highland clans rallied to his side.

Charles took Perth and Edinburgh almost without resistance and defeated the English at Prestonpans, near Edinburgh on September 20. He then invaded England reaching Manchester at the end of November and Derby by December 4. Here his officers insisted that the invasion could not succeed and the army retreated on December 6. Once he was back in Scotland Charles scored a victory at Falkirk, but pursued by the Duke of Cumberland and his troops, he was forced to retire to the Highlands where his army was completely routed at the Battle of Culloden Moor.

For five months he hid in the Highlands with a price of £30,000 on his head. In spite of this enormous reward he was never betrayed and he eventually escaped to France. With his departure the Jacobite movement came to an end.

1749

Publication of *Tom Jones*

Tom Jones, the epic masterpiece by the English novelist Henry Fielding (1707–54), has been described as the greatest novel written. It relates the adventures of its hero with a reality and verve that some say has never been equalled. Fielding's other novels which include *Joseph Andrews* (1742), *Jonathan Wild the Great* (1743), and *Amelia* (1751) do not have the same sparkle.

1750

Publication of Gray's *Elegy*

Elegy Written in a Country Churchyard, the greatest work by the English poet Thomas Gray (1716–71), is perhaps the most beautiful poem in the English language. Inspiration for the elegy (a song of mourning) came from the churchyard at Stoke Poges in Buckinghamshire where Gray was, himself, buried.

1750

Publication of *L'Encyclopédie*

One of the world's most famous encyclopedias, *L'Encyclopédie*, was published in France in 1750.

Two publishers, Le Breton and Briason, decided to produce a translation of Ephraim Chambers' *Cyclopaedia* (1728) and they commissioned the French philosopher and scholar Denis Diderot (1713–84) to produce the work. Diderot persuaded them to produce a new work with wider scope.

The contributors to the new work included all the brilliant French writers of the day such as Rousseau (1712–78), Voltaire (1694–1778), Buffon (1707–88), and Montesquieu (1689–1755). In addition to providing factual material on a wide variety of subjects *L'Encyclopédie* contained a great deal of current philosophical thought. It contained only subjects to which there would be offered a rational explanation and in so doing aroused considerable hostility from officialdom and the clergy and publication was prohibited in 1752 and 1759.

L'Encyclopédie captured the spirit of the new age of reason that was dawning in France – an age of enlightenment that was eventually to result in revolution. This spirit is also evident in the condemnation of the corrupt and poverty stricken society and the welcoming of a new freedom that features in other works produced by the Encyclopaedists.

1750
Walpole builds Strawberry Hill

In 1750 the English author Horace Walpole (1717–97) began converting his cottage, Strawberry Hill, in Twickenham into a mock gothic castle and that area of London is still known as Strawberry Hill. Fifteen years later he wrote the tale of terror *The Castle of Otranto*, but he is best known for his letters.

1752
Franklin invents the lightning conductor

The lightning conductor was invented by the American statesman, scientist, and writer Benjamin Franklin (1706–90) in 1752. He also invented a heating stove and bifocal spectacles,

Benjamin Franklin

started a fire service, a subscription library, and the college that was to become the University of Pennsylvania.

Born in Boston of poor parents Franklin had only two years' schooling. He was apprenticed to his father as a soap and candle maker and then to his brother in a printing shop. He was so successful as a printer that in 1749 he retired to devote his energies to science. By flying a kite during a thunderstorm he was able to prove that lightning is a form of electricity.

In 1753 he was appointed postmaster general to the British colonies in North America and was elected to the Pennsylvania Assembly. From 1776 to 1785 he was ambassador to France and then President of Pennsylvania.

1753
British Museum founded

A national lottery provided the money for the purchase in 1753 of the books, coins, medals, and natural history specimens collected by Sir Hans Sloane (1660–1753). In 1754 Montagu House was bought to house the collection together with those of Lord Oxford Harley, and Sir Robert Cotton, and the royal collections. The British Museum opened to the public on January 15, 1759.

1755
The Lisbon earthquake

On November 1, 1755 about thirty thousand people died in the earthquake that struck Lisbon in Portugal. As buildings collapsed people rushed to a nearby quay for safety but all were killed when a second shock wave destroyed the quay. A third shockwave caused giant waves which completed the destruction.

1755
Publication of Johnson's *Dictionary*

The English writer Samuel Johnson (1709–84) first proposed his *Dictionary of the English Language* in 1747, but it was not published until

1755. Johnson received £1,575 for the work which was the first standard English dictionary. It did much to consolidate the meanings of English words as we know them today.

1756

Founding of Sèvres porcelain factory

Sèvres porcelain includes classically designed decorative pieces, large vases, and dinner services. The factory at Sèvres, near Paris was opened in 1756 to produce 'soft paste', an artificial porcelain, but in 1768 hard paste made of kaolin (china clay) and feldspar, which was closer to the original porcelain invented by the Chinese, was introduced.

1756

The Seven Years' War

This was a renewal of the fight between Britain and France and between Austria and Prussia (see 1740 The War of Austrian Succession).

Between Britain and France the struggle concerned the colonies in India and America and resulted in the collapse of France as a colonial power and the founding of the British Indian Empire. The main issue of discontent between Austria and Prussia was Austria's resolve to recapture Silesia taken from them during the War of Austrian Succession. The fighting started when the French captured Minorca in 1756 and later, the same year, Frederick, fearing that Austria was about to attack, attacked Saxony with a view to invading Bohemia.

Britain's part in the war was, in the main, confined to the colonies in India and North America. In India, where fighting had been continuous since 1748, the decisive incidents occurred at Plassey (1757) and Wandewash (1760). In North America the principal event was the siege and capture of Quebec (1759).

1756

The Black Hole of Calcutta

The outbreak of the Seven Years' War in Europe brought renewed fighting between the French and English in India.

On June 20, 1756 the Nawab of Bengal attacked the English settlement at Calcutta. He imprisoned 146 Europeans in a small dungeon, the Black Hole of Calcutta, but conditions were so cramped and airless that only twenty-three survived the night. Robert Clive (1725–74) and Admiral Charles Watson sailed from Madras and recaptured Calcutta on January 2, 1757.

Clive promised Mir Jaffir, the Nawab's commander-in-chief, that he would be given the throne of Bengal and in June he advanced to Bengal with one thousand troops and two thousand sepoys (native soldiers) and only ten guns. At Plassey in West Bengal, Clive attacked the Nawab's fifty thousand-strong force and scored a resounding victory. Mir Jaffir was made Nawab but the real power in Bengal belonged to the British.

1759

Wolfe takes Quebec

British victories in Canada during the Seven Years' War were brought about largely through the absolute co-operation of the sea and land forces. This was particularly illustrated by the taking of Quebec in 1759.

A fleet of ships carried James Wolfe (1727–59) and nine thousand men up the St Lawrence river to the Isle of Orleons. After waiting for several months Wolfe sent a contingent of men to make a mock attack against Quebec whilst he and the rest of the force were conveyed in boats further up the river. On the following day Wolfe engaged the French on the Plains of Abraham.

Both Wolfe and the French leader, General Montcalm (1712–59) were mortally wounded on the same day, September 13, 1759. Four days later Quebec surrendered to the British and thus paved the way for the complete British conquest of Canada in the following year.

1761

Opening of Bridgewater Canal

Transport systems in Britain were not sufficiently effective to cope with the new demands for increased communications brought about by the Industrial Revolution in the eighteenth

Robert Clive achieved British dominance in Bengal at the Battle of Plassey in 1757.

century. The roads were extremely bad and the railway had not yet been invented.

Francis Egerton, third Duke of Bridgewater (1736–1803), found the answer to the problem. He wanted a cheap method of transportation to carry coal from his mines at Worsley to Manchester so he commissioned James Brindley (1716–72) to design and construct a canal to do the job. Within two years the sixty-seven kilometre-long canal was completed and was filled on July 17, 1761.

The building of this waterway marked the beginning of the canal era in Britain and very soon a network of canals covered much of the country. As a result of his initiative the Duke of Bridgewater is often regarded as the 'father of British inland navigation'.

1762

John Harrison's chronometer

Until 1762, when a clockmaker called John Harrison (1693–1776) produced his chronometer (a clock for use at sea), ships sailing the world's oceans had no reliable method of reckoning longitude. Longitude appears on maps as lines running north-to-south over the globe. They cross east-to-west lines of latitude and ships' positions are calculated from the points at which the two lines cross.

Methods of reckoning latitude had been known for centuries but without knowing longitude as well, ships' captains often did not know precisely where they were. The methods they used, such as reckoning longitude from the position of heavenly bodies, were not nearly accurate enough because, to get accurate information from their nautical charts, they needed an accurate measure of the time of their observations. Many ships were lost or wrecked or delayed on voyages as a result. In 1714, the British government offered a £20,000 prize for an accurate marine clock.

John Harrison began working on his chronometer in 1726 and spent the next 33 years perfecting it. He won the government prize in 1762 when, on a test voyage across the Atlantic from England to Jamaica, his chronometer proved to be only five seconds out.

1762

Mozart the child prodigy

Wolfgang Amadeus Mozart (1756–1791) was born in Salzburg, Austria and is thought by many to be the greatest musical genius who ever lived. In 1762, he toured the royal courts of Europe, where his father, Leopold, had taken him to show his extraordinary ability to the rich and noble people of Europe. Mozart also played before the Pope. He began to compose music when he was only five, and at fourteen, his opera *Mitradate* was a great success in Milan, Italy.

Unlike many child prodigies, Mozart's genius did not fade as he grew up. In his short life of less

than thirty-six years, he composed symphonies, operas, concertos and other works of great beauty and brilliance. Mozart in fact, invented the piano concerto. Mozart produced more than 600 compositions in all.

Unfortunately, despite his success, Mozart and his wife Constanza were often short of money. This was mostly due to Mozart's extravagance and impracticality, though sometimes because he was not paid for compositions by those who had commissioned them.

1764

Hargreaves invents the spinning jenny

The second half of the eighteenth century marked the start of the Industrial Revolution in Britain, a period in which the economy changed from being primarily agricultural- to an industrial-based society. As the amount of industry increased new inventions emerged making work more automated and efficient.

One such device was the 'spinning jenny' invented by James Hargreaves (1720–78) in 1764. Turned by hand, the 'spinning jenny', which Hargreaves named after his wife, enabled one person to spin eight threads at the same time. Combined with the flying shuttle that John Kay patented in 1733, it revolutionized the cotton industry.

Cotton workers, worried that these machines would threaten their livelihood, raided Hargreaves's house in 1768 and smashed his equipment but they could not stop the wind of change that was sweeping the country.

1765

Robert Adam designs Kenwood

Robert Adam (1728–92) and his brothers John, James, and Charles brought about great improvements in architectural style in eighteenth century Britain. Robert, the most celebrated of the four, designed several notable houses including Lansdowne House, Luton Hoo, Harewood House, Syon House, and Kenwood House in Hampstead.

1765
Watt improves the steam engine

Contrary to popular belief, James Watt (1736–1819) did not invent the steam engine. He did, however, make it more efficient.

Earlier engines used steam travelling through a cylinder to push a piston within the cylinder. Cold water was then poured on to the cylinder to condense the steam and created a vacuum to pull the piston back before the operation was repeated. Watt reasoned that the system was

James Watt.

inefficient: in condensing the steam, the cylinder also was cooled so that when steam re-entered a great deal of its energy was being wasted in reheating the cylinder.

Watt solved the problem by using a separate vessel as a condenser so that the main cylinder remained at an even temperature. He also encased the cylinder in a steam jacket to prevent heat loss and he used steam instead of a vacuum to push the piston down as well as up.

1768
Royal Academy founded

This famous British art institution was founded by George III (1738–1820) on December 10, 1768 'for the purpose of cultivating and improving the arts of painting, sculpture, and architecture'. It provided for the appointment of a president and forty members, annual exhibitions of work, and the setting up of schools of instruction.

The first president of the Royal Academy was Sir Joshua Reynolds (1723–92), the English artist famous for many types of painting although he is generally associated with portraiture. His subjects included many of the famous personages of the day including Goldsmith, Garrick, and Johnson. He was knighted in 1768.

One of the original members of the Academy was Thomas Gainsborough (1727–88) whose reputation gained ground after his acceptance. Among his best known paintings are *The Blue Boy* and *The Harvest Wagon*. He was principally a portrait painter, that being the main requirement of his wealthy patrons, although he himself preferred to produce landscapes.

1768
Arkwright invents the spinning frame

The spinning frame of Richard Arkwright (1732–92) made possible the British cotton industry of today. Initially he met with the same resistance encountered by Kay and Hargreaves (*see 1764 Hargreaves invents the spinning jenny*). His machines were smashed, but his invention had already proved its usefulness and the cotton industry progressed rapidly as a result of its introduction.

1768
Cook's voyages of discovery

One of the greatest names in the history of exploration is that of James Cook (1728–79). He made three epic voyages during which he discovered many new places, charted coastlines, and paved the way for the British colonization of Australia and New Zealand.

During his first voyage (1768–71) in the *Endeavour*, he charted the coastline of New Zealand and surveyed the east coast of Australia, claiming it for Great Britain. The second expedition (1772–75) with the *Resolution* and *Adventure* covered over ninety thousand kilometres during which Cook became the first man to cross the Antarctic Circle.

With the *Resolution* and *Discovery* Cook commenced his third voyage on June 25, 1776. He sailed to New Zealand, discovered several of

This portrait of Cook was painted in 1776, soon before he left England on his final voyage.

the Cook Islands, rediscovered the Hawaiian or Sandwich Islands, and surveyed a large stretch of the American coastline. He returned to Hawaii in 1779 but was clubbed to death by natives on February 14.

1769

Cugnot builds his steam carriage

The first successful steam-powered road vehicle was invented in 1769 by Nicolas Cugnot (1725–1804), a French military engineer. Although the three-wheeled carriage had to be stopped every fifteen minutes to get up steam it could travel at up to about three kilometres per hour.

The French government was so impressed with the machine's possibilities that it ordered a similar vehicle for use by the army. Unfortunately it was never used by the army because it had several accidents and knocked down a wall during its trials and the government decided it was too dangerous to use.

Other inventors produced steam road vehicles with varying degrees of success. Principal among these was Richard Trevithick (1771–1833) but after some considerable success he decided that there was no future in road transport and he turned his attentions to the railway (*see 1804 The first steam railway*).

1769

Wedgwood opens Etruria factory

Prior to the time of Josiah Wedgwood (1730–95) English pottery was rather nondescript, but Wedgwood raised it to such heights that it became known and admired throughout the world.

Born at Burslem, in Staffordshire, Wedgwood was only nine years old when he started work in the family pottery. In 1754 he teamed up with Thomas Whieldon, a well known potter. During this partnership Wedgwood produced the melon and cabbage styles of earthenware. Five years later he became a master potter, set up on

his own, and in 1762 was appointed Queen's potter. In 1769 he opened his Etruria works at Stoke on Trent.

At Etruria Wedgwood made the green glaze and cream-coloured pottery known as Queen's ware because Queen Charlotte liked it. Later he invented Jasper ware, a coloured porcelain bearing cameo-type embellishments, for which he is best known, and which is still produced by the company he founded.

1770

Goethe starts work on *Faust*

There are several versions of the story of Dr Faustus, the sixteenth century German scholar said to have sold his soul to the Devil, but possibly the greatest is the two-part drama by Johann Wolfgang von Goethe (1749–1832). He started part one of *Faust* in 1770 and it was published in 1808 but the second part was not published until 1831.

Goethe's earliest works were produced during a period of German literary tradition known as *Sturm und Drang* (storm and stress) which was a precursor of the romantic movement that swept Europe in the nineteenth century. From 1786 to 1788 Goethe visited Italy and was inspired to write classical dramas of formal purity and restraint. His poetry is the finest ever produced in the German language.

Goethe was also extremely interested in science. His life at the Wiemar court marks a unique cultural achievement in many fields.

1772

Priestley publishes his experiments

Although Joseph Priestley (1733–1804) was an English Nonconformist minister with views ahead of his time it is as a scientist that he is remembered. In 1767 he published a *History of Electricity* which was followed by several brilliant experiments in electricity and he proposed several suggestions that were not to be proved for another hundred years.

In 1772 Priestley published a paper in which

he set out his discovery of hydrochloric acid, nitrous oxide, and outlined the possibility of forcing carbon dioxide into water – a product now known as soda water.

In 1774 Priestley discovered oxygen and showed its importance, and he also discovered sulphur dioxide and ammonia. His work, and that of his contemporaries, formed the foundations of modern chemistry.

1773

The Boston Tea Party

Trade in the American colonies was regulated by Great Britain and, as this inevitably meant the imposition of restrictions in trade, the settlers turned to smuggling. The British tried re-enforcing the Navigation Acts which controlled trading – but with little success.

In 1765 the British government passed the Stamp Act which required all legal documents in North America to bear an official stamp. The colonists objected so violently to this imposition that the Act was repealed a year later.

In 1767 tea and other imported goods were taxed in America. Although most of the taxes were later abolished, that on tea remained. In 1773 some of the colonists demonstrated their objection. Their slogan was 'no taxation without representation', that is without their own members of parliament in London. Dressed as American Indians they boarded British ships in Boston harbour and threw cases of tea overboard. As a result of this 'Boston Tea Party', Boston was placed under military control. The seeds of the American War of Independence had been sown.

The American colonies' discontent with British legislation came to a head with the Boston Tea Party. Colonists dressed as American Indians threw chests of tea overboard in protest against tea taxes.

Catherine the Great, Czarina of Russia, an able yet ruthless ruler.

1773

The Pugachev Revolt

Catherine II (1729–96), known as Catherine the Great, ruled Russia for thirty-four years after her husband Czar Peter III, an unbalanced weakling, had been deposed and murdered. During her reign Russia extended its territories to include parts of Turkey, Sweden, and Poland.

She was said to be in favour of better treatment for the serfs (peasants) but she did little to help them. In fact life for them became even more intolerable during her reign and they were taxed heavily. As a result there were several revolts, including the Pugachev Revolt in 1773.

1775

First performance of *The Rivals*

The Rivals, the five-act comedy by English playwright Richard Brinsley Sheridan (1751–1816), was not very well received when it was first performed at Covent Garden Theatre, London on January 17, 1775. However it soon achieved success and remains popular to this day as do *The School for Scandal* (1777) and *The Critic* (1779).

1775

First performance of *The Barber of Seville*

Le Barbier de Séville ('The Barber of Seville'), a comedy by Pierre Augustin Caron de Beaumarchais (1732–99), was first performed in Paris on February 23, 1775. The Italian composer Rossini used it as the basis for an opera in 1816 and Mozart bestowed the same honour on Beaumarchais' other great work *Le Mariage de Figaro* ('The Marriage of Figaro') in 1786.

1776

American Declaration of Independence

Great Britain regulated trade in the American colonies to such a great extent that the settlers began to grow annoyed at the controls imposed upon them. There were acts of rebellion (*see 1773 The Boston Tea Party*) and this hostility flared into war when, on April 19, 1775, shots were fired at Lexington.

The first battle of the war, fought at Bunker Hill, Charlestown, was won by the British who also scored decisive victories in New York (1776) and Philadelphia (1777). But the American Continental Congress had appointed George Washington (1732–99) to take charge of the untrained American soldiers and he inspired them to fight for their freedom. Further inspiration was provided on July 4, 1776 when the Congress issued the Declaration of Independence.

The Declaration renounced allegiance to the British throne and resolved that these United

Emelian Pugachev (*c.* 1744–75) claimed that he was Peter III, miraculously still alive, and, although others had made the same claim, the people, to whom he had promised an end to serfdom, rallied to his side. They captured fortified posts, burned the homes of landowners, and headed for Moscow. As the peasants approached, a party of hand-picked troops attacked them and the rebellion was quashed. Pugachev was taken to Moscow in an iron cage and executed there in January 1775.

1773

First performance of *She Stoops to Conquer*

On March 15, 1773 the first performance of *She Stoops to Conquer* by Oliver Goldsmith (1728–74) took place at the Covent Garden Theatre, London. This five-act play concerns the hilarious adventures of a lady who dresses as a serving maid to win the man she loves.

HISTORY OF THE UNITED STATES

1776 July 4: thirteen colonies in America declared independence from Britain.

1783 End of the eight-year War of Independence. Britain recognizes independence of the new United States.

1789 George Washington becomes first President of the United States of America.

1791 Vermont becomes the fourteenth state of the USA. Ultimately, there were fifty states. The last to join was Hawaii, in 1959.

1804-1806 Explorations by Lewis and Clark, who traversed North America from east to west.

1812-1814 War between Britain and the United States of America, after which a 'special relationship' developed between them.

1823 The Monroe Doctrine.

1830 Indian Removal Act

passed. Indians sent to reservations.

1848 Californian Gold Rush.

1860 Abraham Lincoln becomes President.

1861-65 American Civil War: anti-slavery North defeats the pro-slavery Confederates in the South.

1865 Assassination of Lincoln.

1869 Completion of railway coast to coast across the USA.

1898 Spanish-American War.

1917 The USA enters the First World War.

1929 Stock market crash on Wall Street. Start of the Depression.

1932 Franklin D. Roosevelt elected President, and after inauguration in 1933, embarks

on New Deal to restore prosperity in the USA.

1941 USA enters Second World War, which ended in 1945.

1950 USA intervenes in the Korean War.

1960 Start of Dr Martin Luther King's agitation for Black rights.

1960 John F. Kennedy elected President.

1969 USA puts first man on the moon.

1973 US troops withdraw from Vietnam.

1974 US President Richard Nixon resigns after Watergate scandal.

1987 December 8: Disarmament Treaty signed by US President Ronald Reagan and Russian leader Mikhail Gorbachev.

Colonies are, and of right ought to be, free and independent States'.

The Americans were aided in their fight by Britain's enemies in Europe and in 1777 the British general, Burgoyne (1723–92), was forced to surrender at Saratoga. In 1781 General Cornwallis (1738–1805), cut off at Yorktown with French ships preventing aid reaching him by sea, surrendered and the fighting ended. America was granted its independence in 1783.

1776

Publication of *The Wealth of Nations*

The Wealth of Nations by the Scottish economist Adam Smith (1723–90) was largely responsible for the creation of economics as a separate

science. Although many of its theories have now been superseded it remains the most famous work on the subject and is still required reading for political economists.

1777

Lavoisier's experiments with oxygen

Oxygen was discovered in 1774 by Priestley (*see 1772 Priestley publishes his experiments*) and given the name 'dephlogisticated air'. It was also discovered at about the same time by the Swedish scientist Scheele who called it 'empyreal' or 'fire air', but the French chemist Antoine Laurent Lavoisier (1743–94) gave the element its modern name. He considered it to be an essential constituent of acid and so he called it *oxygène* (acid former).

In addition to repeating the experiments conducted by Priestley, Lavoisier carried out several of his own. In one of them he showed that mercury, heated in a small amount of oxygen, was transformed into a red powder which he called 'mercury oxide'.

1779
Crompton invents the spinning mule

To help his mother the Englishman Samuel Crompton (1753–1827) spun cotton at home. But he found the job awkward so he tried to improve the equipment. The machine he invented combined features from Arkwright's jenny and Hargreaves' frame and because of this cross between the two, Crompton's machine was known as a 'mule'.

1779
The first iron bridge

The first iron bridge in the world was completed in 1779 near Coalbrookdale, Shropshire, England. The whole of the surrounding area, which is rich in other reminders of the Industrial Revolution including a canal complex, coal mine, coking works, and furnaces, has been developed as an environmental museum of science and technology.

The Industrial Revolution introduced new technology in every sphere: the first iron bridge near Coalbrookdale, erected in 1779.

1780
The Gordon Riots

The Gordon Riots were an appalling explosion of violence in London in June, 1780. They began as an attempt to force Parliament to repeal an Act it had passed in 1778 to stop some forms of discrimination against Roman Catholics.

Lord George Gordon (1751–93) a fanatical young aristocrat, led a great procession of Protestants to Westminster in protest against the Act on June 2. The procession became a mob which, shouting furious cries of 'No Popery!', began attacking the Catholic chapels of foreign embassies. The mob soon extended its activities to the houses of well-off Catholics, then to prisons, the Bank of England and even to the home of the prime minister, Lord North.

For a week the 'No Popery' mob was in charge of London, until order was restored. The memory of those days and nights of fire and terror remained for many years.

1780
The first Derby

The Derby, one of the five Classics of English horse racing, was first run at Epsom, Surrey, in 1780, and has been run every year since.

Named after the 12th Earl of Derby, it is a flat race for three-year-old colts and fillies. In the 1913 Derby, Emily Davidson, a Suffragette, was killed when she threw herself under George V's horse. Famous winners include Sir Ivor, Nijinsky, Hyperion and Shergar.

1781
Herschel discovers Uranus

William Herschel (1738–1822) was born in Hanover but moved to England in 1757 and taught music. In his spare time he studied astronomy and, as he earned very little money, he had to make his own telescope.

His first (1774) was so successful that he devoted a great deal of the rest of his life to the improvement and manufacture of telescopes. By 1789 he was using for his observations a forty-eight-inch reflecting telescope, the largest in the world at that time.

Herschel made several important astronomical discoveries including several double stars and two satellites of Saturn. He raised the number of known nebulae from 180 to 2,500 and, in the field of physics, he was the first to discover infra-red rays. But his most spectacular achievement was the discovery, on March 13, 1781, of the planet Uranus. A year later he was appointed private astronomer to George III.

1781
Kant's *Critique of Pure Reason*

Kritik der reinen Vernunft ('Critique of Pure Reason') was the first of three books in which Immanuel Kant (1724–1804) expounded his influential idealist philosophy. Unlike other thinkers of his day who said that man could understand all things purely by reason, Kant suggested that there was certain knowledge, such as the existence of God, which men could not understand in this way because they could not experience it.

1782
Burke's Economic Reform Act

One of the great causes which Edmund Burke (1729–97) pursued throughout his outstanding career in British political life was that of economical reform. By this, Burke meant the freeing of the House of Commons from the influence of, and exploitation by, the king.

George III was able to influence the way the House of Commons voted by putting his own supporters and friends into certain government offices and places, including parliamentary seats.

The economical reform movement in the 1770s and 1780s, of which Burke was one of the leaders, demanded parliamentary, not royal, control of the choice of people to fill various positions and of the salaries they were paid. Burke's Economic Reform Bill, which became law in 1782, was one step on the way to fulfilling this demand. The Act regulated the pensions and payments of a number of posts in the royal household, and abolished about forty others.

1782
Pitt the Younger becomes Chancellor

William Pitt the Younger (1759–1806), so-called to distinguished him from his famous father William Pitt, Earl of Chatham, became Chancellor of the Exchequer in 1782. Although Pitt had shown great talent as an orator and politician, it was a very quick promotion for a young man who had entered Parliament less than two years before. In 1783 George III chose the twenty-four-year-old Pitt to be First Lord of the Treasury (the official title of the king's first minister) and Chancellor of the Exchequer.

Pitt held office until 1801, and was in power again when he died in 1806. No British prime minister since then has been so young when appointed to the office.

Pitt's time in office, much of it overshadowed by war with France, was distinguished by the wide-ranging administrative and economic reforms he introduced. It was Pitt who first made the British pay income tax, from 1799 to 1816.

1783
The Montgolfier balloon ascents

The Montgolfier brothers, Joseph (1740–1810) and Etienne (1745–99), from Annonay in France, made aviation history with their hot-air balloons in 1783. They were convinced that the same kind of heated air which sent pieces of paper wafting up the chimney from their home fire could also be used to lift men up into the air.

After several months' work, they felt confident enough to give a public demonstration of their experiments on June 4, 1783. They released a large balloon over the heads of the astonished citizens of Annonay. The balloon was made of linen lined with paper and filled with hot air from a straw and wool fire.

The Montgolfier balloon.

At Versailles in September, Louis XVI and Marie Antoinette witnessed the first flight by living creatures, when the Montgolfiers sent a sheep, a duck and a rooster into the air in a basket suspended from their balloon. A month later, the first person to fly, Pilâtre de Rozier, went up in a Montgolfier balloon.

1783
The *Pyroscaphe*

Several attempts had been made to propel boats by steam power before the Frenchman, Claude, Marquis de Jouffroy d'Abbans (1751–1832) achieved the first real success in 1783.

Earlier, he had had a boat built which carried paddles designed on a system similar to the paddling movement of water birds. When this proved unsuccessful, Jouffroy returned to the paddle wheels with which others had experimented before him.

His new boat, the 182-tonne *Pyroscaphe*, carried a double-acting steam engine, on the basis of James Watt's recent improvements, to activate the ratchet mechanism which turned the paddle wheels. On July 15, 1783 the *Pyroscaphe* steamed upstream on the river Saône near Lyons for fifteen minutes, the first boat ever to be propelled by steam power against a current.

Jouffroy did not have the capital to carry his experiments further, and the steamboat was perfected instead in the USA and Britain.

1786
Burns's *Poems*

Robert Burns (1759–96), a young farmer from Ayrshire, published his *Poems Chiefly in the Scottish Dialect* in Kilmarnock in 1786. The poems brought him immediate fame, which was consolidated by his magnificent narrative poem *Tam O'Shanter* (1790) and his many beautiful lyrics, including *Comin' thro' the Rye*, *A Red, Red Rose* and *Auld Lang Syne*. Today, Burns is revered as Scotland's national poet.

1787
Formation of the MCC

The Marylebone Cricket Club (MCC), the first international administrative body of world cricket, was formed in 1787. An historic meeting of the club in 1788 revised cricket's existing rules and laid the basis of the modern game. MCC first met on Thomas Lord's ground in Dorset Square, London. When Mr Lord moved to St John's Wood in 1809, MCC also moved there.

1788
The impeachment of Warren Hastings

The trial of Warren Hastings (1732–1818) for corruption and atrocities while he was Governor General of India from 1774 to 1785, began in Westminster Hall in February 1788.

Hastings had been a very able administrator in India, but had been high-handed in his efforts to raise money to defend British possessions there against the French. He had been forced to desperate measures because British resources were stretched to their limit by the War of American Independence. The English politicians, led by Edmund Burke, Charles James Fox and Richard Sheridan, who demanded Hasting's impeachment, had misunderstood his activities and greatly exaggerated their evils.

Hastings was found not guilty in 1795, seven years after the trial had begun. Although the impeachment had been unjust, it did draw attention to India's problems.

1788

Hepplewhite's *Guide*

George Hepplewhite (d. 1786) was an English cabinet-maker who planned his book, *The Cabinet Maker and Upholsterer's Guide, or Repository of Designs for Every Article of Household Furniture* simply as a catalogue to attract buyers to his furniture designs. It was published in 1788, two years after his death, and is now regarded as a major expression of eighteenth-century English furniture design.

1789

The mutiny on HMS *Bounty*

The *Bounty* was a Royal Navy ship which in 1789 became the centre of the most famous mutiny in naval history.

Her captain, William Bligh (1754−1817), had been ordered to Tahiti in 1787 to obtain breadfruit trees and take them to the West Indies for cultivation. The ship had left Tahiti and was far out in the Pacific near Tofua when the majority of the crew, led by the master's mate Fletcher Christian, mutinied on April 28, 1789, probably because they wanted to stay in Tahiti and not return to England. They set Bligh and eighteen members of his crew adrift in the ship's longboat. With only a compass to help him, Bligh arrived safely in Timor in June 1789 − a journey of nearly 6,500 kilometres in an open boat. It was a remarkable feat of navigation.

Bligh later became Governor of New South Wales. Some of the mutineers, led again by Christian, settled on remote Pitcairn Island. Others were caught and hanged.

1789

King Louis XVI calls the Estates General

Louis XVI (1754−93) ascended the throne in 1774 and by 1788 the public treasury was empty, the State was burdened with a huge debt, and the people were crushed under heavy taxes. Louis and his ministers were therefore forced to call together the Estates General − nobility, clergy, and Third Estate (the people) − for the

first time since 1614 to try to find a way to pay the nation's debts.

The Estates General met at Versailles on May 5, 1789. The Third Estate hoped that this meeting would begin granting them the equality and freedom to take part in government which they had long been denied, but it soon became clear that they could expect no such results.

The Third Estate broke away and joined by some of the clergy, on June 17th, proclaimed itself the National Assembly, representing the majority of the French people. The alarmed king had the delegates locked out of their usual meeting place, but the new National Assembly moved to a nearby indoor tennis court where, on June 20, they took the famous *Jeu de Paume* oath not to separate until 'the Constitution of this realm has been established on solid foundations'.

By the end of June most of the clergy and many nobles had joined the Assembly. On July 7 it became a Constituent Assembly and began planning a new constitution for France.

1789

The fall of the Bastille

When Louis XVI dismissed his chief minister Necker on July 11, 1789, replacing him and other officials with aristocrats, the people of Paris rose in revolt. They were already discontented with soaring bread prices and unemployment, and were by now inspired by the activities of the Third Estate at Versailles. To fight the king and the troops he was placing round Paris, they needed weapons. One place which might provide them was the massive, brooding Bastille prison, where many people had been imprisoned without trial.

A mob demanding arms arrived at the Bastille early on July 14, and swarmed into the outer courts. The Governor, Launay, ordered his small garrison force to fire and many people fell dead. Provoked to fury by news of this, more people, including French Guards with cannon, surged to the Bastille. Late in the afternoon Launay surrendered. He was dragged off to prison but was beheaded by the mob on the way.

The Bastille held only seven prisoners. The real significance of its fall was symbolic: the king had been defeated by Paris. The people of Paris emphasized their victory over the king when a great crowd marched to Versailles in October and forced the royal family and the National Assembly to return to Paris.

The people of Paris storm the Bastille at the start of the French Revolution, assisted by mutinous troops.

1789
Discovery of uranium

Uranium, a heavy, radioactive metallic element, was discovered in 1789 by a German scientist, Martin Klaproth (1743–1817) who had no inkling of the momentous nature of his discovery. It was not until 1938 that scientists realized uranium's very special properties. It is the only element so far known to science which can readily be used in the creation of nuclear (atomic) energy.

1789
Bentham's theories published

Jeremy Bentham (1748–1832) was one of the most influential philosophers of his age. He constantly questioned and criticized the British law and constitution, saying they should be improved and that the purpose of law and government should be to create 'the greatest happiness of the greatest number'. He explained his theory in *Introduction to Principles of Morals and Legislation*.

1791
Blake's *Songs of Innocence*

William Blake (1757–1827) published his second book of poems, *Songs of Innocence*, in 1789. Although the poems were bright, fresh lyrics about innocence, they still contained the mystical, magical thoughts which were to set

Blake's poems apart from the writings of most of his contemporaries. An engraver, he etched his poems and their decorative designs on copper plates himself.

William Blake was a mystic, a poet and a remarkable artist, as shown by this illustration for Dante's *Divina Commedia* (Tate Gallery, London).

1791
Galvani's experiments with electricity

In 1786, Luigi Galvani (1737–98), anatomy professor at Bologna University, was using a steel scalpel to dissect a frog's leg when an assistant in his laboratory produced a spark with a static-electricity machine. The frog's leg twitched.

Galvani thought this phenomenon so intriguing that he tried other experiments. Once he went out in a thunderstorm to see if lightning would also cause a dead frog's legs, attached by a brass hook to an iron fence, to contract. It did.

Galvani thought he had discovered 'animal electricity' and that it was present in the material of an animal's nerve and its corresponding muscle. In fact, he was observing electricity in motion: the frog's legs were acting as electrolytes allowing electrons to flow from one piece of metal to the other, causing a momentary current.

The publication of Galvani's experiments in 1791 helped lead other scientists to the discovery of electric currents.

1791
Paine's *The Rights of Man*

Thomas Paine (1737–1809) was an English radical thinker who played a part in both the American and the French Revolutions.

He went to America in 1776, and was soon in the midst of the colonists' struggle for independence, writing a series of pamphlets encouraging resistance to the British (*see 1776 American Declaration of Independence*).

He returned to England in 1787, but was forced to flee, this time to France, to avoid being arrested because of the extreme language of his book *The Rights of Man*, published in two parts in 1791 and 1792. In the book, Paine supported the French Revolution and said that Britain, too, should rid herself of her monarchy and set up a revolutionary government. He also suggested a number of reforms to help the aged and poor in Britain which seemed revolutionary then, but which have since been adopted.

Paine was made a member of the Convention in France, and returned to the United States in 1802.

1791
Sheraton's *Drawing Book*

Thomas Sheraton (1751–1806) had, with Chippendale and Hepplewhite, major influence on English furniture design in the eighteenth century. His *Cabinet Maker's and Upholsterer's Drawing Book*, published in parts between 1791 and 1794, included designs for many types of furniture, much of it decorated with veneers and inlays rather than carving. He seems to have been a designer rather than a maker of furniture; nothing actually made by him is known to exist.

1792
France becomes a Republic

Growing political activity in Paris, a serious economic crisis, and a threat of war from other countries in Europe, combined to move the journeymen, craftsmen and wage-earners of the city, the *sans-culottes*, to revolt in 1792. Early on

August 10, great crowds surrounded the Tuileries Palace, where Louis XVI and his family had virtually been prisoners since their attempted flight from France in June, 1791. They had been recaptured at Varennes and had been completely mistrusted by the French people since.

The king and his family took refuge with the Legislative Assembly, but the *sans-culottes*, armed with pikes, moved in and forced the Assembly to suspend the king from his duties. They also demanded that a National Convention be elected to plan a new constitution.

The Convention met on September 20, and the next day voted unanimously to abolish the monarchy. In December Louis was brought to trial and called upon to answer for repeated acts of treason against the Republic. A death sentence was passed and Louis was executed on January 21, 1793 at the Place de la Révolution.

1793

The Reign of Terror

The Reign of Terror (1793–94) took place in France at a time of great crisis, when exiled royalists were plotting against the government and foreign powers, including Prussia, Austria and Great Britain, were threatening invasion.

The makers of the Terror were the extreme republican Jacobins, dominated by Maximilien Robespierre (1758–94), who were swept into power by mob violence in June 1793. Working through the Committee of Public Safety which had been set up by the Paris revolutionary, Georges Jacques Danton (1759–94), the Jacobins imposed a dictatorship on France.

In the name of 'public safety', their Revolutionary Tribunal sent hundreds of people including Queen Marie Antoinette, aristocrats, priests, officials and ordinary citizens to the guillotine. Those who protested, like Charlotte Corday (1768–93) were guillotined (she had stabbed to death the Jacobin Jean Paul Marat (1743–93) in his bath) and eventually even Danton was executed.

It was not until July 1794 that anarchy in the provinces, financial and economic chaos and a general horror at the bloodshed, combined to bring Robespierre down. The French army had begun to win victories against their enemies, too, and Robespierre's repressive rule was no longer needed. He was executed without trial on July 28, as were many of his followers.

Marie Antoinette, wife of Louis XVI, is led to the guillotine.

1795

Mungo Park explores Africa

In 1788 the African Association was formed to encourage exploration and promote British interests in the virtually unknown continent of Africa. One of its first objectives was 'to ascertain the course and, if possible, the rise and termination of that mysterious river – the Niger'.

A Major Houghton responded to the call in 1790 but, as nothing was heard from him after 1791, he was presumed killed. Mungo Park (1771–1806), a Scottish surgeon, requested that he be allowed to step into Houghton's place and the African Association accepted.

Park began his expedition in December 1795, and had several narrow escapes. But he collected the required information and published his adventures in *Travels in the Interior of Africa* (1799).

The book aroused so much interest that Park was commissioned to make another expedition in 1805. During this journey his canoe overturned and he and his companions were drowned.

1796
The first cowpox inoculations

Country people in England had long suspected that there was a connection between cowpox and smallpox. They had noticed that people who worked with cattle and who contracted cowpox never seemed to catch smallpox.

Edward Jenner (1749–1823), a doctor in Berkeley, Gloucester, set out to find if there was

This drawing of a sculpture of Jenner shows the first cowpox inoculation.

any truth in the belief. In May 1796 he injected liquid from cowpox sores into a young boy, James Phipps, who caught cowpox: however, the resulting sores soon healed. Later Jenner injected Phipps with smallpox but it had no effect on the boy's health: the cowpox had made him immune.

In spite of initial opposition the practice of vaccination in which the surface of the skin is scratched with vaccine gained steady support both in Great Britain and abroad, so that today smallpox has been virtually eradicated all over the world.

1797
The Spithead Mutiny

The English writer Samuel Johnson described life at sea in the eighteenth century as follows: 'No man will be a sailor who has contrivance enough to get himself into jail; for being in a ship is being in a jail, with the chance of being drowned. A man in a jail has more room, better food, and commonly better company.' Quite often, in fact, criminals were the only men who could be persuaded to go to sea.

Conditions in the navy were virtually intolerable and led the men to mutiny at Spithead and the Nore in 1797. Of the two mutinies, that at Spithead was conducted in the most sensible manner; the mutineers put a deliberate plan into action and appointed delegates to negotiate. When their chief demands were met they returned to duty. The Nore mutiny, however, was little more than a dangerous and unnecessary brawl.

As a result of the mutinies several changes were made to Navy regulations. Conditions and pay were improved and the British sailor became a respected member of society instead of a social outcast.

1798
Publication of *The Ancient Mariner*

Lyrical Ballads (1798) published anonymously by the poets William Wordsworth (1770–1850) and Samuel Taylor Coleridge (1772–1834) contained one of the finest magical English poems – *The Ancient Mariner*. The poem was based on a dream related to Coleridge by a friend. At about the same time Coleridge wrote his magnificent *Kubla Khan* and the first part of *Christabel*.

1798
Publication of Malthus's theories

The publication of *Essay on the Principle of Population* by Thomas Robert Malthus (1766–1834) aroused considerable controversy – largely because his theories were misunder-

THE MODERN FRENCH EMPIRE

The French Empire

The French Empire lost several territories to Britain after the Seven Years' War (1756–63). The most important were settlements in India and Canada, held by France since the 17th century.

Later territories acquired by France were:

Territory	Colonized/Protectorate	Independent/Annexed	New Name
AFRICA			
Dahomey	1894	1958	1959
Ivory Coast	1904	1958	
Niger	1904	1958	
Senegal	1895	1958	Part of Mali,1959
Upper Volta	1919	1958	
French Sudan	1904	1958	
French Guinea	1882	1958	
Morocco	1912	1956	
Algeria	1830	1962	
Tunisia	1881	1956	
Madagascar	1896	1958	Malagasy
Reunion Island	1643	Part of France 1947	
Somaliland	1881	Part of France 1946	Afars and Issas
Comoro Island	1886	Part of France 1946	

Territory	Colonized/Protectorate	Independent/Annexed	New Name
ASIA – Indochina			
Vietnam	c.1884	1949	
Laos	1893	1962	
Cambodia	1863	1953	Kampuchea
AMERICA – Part of France			
French Guiana	1674	1946	French Polynesia
Martinique	1635	1946	French Polynesia
St Pierre/Miquelon	1660	–	
PACIFIC OCEAN			
Oceanic Settlements	1801	Part of France 1958	
New Caledonia	1853	French Polynesia	
Wallis & Futuna Islands	1842	Part of France 1959	

stood. He stated that population increases at a faster rate than food supplies increase and that ultimately there would be insufficient food to go round.

1798
First performance of Haydn's *Creation*

The *Creation*, the popular oratorio by the Austrian composer Franz Joseph Haydn (1732–1809) was first produced in Vienna in 1798. Written to words from *Genesis* and a poem by Lidley, the work was first performed in London in 1800. It became so popular in England that several choral societies were formed specially to sing it.

1798
Rebellion in Ireland

In 1790 the Irish patriot Wolfe Tone (1763–98), inspired by the French Revolution, helped to form the United Irishmen. This society was devoted to the creation of a United Ireland and the elimination of English rule. Tone believed that armed rebellion was the only way to achieve these objectives and he enlisted the aid of the French.

In December, 1796 he sailed from Brest with French troops under the command of General Hoche, but bad weather forced them back.

Two years later an uprising was attempted in Dublin but the leaders were arrested and on June 26, 1798 Vinegar Hill, the headquarters of the United Irishmen, was stormed. A last attempt was made by Tone in October when he landed with a small force at Lough Swilly in the north, but he was captured by the British. He was sentenced to be hanged but on November 19 he took his own life.

1798
The Battle of the Nile

British attitude towards the French Revolution was largely sympathetic until the execution of Louis XVI (*see 1793 The Reign of Terror*). When the revolutionaries began interfering in the affairs of other countries, Britain and other nations declared war on France in 1793.

At the same time a young officer, Napoleon Bonaparte (1769–1821) was beginning to make a name for himself and in 1798 he invaded Egypt, capturing Malta on the way, with a view to threatening British power in India.

Prior to Napoleon's departure for Egypt the British became aware that he was preparing a fleet at Toulon and they sent a squadron under Horatio Nelson (1758–1805) to investigate. Unfortunately Nelson's ship, *Vanguard*, was damaged in a storm and whilst it was being repaired at Sardinia the French set sail.

Not knowing Napoleon's destination Nelson had to search for the French ships. It was to be two months before he finally caught up with them – at Aboukir Bay, near Alexandria.

On August 1, 1798 Nelson engaged with the French and all but four of the enemy ships were taken or destroyed in the battle at the mouth of the Nile. Napoleon's army was cut off in Egypt and all thoughts of advancing to India had to be abandoned.

1800
Volta invents first battery

Count Alessandro Volta (1745–1827), the Italian physicist, made several important discoveries in electricity. Among them was that if two different metals placed in a salt solution are connected by a wire an electric current runs along the wire. In 1800 Volta took this a stage further by placing several pairs together to produce what is now known as the voltaic pile, or battery.

1800
Owen takes over New Lanark Mills

The British industrialist and social reformer, Robert Owen (1771–1858), was convinced that if working and living conditions were of a high standard the character of people would improve and they would work for the good of the community. In 1800 he moved to New Lanark, Scotland, to manage the cotton mills. By improving conditions and providing schools he created a model community and the mills prospered. In 1817 he advocated the creation of self-supporting 'villages of co-operation' but people in England were not interested. He went to America to form such a community at New Harmony, but the project failed.

After returning to Britain he joined a working class movement which led to the formation of large trade unions, but they collapsed in 1834. Owen's concept of co-operation did, however, eventually lead to the formation of the co-operative movement that flourishes to this day.

1801
Union of England and Ireland

Following the unsuccessful rebellion of 1798 (*see 1798 Rebellion in Ireland*) the British prime minister William Pitt (1759–1806) decided that the only way to restore law and order was for Britain and Ireland to be united.

The Act of Union was passed by the British government on July 2, 1800. The Irish, reacting favourably to the promise of Roman Catholic emancipation (and a fair amount of bribery), passed the Act on August 1. The new Act became law on January 1, 1801. It formed the two kingdoms into one under the same flag, monarch, and parliament.

About a month later the cabinet began considering its promise to the Catholics. But George III heard of their proposals and flatly refused to accept the idea of allowing the Catholics any political rights and Pitt resigned in protest. Catholics were not emancipated (given civil rights) until 1829, and were not allowed to sit in Parliament until 1895.

1801

Flinders circumnavigates Australia

For many centuries, geographers speculated about a large land mass which they called Terra Australis Incognita – Unknown Southern Land. Later, parts of the continent we know as Australia were explored by various navigators. Captain James Cook discovered the province of New South Wales. Dutch navigators called those parts of Australia they knew 'New Holland'. It was the British sailor Matthew Flinders (1774–1814) whose explorations covering the whole coastline of the continent, gave it the name by which it is known today – Australia.

Whilst serving as a surveyor in the Royal Navy at Sydney from 1795–99, Flinders mapped the eastern coast of Australia and circumnavigated Tasmania which up to that time had been regarded as part of the mainland. In 1801 he was sent again to Australia and spent the next two years charting the whole of the south and east coast and most of the north. In carrying out this survey he sailed all the way round Australia. Returning home in 1803 he was captured by the French, remaining a prisoner for six years, so it was not until 1810 that he was able to announce his discoveries.

1803

Dalton develops his atomic theory

John Dalton (1766–1844), the English chemist, began work on his atomic theory in 1803. He proposed that all elements were made up of atoms, that atoms were so small they were indivisible, that elements combined because their atoms joined together, and he gave each element an atomic weight.

1804

The first steam railway

The first iron railway (cast-iron bars on top of wooden rails) was laid at Coalbrookdale, Shropshire and the trucks were pulled by horses.

Richard Trevithick (1771–1833), a Cornish mining engineer, who had experimented with steam powered road vehicles (until one blew up!) was the first to use a steam engine to haul the trucks, running on flanged iron rails.

On February 11, 1804, at the Pen-y-Darren ironworks in Wales, the engine hauled a twenty tonne load from Merthyr Tydfil to Abercyon, a distance of over fifteen kilometres. In spite of the pessimists' predictions that the wheels would slip on the iron rails, the trial was successful.

Trevithick was convinced that the railway could also be used for passenger travel and in 1808 he set up a small railway in London. The engine, the *Catch-me-who-can*, carried people around a circular track at one shilling a ride – until one day an engine wheel broke and Trevithick dropped the scheme.

1804

Napoleon becomes emperor

On May 18, 1804 Napoleon Bonaparte was declared Emperor of France. At a ceremony in Notre Dame, Paris on December 2, Napoleon crowned himself emperor and the republican constitution for which the people of France had fought the revolution existed no longer (*see 1792 France becomes a Republic*).

Napoleon as First Consul.

Napoleon's meteoric rise to power began in 1785 when he received a commission in the La Fère artillery regiment. In 1793 he was put in charge of the artillery at Toulon which was being invaded by English and Spanish forces and he was largely responsible for the recapture of the city. Two years later he easily crushed the royalist rising in Paris and soon after he set out on his Italian Campaign before proceeding to Egypt (*see 1798 The Battle of the Nile*).

In 1799 Napoleon returned to France, overthrew the Directory (the executive group which held power in 1795–99), and set himself up as leader. By 1802 he had secured the consulate for life together with the power to name his successor. At the same time he secured peace with Britain, the first time France had been at peace since 1792. He could now concentrate on the reorganization of France: he established the Bank of France, simplified the law, encouraged trade and industry, and introduced a system of public education.

1805
The Battle of Trafalgar

Napoleon utilized the peace of 1802 to strengthen internal matters in France (*see 1804 Napoleon becomes Emperor*), but he also extended French influence abroad. Britain realized the danger inherent in Napoleon's increasing strength and decided to make the first move in 1803 by declaring war.

The French reasoned that the only way to defeat Britain was by invasion, so troops were made ready at Boulogne. But the British ruled the seas, so Napoleon had first to get the British fleet out of the Channel.

French and Spanish ships were ordered to sail for the West Indies in the hope that Britain would give chase, but only thirty-three, under Admiral Villeneuve (1763–1806), managed to evade the British fleet that was lying in wait. Those that did escape were pursued by Admiral Lord Nelson in the *Victory* and Villeneuve returned to Cadiz in Spain.

Napoleon then ordered the French and Spanish fleets to the Mediterranean and two days later, October 21, 1805, the British attacked off Cape Trafalgar. The French were completely

Nelson, Britain's greatest admiral, was killed at Trafalgar.

defeated and Napoleon's invasion plans duly thwarted. But the victory was won at the cost of the life of Britain's greatest admiral, Nelson, who was killed during the battle.

1805
The Battle of Austerlitz

In July 1805 Britain, Austria, Russia, and Prussia formed a coalition against France. Napoleon's immediate reaction was to invade Germany and Austria. On October 22 he inflicted a serious defeat upon Austria at Ulm and also took Vienna. On November 28 he met the combined Russian and Austrian forces at Austerlitz. There were three emperors on the battlefield: Napoleon of France, Alexander (1777–1825) of Russia, and Francis II (1768–1825) of Austria.

Napoleon's army of 65,000 men was outnumbered by the Russians and Austrians who had some 83,000 troops at their command. Nevertheless the French were the overwhelming victors in the battle on December 2. They lost only about 7,000 men whereas some 35,000 Russians and Austrians were killed or captured. It was one of Napoleon's greatest victories.

As a result, Alexander's army was forced to retreat to the east, the Austrians signed the Peace of Pressburg, and the coalition ended.

1805
Wordsworth writes *The Prelude*

Some of the best loved English poems such as *Daffodils*, *On Westminster Bridge*, and *The Solitary Reaper* were written by William Wordsworth (1770–1850). In 1805 he wrote one of his longest poems, *The Prelude*, an autobiographical work, but it was not published until 1850. Wordsworth was made Poet Laureate in 1843.

1806
End of the Holy Roman Empire

The Holy Roman Empire is sometimes regarded as originating with Charlemagne (*see AD 800 Charlemagne crowned Holy Roman Emperor*) although some claim it began with the coronation

in AD 962 of Otto the Great, King of Germany, as Roman Emperor. The last emperor, Francis II of Austria, abolished the title following the defeat at Austerlitz, so that it would not pass to Napoleon.

1808
The Peninsular War

In July 1808 the Spanish, ruled by Napoleon's brother Joseph, rebelled and defeated the French at Baylen. The British realized that this was an opportunity to attack France through Spain and sent Sir Arthur Wellesley (1769–1852), later Duke of Wellington, to Portugal. He defeated the French at Vimeiro and then returned to England.

Sir John Moore (1761–1809) then took command and advanced into Spain to cut French lines of communication but Napoleon was in Spain at the time and he forced Moore to retreat to Corunna on the coast, where Moore was killed in 1809.

Wellington took a new army to Portugal and marched towards Madrid. He beat the French at Talavera but then had to retreat and he remained on the defensive until he achieved a victory at Salamanca in 1812. Wellington then took Madrid and, by a victory at Vittoria in 1813, drove the French out of the country.

1809
Metternich becomes Austrian chancellor

Prince Clemens Wenzel Lothar Metternich (1773–1859) was the principal figure in European politics following his appointment as Chancellor and Foreign Minister of Austria in 1809.

It was largely through his efforts that the Austrian Empire remained intact for the next thirty-nine years until the revolution of 1848 (*see 1848 European Revolutions*). The spirit of revolution had been rife in Europe ever since the French Revolution in 1789 and Metternich did his utmost to suppress it wherever it occurred. As foreign minister he raised the international status of his country and led the countries of Europe in a coalition that checked the career of

Napoleon; as a dedicated Austrian he always put the interests of his own country first.

In many ways Metternich was not typical of the time in which he lived, for he represented an age that was almost past. Many people resented his methods of preserving that age, but in so doing he ensured peace in Europe during the period of his office.

1810
Prizefight between Cribb and Molineaux

Tom Cribb (1781–1848) from Hanham, near Bristol, was the first of the bare-knuckled prize-fighters to achieve everlasting acclaim. This reputation was gained principally through his two fights with Tom Molineaux (1784–1818), a freed black slave. Cribb won both although he received a sound beating in the first and won the second only because Molineaux had an upset stomach.

1810
Northumberland miners' strike

Coal miners in Northumberland, England, ceased work in 1810 in support of their protest against an alteration of their terms of yearly binding.

This annual bond had been a cause of contention for many years and was largely responsible for a long-term strike in 1765.

In 1810 troops were called in but the strike was eventually settled through the intervention of a clergyman, William Nesfield.

1811
Luddite Riots

The first outbreaks of the Luddite Riots occurred in and around Nottingham, England, in 1811. They were possibly named after a workman, Ned Ludd. Historians have never agreed as to whether the riots were the result of a secret, national movement with branches throughout Britain, or whether they were a series of disconnected movements.

The members were factory hand-workers whose objective was to destroy new factory machinery. As the Industrial Revolution developed, men began to realize that the machines could work faster and more efficiently than they could and their jobs were seriously threatened.

Masked members of the movement broke into factories in the night and smashed up the new machines. The movement soon spread, and by 1812 machinery was being destroyed in Yorkshire, Lancashire, Derbyshire and Leicestershire. By 1813 many Luddites had been brought to trial at York Assizes where many were sentenced to death or transported overseas.

Napoleon's retreat from Moscow.

1811
Nash designs Regent's Park

John Nash (1752–1835) had already gained a considerable reputation as an architect when he came to the notice of the Prince Regent who engaged him to plan the new Regent's Park in London in 1811. Nash's greatness lay in his ability to plan whole districts of London as through they were landscape gardens.

1812
Battle of Borodino

The Battle of Borodino is remembered chiefly for the tremendous loss of life incurred by both the French and Russian armies. But it is also remembered as Napoleon's ill-fated attack on Moscow and the beginning of defeat for the French emperor.

Napoleon invaded the vast land mass of Russia with a huge army, narrowly defeating the Russians at Borodino, just west of Moscow. But when his army finally reached Moscow he found the Russians had burned the city and deserted it. His army was cold, hungry and sick; and forced to retreat, his men suffered miserably from the effects of the harsh Russian winter. Only 32,000 of his 600,000 strong army were to survive and the Russians were to lose 42,000 men out of 121,000. Meanwhile Napoleon hurried back to Paris to raise new levies.

This humiliating expedition encouraged the nations of Europe, who now saw some hope in massing their armies against Napoleon.

1812
Grimms' *Kinder- und Hausmärchen*

The brothers Grimm, Jacob Ludwig Carl (1785–1863) and Wilhelm Carl (1786–1859) both studied law at Marburg in Germany and both were students of folk-lore. In 1812 they published their first edition of *Kinder- und Hausmärchen* ('Fairy Tales'), which includes *Rumpelstiltskin* and *Hansel und Gretel*. The tales have been translated into many languages, so that children from all over the world are familiar with them.

1813
Battle of Nations

Encouraged by Napoleon's crushing setback in Russia, a new form of nationalism began to grow among the peoples of Europe. In Holland, Belgium and Italy, people increasingly wanted to be rid of Napoleon. Prussia reorganized its army, encouraging its people 'to defend the state'.

In October 1813 the combined armies of Prussia, Russia and Austria aided by Great Britain and Sweden defeated Napoleon near Leipzig, Germany, in the Battle of Nations. On March 21, 1814 Paris was taken and in April Napoleon abdicated. He was sent into exile on Elba, a little island off the coast of Italy.

Meanwhile the Bourbon monarchy was restored. Louis XVIII (1755–1824), brother of the executed Louis XVI was made king, but it was not long before he had made himself extremely unpopular by reversing some of the achievements of the Revolution. This opened the way for Napoleon's return from Elba (see 1815 Battle of Waterloo).

1813
Jane Austen's *Pride and Prejudice*

Jane Austen (1775–1817) was born in Hampshire, England, the daughter of a rector. She was a quiet, sensitive person and the author of six novels, the first of which, *Pride and Prejudice* did not appear until 1813. Her novels are wonderful documentaries of the English comfortable middle-class life in the nineteenth century, and her caustic wit and ability to depict rounded, three-dimensional characters have made her one of England's best-loved novelists.

1813
Elizabeth Fry visits Newgate Gaol

Elizabeth Fry (1780–1845) was an English Quaker. In 1813 a friend told her about the miserable conditions of prisoners in London's Newgate Gaol. Elizabeth went straight to the gaol where she found three hundred women, tried and untried, herded together with their children in filth and squalor. From that day she devoted herself to prison reform.

1814
Kean plays Shylock

Edmund Kean (1787–1833) was an extraordinary man who established a reputation on the English stage as the greatest tragic actor of his day. In 1814 he appeared as Shylock in Shakespeare's *Merchant of Venice* at Drury Lane. The supporting cast was poor, but Kean was an overwhelming success and for several years he dominated the English theatre.

1815
McAdam begins road construction

John Loudon McAdam (1756–1836) revolutionized road making in Britain. He first began experimenting in 1798 and concluded that roads should be made of successive layers of broken stone, each of them packed down tight by pressure before the next was laid. In 1815, as surveyor-general of Bristol roads, he began employing his method and it was soon in general use.

1815
Battle of Waterloo

When allied forces captured Paris in March 1814, the great French emperor, Napoleon Bonaparte was sent into exile on the Mediterranean island of Elba. Ten months later he escaped. He landed in France and advanced towards Paris. Old soldiers flocked to him and King Louis XVIII, so recently restored to his throne, fled abroad.

The allies gathered their forces. An Austrian force prepared to attack in the south, a vast Russian army advanced from the north. In Belgium, Marshal Blücher (1742–1819) commanded a Prussian army of over one hundred thousand while the Duke of Wellington had almost as many British, Dutch, German and Belgian troops assembled near Brussels. Napoleon moved fast. With 120,000 men he

Arthur Wellesley, 1st Duke of Wellington.

marched into Belgium to attack his enemies before they could unite.

Wellington had defeated most of Napoleon's best marshals during his campaign in Portugal and Spain (1808–14). He had not met Napoleon before the four-day campaign of Waterloo. The battle was a famous one, though neither general was at his best. Wellington did well to hold off the main French attack all day on June 18, forcing the Imperial Guard, the cream of Napoleon's army, to retreat.

Before sunset Blücher's Prussians began to arrive, and the French were doomed. Napoleon abdicated, and this time his enemies sent him farther away – to the island of St Helena in the South Atlantic. He did not return again.

1815
Congress of Vienna

The congress met in order to settle the affairs of Europe after the defeat of Napoleon in 1814. France was represented by the great Talleyrand (1754–1838), but the congress was dominated by Prince von Metternich (1773–1859) of Austria and Viscount Castlereagh (1769–1822) of Britain.

Both these men were strong conservatives, who believed that the revolutionary ideas released all over Europe after the French revolution of 1789 were responsible for the troubles throughout the continent since then, and ought

to be suppressed. Napoleon's escape from Elba forced the congress to reach a settlement, which it did just before Waterloo.

Most of the representatives at Vienna wanted to restore the balance of power and to restore rulers to the thrones they held before the French Revolution. The settlement was therefore a victory for the big powers over small states and for the old form of kingly government over republicanism. But it could not completely suppress the new ideas of freedom and democracy which the French Revolution had introduced and further uprisings occurred later. However, the settlement at Vienna did prevent a general, widespread war breaking out in Europe for a century.

1815
The Davy lamp

Sir Humphrey Davy (1778–1829), the British chemist, was a brilliantly inventive scientist who suggested (among other ideas) the use of nitrous oxide (laughing gas) as an anaesthetic (first used long after his death). He invented the miners' safety lamp in 1815 and refused to patent it, so that everyone might benefit quickly. Others invented similar lamps, notably George Stephenson, the railway engineer.

1816
Invention of the stethoscope

A stethoscope is the instrument used by doctors to listen to the sounds made by the heart, lungs or other organs inside a patient's body. Its inventor was a French doctor, René Laënnec (1781–1826), who first used a paper tube and later a wooden pipe. The modern stethoscope which hooks into both ears was developed later.

1818
Grillparzer's *Sappho*

Franz Grillparzer (1791–1872), Austria's greatest playwright, wrote chiefly poetic dramas, some of which are better read than acted. Grillparzer suffered intellectual persecution as a result of strict censorship in Austria,

A detail from *The Battle of Waterloo*, by Felix Philippoteaux (1815–84).

and he eventually stopped writing plays altogether. *Sappho*, written very quickly, is about love doomed to disappointment and the impossibility of reconciling life with art – themes that troubled Grillparzer personally.

1819
Peterloo Massacre

The years after the Battle of Waterloo were turbulent times in Britain. High unemployment brought the poorest workers close to starvation; there were strikes, riots and cases of machine-breaking (machines were blamed for unemployment). Calls for reform of politics and society were loud and continuous; cities like Manchester and Birmingham had a special grievance because they were not represented in Parliament. The government was worried by the disturbances and feared violent revolution.

On August 16, 1819 a large meeting was held on St Peter's Field, Manchester, to organize a petition for reform. The local magistrates, hearing talk of military drill and revolutionary flags, sent in soldiers to arrest the chief speaker, Henry Hunt (1773–1835). The soldiers were jostled by the angry people, cavalry went in to help them, discipline broke down and in the panic eleven people were killed and several hundred injured. The incident caused great anger; opponents of the government called it the 'Peterloo Massacre', recalling the slaughter at Waterloo.

1819
Géricault's *Raft of the Medusa*

This overwhelming picture, the most famous painting of the French artist Jean Louis Géricault (1791–1824), hangs in the Louvre, Paris. It shows survivors of the ship *Medusa*, desperate and dying, and others lying dead on their raft. The painting combines classical forms and Romantic intensity with the use of strange colouring. Géricault was also a remarkable painter of horses (in England he painted *Derby Day*). He died aged thirty-three – after falling from his horse.

1819
Voyage of the *Savannah*

The *Savannah* crossed the Atlantic, from Savannah, Georgia, to Liverpool, England, in twenty-five days. That was a very fast time, but what made her voyage important was that the *Savannah* was a steamship – the first to make the Atlantic crossing.

The *Savannah* was built in New York as an ordinary sailing ship with masts and, like all ships then, a wooden hull. But before she sailed she was fitted with steam power and two enormous paddle wheels. She still kept her sails and on her trans-Atlantic crossing she probably covered a greater distance under sail than steam. Her paddle wheels could be drawn up and laid on the deck when not in use.

All the early steamers were fitted with sails as well as steam-driven paddle wheels, because the early steam engines were not perfectly reliable and because sail-power saved coal, which was expensive and took up a lot of cargo space. By the end of the century, using screw-propellers instead of paddles, steamers were crossing the Atlantic in one-fifth of the time taken by the *Savannah*.

1819
Keats's *The Eve of St Agnes*

Though he died at twenty-six of tuberculosis, John Keats (1795–1821) is one of the greatest and most loved of British Romantic poets. He brought a sense of delight to English verse hardly known since the Elizabethans. The *Eve of St Agnes*, written like most of his best works during his passionate love for Fanny Brawne, is (said the poet Swinburne) 'a perfect and unsurpassable study in pure colour and clear melody'.

1819
The British acquire Singapore

The island of Singapore lies at the tip of the Malay peninsula. In 1819 it was a swampy, unattractive place, where no one lived except a few fishermen. The Dutch, who were the chief European power in the region, had overlooked the island when they were taking over all the important points in the Malay archipelago.

Stamford Raffles (1781–1826), an official of the British East India Company, persuaded Warren Hastings, then governor-general of India, that the place was worth having. The East India Company bought it from the Sultan of Johore, Raffles was appointed governor, and within four years he had made the settlement so prosperous that its annual trade was worth £2,500,000.

Situated approximately midway between India and China, Singapore was one of the most important British bases on the Far Eastern trade route for over 130 years.

1819
The start of the *Zollverein*

At the settlement of Europe made at the Congress of Vienna (1814–15) after the defeat of Napoleon, Germany became a confederation of independent states. A contest began between Austria and Prussia, the two largest, to decide which should dominate the new Germany.

One major economic problem in Germany was the existence of so many customs' barriers, not only between the different states but also between different provinces. The Prussians decided on a major reform of the customs' system, abolishing or reducing most tariffs.

It soon became obvious that if the system were to work well, the numerous small states around Prussia, or in some cases actually surrounded by it, would have to be included. Pressure was brought to bear on these states to join the Prussian *Zollverein* (customs' union). The first one to join was the tiny principality of Schwarzburg-Sonderhausen. Gradually, more and more German states were drawn into the *Zollverein*. In less than forty years, nearly all of modern Germany belonged, preparing the way for the foundation of the German Empire in 1871.

1820
Shelley's *Prometheus Unbound*

Percy Bysshe Shelley (1792–1822), friend of Keats and Byron, was full of boundless love for mankind, but contempt for most of man's institutions (church, government, etc.). Above all he was a brilliant Romantic poet, the equal of Keats and Wordsworth, perhaps for some people greater than either. *Prometheus Unbound* is a long, difficult, philosophical drama; the book also contains some of Shelley's sweetest lyrics.

1820
Lamartine's *Méditations* published

In his *Méditations poétiques et religieuses*, Alphonse de Prat de Lamartine (1790–1869) gracefully expressed feelings of love and despair, hope and melancholy, and man's affinity with nature. Lamartine was a politician as well as a poet, a stirring speaker and one of the leading spirits of the revolution of 1848. He later wrote many volumes of history in a vain attempt to pay off his debts.

1820
The Brontës settle at Haworth

The Rev Patrick Brontë had three extraordinary daughters, Charlotte (1816–55), Emily (1818–48) and Anne (1820–49), who passed almost their whole, sadly short, lives at Haworth parsonage. Charlotte wrote *Jane Eyre* (1847) and three other novels; Emily wrote *Wuthering Heights* (1847) and Anne *The Tenant of Wildfell Hall* (1848). Their brother Branwell showed talent as a painter, but drank himself into an early grave.

Charlotte Brontë in 1850.

The Hay Wain by Constable.

1821
Greek nationalist revolt

Throughout the nineteenth century the empire of the Turks, which included south-east Europe and the Middle East, seemed to be on the point of collapse. The first people to launch a major war of independence against their Turkish masters were the Greeks. The Greeks attracted much sympathy in Europe, but the situation was complicated by the conflicting interests of the major powers, and by the tendency of the Greeks to fight each other no less bloodily than they fought the Turks.

Russia supported the Greeks; Britain and France favoured a compromise. In 1827 these three powers joined in destroying the Turkish-Egyptian fleet at Navarino, when it refused to obey instructions to withdraw from Greek waters. Next year Russia attacked by land and the Turks were forced to yield.

The Greeks gained their independence in 1830, though within limited boundaries. The modern frontiers were not achieved until the Balkan wars of 1912–13.

1821
Constable paints *The Hay Wain*

Exhibited in Paris three years later, this painting of a waggon fording a mill stream caused a sensation such as English artists have seldom achieved in France. John Constable (1776–1837) was perhaps the greatest painter of the English countryside especially the broad landscapes of his native Suffolk. With his contemporary, Turner, Constable influenced the great French school of Impressionism.

1822
Ampère's *Observations electro-dynamiques*

The unit for measuring an electric current is called an 'ampere', or 'amp' for short. It is named after the great French physicist and mathematician, André Marie Ampère (1775–1836), who was one of the founders of the science of electromagnetism. In 1822 he published his discoveries in a work called *Observations electro-dynamiques*.

1823
Beethoven's ninth symphony

The ninth and last symphony of Ludwig van Beethoven (1770–1827) was written when the composer was almost totally deaf and gloom was gathering about him. But there is no gloom in this noble and glorious choral symphony.

Ludwig van Beethoven

Written for the London Philharmonic Society, it was planned as early as 1816, as the third of a group of three symphonies.

The great events of Beethoven's sad but heroic life are all musical. Born in Bonn of Flemish descent, he went to Vienna in 1792 to study with Haydn (who was too upset by the recent death of Mozart to be much help), and was soon very popular as a pianist.

Growing deafness made Beethoven feel depressed and persecuted, though his fame increased rapidly after about 1800. He never gave up: 'I will seize Fate by the throat', he swore, and for nearly thirty years he produced a stream of marvellous works. He revolutionized most forms of orchestral and choral music; his influence on music is as impossible to measure as Shakespeare's influence on literature.

1823
The Monroe Doctrine

This principle of United States foreign policy declared that no interference by European powers would be tolerated in North or South America. It was proclaimed by President James Monroe (1758–1831) but its real author was John Quincy Adams (1767–1848), the Secretary of State.

It was provoked by European threats to reconquer the Spanish colonies in South America, which had recently gained independence. The doctrine was supported by Britain, and in practice it could be enforced only by the British navy.

Since 1823 the Monroe Doctrine has been often modified, restated, and occasionally challenged. The most recent example was the construction of Soviet Russian missile bases in Cuba; the United States government forced the Russians to dismantle them in the 'Cuba Crisis' of 1962 (*see 1961 Kennedy becomes US President*).

1823
Babbage's calculating machine

Charles Babbage (1792–1871), 'father of the computer', was a professor of mathematics at Cambridge University. In 1823 he began work on a calculating machine. It was never completed, nor was his second machine, which he called an 'analytical engine'. Nevertheless, Babbage's 'engine' was the direct ancestor of the modern digital computer.

Part of Babbage's 'analytical engine'.

1824
Death of Byron

Many people were shocked by Lord Byron (1788–1824): 'mad, bad and dangerous to know', someone called him. Extremely handsome, fearlessly outspoken, and determined to experience everything that life offered, he was a romantic man as well as a Romantic poet (*Childe Harold, Don Juan*). When the Greeks rebelled against their Turkish overlords (*see 1821 Greek nationalist revolt*) Byron threw himself into their struggle, but he died of marsh fever at Missolonghi.

1825
Opening of the Stockton and Darlington Railway

The Stockton and Darlington Railway was the first public railway in the world which carried goods and passengers by locomotive. But it was not much of a railway by modern standards. Its real purpose was to carry freight, and for fifteen of its forty kilometres the carriages could run downhill without the help of the engine.

Few passengers used the railway, and most of those who did hired a carriage which was drawn by horses (half the line was already built before the company decided that a steam locomotive should be used at all). There was no regular passenger service until some years later.

Still, the little Stockton–Darlington Railway marked the beginning of the great age of railway-building: twenty years later Britain had a railway network of over three thousand kilometres of track.

1825
Portugal acknowledges Brazilian independence

When Portugal finally recognized Pedro I as emperor of its former colony of Brazil, the largest country in South America became an independent state. In the same year Bolivia, taking its name from the great liberator, Simón Bolívar (1783–1830), the 'George Washington of South America', declared its independence from Spain. The colonial era in South America was over.

Except for Brazil, all South America had been under Spanish control, and the eclipse of Spain during the Napoleonic period (1808–14) encouraged nationalists throughout the continent to fight for independence. Besides Bolívar, the liberators of South America included José de San Martín (1778–1850) and Bernardo O'Higgins (1778–1842). San Martín's leadership was especially important in Argentina (independent 1816), while O'Higgins took the leading role in Chile (independent 1818).

Simón Bolívar

1826

Menai Bridge opened

This 175 metre suspension bridge linking Wales with the island of Anglesey was the world's longest suspension span. Still in use, it was built by Thomas Telford (1757–1834), the most famous British engineer of his day. Telford built the Conway Suspension Bridge at about the same time, but this Scottish civil engineer also built roads, bridges, canals, docks, harbours and waterways, many of which are still in use today.

1826

Cooper's *The Last of the Mohicans*

James Fenimore Cooper (1789–1851) was reading an English novel one day in 1819 and said to his wife he could write a better book himself. She challenged him to try, and in the next thirty years he wrote more than forty. Many were adventurous novels about pioneer life in America, including *The Last of the Mohicans*, but he also wrote several books about the young American republic.

1826

Niépce prints photographic image

Joseph Nicéphore Niépce (1765–1833) was one of the French pioneers of photography. He discovered that an image could be permanently recorded by the action of sunlight on a metal plate coated with asphaltum – a substance used as a ground in etching. Such a plate was printed in Paris in 1826, when Louis Daguerre approached Niépce to form a partnership. The successful daguerreotype process was perfected after Niépce's death (*see 1839 Daguerre demonstrates daguerreotype*).

1827

Schubert: *Die Winterreise*

Die Winterreise (The Winter Journey) was one of the last works of the prolific Austrian composer Franz Schubert (1797–1828), who died of typhoid in the following year. In Schubert's mind poetry turned itself into music as soon as he read it. He composed at terrific speed (though he often revised carefully) and he is probably the greatest writer of *lieder* (German songs) who ever lived. He composed more than 600 songs, as well as nine symphonies and much chamber music.

1827

Ohm's law is published

One of the basic laws of electricity was discovered through the experiments of the German scientist Georg Simon Ohm (1787–1854), and published in a pamphlet in 1827.

Ohm's law is concerned with the relationship of resistance to potential difference and current in an electrical circuit. It is sometimes written as $I = \frac{E}{R}$, in which I is the current measured in amperes, E is the potential difference, and R is the resistance. The unit used for measurement of electrical resistance is now called an ohm, in honour of the discoverer of this law.

1827
Mendelssohn's *Midsummer Night's Dream*

Felix Mendelssohn (1809–47) wrote this as an overture to Shakespeare's play but besides his own compositions, he was famous as a pianist, as a conductor, and for his revival of the music of Bach. This German composer was especially popular in England, and once entertained Queen Victoria by playing (on the piano) *Rule Britannia* with his right hand, whilst his left played the Austrian national anthem.

1827
Manzoni's *I promessi sposi*

Alessandro Manzoni (1785–1873) was the greatest Italian writer of the Romantic period and *I promessi sposi* ('The Betrothed') was his greatest work, perhaps the greatest Italian work of the century. It was an historical novel set in seventeenth-century Milan during the Spanish occupation. Manzoni was already well-known as a poet, but after the last volume of *I promessi sposi* was published in 1827 he became a great national figure.

1828
Death of Chaka

Chaka was the warrior-king of the Zulus. He turned them from a humble little tribe into a powerful military nation. Under his rule, which began soon after 1800, the Zulu *impis* (regiments) controlled almost the whole of Natal.

Chaka introduced the 'buffalo's horns' formation (troops drawn up in a crescent) and the short-bladed *assegai* (spear) for fighting at close quarters. He liked Europeans and allowed the British to settle at Port Elizabeth. In 1828 Chaka was assassinated by his successor, Dingaan.

1829
Rossini's *William Tell*

The last opera of the Italian composer Gioacchino Antonio Rossini (1792–1868), *Guillaume Tell* ('William Tell'), about the Swiss hero, was produced in Paris, where Rossini lived. Except for the marvellously comic *Il Barbiere di Seviglia* ('The Barber of Seville'), it is his most famous work. During the next few years Rossini wrote some religious music and songs.

1829
Stephenson's *Rocket*

This rugged little railway engine was built by George Stephenson (1781–1848) and is preserved in the Science Museum, London. It defeated its rivals in trials held to choose a locomotive for the Liverpool–Manchester Railway, winning the £500 prize. It reached a speed of 48km/h and triumphantly proved the efficiency of Stephenson's multi-tubular boiler.

1829
London Metropolitan Police founded

A criminal who got caught in the early nineteenth century was likely to suffer very severe punishment. But most criminals were not caught, because there was no regular police force. Law enforcement was carried out by two or three constables appointed by each parish. They had no training and did not wear uniforms.

Many people were afraid that a regular police force would allow the government too much power to suppress the freedom of ordinary citizens. But with crime so high, police seemed necessary.

When he became Home Secretary in 1821, Sir Robert Peel (1788–1850) decided that London had to have a system of police. After a long delay (eight years), a force of three thousand top-hatted constables was created to police the area within twenty kilometres of Charing Cross. Later, the system was introduced to the whole country.

1830
The French capture Algiers

King Charles X of France (1757–1836) hoped that a glorious imperial exploit would make his government less unpopular, but less than a month after the capture of Algiers he lost his throne (*see 1830 The July Revolution*).

The French had been quarrelling with the Dey of Algiers for some time. When the Dey lost his temper with the French consul and hit him in the face with his fan, an expedition was sent against the North African city.

Algiers had once beaten off an attack by the Emperor Charles V, ruler of half Europe in the early sixteenth century, but the French under the Comte de Bourmont (1773–1846) captured it without too much trouble. It took them much longer to conquer the surrounding country. The skilful Arab leader Abd-el-Kader (1807–83) was not captured until 1847. Subsequently the French ruled Algeria until 1962.

Berlioz possessed a genius for large-scale orchestral works that made him one of the great French composers.

1830
Berlioz's *Symphonie Fantastique*

This was the first major work of the great French Romantic composer, Hector Berlioz (1803–69), and its first performance in 1830 revealed an array of new musical ideas. It has always remained the most popular work of this devoted musician. Berlioz gained his musical education against fierce family opposition and earned a living for thirty years as a music critic.

1830
The July Revolution

In 1814 the French monarchy was restored and French aristocrats returned from exile to their estates. But the French people did not forget the ideas of the French Revolution and the liberal reforms of Napoleon.

The Bourbon kings Louis XVIII (1814–24) and Charles X (1824–30) felt little sympathy with the hopes and ideas of most of their subjects. Indeed, before he succeeded his brother, Charles was the leader of a fiercely reactionary party. As king, he put extreme conservatives in charge of

Louis Philippe, King of France 1830–48, came to the throne as a result of the July Revolution.

the government. Many feared that he was about to create a dictatorship.

A general election in which the government lost its majority in the Chamber of Deputies brought matters to a head. The government prepared orders to dissolve the Chamber and change the rules in elections, and to enforce strict censorship of the press.

The printers of Paris, threatened with unemployment, shut up shop, and others soon copied them. Angry crowds gathered in the July heat. The government was taken by surprise, and when the revolt began, there were not enough troops to control it. The tricolour (Revolutionary flag) flew again from the towers of Notre Dame cathedral.

Finally the king realized he would have to abdicate. The Chamber invited Louis Philippe, a member of the junior royal house of Orléans, to take the throne. So began the eighteen-year reign of the 'July Monarchy'.

1830
Belgium wins independence

When the Dutch gained their independence in the late sixteenth century, the southern provinces of the Netherlands (roughly equal to modern Belgium) remained under the rule of Spain, and later Austria. During the Napoleonic wars they were overrun by the French, and when Napoleon was defeated in 1814, they were reunited with the Netherlands as one kingdom.

The union with the Dutch was not popular in Belgium. Although the two peoples had much in common, problems arose out of differences in religion, language, and social customs.

Under the Dutch king, the Belgians felt – and with justice – that they were treated as second-class citizens. Riots broke out against Dutch rule in 1830 and quickly developed into a full-scale revolution. The Belgians declared their independence (*see 1830 Palmerston becomes foreign secretary*), and next year drew up a national constitution, inviting Leopold of Saxe-Coburg (1790–1865) to be their first king.

1830
Liverpool-Manchester Railway opens

This was the first public railway built specially to carry passengers in a train drawn by a steam locomotive. The chief engineer was George Stephenson, who had to build the line across the ten kilometre bog of Chat Moss – one of the great stories of pioneer construction engineering.

The line was opened at a great public ceremony on September 15, with the Duke of Wellington attending. But a horrible accident spoiled the occasion. William Huskisson, a former cabinet minister, was run over by the train and died soon afterwards.

The opening of the Liverpool–Manchester Railway marks the true beginning of the railway age. Until then, few people were certain that steam locomotives could provide a practical form of public transport. The success of the railway put all doubts to rest. Railway companies blossomed like flowers and steel tracks began to spread rapidly across Britain.

Delacroix's painting *Liberty Leading the People* was inspired by the July Revolution in Paris.

1830
Delacroix's *Liberty Leading the People*

This famous painting by the very fine Romantic painter, Eugène Delacroix (1798–1863), was inspired by the July Revolution. 'If I haven't fought for my country at least I have painted for her', Delacroix wrote to his brother, a soldier. His delight in rich colours and physical vigour brought a lively new spirit into painting, and his influence was perhaps even greater than his actual works.

1830
Palmerston becomes foreign secretary

It is as Whig foreign secretary that Viscount Palmerston (1784–1865) gained his reputation, although he did become prime minister of Britain twice (1855–58 and 1859–65). He started his political life as a Tory but in 1830 he changed sides to become foreign secretary under the Whig, Lord Grey.

In his later years Palmerston personified all that was aggressive about Victorian Britain's foreign policy. He was considered a tactless man; always intent on reminding other countries that Britain was a very powerful nation. This earned him the name 'firebrand Palmerston'.

He was nevertheless a great champion of Liberalism. His first major success was setting up Belgium as an independent state, and he later openly criticized the repressive policies of Austria, Prussia and Russia, aiding both Italy and Hungary during the 1848 revolutions that spread through Europe.

All his life he was a great orator, and he was admired even by those who disapproved of his policy.

1830
Sturt explores the Murray river

Captain Charles Sturt (1795–1869), an officer in the British army, was posted to Australia in the 1820s and became interested in exploring the

unknown interior of New South Wales. On his first expedition in 1828 he discovered the Darling river.

Setting off again in 1830 Sturt followed the Murrumbidgee down to its junction with the Murray, the largest river in Australia. He traced the Murray down to Lake Alexandrina, though he failed to discover the mouth of the river.

On his third expedition, 1844–45, he lost his sight completely, and never fully recovered it. He died in England in 1869, just before receiving the knighthood he had been promised.

1830
Hugo's *The Hunchback of Notre Dame*

Victor Hugo (1802–85) became a giant figure in nineteenth century French literature. *Notre Dame de Paris* ('The Hunchback of Notre Dame'), a marvellous recreation of medieval Paris, belonged to his first great period of work in the 1820s and 1830s. Many of his later works were written during nearly twenty years in exile in Guernsey. His funeral in 1885 was a great occasion in France.

1831
Faraday discovers electrical induction

Michael Faraday (1791–1867) once refused to become president of the Royal Society because

Faraday's laboratory at the Royal Institution, where he carried out his research into the nature of electricity.

he was afraid it would delay his research. He was the ideal scientist: calm, careful, clear, humble, but a genius. A blacksmith's son, he had very little education. Through Sir Humphry Davy (1778–1829) he got a job as a laboratory assistant in the Royal Institution, and rose to become professor of chemistry.

Faraday's greatest work was in electricity, not chemistry. From experiments, he deduced that a magnet is capable of producing electricity, and from this followed his famous report to the Royal Society in 1831 of his discovery – electro-magnetic induction. Then it was a short step to his invention of the electrical generator.

Faraday made many other discoveries in electricity and chemistry, including what is now known as electrolysis. He was the first scientist to emphasize the importance of the 'field' rather than the 'particle', and this connects him with Einstein and the theory of relativity.

1831
Pushkin's *Eugene Onegin*

The greatest work of Alexander Sergeievich Pushkin (1799–1837) was at last finished in 1831. Its author called it a 'novel in verse' and it owed much to Pushkin's study of Byron's poetry. He came from an aristocratic family, and married a silly though beautiful girl. Pushkin died in a duel with one of her admirers.

1831
Chopin settles in Paris

Like many great musicians, Frédéric Chopin (1810–49) showed his genius very early (he composed his first *Polonaise* before he was ten). He died of tuberculosis while still young. Born in Poland of a French father, he was a brilliant pianist and perhaps played his own exquisite and lyrical compositions and lively dances (he wrote little orchestral music) better than anyone else.

1832
Morse invents the telegraph

The idea of an electromagnetic recording telegraph came to Samuel Morse (1791–1872) as he was on a ship returning to New York to take up his job as professor of painting. He also devised the system of dots and dashes, now called Morse Code, for sending messages.

Morse did not have much money and he was not able to spend all his time on his invention. It was not until 1844, after the US Congress had voted money to string a copper wire between Washington and Baltimore, that Morse, from the Supreme Court building in Washington, tapped out the first telegraph message: 'What hath God wrought'.

Although the US government refused to buy Morse's telegraph, he sold the system to private companies and, unlike most inventors, made a profit out of his invention.

1832
Great Reform Bill

The cause of 'reform' in Britain was the greatest subject of argument in the early nineteenth century. What people meant by reform was, first and foremost, reform of parliament.

Very few people were allowed to vote in parliamentary elections (about 435,000 out of a population of nearly 20,000,000), and the seats in the House of Commons were allocated in strange and unreasonable ways. A thinly populated county like Cornwall had twenty-four members, while booming industrial cities like Manchester and Birmingham had none. Some 'pocket' boroughs had only ten or twelve voters,

A Morse Code operator. Samuel Morse's code is still used internationally for telegraphic communications.

while other constituencies had several thousand.

Reform had to wait until the Whigs, the party who supported it, formed a government in 1830. Then followed two years of crisis, including another election, two resignations by the prime minister, Earl Grey, and threats against the anti-Reform House of Lords.

The bill was finally passed in 1832. Its first effects were small: pocket boroughs were abolished, big cities gained parliamentary representation, and the number of voters was increased about fifty per cent. The real importance of the Act was that it opened the way for more democratic reforms in the future.

1833
Factory Act

Most people in the early nineteenth century believed that industry would be profitable only if governments did not interfere with it. But some were shocked by the grim working conditions and long hours worked by labourers, especially children.

In England a parliamentary committee in 1832 revealed the horrible truth of child labour in textile factories and gave Lord Ashley (later Earl of Shaftesbury, 1801–85) the opportunity to begin his great career in defence of the poor and helpless.

The Factory Act of 1833 was a disappointment to Ashley, who had hoped to enforce a maximum working day of ten hours for all workers. However, it did stop the employment of children under nine, it limited hours of work for older children, and it introduced a system of inspectors to make sure the law was obeyed by the factory owners.

1833
Abolition of Slavery

News of the passing of the act abolishing slavery in British colonies was brought to William Wilberforce (1759–1833) as he lay dying. Wilberforce had spent his entire political career fighting against the slave trade.

Slavery had been illegal in England since 1772, but the slave trade continued in full flood. About 20,000 Africans were transported to America every year by ships from Liverpool, Bristol and London. The opponents of the trade, called 'Abolitionists', fought long and hard against it. Finally, a motion to declare it illegal was carried by Charles James Fox (1749–1806) through parliament in 1807.

The next step was to persuade other countries to abolish the trade, and to stop illegal trading (profits were so large that slave-traders could afford to lose two ships out of three). France, Spain and Portugal soon agreed to stop trading, but as long as slavery itself was legal, illegal slave-trading went on.

Britain's abolition of slavery cost the government £20,000,000 in compensation to slave-owners. But it was an important step towards ending an ancient evil.

The cruel slave trade, campaigned against by Wilberforce.

1834
Hundred Views of Mount Fuji

Hokusai (1760–1849), the most famous of Japanese artists among Europeans, was born poor and, in spite of the number of his drawings (over thirty thousand) and the popularity of his prints, died poor too. He made plenty of money but spent it fast. His *Hundred Views of Mount Fuji*, the mountain whose beautiful shape might have been designed by Hokusai himself, were published in three volumes, in monochrome (one colour).

1834
Tolpuddle Martyrs

Although trade unions were not illegal in 1834, they were closely restricted by laws against secret political societies. The 'Tolpuddle Martyrs' were a small group of farm labourers in Dorset who formed a union to try to obtain better working conditions and pay.

The British government had been terrified of any sign that workers were getting together, because of the appalling consequences this had had during the French Revolution of 1789. The authorities became suspicious of the Dorset labourers, who were led by George Loveless. They were prosecuted, at Dorchester, because they had carried out a secret initiation ceremony in which oaths were sworn.

The 'Tolpuddle Martyrs' were sentenced to seven years transportation in a penal colony in Australia, but two years later the sentence was remitted. Their case became a famous rallying cry for early trade unions.

1834
Balzac's *Le Père Goriot*

This is one of the most popular novels of Honoré de Balzac (1799–1850). Balzac, who is to France what Dickens is to England, regarded himself as 'secretary' to French society. His vast, detailed *Comédie Humaine* ('Human Comedy'), teeming with characters, was an attempt to portray every aspect of French history in his lifetime. *Le Père Goriot* is one of the most popular masterpieces in this collection.

1835
Mme Tussaud's opens in London

Marie Tussaud (1760–1850) was an expert modeller in wax. In Paris, she made many heads of people executed in the French Revolution, and was imprisoned herself for a short time. After a successful show in London (1802) she travelled around England and eventually settled in Baker Street, and opened her permanent exhibition in nearby Marylebone Road, where it remains today.

1835
Andersen's Fairy Tales published

Hans Christian Andersen (1805–75) had an unhappy childhood. A teacher treated him badly and fellow-students jeered at him. *The Ugly Duckling* was in a way about himself, for he became a famous writer of children's fairy stories, loved all over the world. He wanted to be a famous novelist and playwright, but there he was less successful.

1835
Colt patents revolver

The first successful revolver, the prototype from which all later revolvers are descended, was patented by the American gunsmith, Samuel Colt (1814–62). He also made rifles and shot-guns with revolving chambers, but his first factory went bankrupt and it was not until the 1850s that Colt had a big success with his Navy revolver. His guns were used by the army and the navy in the American Civil War.

1836
The Great Trek

The British took over the Cape Colony, South Africa, from the Dutch in 1814. The settlers of Dutch descent were not happy under British rule and felt that native African peoples were too much favoured. Under Piet Retief and others about ten thousand Boers ('farmers') left Cape Colony and trekked with their ox waggons to the north-east, away from British influence. On the way they came into bloody conflict with the Zulus. Retief and many more were killed.

When Natal was annexed by Britain to prevent the Boers establishing a republic, they moved north, across the Vaal river. Eventually the British acknowledged independent Boer republics in the Transvaal and Orange Free State.

A view of Mount Fuji over a river at sunset, by Hokusai – one of the most famous Japanese artists at the end of the 18th century.

In 1902, after the South African War, the Boer republics became British colonies, and later joined the Union of South Africa.

1836
Battle of the Alamo

In 1835 Texas was part of Mexico, but inhabited by many Anglo-American immigrants. When the Mexican government tried to stop immigration and refused various demands by the white settlers, rebellion broke out. Sam Houston (1793–1863) was appointed the Texan commander.

In February 1836 the Mexican general and president, Santa Anna (1795–1876) marched into San Antonio and besieged the Alamo, a thick-walled fortress covering just over one hectare which had once been a mission settlement. It was defended by less than two hundred men, including Davy Crockett (1786–1836), and was commanded by William Travis (1809–36) and James Bowie (1799–1836).

The siege lasted twelve days, then Santa Anna ordered his 2,400 men to make an all-out attack. Two assaults were beaten off, but the third succeeded, and all the defenders were killed.

Two months later Santa Anna was routed by Sam Houston at San Jacinto, where the Texan war-cry, 'Remember the Alamo!' was first heard. Texas became an independent republic, but nine years later it joined the United States.

1837
Accession of Victoria

The British people thought that the slight, eighteen-year-old girl made a pleasant change after her two fat and foolish uncles who had reigned before her. She was to reign longer than any other English monarch, dying in 1901. Reigning over the richest, strongest country in the world for so long a time, Victoria (1819–1901) grew to be a more interesting person than perhaps she was by nature.

As a young queen she was helped by her first prime minister, the amiable, fatherly Lord Melbourne (1779–1848), and by her dedicated husband, the German prince, Albert (1819–61), whom she married in 1840. After Albert's death in 1861 Victoria retreated into gloomy widowhood, refusing to play her full part as sovereign.

Another prime minister, Disraeli (1804–81), flattered her out of her gloom in the 1870s and in her later years this dumpy, lame, little old lady in a lace bonnet became a figure of prestige, before whom cabinet ministers trembled.

1837
Dickens publishes the *Pickwick Papers*

Publication of *The Posthumous Papers of the Pickwick Club* launched the career of the greatest English popular novelist, Charles Dickens (1812–70). His finest gift was his creation of vivid, often humorous characters, but he was also a powerful critic of the evils of Victorian society. Novels by Dickens include *Oliver Twist* (1839), *Nicholas Nickleby* (1839), *David Copperfield* (1850), *A Tale of Two Cities* (1859) and *Great Expectations* (1861). Many were first published as serials, appearing monthly.

A scene from *Oliver Twist*.

1838
The People's Charter

The Chartist movement, a working-class movement for reform, grew out of disappointment at the results of the Reform Act of 1832 and the failure of Robert Owen's trade unionism. The Charter was drawn up by William Lovett

Victoria in old age. Her reign, which lasted into the twentieth century, saw Great Britain as the most powerful and industrially advanced nation in the world. Victoria's empire covered a quarter of the world.

(1800–77), founder of the London Working Men's Association, and Francis Place (1771–1854), a well-known radical. Most of the reforms it demanded – votes for all adult males, constituencies of equal size, salaries for MPs etc. – now seem moderate; but in 1838 they seemed too dangerously democratic.

Chartism also attracted more militant figures, like Feargus O'Connor (1794–1855), who was particularly active in the movement.

A national convention was held in 1839 and a Chartist petition with over a million signatures (some, it turned out, forged) was presented to parliament, which rejected it. O'Connor's call for violence resulted only in a few small riots and strikes. The Chartist movement remained very active and was revived in 1848. After that, its cause was taken up by other organizations.

MUSIC 1720–1920

1720 First mention of clarinet as orchestral instrument.
1721 Johann Sebastian Bach writes his six Brandenburg concertos.
1722 Jean Philippe Rameau lays foundations of modern musical harmony.
1727 Development of sonata form with two themes.
1729 J.S. Bach writes St. Matthew Passion; George Frederick Handel writes six oboe concertos.
1732 Birth of Franz Joseph Haydn, composer and 'father' of the orchestral symphony.
1741 Handel composes his Messiah.
1750 Death of J.S. Bach; first printed music (Leipzig).
1756 Birth of Wolfgang Amadeus Mozart, composer and 'father' of the piano concerto.
1759 Death of G.F. Handel.
1767 Earliest mention of a piano in England.
1770 Birth of Ludwig van Beethoven, composer.
1782 Birth of Niccolo Paganini, violinist.
1787 Mozart writes opera The Marriage of Figaro.
1791 Death of Mozart.
1792 Haydn's oratorio The Creation performed in Vienna.
1795 Pedro Albeniz, founder of modern piano style, born, in Spain; Beethoven composes two piano concertos.
1797 Birth of Franz Schubert, composer.
1803 Birth of Hector Berlioz, French composer.
1804 Beethoven writes his Eroica symphony.
1809 Death of Haydn; Felix Mendelssohn, composer, born.
1810 Birth of Frederick Chopin pianist/composer and Robert Schumann, composer.
1811 Birth of Franz Liszt, pianist and composer.
1813 Birth of Richard Wagner and Giuseppe Verdi, both opera composers.
1814 Maelzel invents metronome – musical timekeeper; Schubert writes his famous song The Erl King.

1822 Schubert's Unfinished Symphony; Royal Academy of Music founded, London; Liszt makes debut as a pianist.
1823 Sebastian Erard makes a grand piano.
1824 Beethoven's Choral Symphony performed in Vienna.
1825 Johann Strauss, waltz composer, born.
1826 Mendelssohn composes overture to A Midsummer Night's Dream, and Berlioz his Fantastic Symphony.
1827 Death of Beethoven.
1828 Death of Schubert.
1829 Mendelssohn revives the music of J.S. Bach.
1830 Development of Romantic (expressive) music.
1833 Chopin writes his 12 études (concert studies); birth of Johannes Brahms, composer.
1835 Charles Camille Saint-Saëns, French composer, born.
1837 Berlioz writes Requiem; tuned kettledrums first used in orchestras.
1838 Jenny Lind, singer known as 'The Swedish Nightingale' made her debut in Stockholm; Georges Bizet, composer, born.
1839 Verdi's first opera performed at La Scala, Milan.
1840 Adolphe Sax invents the saxophone; birth of Peter Ilytch Tchaikovsky, famous Russian composer; death of Niccolo Paganini, violinist.
1841 Birth of Antonín Dvořák, Czech composer.
1843 Wagner's opera The Flying Dutchman performed; tuba first used in orchestras; birth of Edvard Grieg, Norwegian composer.
1846 Death of Mendelssohn.
1849 Death of Chopin.
1856 Death of Schumann.
1858 Giacomo Puccini, Italian opera composer, born.
1860 Birth of Gustav Mahler, Austrian composer.
1861 Brahms' first piano concerto.
1862 Birth of Claude Debussy, French composer.

1865 Birth of Jean Sibelius, Finnish composer.
1866 Berlioz writes his famous opera The Trojans.
1868 Modest Mussorgsky writes Boris Gudanov, the famous Russian opera.
1869 Death of Berlioz.
1871 Verdi's opera Aida first performed in Cairo.
1873 Birth of Sergei Rachmaninov, composer.
1875 Bizet dies a few days after the first performance of his controversial opera Carmen; Tchaikovsky's first piano concerto; Trial by Jury the first Gilbert and Sullivan opera, produced.
1876 Birth of Spanish cellist Pablo Casals; first complete performance of Wagner's 'Ring' cycle of operas based on German legends.
1877 Saint-Saëns' Samson and Delilah opera; Tchaikovsky's Swan Lake ballet performed.
1880 Tchaikovsky's 1812 Overture; Brahms' Hungarian dances.
1882 Birth of Igor Stravinsky, Russian composer.
1883 Metropolitan Opera House, New York, opened; death of Wagner.
1886 Death of Liszt.
1891 Birth of Sergei Prokofiev, Russian composer.
1893 Death of Tchaikovsky; Verdi's last opera, Falstaff.
1897 Death of Brahms.
1900 Puccini's opera Tosca.
1902 Enrico Caruso, Italian opera singer, makes his first recordings.
1906 Dmitri Shostakovitch, Russian composer, born.
1910 Stravinsky's Firebird ballet music.
1916 Birth of Yehudi Menuhin, violinist.
1917 Salzburg Music Festival founded.
1918 Edward Elgar, English composer writes Cello Concerto; death of Debussy, founder of Impressionist music.
1920 Stravinsky's Symphonies of Wind Instruments.

1838

Archimedes is launched

Though not the first steamship to be built with a screw-propeller, the SS *Archimedes* proved that a propeller was more efficient than paddle-wheels. Built in England by the inventor Sir Francis Pettit Smith (1808–74), the 207-tonne *Archimedes* could maintain an average speed of 7.5 knots. This success persuaded I.K. Brunel to fit a propeller to his great ocean-going steamer, the *Great Britain* (*see 1858 Brunel launches Great Eastern*).

1838

Wreck of the *Forfarshire*

On September 7, 1838 the *Forfarshire*, bound from Hull to Dundee, was wrecked on the rocks of the Farne Islands. The lighthouse keeper and his daughter, Grace Darling (1815–42), a frail girl, bravely set out in a small, flat-bottomed boat and succeeded in rescuing five people.

Grace's father made a second trip with two of the rescued, and took off four more people – the last alive out of sixty-three on board. The exploit made Grace Darling a national heroine.

1838

First Afghan War

Fear of Russian expansion caused some strange policies in British India, none more disastrous than the attempt of the governor-general, Lord Auckland (1784–1849), to replace Dost Mohammed (1793–1863) as emir of Afghanistan – he had made himself ruler in 1826.

The British expedition, though badly organized, took the Afghan capital of Kabul in April 1839, but foolishly remained in occupation after Dost Mohammed had surrendered. Communications across the North-West Frontier began to crumble and rebellion broke out in Kabul. Early in 1842 the British began a disorderly retreat, under constant attack by Afghan tribesmen. Only one man reached safety.

A subsequent campaign restored British prestige somewhat by recapturing Kabul to release British prisoners, before withdrawing to India.

The second Afghan War (1878–80) resulted in British occupation and control of Afghan foreign relations. The emirs kept internal self-government, and after the brief, third Afghan War, Britain recognized the full independence of Afghanistan in 1921.

1839

Daguerre demonstrates daguerreotype

With others, Louis Daguerre (1789–1851) had been experimenting for many years with methods of recording a picture, and in 1839 he displayed the method he had invented to the Paris Academy of Sciences.

A polished silver plate, coated with silver iodide, was exposed, in a camera, for three or four minutes. The image was developed by mercury vapour, which condensed on the plate in proportion to the amount of light that had reached it, and was 'fixed' by a salt solution. Prints could then be made from the plate.

The daguerreotype, as it was called, immediately became very popular. A number of improvements in the process were made by Daguerre and others. Modern photography, however, is more directly descended from the method of W. H. Fox Talbot (1800–77) who recorded images on paper and published his results a few months before Daguerre.

1839

Liszt's European tour begins

Franz Liszt (1811–86) was acknowledged, even by Chopin, as the world's greatest pianist. His European tour was a huge success, though the profits were soon dissipated by Liszt's openhanded generosity. As a composer he is probably best remembered for his Hungarian rhapsodies and symphonic 'tone poems', a form he virtually invented.

1840

McMillan's bicycle

The bicycle developed from the 'velocipede', which had no pedals and was propelled by the rider, sitting on a cross-bar, pushing his feet against the ground. One variety, called a *draisine*, had a pivoting front wheel and primitive handlebar. It was to one of these machines that a Scottish blacksmith, Kirkpatrick McMillan, fitted pedals to drive the rear wheel.

Penny post is introduced

Although the British Post Office has benefited from many good ideas, it has usually resisted them as hard and as long as possible. That was certainly true of John Palmer's idea of using mail-coaches, which began (in 1784) only when the prime minister insisted. It was also true of the penny post, which Rowland Hill (1795–1879) had been urging for years.

In those days, the person who received the letter paid the postage, but this was so expensive that very few people were able to accept the letters that were delivered to them. The Post Office was therefore losing a great deal of money. Hill said that a single, cheap, one-penny rate would actually be more profitable, because of the great increase in business that would follow. He also suggested using something quite unknown: an adhesive (stick on) postage stamp which was bought by the sender. This meant that postage was pre-paid.

Of course he was right. The number of letters posted rose eight hundred per cent in twenty-five years, while the use of stamps and standard rates made the whole system much more efficient. Hill's innovation gave rise to a new hobby, stamp collecting.

First China War

This sordid war between Britain and China had complicated origins. It was fought over trade, and it is sometimes called the Opium War, because this drug was being illegally traded by British and Chinese merchants. All British opium was surrendered on the command of the Chinese government in 1839, but Britain spoiled its case by later demanding compensation. There were other grievances, including an attack on a British warship, which led to war.

At the Treaty of Nanking (1842), the Chinese made concessions to British and other foreign merchants, but neither side was happy, and war began again after the Chinese had imprisoned the crew of a British-registered ship. The British foreign secretary was Lord Palmerston, an aggressive patriot who believed in protecting British nationals at any cost. Although the men were released the Chinese refused to apologize and rejected other demands.

Britain and France, passively supported by other countries, then resorted to force, and the Chinese were compelled to give way when a military expedition reached Peking in 1860. The opium trade was reinstated on the grounds – cynical but true – that the Chinese authorities were incapable of stopping it.

New Zealand becomes British

European settlement in New Zealand after Captain Cook explored the coasts in 1769 was slow and confined to the coast. Most of the immigrants were adventurers and criminals, who badly disrupted the native society of the Maoris.

Properly planned colonization began with the formation of the New Zealand Company in 1838, and in 1840 Captain William Hobson was sent out to make a treaty with the Maoris granting sovereignty over the two islands to Great Britain. The government was reluctant to take responsibility for New Zealand, but feared that otherwise the French would do so. It was also necessary to protect the Maoris from lawless Europeans though, as later events proved, the protection was not sufficient.

The colony became self-governing only twelve years after it was founded.

Discovery of Antarctica

In 1775 Captain Cook (1728–79) had circled the Antarctic continent without sighting land. In his wake sailed many whaling and sealing ships, and it may have been one of them that first glimpsed the mainland of Antarctica. The long peninsula that points towards South America was certainly seen by an American sealer, Nathaniel Palmer, in 1820, but it had probably been marked down earlier by a British ship commanded by Captain Edward Bransfield. The Russian expedition of F. B. von Bellingshausen in 1819–21 may have beaten both of them.

However, nothing was known about Antarctica until the late 1830s, when three large expeditions sailed to explore it. The French under J. C. S. Dumont d'Urville (1790–1842) planted their flag on an island off the coast of Adélie Land in 1840. The Americans under Charles Wilkes (1798–1877) discovered Wilkes

Land in the same year. The third and most successful expedition was British. Commanded by James Clark Ross (1800–62), it discovered the Ross Ice Shelf and Mount Erebus in 1841.

1841
The British occupy Hong Kong

Hong Kong, which means 'fragrant harbour', is a rocky island, forty-eight square kilometres in area, lying off the south-east coast of China. Having an excellent harbour, it has long been an important place for trade. The British occupied it in the China War (*see 1840 First China War*) and the Chinese recognized British sovereignty at the Treaty of Nanking the following year. Later, considerably more territory was added to the colony, and a lease was granted, which is due to run out in 1997. In that year, under an agreement between the British and Chinese prime ministers signed in December 1984, Hong Kong will once more become Chinese territory.

1842
Ether is used as an anaesthetic

Anyone who had an operation in 1842 was cut up while still conscious, although with luck (and money!) he or she would be doped with opium or some other pain killer. General anaesthesia (making the patient unconscious) was demonstrated in public by two American dentists, using nitrous oxide (1844) and ether (1846). But anaesthetics had been used earlier: probably the first use of ether for this purpose was by another American, Crawford Long (1815–78), in 1842.

Chloroform was developed for women in childbirth by the Scottish physician Sir James Simpson (1811–70) in 1847. Many were against its use, because it contravened the statement in the Bible that 'in pain shall you bring forth children'. However, Queen Victoria, who bore six children before being given chloroform during the birth of Prince Leopold, in 1853, had no patience with such ideas. She called it, gratefully: 'That blessed chloroform!'

Gogol publishes *Dead Souls*

This macabre but amusing satire of Nikolai Gogol (1809–52), which relates an attempted swindle by a villain who buys dead serfs, is the masterpiece of the great Russian humorist. Less realistic and less optimistic about human nature than Dickens, he shared with him a teeming imagination that poured forth a gallery of grotesque characters.

1844
O'Connell imprisoned

Daniel O'Connell (1775–1847), the Irish statesman, was largely responsible through his Catholic Association, for ending political discrimination in Britain against Roman Catholics (Roman Catholic Emancipation Act, 1829).

Though it righted one wrong, the Act did not end Irish dissatisfaction, and in the 1840s O'Connell led the call for a repeal of the Act of Union, which had joined Ireland to England in 1800. The movement was not supported by all Catholic Irish, but enormous mass-meetings were held to demand repeal.

The fiercer, more anti-English propaganda of the 'Young Ireland' movement, with which O'Connell was not in sympathy, made the situation very dangerous in the eyes of the government, and troops were moved to Ireland in case of rebellion.

In October 1843, a large meeting called by O'Connell was banned by the government. He obeyed the order but was arrested nevertheless and, after a very biased trial, sentenced to a year in prison. The verdict was reversed on appeal and O'Connell freed. But the few months he had been held in prison without bail harmed his health (he was sixty-eight), and his great influence over the Irish people had practically vanished.

1844
Turner's *Rain, Steam and Speed*

The later works of J. M. W. Turner (1775–1851), to which this vibrant red-and-gold study of a train on a bridge belongs, were regarded as decadent, but are now seen as a striking development foreshadowing the French Impressionist school. Turner was the most gifted of artists and, with Constable, the greatest of English landscape painters.

1844
Dumas' *The Three Musketeers*

This romantic story, full of colour and adventure, was written by a romantic French character, Alexandre Dumas (1802–70). He is often called Dumas *père*, to distinguish him from his son who, like the father, was a popular playwright. *Les Trois Mousquetaires* ('The Three Musketeers') was soon followed by *Le Comte de Monte Cristo* ('The Count of Monte Cristo'), eighteen volumes long.

A scene from *The Three Musketeers*.

1845
Poe's *Tales of Mystery and Imagination*

This was a vintage year for the American writer of grisly and ghostly stories, Edgar Allan Poe (1809–49). His poem *The Raven* (that grim bird for ever croaking 'Nevermore!') appeared the same year. Poe's literary reputation now stands very high. Although Poe became famous, he remained poor, ruining his health and killing himself with drink and drugs.

1845
Engels: *The Condition of the Working Class in Britain*

The German socialist, Friedrich Engels (1820–95) is best remembered as the partner of Karl Marx, although his clear style makes him a simpler guide to Marxism than Marx himself. Engels's description of working-class conditions in England, where he lived most of his adult life, was written in the year that he began his collaboration with Marx.

1845
The Irish Famine

Potatoes and very little else were all that many people in Ireland had to eat during the 1840s. So, when a blight rotted and ruined the potato harvest in 1845, some four million people faced starvation. To make matters even worse, the British government was unable or unwilling to provide the Irish with food. As a result, men, women and children died in their thousands. There were so many deaths that people had to be buried in mass graves. The blight also ruined the potato crops in 1846 and subsequent years until, by 1851, about one million Irish people had perished.

To escape the disaster, many emigrated to America. Large numbers of them died at sea because the ships in which they sailed, known as 'coffin ships', were not fit for the voyage. Those who survived took with them a burning hatred of the British for their failure to cope with the famine.

1846
Lear's *Book of Nonsense*

Edward Lear (1812–88) was a funny, eccentric Englishman, who made popular the type of comic verse called a limerick. He was also a talented artist, and was hired by the Earl of Derby to draw the animals in his private zoo. He became a great favourite of the Earl's family and wrote his first *Book of Nonsense* for the Earl's grandson. A further book, *Nonsense Songs, Stories, and Botany*, was published in 1870.

1846
Repeal of the Corn Laws

The greatest argument in Britain after the Reform Act of 1832 was: 'free trade' versus 'protection' (high duties on imports). At the centre of that argument lay the Corn Laws. The Corn Laws attempted to protect British farmers by keeping the price of wheat – and therefore bread – high, by duties on imported corn. The Tory party, representing landowners and farmers, favoured the Corn Laws. The Whigs, representing manufacturers and businessmen wanted to abolish them, to make bread cheap and thus keep wages down.

Sir Robert Peel (1788–1850) although head of a Tory government, had come to believe in free trade. The failure of the potato crop, causing famine in Ireland, convinced him that cheap bread was necessary, and he brought in a bill to repeal the Corn Laws. With the help of Whig votes, the bill was passed, although a majority of Peel's party voted against it. Soon afterwards, the Tory government fell, and Peel's career was finished.

Repeal of the Corn Laws made very little difference to the immediate situation, but it represented the decisive victory of free trade over protection.

1848
The Communist Manifesto

The Communist Manifesto was in fact written by Marx, although he often described his friend Engels as its joint author. A masterpiece of political propaganda it summoned the working classes of Europe to rebel against their capitalist masters. Its argument is clearly stated, neatly summed up in the sentence: 'The history of all hitherto existing society is the history of class struggles.'

1848
California gold rush

In the great gold rushes of the nineteenth century, many people made their fortunes, but many did not. The discovery of gold in California sent thousands of Americans rushing westwards; the population soared and California was on its way to becoming one of the world's richest – and most violent – places. Other great gold rushes include those in Victoria, Australia (1851), on the Witwatersrand, South Africa (1886) and the Klondike in Alaska and northwest Canada (1897).

1848
Pre-Raphaelite Brotherhood

The name was chosen by a group of English artists, including Dante Gabriel Rossetti (1828–82), John Everett Millais (1829–96) and William Holman Hunt (1827–1910). Reacting

The Death of Ophelia, by Sir John Everett Millais, is in the Tate Gallery, London.

against early Victorian standards of academic painting, they wanted to get closer to Nature, and identified themselves with what they regarded as the ideals of artists before the Renaissance (or 'pre-Raphael'). The PRB (formed c.1848) had very great influence; the brilliant detail of early disciples achieved a striking realism.

The ideas of the PRB later became associated with the 'arts and crafts' movement – a reaction against industrialism of which the leading advocate was William Morris (see 1884 William Morris forms Socialist League). It was in this field – design rather than painting – that the ideas of the PRB proved most fruitful.

1848
February Revolution

Louis Philippe (1773–1850) came to the French throne via revolution (1830) and left it the same way. The February Revolt grew out of protests against the government's suppression of the cause of liberal reform. Faced with a hostile combination that included many of the middle class, on whom his monarchy relied, Louis Philippe abdicated.

Left-wing leadership plus working-class pressure ensured that the monarchy would not this time be restored. A republic was declared and an election held in which all males were allowed to vote (previously, only about one in thirty could vote). The result, however, was a thoroughly conservative Chamber of Deputies. The Left wing was defeated, and the barricades went up in the streets again in June. This second rising was suppressed by troops, with many dead and wounded, and socialism was repressed.

The constitution of the Second Republic was ratified in November, and the difficult question of finding a suitable president was solved by the election of Prince Louis Napoleon (1808–73), a nephew of the emperor, who appealed to a sufficient number of people. Hardly anyone was satisfied with the Second Republic, and it lasted less than four years. As his elected spell neared its end, Louis Napoleon carried out a coup d'état which made him, in effect dictator. In 1852 he proclaimed himself emperor, as Napoleon III.

1848
European Revolutions

In 1848 every important country in Europe, except Britain, was shaken by revolt. The frustration of popular liberal and national ambitions formed the background; an economic slump, with failed harvests and rising unemployment, provided more immediate causes. The revolts were not planned, though they took place as a chain reaction following outbreaks in France and the Austrian empire. Revolutionaries like Marx were taken by surprise; The Communist Manifesto had little effect.

The first outbreaks occurred in northern Italy and Sicily. The French revolt followed in February, and it was promptly echoed in Belgium, Holland, and various German states, including Prussia. Within the Austrian empire, the Hungarians and the Czechs rebelled, and Metternich fell from power after almost forty years. Venice seized brief independence, and the Papal States gained constitutional government.

None of these revolutionary movements was wholly successful, and in two years the old systems of government were restored nearly everywhere. However, the despots of Europe were never again able to feel quite so secure.

1848
Millet's *The Winnower*

Jean François Millet (1814–75) was one of the leaders of the Barbizon school, so-called after the French village where these painters lived. They wanted to depict, realistically, the natural landscape, though Millet, the son of a peasant family, was more interested in the hard life of the peasants who inhabited that landscape. His best-known works include The Winnower (1848), Peasants Grafting and The Gleaners.

1851
The Great Exhibition

Housed in a glass palace so large it enclosed several elm trees in Hyde Park, London, the Great Exhibition was at once a celebration and an advertisement of British trade and industry, both of which at that time were at a peak.

The chief organizer of the Exhibition was Prince Albert, Queen Victoria's husband, who may have damaged his health by his immensely hard work. The 'Crystal Palace' was designed by Sir Joseph Paxton (1801–65), a gardener by trade who had already designed greenhouses, an arboretum, the great conservatory and magnificent fountains at Chatsworth House for the

Duke of Devonshire.

The basis of the Exhibition was machinery and raw materials from Britain, the empire and other countries; but it included some oddities, like rhubarb champagne, stuffed frogs and a garden seat made of coal. The Exhibition was a tremendous success, and in memory still symbolizes Britain at the height of her greatness.

The Great Exhibition of 1851, organized by Prince Albert, Queen Victoria's husband.

1851
Melville's *Moby Dick*

One of the greatest of American novels, this story of the struggle between a man and a fierce white whale can be read in many different ways. On one level, the contest stands for man's struggle with fate. The author of *Moby Dick*, Herman Melville (1819–91), was never particularly successful during his lifetime; recognition came about thirty years after his death.

1852
Giffard's aero-engine

The French inventor Henri Giffard (1825–82) was the first man to control the movements of a flying machine in the air. All previous airships could not be properly steered or propelled because they had no suitable engine. Giffard mounted a steam engine to drive a propeller in his forty-five-metre-long airship and flew it at nine km/h, steering his own course.

1852
Stowe's *Uncle Tom's Cabin*

This novel about slaves in the American South helped to rouse opposition to slavery. Today it seems sentimental, and 'Uncle Tom' has become an insulting name for a black man who humbles himself in white society. Harriet Beecher Stowe (1811–96) became famous through this book.

1852
Wells Fargo founded

Henry Wells (1805–78) and William George Fargo (1818–81) founded Wells, Fargo and Company to provide safe banking and fast communications for California gold-miners. Their fast overland stage-coaches began to run a few years later.

Although their long-distance business was affected by the building of railways, as late as 1916 Wells Fargo and other similar companies covered well over sixty-thousand kilometres of western routes.

1852
Independence of the Transvaal

The Transvaal was first settled by the descendants of Dutch colonists from the Cape Colony in 1838, anxious to escape British control.

At the Sands River Convention Britain recognized the independence of the Transvaal settlers, who were led by Andries Pretorius (1799–1853). The new state was called the South African Republic (1856).

However, all was not well in the Transvaal. The British suspected the Boers ('farmers') of enslaving Africans and coveting Bechuanaland (Botswana). The Boers quarrelled among themselves, especially over efforts to unite with the Orange Free State. The discovery of gold led to new territorial claims, more trouble with Africans, and the breakdown of government.

In 1877 Britain annexed the Transvaal, thereby becoming involved in war with the Zulu and, three years later, with the Boers themselves. By the Pretoria Convention (1881), Britain allowed self-government to the Transvaal but kept overall sovereignty.

1853

The start of modern Japan

In 1638, fearing the influence of Christian missionaries, the Emperor of Japan issued a decree isolating his country from the outside world. Foreign books, foreign ideas and foreign goods as well as foreigners were banned. Japan therefore remained a feudal, medieval society while in other parts of the world, great progress was made in science and technology. Then, in 1853, the American Commodore Perry arrived in Japan with a fleet of steamships. A steamship route was about to be established in the seas near Japan, and the Japanese reputation for ill-treating foreign sailors was so fearsome that Perry demanded the authorities conclude a treaty to open up their country to foreign trade.

The Japanese government were aware of the humiliating fate of the Chinese at the hands of Europeans (see 1840 First China War) and were afraid that if they refused the treaty, the same thing might happen to them. So, they agreed and signed a treaty with the United States in 1854. Similar treaties with Britain, Russia and the Netherlands followed in 1856. Now that Japan was open to the modern world, a great transformation took place, Japan became 'westernized' which meant that, in due time, it acquired a modern army and navy, political system and railways, factories, electric power, telephones, the cinema, aviation and other technology.

The new modern Japan was pioneered by the Emperor Meiji who came to the throne in 1867. Previously, the Japanese Emperor had been a figurehead, while Shoguns, or warlords, ruled the country. Now, the Shoguns were overthrown and the samurai class of warriors, from which they came, was abolished.

1853

Verdi's *La Traviata*

It is primarily his gift for melody that makes Guiseppe Verdi (1813–1901) so continually popular as a composer of opera. *Rigoletto* (1851) was his first great international success. *Il Trovatore* ('The Troubadour', 1853) and *La Traviata* ('The Strayed One', 1853) confirmed his reputation. But Verdi's greatest work was done late in life: *Otello* first performed when he was seventy-four, *Falstaff* when he was eighty.

1854

Outbreak of the Crimean War

The war in the Crimea — the peninsula of Russia that projects into the Black Sea — arose out of the weakness of the Turkish empire and the fear of Russian expansion at Turkish expense. It began with a dispute over the rights of Christians, whom Russia claimed to protect, in the Turkish empire. Russian troops moved into outlying provinces and the Turkish sultan declared war (October 1853). Britain and France came to Turkey's aid six months later, and their forces reached the Crimea in September 1854.

The allies defeated the Russians on the River Alma and advanced towards Sebastopol. Their campaign was badly organized and badly led: the most famous disaster, the result of an order misunderstood, was the suicidal charge of the Light Brigade (cavalry) straight at the Russian artillery during the battle of Balaclava (October). The Battle of Inkerman (November) was an allied victory, but Sebastopol still held out. During the winter siege, thousands died of cold and disease, and the city's defences did not fall until September 1855.

There were no more major battles, and peace was arranged in 1856 (Treaty of Paris). With minor changes, it left the situation much the same as it was when war began. But Nicholas I, the Russian Czar whose ambitions had sparked off the war, was dead and the Russian threat to Turkey had greatly diminished.

1854

Florence Nightingale goes to the Crimea

In the nineteenth century hospitals were filthy and fever-ridden, and nurses were often ignorant, brutal and drunk. When Florence Nightingale (1820–1910), a beautiful, wealthy girl decided to become a nurse, her parents were horrified.

Florence Nightingale's opportunity to help the nursing profession came with the outbreak of the Crimean War. She took a party of thirty-eight nurses to the hospital at Scutari, near

Florence Nightingale administering medicine to soldiers at Scutari Hospital, near Constantinople, during the Crimean War.

Constantinople, where conditions were foul and miserable for the thousands of sick and wounded. She soon devoted herself to re-organizing the hospital, and provided blankets, medicines, soap and scrubbing brushes, nursing all the worst cases herself.

When she finally returned to England in 1856, Florence Nightingale had gained such a reputation for herself that a sum of £50,000 was collected to found the Nightingale Training School for Nurses attached to St Thomas's Hospital, London. This training by Florence Nightingale was to set new standards of skill, good behaviour and discipline in nursing.

1854
Emily Dickinson starts to write poetry

The American poet, Emily Dickinson (1830–86), was the daughter of a lawyer. In 1854 she withdrew completely from society and began to write poetry: at her death she had written over a thousand poems, most of which were published posthumously. Her intensely personal and often spiritual lyrics were almost immediately recognized as the work of a great poet.

1855
Hiawatha is published

Henry Wadsworth Longfellow (1807–82) was an American poet. He was professor of modern languages at Harvard University for twenty years but finally gave up his academic career to devote his life to poetry. *Hiawatha*, his long poem about American Indians, is perhaps his most famous. Longfellow has always been extremely popular as a simple, romantic, story-teller.

1856
Invention of the Bessemer converter

In the mid-nineteenth century very little steel was being produced in Britain. In 1855 only about fifty thousand tonnes were being home-produced and that at the exorbitant average cost

of £75 a tonne. Wrought iron was at that time still the main product of the British iron industry.

During the Crimean War (*see 1854 Outbreak of the Crimean War*) an English inventor called Henry Bessemer (1813–98) designed a new rotating artillery shell. Bessemer found his invention unsatisfactory because the traditional cast-iron cannon was too weak. As a result he developed his famous steel-making process.

To produce steel, impurities such as silicon, manganese and phosphorus have to be removed from the pig-iron. Bessemer's idea was to blow a blast of air through the converter containing the iron, so oxidizing the silicon and manganese. This revolutionary process meant that steel could now be produced cheaply and swiftly.

1857
Madame Bovary is published

Gustave Flaubert (1821–80) is regarded by many as being France's greatest nineteenth century novelist. Born in Rouen, the son of a doctor, his literary aim was to produce a work of perfectly balanced prose. This he achieved in many ways with *Madame Bovary*, published in 1857, the tragic story of a young, unhappily married woman.

1857
Publication of *Les Fleurs du Mal*

Charles Baudelaire (1821–67) was not greatly appreciated during his lifetime, but is regarded now as one of France's finest poets and an important influence on modern European poetry. In 1857 Baudelaire's volume, *Les Fleurs du Mal* ('Flowers of Evil') was condemned and he was prosecuted for obscenity. The poems were written at various dates and express superbly the eternal conflict between good and evil in man.

1857
British enter Canton

There was already tension regarding trade between China and Great Britain when the

British entered Canton in 1857.

Dissatisfied with the terms of the Treaty of Nanking (*see 1840 First China War*) the British wanted free travel in China, the residence in Peking of diplomatic representatives and the right of way in the Yangtze river for their merchant vessels. China, on the other hand, felt that it had ceded quite enough to the British and other European traders.

In the midst of civil war, China was not able to cope with these British demands, and war finally broke out over a comparatively minor incident. In 1856 the Chinese boarded a Chinese-owned but British-registered craft, the *Arrow*, which they suspected of piracy. The British retaliated the next year by taking Canton, and pressing on to Tientsin, they threatened Peking. In order to save their capital, the Chinese finally gave in to the demands of the British.

1857

The Indian Mutiny

During the century which elapsed after the Battle of Plassey in 1757 (*see 1756 The Black Hole of Calcutta*) great tension and mistrust developed between the British and the Indians. Large areas of India were controlled by the British East India Company and there were many differences in belief and culture beween the two peoples.

In 1857 the *sepoys*, Indian troops serving under British officers, revolted in Bengal. They had refused to handle cartridges which they believed the British officers had coated in cow and pig grease: the cow is a holy animal for the Hindus and the pig is considered too unclean to be touched by the Moslems. This, combined with other grievances, was a major cause of the Indian Mutiny which involved about eighty thousand native soldiers.

Ghastly atrocities were committed by both sides. The British troops were slow to grasp the gravity of the situation, while the mutineers took Delhi and Lucknow, a city where the British were beseiged for months. The massacre of European women and children at Cawnpore caused more outrage than any other event.

When the mutiny was quelled under John Lawrence, chief commissioner of the Punjab, the British took away the political power of the East India Company. The Crown took over direct control under the Government of India Act (1858).

1858

Burton discovers Lake Tanganyika

Sir Richard Francis Burton (1821–90) was an exceptional British explorer. He served in Sindh, India, where he mastered several languages including Hindustani, Persian and Arabic, and wrote vivid and faithful accounts of his life there. In 1853 he made a pilgrimage to Mecca disguised as an Indian Pathan.

Burton's most hazardous and dramatic expedition was his exploration of the Somali region of East Africa in 1854. Although accompanied by John Hanning Speke (1827–64), he accomplished the most dangerous part of his journey alone. No white man had entered Harrar, the Somali capital, but Burton stayed with the king for ten days, riding back over the desert, almost without food and water. It was in 1857 that he and Speke set off to find the equatorial lakes of Africa. Quite independently Burton found Lake Tanganyika in 1858 and Speke found Victoria Nyanza. This infuriated Burton and the two went their separate ways.

1858

Brunel launches *Great Eastern*

Isambard Kingdom Brunel (1806–59) was a British engineer. Throughout his life he took an interest in the development of ocean steam navigation and in 1823 began work on the first Thames tunnel project.

Brunel was responsible for building three of the century's greatest ships. The first, the *Great Western*, built in 1838, was the first steamship to make regular trips across the Atlantic and it was followed in 1845 by the *Great Britain*. This was a huge, iron steamship the largest of its time. Recently restored, this ship may be seen at Bristol.

In 1858 his greatest ship was launched. Brunel's *Great Eastern* was a massive ocean liner, the only ship to be powered both by a propeller and paddle-wheels. She was five times bigger than anything already built and was intended to be the finest passenger-carrying ship in the world. Unfortunately, she was a commercial failure and after several years as a cable-laying vessel, in 1888 was sold and broken up.

Garibaldi led his red-shirted volunteers. Within three months they had captured Sicily.

1859
On Liberty is published

John Stuart Mill (1806–73) was one of the principal British intellectual thinkers behind modern Liberalism. He was a humanitarian who felt that the greatest good was to serve society, and he is best remembered for his brilliant essay, On Liberty. His belief in votes for women and the freedom of thought and speech influenced both his own and future generations.

1859
Tennyson's Idylls of the King

Born in Lincolnshire, Lord Tennyson (1809–92) was one of England's most respected Victorian poets. Following the publication of his poem In Memoriam (1850) he became Poet Laureate in succession to Wordsworth. The first Idylls of the King, long poems based upon the legend of King Arthur, appeared in 1859, establishing him as a great poet of his age.

1859
Publication of Darwin's *Origin of Species*

Charles Darwin (1809–82) was always an enthusiastic naturalist and in 1831 he set off on a voyage as official naturalist on board the naval survey ship *Beagle*. It was as he sailed through the Galapagos Islands and across the Pacific to Australia that Darwin made detailed observations of different animals and fossils.

Years after his trip Darwin published his findings in his *Origin of Species*. He had noticed the constant struggle for survival in nature; how the fittest of a species would survive and reproduce its own kind, while the naturally weak would die out. He concluded that over millions of years species had adapted to survive their ever-changing environment.

A storm of controversy broke out; it was felt Darwin was denying the biblical account of the origins of man as found in *Genesis*. Although Darwin's theory of natural selection is now widely accepted, there are still 'creationists' who dispute its validity.

1860

Garibaldi invades Sicily and Naples

Giuseppe Garibaldi (1807–82) was an important Italian patriot and liberator. In 1834 he joined the 'Young Italy' nationalist movement and, condemned to death for his revolutionary activities, he escaped to South America where he fought in two civil wars.

Garibaldi's most spectacular achievement was in 1860, when the nationalists were busy unifying the small states of northern Italy. Leading red-shirted volunteers known as 'the thousand heroes', Garibaldi, aided by Count Cavour (1820–78), set out to capture the south which was held by the King of Naples. Within three months he had conquered Sicily; he soon entered Naples in triumph, and Victor Emmanuel was proclaimed King of Italy.

Twice in later years Garibaldi tried to take the city of Rome from the Pope, believing that only then would Italy be truly independent. Both attempts failed and Garibaldi devoted his last years to writing on behalf of oppressed nations.

THE BRITISH EMPIRE

The British Empire was the largest of the modern empires. At its greatest extent in the 19th century, it covered one quarter of the earth's surface and included one quarter of its population. The first British territory overseas was Newfoundland (1583) which became part of Canada in 1949. This was followed by: The thirteen American colonies (from 1607), independent as the United States, 1783. India (after 1757), independent as India and Pakistan, 1947. (Pakistan divided into Pakistan and Bangladesh (formerly East Pakistan) 1971.) Canada (1763) Dominion status, 1867. Australia (1788) Federal Commonwealth, 1900. New Zealand (1840) Dominion of the British Commonwealth 1907. South Africa (Cape Colony, Orange Free State, Transvaal, Natal, Cape of Good Hope: came under British rule 1896–1902) Union of South Africa, 1910. Left British Commonwealth 1961. In addition to many islands in the Mediterranean Sea, e.g. Malta; Atlantic, e.g. Ascension; Pacific, e.g. Samoa; Indian Ocean, e.g. Mauritius; West Indies (Caribbean), e.g. Antigua and colonies on the American mainland, viz. British Guiana (now Guyana) and British Honduras (now Belize), other territories of the British Empire included:
ASIA: Singapore (1824) one of the Straits Settlements, independent 1965; Hong Kong (leased from China 1841), to return to China 1997; Sarawak (1841), Straits Settlements (1867) and Malay States (1873), independent as Malaysia 1963; Burma (1886), independent 1948; Ceylon (1801), independent 1948 (now Sri Lanka); Aden (1839), independent 1967 (now South Yemen); North Borneo (1888), independent 1963.

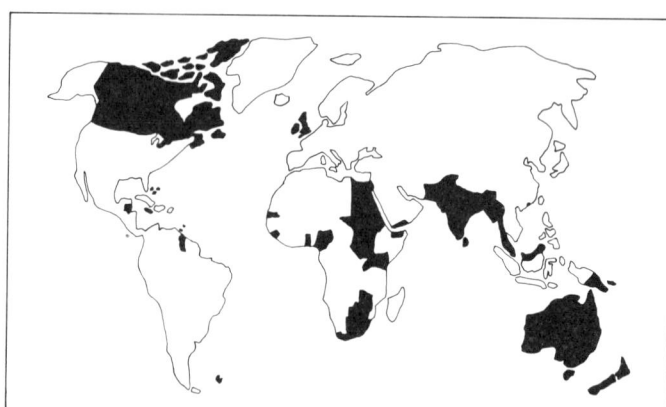

The British Empire at its greatest extent.

AFRICA

Territory	Protectorate/ colony	Independent	New name
Sierra Leone	1787: former slaves settled in. Protectorate: 1896	1961	
Gambia	1843	1965	
Nigeria	from 1861	1960	
Anglo-Egyptian Sudan	1898	1956	Sudan
Gold Coast	1874	1957	Ghana
Somaliland	1884	1960	part of Somalia
N. Rhodesia	1889	1961	Zambia
S. Rhodesia	1889	1980	Zimbabwe
Nyasaland	1891	1962	Malawi
Bechuanaland	1885	1966	Botswana
Basutoland	1868	1966	Lesotho
Kenya	1920	1963	
Uganda	1894	1962	
Tanganyika	1917 (former German East Africa, Trust territory from League of Nations. British rule from 1946	1961	Tanganyika and Zanzibar joined as Tanzania 1964
Zanzibar	1890	1963	
Swaziland	1906	1968	

Territories of the British Empire became members of the British Commonwealth except South Africa, Burma, Pakistan, Fiji (left Commonwealth 1987) and Sudan.

Other European countries with overseas territories included Germany (Africa/Pacific islands), Italy (Africa), Belgium (Congo, Africa) and Denmark (Danish West Indies).

1860

Introduction of antiseptics

In 1846 Joseph Lister (1827–1912) attended the first operation ever performed with the aid of anaesthetics (*see 1842 Ether is used as an anaesthetic*). Although this was to make surgery easier, it did not do much to make it safer; more patients still died from infections caused by inflamed wounds than from the actual operations. No one had yet discovered why these post-operative infections occurred, or how they could be treated.

Lister worked for twelve years to solve the problem. In 1860 he became Professor of Surgery at Glasgow, Scotland, and at the Royal Infirmary he showed how carbolic acid mixed with water or oil could be used to kill germs before they multiplied; hands, dressings and instruments were to be disinfected in the mixture.

The results of Lister's work were tremendous. Patients began to recover without the earlier post-operative complications and the number of deaths fell rapidly. The introduction of this antiseptic system is often known as the 'Listerian revolution'.

1860

Golf: The first British Open

It has never been clearly established when golf started, but it seems that it was almost certainly Scottish in origin; there is a recorded sale of a golf ball for ten Scottish shillings in 1452. The British Open Championship is the oldest championship in golf, dating from 1860; the National Open Championship in the USA started in 1895.

1860

First internal combustion engine

Attempts to develop efficient types of engines continued during the eighteenth and nineteenth centuries (*see 1765 Watt improves the steam engine*). The internal combustion engine followed on as an improvement to the steam engine.

Like so many other mid-nineteenth century inventions, no single person can be said to have invented the internal combustion engine. It was more the result of one hundred years' research. The varieties of steam engines soon proved unsatisfactory for road transport because huge amounts of coal or wood had to be carried to keep the fire in the engine alight.

In 1860 Etienne Lenoir (1822–1900) a Frenchman, built an internal combustion engine that gave a reasonably satisfactory service operating on illuminating gas. It worked on a two-stroke cycle and several hundred were sold over the next few years.

The modern engine used in cars, however, is based on a four-stroke petrol engine built by Nikolaus Otto in 1876. The age of the automobile had begun.

1861

Krupp's first gun

Krupp was the name of a German industrial family which owned one of the largest steel and armaments works in Europe, producing its first gun in 1861. The firm was well-known for its social welfare; good schools, houses and co-operative stores were available for the workers. During World War I the firm became internationally famous when it produced heavy guns like *Big Bertha*, a 42-cm howitzer.

1861

George Eliot's *Silas Marner*

Mary Ann Evans was born in Warwickshire, England, and had a severely religious upbringing. Adopting the pen-name of George Eliot (1819–80), she wrote stories which revealed both a sense of humour and compassion for the terrible tragedies that strike at ordinary, simple people. *Silas Marner*, published in 1861, is the story of a weaver who brings up a child whom he finds on his doorstep.

1861

Expedition to Flinders river

One of the most tragic events in the story of Australian exploration was the expedition led by Robert O'Hara Burke (1820–61), an Irish-born police officer. The party was given a grand farewell as it set off for the Australian interior. When the second-in-command resigned, he was replaced by William Wills, the party's astronomical observer.

While waiting for members of his party at Cooper's Creek, Burke grew impatient and set off with only Wills, King and Gray as companions. It was a foolhardy and ill-fated decision, but the men finally reached Flinders river in 1861, hungry and exhausted.

The return journey was a nightmare; Gray died and the remaining three found their camp at Cooper's Creek deserted. Their food supplies had run out, yet starving and weak from exposure they set off towards Adelaide. They struggled on, but Burke and Wills died. Only King survived, cared for by natives.

A Union soldier (left) and Confederate soldiers (right) from the American Civil War.

(Right) Abraham Lincoln with General McClennan after the Battle of Antietam, September 1862.

1861

Outbreak of the American Civil War

The American Civil War took place between the eleven states in the south and the rest of the Union, when tension over the question of slavery rose to a head. For two centuries African slaves had been shipped to America. The northern states now joined Europe in their belief that slavery should be abolished; the southern states disagreed, and wanted to leave the Federal Union, calling themselves the Confederate States of America.

The army of the north was wealthier, better equipped and bigger than that of the south, but it took bitter fighting and the loss of nearly seven hundred thousand lives before the quarrel was resolved.

The southerners fought with grim determination led by several exceptional men such as 'Stonewall' Jackson and Robert E. Lee. Abraham Lincoln (1809–65) President of the United States, led the north. In 1863, after the north's victory at the battle of Gettysburg, Lincoln delivered his famous speech on democracy: '. . . that government of the people, for the people, by the people, shall not perish from the earth . . .' In 1864 the north took the offensive and the south surrendered to General Grant in 1865. Five days later, Lincoln was assassinated. After the war slavery was abolished.

1862

Turgenev's *Fathers and Sons*

When *Fathers and Sons* was published in 1862, Ivan Sergeievitch Turgenev (1818–83) was already a well-known novelist and short story writer. Disliked in Russia by both revolutionaries and reactionaries, his book was immediately recognized as a great work abroad, especially in England. His attack on Russian serfdom, *Sportsman's Sketches* (1852), brought him into disrepute with the Russian government.

1862
Bismarck becomes prime minister

Many factors inspired the unification of the German states (*see 1819 The start of the Zollverein*), but the man who finally created a powerful German nation was Count Otto von Bismarck (1815–98).

Bismarck became prime minister of Prussia in 1862. His methods of government were harsh and often unscrupulous and he believed in rule by 'blood and iron' rather than rule by Parliament. Bismarck's determination to do everything possible to unite Germany under Prussia and to drive Austria out of the German states was in later years to earn him the name 'Iron Chancellor'.

In 1864 Bismarck successfully fought a war with Denmark to decide who should own Schleswig-Holstein, and the Danish defeat gave Prussia an important naval base at Kiel. After his victorious 'Seven Weeks' War' with Austria, Bismarck had a freer hand in Germany: he annexed some of the smaller states and united the remaining ones with Prussia under the North German Confederation.

1863
First underground railway

The world's first underground railway was opened in London in 1863 as the Metropolitan railway. This early underground line ran from Bishops Road to Farringdon Street (about six kilometres); the lines were in cuttings beneath the street, roofed over to take the road surface. The first Continental European underground railway (in Budapest) was opened in 1896.

1863
Maximilian becomes Emperor of Mexico

In 1860 Benito Juárez, a Zapotec Indian, led a revolt against the dictatorship of Miramón in Mexico and with the support of the USA succeeded in overthrowing the dictator. When Juárez declared that he could not pay the national debts of Miramón's regime to France,

Britain and Spain, all three countries sent troops to occupy Mexico.

Britain and Spain soon came to an agreement with Juárez and as a result withdrew their troops. France, however, remained, largely because Emperor Napoleon III felt he could establish a colony there and on June 7, 1863 French troops entered Mexico City and overthrew Juárez. Napoleon persuaded Archduke Maximilian, brother of the Emperor of Austria, to become Emperor of Mexico in 1863.

The USA was outraged by Napoleon's actions (*see 1823 The Monroe Doctrine*) and sent troops to support Juárez. When the French were forced to withdraw, Juárez and his men captured Maximilian and executed him in 1867.

1863
Football Association founded

In the mid-nineteenth century football clubs started spreading through Britain and it was soon felt that a definitive set of rules for the game should be prepared. In October 1863, representatives of the clubs met to form the Football Association. The Association grew slowly; in 1871 it introduced the FA Cup competition, and today it is respected throughout the world.

1864
The First Socialist International

Marx was largely responsible for founding the First Socialist International in London in 1864, a union of communist or socialist movements. His ideas on subjects such as education, trade unions and co-operatives were to prove invaluable.

The International soon split up, leaving Marx time to write *Das Kapital* ('Capital'). The International failed partly because Marx quarrelled with the rival leaders, but also because Marx's theories (*see 1848 The Communist Manifesto*) clashed with the anarchists' theories. Mikhail Bakunin (1814–76), the leading anarchist, was Marx's most vigorous opponent. He believed that instead of a government, a self-controlling system of little societies, undisturbed by outside forces, would form the ideal basis for society.

adopted, as well as the motto 'Charity in War'.

The Convention agreed that the wounded should be respected; that military hospitals should be regarded as neutral and that buildings or vehicles marked by the Red Cross should be safe from attack.

In the Middle East today, a Red Crescent replaces the Red Cross (in Iran a Lion or Sun is used).

Karl Marx lived for a period in London, preparing his theories on international communism in the British Museum reading room.

Marx believed in the 'dictatorship of the proletariat', a belief which forms the basis of modern communism. This theory advocated a situation where the proletariat (the industrial working class) makes and controls a new state of its own. Bakunin, however, rejected the idea of the state altogether.

1864
Dunant founds Red Cross

In 1859, Henri Dunant, a Swiss humanitarian (1828–1910), witnessed the horrific slaughter that took place at the battle of Solferino, and also the lack of medical attention for relieving the sufferings of the wounded. Dunant resolved to create an organization which would provide medical services to all combatants in battle, no matter what their nationality.

In 1862, Dunant published a booklet setting out his ideas and in 1863, an international conference was held at Geneva, Switzerland, at which twenty-six governments were represented. This conference led in 1864 to the adoption of the Geneva Convention for the treatment of combatants in war, especially prisoners, and the foundation of the Red Cross Movement. The emblem of a red cross on a white background – the Swiss flag colours reversed – was

1865
Booth founds Salvation Army

William Booth (1829–1912) was a strongly religious Englishman. In 1852 he became a regular preacher of the Methodist Church but he broke away nine years later to become an independent preacher.

In 1864 Booth went to London where he conducted services in tents and in the open air. In Whitechapel he then founded the Christian Mission (1865) which later became known as the Salvation Army, modelling the organization along the lines of the army, with himself as 'General'.

Booth was a man who believed that unconverted people would be eternally damned. However, he had great compassion for those who were less fortunate than himself and who lived in filth, misery and squalor. Above all, his Army was devoted to bringing people to salvation.

Music, especially brass bands, has always been an attractive and important feature of the Salvation Army, as has its charitable work. Today there are branches throughout the world.

Following pages: *The Execution of the Emperor Maximilian*, from a painting by Manet, painted about 1868. Maximilian, with two of his generals, was executed in 1867.

1865

Mendel announces heredity laws

Gregor Johann Mendel (1822–84) was an Austrian monk who lived in what is now Czechoslovakia. In the monastery garden he performed experiments leading to the basic principles of heredity.

Mendel's work involved the crossing and subsequent observation of various kinds of garden pea. He showed that inheritance involved pairs of contrasting characteristics such as tallness and shortness. These characteristics were described as either dominant (strong) or recessive (weak) and Mendel showed how a tall pea crossed with a short one resulted in a tall offspring. This was unexpected; it had been believed that a medium-sized plant would be the result of such a union.

Mendel achieved fame only after his death, when in 1900 three other botanists obtained results similar to his. Mendel has since taken his place in history as one of the great influences in the story of genetics (the science of heredity).

1865

Alice in Wonderland

Alice's Adventures in Wonderland is a strange and fantastic tale written for children by a shy and retiring man, known as Lewis Carrol (1832–98), whose real name was Charles Lutwidge Dodgson. The story was published in 1865 with wonderful illustrations by Sir John Tenniel (1820–1914) and was followed in 1872 by *Through the Looking Glass and What Alice Found There*.

1866

Queensberry rules set up

By the 1860s people in Britain were rather disgusted by the brutality of the professional 'bruisers', as boxers were called, and were in favour of laws being enforced. In 1866 the Amateur Athletic Club was founded and in the same year Lord Queensberry drew up a code of laws which came to govern all contests in Britain.

1866

War and Peace completed

Leo Tolstoy (1828–1910), Russian novelist and moral philosopher, wrote two masterpieces: *War and Peace* (about Napoleon's invasion of Russia) and *Anna Karenina*. When he grew uneasy about his prosperous life, he renounced his wealth, and evolving his own pure form of Christianity, took up the life of an ordinary peasant.

1866

US Civil Rights Act

Tension soon grew concerning the political and civil rights of Negroes (*see 1861 Outbreak of the American Civil War*). In 1865 slavery was abolished in the USA but the southern states immediately tried to restrict the freedom of the Negroes. In 1866 Congress adopted the Civil Rights Act.

The act gave the Negro the right to vote, to sign contracts, to sue and to give evidence. It gave him rights in the face of the law and protection from violence. An attempt was made to rehabilitate the whites and Negroes in the devastated south, but it failed. The southern states were determined to keep the Negroes in an inferior position and on principle always opposed the politics of the north.

1866

Crime and Punishment

Fyodor Mikhailovich Dostoevsky (1821–81) was born in Moscow. Arrested in 1849 for belonging to a socialist society, he was sent to Siberia for four years. The theme of his novels centres round his sympathy for ordinary people humiliated at the hands of society. His greatest works include *Crime and Punishment* (1866), *The Idiot*, *The Brothers Karamazov* and *The Possessed*.

1867

Fenian Rising

The Fenians were an Irish-American secret society formed to remove British control from Ireland. It was founded in 1858 in the United

States and its name was derived from the legendary band of warriors in Ireland led by Finn Mac Cumhaill.

When Irish-Americans flocked to Ireland after the American Civil War there was an increase in Fenian activities and plans for a rising. The government heard of the plans, however, and took immediate action: the Fenian newspaper was suppressed and several members of the society imprisoned.

In 1867 several minor risings broke out in Ireland and there was an attempt to take Chester Castle. A policeman was killed in Manchester and the three Fenians hanged for this became known as the 'Manchester martyrs'. Clerkenwell Prison, London, was then blown up in an attempt to free Fenian prisoners, and twelve people were killed.

1867
The Blue Danube waltz

There is no formal western European dance that has been more adored than the waltz. The peak of its popularity was in nineteenth century Vienna, a city of fashionable and glamorous dances. Perhaps the best-known symbol of Romantic Vienna is Johann Strauss's full-blooded waltz, *Die Blaue Donau* ('The Blue Danube'), which he wrote in 1867.

1868
Disraeli and Gladstone come to power

From about 1865 British politics were dominated by the great political duel between two famous men, Gladstone and Disraeli. William Gladstone (1809—98) was a Liberal, serious, earnest and very conscientious. His rival, Benjamin Disraeli of the Conservative party, was clever, witty, colourful and very romantic.

In 1868 Disraeli became prime minister for the first time (his second period was 1874—80), but there was a strong demand for reform throughout Britain and in the same year he lost the General Election to the Liberals led by Gladstone. Gladstone was prime minister four times, and was to carry through a programme of overdue reforms before a real age of Conservatism could set in.

Gladstone and Disraeli disliked one another intensely. Disraeli accused Gladstone of not being a 'gentleman' and Gladstone thought Disraeli was immoral. Gladstone's main interest lay in the right of the individual and the right to vote, while Disraeli's thoughts moved on a larger scale, concerned with general social conditions. In foreign affairs Gladstone disapproved of British expansion, but Disraeli was a true Victorian Imperialist.

Despite these personal differences both men can be regarded as great British statesmen, who in their own ways were responsible for some very important social changes. Disraeli, who was greatly admired by Queen Victoria, was the founder of the Conservative party in its present form.

1869
Suez Canal opened

Plans to connect lower Egypt to the Red Sea go back to ancient times. France looks out onto the Atlantic and the Mediterranean, and this, combined with her economic and political rivalry with England in the nineteenth century, encouraged her plans to pierce the isthmus of Suez with a waterway.

Gladstone addressing Parliament.

218

The Suez Canal, the work of French engineer Ferdinand de Lesseps, was the key to trade with the East, by-passing the lengthy route round the Cape.

In 1854 a French engineer, Ferdinand de Lesseps (1805–94), conceived his scheme for the Suez Canal and in 1860 work began on it. The British government refused to help the scheme, as it feared France's expansion in Egypt. The French continued, nonetheless, using Egyptian labour, and by 1869 some 432,807,882 French francs had been spent on the project. In August the Canal was completed.

On November 17, 1869 there was a grand ceremony to open the Canal, headed by the French imperial yacht, *Aigle*. The British, by now grateful to de Lesseps for his good work, gave him a British knighthood. Meanwhile, Prime Minister Benjamin Disraeli had seen to it that Britain purchased a large shareholding in the Suez Canal Company, so giving Britain an important say in the running of the canal.

1869

Brahms's *Requiem* performed

Johannes Brahms (1833–97) the German composer, always maintained a dislike of opera, but his *German Requiem*, first performed in 1869, is a very great choral work. Brahms's music was solidly based on classical foundations; he acts as a link

between Beethoven, the classical composer, and Schumann the romantic. Brahms's Violin Concerto and his Double Concerto for violin and cello are amongst the greatest ever written.

1870
Smetana's *Bartered Bride*

1870, the date of the premiere of Smetana's *Bartered Bride*, marks the birth of a truly Czech national school of music. Bedřich Smetana (1824–84) was one of Czechoslovakia's greatest composers and in 1866 he became conductor of the new National Theatre for which he wrote most of his operas. He became deaf in 1874, but continued composing until 1883.

1870

Franco-Prussian War

Bismarck decided on one more war to unite Germany under Prussian leadership (*see 1862 Bismarck becomes prime minister*). He chose France as his enemy, making the dispute over who should inherit the Spanish throne the immediate cause. A Hohenzollern Prussian prince was a candidate, but France created such a storm of protest that the prince withdrew. Prussia refused to guarantee that it would not oppose any similar future event and so France declared war in 1870.

The war was disastrous for France: Napoleon III surrendered and became a prisoner and the main army, besieged at Metz, capitulated in October. Meanwhile the Second Empire was overthrown and the Prussians besieged Paris.

In September 1870 Leon Gambetta (1832–82) had with others declared France a Republic. He had escaped from Paris to Tours in a balloon, where he set up the headquarters for France's defence and he became dictator for five months. Gambetta's determination was remarkable; even when Paris capitulated through famine and internal discontent, he wanted, in vain, to continue the war.

After their victory, the united German Empire was proclaimed at Versailles in 1871. The victors imposed heavy peace terms on the French in the Treaty of Frankfurt. France lost Alsace-Lorraine and had to pay a war indemnity.

(Right) The Battle of Mt. Valerien, January 19 1871, sealed the fate of the French, who capitulated on January 28.

1870
Education Act

The nineteenth century was a period of change as far as British education was concerned; change from minor concern about children's education to wide control. There had been an Act in 1833 which made part-time education compulsory for children working in factories, but it did nothing for children working elsewhere.

The first real Education Act was in 1870. School boards were set up and each board had to arrange for children under ten years of age to attend school. The board also had to arrange to pay school fees for the poorest parents. By 1876 school attendance was compulsory all over Britain and by 1891 all elementary schools were made free.

Between this act of 1870 and the one of 1944, the State became more and more aware of the necessity for full-time education for children between the ages of five and fifteen.

1871
William becomes Emperor of Germany

During the Franco–Prussian War negotiations were pushed on for the uniting of all Germany outside Austria. When France had declared war, the German states had rallied round William, the King of Prussia (1797–1888), so that he knew he had the support of a united nation. On January 18, 1871, during the siege of Paris, William was finally proclaimed Emperor of Germany at his headquarters in Versailles.

The question of what the new state should be called was a problem. Bismarck wanted to revive the title of German Emperor, although William disliked the idea and Bavaria was unhappy too. Yet as always, Bismarck had the last word.

A new *Reichstag* (parliament) was elected from all Germany, but its powers were not clearly defined in the beginning. Nor was it clear to whom Bismarck, now Chancellor, was responsible; Bismarck felt he was responsible to the emperor, while the politicians felt he was answerable to the *Reichstag*. The parliament was opened by William on March 21 and on June 16 he entered Berlin at the head of his troops. After this William tended to leave the destiny of Germany in Bismarck's capable hands.

Bismarck reviewing Prussian troops before the Franco–Prussian War.

1871
Paris Commune

At the close of the Franco–Prussian War, the agreement that German troops should march in triumph through Paris humiliated the French, and prompted the outbreak of the Paris Commune on March 18, 1871.

Throughout the war the French had been split in two: the more reactionary loyalists in the provinces wanted peace with Prussia, while the revolutionaries in Paris had wanted war and to set up a more extremist Republic. The Commune was like a second siege of Paris, with the revolutionaries barricading themselves inside the capital.

It was Adolphe Thiers (1797–1877) who had persuaded the National Assembly to agree to peace, and now it was he who crushed the 'communards'. His troops stormed Paris on May 21. The violent fighting and massacre that followed (known as 'bloody week') resulted in the death of over twenty-six thousand Parisians. It was the end of what the French Socialists called the first 'workers' republic'.

find the source of the Nile. In constant danger from Arab slave traders, he suffered terrible hardships, especially when his medical chest was stolen. In Europe he was given up for lost, but in November 1871 H. M. Stanley (1841–1904), who had been sent to Africa by an American newspaper, found Livingstone on the east coast of Lake Tanganyika and greeted him with the now famous words: 'Dr Livingstone, I presume'.

1871

Zola starts *Les Rougon-Macquart*

Emile Zola (1840–1902), the French novelist, evolved his pseudo-scientific theory of the 'naturalistic' novel around 1868. He believed that birth, background and circumstances formed a character and felt that the novel should be a form of human case history. The *Rougon-Macquart* series was a cycle of twenty novels, some quite brutal, based around the members of one family.

1871

Rugby Football Union founded

Football was played in English public schools, yet no two schools had the same rules. All agreed, however, that the ball must never be carried or passed by hand. This rule was violated in 1823 in Rugby School, leading to the modern Rugby football. Its rules were codified in 1871 when a group calling itself the Rugby Football Union met in London.

1871

Livingstone meets Stanley

David Livingstone (1813–73) was a Scottish medical missionary and explorer. In 1858 he was commissioned by the British Government to explore eastern and central Africa, and it was on this trip that he discovered Lake Nyasa. For the first time he entered an area devastated by the slave trade and determined then to rid Africa of this human sacrifice.

In 1866 he set out on a private trip to continue his fight against the slave trade and to

1871

Trade Unions legalized in Britain

British trade unionism grew very fast after 1825 when the Combination Acts were repealed, which meant that they were no longer regarded as criminal associations. They still had no legal status, yet in spite of this, unionism spread.

In 1851 the Amalgamated Society of Engineers was formed, one of the most famous of the early trade unions. This union was to act as a model for others for it included several separate unions such as machinists, blacksmiths and fitters. The fight was now really on, and several other similar unions were formed; they were powerful and determined to make unions recognized, legal bodies and to strengthen themselves they elected a special committee to represent them.

Their determination was soon rewarded when in 1871 the Trade Union Act recognized them as legal associations. The Act also granted workers the right to strike and the right to picket.

The Trade Unions, legalized in Britain in 1871, had grown to a powerful movement by the 1920s. The sense of pride in belonging to a Union was typified by the banners of each branch.

1872
The Ballot Act

South Australia was the first state to introduce the Secret Ballot Act (1856), since when it is usual to refer to it as the Australian Ballot. The system then spread to Europe and America, reaching Great Britain in 1872. It was introduced through the Ballot Act to meet the growing public and parliamentary demand for the protection of voters who had often been terrorized in the days when announcing votes in public was the rule.

1873
Ashanti War

In the nineteenth century the people of Ashanti (today a region in Ghana) conquered many of their coastal neighbours, hoping to increase their slave trade with Europeans. Britain abolished the slave trade and made peace with the coastal peoples, so the humiliated Ashantis attacked their neighbours. British troops soon moved in and destroyed the Ashanti capital, Kumasi, in 1874.

1873
Verne's *Around the World in Eighty Days*

Jules Verne (1828–1905) was the French author of innumerable adventure stories, combining a vivid imagination with a gift for popularizing science.

Le Tour du Monde en quatre-vingt Jours ('Around the World in Eighty Days') was the story of Phileas Fogg who, accompanied by his valet Passepartout, wins a bet to travel round the world in eighty days.

1874
The first Impressionist Exhibition

In 1863 a painting called *Déjeuner sur l'herbe* was shown at the Salon des Refusés in Paris – established by Napoleon III for artists turned down by traditional exhibitions. It was by Edouard Manet (1832–83); the nude woman in the painting shocked the public, but the technique amazed the experts. With Manet, a number of artists who sympathized with his ideas, formed a new school, and in 1874 they held an exhibition at the studio of the photographer, Nadar.

Café-Concert at the Ambassadeurs painted by Edgar Degas in about 1876–77.

A weekly paper ridiculed the artists for deserting the traditional school and called them 'Impressionists'. The name stuck — and Impressionism turned out to be one of the most revolutionary and lively experiences of nineteenth century art.

The Impressionists advocated painting in the open air, emphasizing the effects of light, and the use of a light palette. Claude Monet (1840–1926) who first painted in sunlight in 1866, painted the effects of sun and the smoke of the engines of the Gare St Lazare. Renoir (1841–1919) painter of the *Swing* had similar ideas to Monet, as did Pissarro and Sisley.

Other famous Impressionists include Edgar Degas, who painted several lovely ballerinas and a masterpiece, *l'Absinthe*, and Paul Cézanne, painter of the beautiful landscape *Montagne de Ste Victoire*.

1874
Mussorgsky's *Boris Godunov*

Modest Petrovich Mussorgsky (1835–81) resigned his commission in the army to devote his life to music. He was a member of a Russian nationalist group of musicians known as 'The Five' which included Rimsky-Korsakov, and first made his name with his songs. The opera *Boris Godunov*, his masterpiece, was based on a play by Pushkin and was performed in St Petersburg in 1874.

1875
Gilbert and Sullivan's *Trial by Jury*

Sir Arthur Seymour Sullivan (1842–1900), the English composer, and Sir William Schwenck Gilbert (1836–1911) playwright and humorist, first met in 1871. In 1875 Richard D'Oyly Carte of the Royalty Theatre, London, commissioned them to write an operetta. The result was *Trial by Jury*; it was an immediate success, making their partnership one of the most brilliant in the history of light opera.

1876
Wagner's *Ring* at Bayreuth

Richard Wagner (1813–83) was a poet and one of Germany's greatest dramatic composers. He reformed the whole structure of opera, abandoning the traditional use of aria and recitative in favour of a perfect fusion of drama and music.

Wagner was the first to use the *leitmotif* successfully: musical themes introduce and identify different characters in his operas and this both aids dramatic development and psychological exposition.

In 1870 a theatre was built at Bayreuth and Wagner gave a full performance there of his work *The Ring of the Nibelungs* in 1876. This vast work is a cycle of four full-scale operas in which Wagner draws upon Teutonic mythology, using gods, dwarfs and giants to illustrate the corrupting effect of the lust for power in hearts which have renounced love.

Other operas by Wagner include *The Flying Dutchman, Parsifal, The Mastersingers* and *Tristan and Isolde*.

Richard Wagner

1876
Grieg's *Peer Gynt*

Edvard Hagerup Grieg (1843–1907) was born in Norway and is Scandinavia's best known nineteenth century composer. Greatly inspired

GREAT INVENTIONS

1450 Printing press with moveable type invented.

1589 First knitting machine.

1698 First steam engine developed by Thomas Savary.

1701 Seed drill for planting seeds in rows invented by Jethro Tull.

1712 First low-pressure steam pump developed by Thomas Newcomen.

1783 First steamboat.

1800 Electric battery invented.

1802 High-pressure steam engine built by Richard Trevithick.

1806 Gas lighting used in cotton mills.

1810 First power-driven printing press.

1811 Method for preserving food in cans developed.

1825 Opening of the Stockton to Darlington railway, the world's first public steam railway.

1826 Invention of photography.

1827 Development of the water turbine.

1837 Invention of the telegraph.

1851 Domestic sewing machine invented.

1856 Process for producing artificial dyes from coal-tar successful. The first artificial dye was mauve.

1865 Refrigerator first successfully developed.

1867 Dynamite manufactured by Alfred Nobel.

1869 Vacuum cleaner developed.

1872 The first manufacture of celluloid film.

1873 The first typewriter manufactured.

1876 The first practical gas engine.

1876 Invention of the telephone by Alexander Graham Bell.

1878 Thomas Alva Edison developed his phonograph recording machine.

1878–79 Development of the electric light bulb.

1880 Chemical fertilizers developed.

1882 Electric fan and electric iron developed.

1884 Steam turbine developed, and rayon, the first artificial fibre, produced.

1885 Production of the first automobile and the first 'safety' bicycle.

1895 Marconi first developed his wireless.

1907 First washing machine manufactured.

1909 Bakelite, the first polymer (chemical mixture), discovered.

1913 Diesel-electric railway engines first used in Sweden.

1922 Technicolour film process developed.

1926 John Logie Baird develops his television process.

1931 The caterpillar tractor developed.

1938 RADAR (Radio Detecting and Ranging) method of detecting aircraft was first used.

1944 Automatic digital computer built.

1948 Long-playing record developed, and transistor invented.

1951 First commercial electronic computer developed.

1956 Nuclear energy used to produce electricity.

1959 First public demonstration of hovercraft.

1960 Development of the laser beam.

The Industrial Revolution

This revolution in work took place between the mid-18th and mid-19th centuries, when the making of textiles was transferred from weavers working in their homes, to machines producing cloth in factories. Later, other industries such as iron, pottery and mining made use of the steam power and railway transport which were also part of the Industrial Revolution. The main developments which put the textile industry into factories were:

1733 John Kay's 'Flying Shuttle'. This could throw a weaving shuttle from one side of a loom to the other faster than weavers could do it by hand.

1764 'Spinning Jenny' devised by James Hargreaves. This could do the same work as eight spinners.

1765 The steam engine, improved by James Watt, enabled factory machines to be driven by steam – instead of water-power.

1769 Richard Arkwright's water-driven frame for twisting yarn.

1784 Samuel Crompton's 'Spinning Mule' combined the features of 'Spinning Jenny' and Richard Arkwright's frame.

1785 Edmund Cartwright's power loom doubled the output of cloth achieved by hand-weavers.

by folk music, he was a delightful miniaturist. His most celebrated works are his incidental music to Ibsen's play *Peer Gynt* and his later Piano Concerto.

1876
The Battle of Little Big Horn

The massacre of the North American Indians by white men remains to this day a controversial issue, although it is generally believed that the Indians were justified in protecting their rights to live as they pleased. The Battle of Washita (1868) was the beginning of the end for the southern Plains Indians. George Armstrong Custer (1839–76) led his cavalry in this slaughter of the Cheyenne and it has since been called 'Custer's Massacre'.

Hostilities between Red Man and White Man continued. When Custer and the Seventh Army were ordered against the Sioux, Custer was taken by surprise when he reached the valley of Little Big Horn. Instead of a few Indians, he was confronted by a well-prepared force and was soon hemmed in. It was to be 'Custer's last stand', for as he and his two hundred and twenty-six men rode into the midst of the enemy, they were slaughtered.

1876
Tchaikovsky's *Swan Lake*

Piotr Ilyich Tchaikovsky (1840–93), the Russian composer, wrote ten operas, six symphonies, four concertos and three ballets, amongst his major works. His ballets include *The Sleeping Beauty*, *Nutcracker* and *Swan Lake* (1876). Tchaikovsky died of cholera soon after the first performance of the *Pathétique* symphony, a work reflecting his melancholy nature.

Tchaikovsky

1876
Bell invents the telephone

Alexander Graham Bell (1847–1922) was a Scottish-American physicist and inventor. In 1876 he exhibited an apparatus embodying the results of his studies in the transmission of sound by electricity – the basis of the modern telephone. The first telephone message transmitted was from Bell to his assistant: 'Mr Watson, please come here: I want you'.

1876
Tom Sawyer is published

Mark Twain's real name was Samuel Langhorne Clemens (1835–1910). He was an American writer, who took his pen-name from the cry Mississippi pilots used when they were taking soundings ('mark twain', meaning 'by the mark two fathoms'). His famous novels *Tom Sawyer* and *The Adventures of Huckleberry Finn* (1884) have become world classics and give a wonderful picture of life on and around the Mississippi.

The world of Mark Twain: Huckleberry Finn and a Mississippi riverboat.

1876
Mallarmé's *L'Après-midi d'un faune*

Stéphane Mallarmé (1842–98), a French poet, has been described as 'the crown and conclusion of the Symbolist Movement'. He believed that poems should suggest rather than describe and that words had meanings beyond their everyday significance. His masterpiece, the pastoral short poem *L'Après-midi d'un faune* ('The Afternoon of a Faun'), which inspired the musician and composer Debussy, was published in 1876.

1877
Whistler v. Ruskin

In 1877 James Whistler (1834–1903), an American artist, sued John Ruskin, English author and art critic, for libel. Ruskin (1819–1900) had accused Whistler of flinging a pot of paint in the public's face, and the lawsuit that followed was subsequently famous for representing two opposing nineteenth century attitudes to art. Whistler won the lawsuit and was awarded a farthing damages.

Whistler believed that a painting must, above all, be a work of art; that it should be a 'harmony' of perfect shapes and colours which would give pleasure independently of the subject matter. This kind of thinking led to the battlecry 'art for art's sake'.

Ruskin on the other hand, opposed this philosophy fiercely. A Victorian moralist, he was interested in social problems, education, morals and religion. He never sought to produce anything that he would call a 'work of art', but largely drew buildings or natural objects as they appeared to his eye.

1878
Edison patents the phonograph

Thomas Alva Edison (1847–1931), American inventor, was by the age of thirty, already highly successful. After producing many new devices to increase the efficiency of the Western Union Company's telegraph and telephone services, he went on to invent and patent an automatic repeater which sent messages from one wire to the next. His phonography, or talking machine, was an early type of record player.

The phonograph used a revolving cylinder covered with tin foil which Edison had to turn by hand, as electric motors were not then in common use. Mechanical vibrations were created when the operator spoke into the recording tube and a needle transferred these on to the tin foil. The impressions on the tin foil represented the loudness and pitch of the

Edison and his phonograph.

recorded voice. Another needle was then moved along the impressions and the vibrations reproduced the voice in the hearing tube.

1878
Edison and Swan produce light bulb

In 1860 Sir Joseph Wilson Swan invented an electric lamp, so it can be said that he was the real pioneer of electric lighting as we know it. Swan (1828–1914) was an English physicist and chemist, who also patented the carbon process for photographic printing.

Swan's lamp had contained a carbon filament which glowed, though not brightly. Nearly twenty years later both Edison (*see 1878 Edison patents the phonograph*) working on Swan's idea, and Swan himself, produced a greatly improved lamp.

The aim had been to produce a bulb which could be manufactured cheaply and easily: the secret lay in the filament. The 'Edison and Swan bulb' used a filament made from a length of carbonized sewing thread, mounted in an evacuated glass tube. This bulb produced a glow for forty hours. In 1882 the people of New York watched as Edison switched on the world's first electric light system powered from his generating station at Pearl Street.

The Zulus strongly resisted the encroachment of European settlers.

1879

Zulu War

European powers did not hesitate to grab African territory to further their own trade. The British and Dutch fought over the south and in so doing the British confronted the Zulu people of the Bantu tribes. The Zulus were finally crushed by the British, and the government annexed Zululand (now a part of South Africa) to the crown in 1887.

1879

Panama Canal started

When explorers after Columbus found that the two American continents were a barrier to the Far East, interest in the possibility of an inter-oceanic waterway across the Isthmus of Panama was aroused. In 1879 the Panama Canal company was founded with de Lesseps as president (*see 1869 Suez Canal opened*).

By 1889, work had stopped because the level canal that de Lesseps wanted to build was not suitable for the hilly terrain of the Panama Isthmus, and the workings were constantly flooded. In 1904, the United States purchased the old French workings and, to overcome the problem of the hilly terrain, built a canal with locks; the locks raised the water to 26 metres

above sea level. The canal opened 15 August 1914 and was 64 kilometers in length, linking the Atlantic and Pacific Oceans.

1880

Death of Ned Kelly

After 1788 the British began to use Australia as a penal colony, even though a number of the criminals sent to Australia were guilty of only petty offences such as poaching. Much of Australia was therefore colonized by freed prisoners and gold diggers. These were lawless times and many lawbreaking colonists were ruthlessly hunted down by the police and their Aborigine scouts. Life generally became very difficult for them in this repressive situation.

As a reaction to their hardships many of these men became outlawed bushrangers. Their spectacular raids on banks and towns, their horse-thieving and attacks on policemen made them notorious – and over the years many became national heroes.

The most famous and often-told story is that of the bushranger Ned Kelly (1855–80) who fashioned himself a suit of armour as a protection in gunfights. His knees, unfortunately for him, were unprotected and at a shoot-out at Glenrowan, he was shot in the legs and captured. Ned Kelly who has become a legendary figure in Australian folklore, was afterwards hanged.

(Left) Laying the floor of the Pedro Miguel Lock in 1912, one of the most important parts of the Panama Canal. Some men can be seen laying the concrete floor, others working on the enormous armour-plated gates.

1881

The First South African War

In 1881 the descendants of Dutch settlers in South Africa, known as Boers, rose against the British in an attempt to regain the independence that they had previously given up in return for protection against the warlike Zulus. The British were defeated at Majuba, and at the Convention of Pretoria, the Transvaal received a degree of self-government, pioneer Paulus Kruger (1825–1904) becoming president in 1883.

The quarrel was not over. Non-Boer European settlers (or *Uitlanders*, mainly British) swarmed into the Transvaal, threatening to out-number the Boers. Kruger denied them an effective vote. In 1895 L. S. Jameson (1853–1917) of the British South Africa Company led an unofficial raid into the Transvaal with the connivance of Cecil Rhodes (1853–1902) premier of Cape Colony. The raid did not succeed, and the hoped-for *Uitlander* uprising did not occur. (*See 1899 The Second South African War*).

1881

Ibsen's *Ghosts* published

Henrik Ibsen (1828–1906) was a Norwegian poet and an outstanding pioneer of social drama. His *Dukkehjem* ('A Doll's House') and *Genganere* ('Ghosts') were disliked at the time as they dealt with very controversial issues. A stroke in 1900 ended his literary career, but he had already caused a revolution in the world of drama.

1881

Parnell imprisoned

As an MP Charles Stewart Parnell (1846–91) was a leading figure in the struggle to win independence for Ireland. He used two methods to focus attention on Irish grievances: he deliberately obstructed debates at the House of Commons; and he organized the Irish peasants into boycotting unpopular, absent landlords.

In October 1881 Parnell was imprisoned for a short time for inciting the Irish, but while he was in prison disorders in Ireland grew worse and so Gladstone released him. In 1882 Irish terrorists murdered the Chief Secretary and Under-Secretary for Ireland as they were walking through Phoenix Park in Dublin. Parnell denounced the murders and later won a libel action against *The Times*, which had maintained that he had been involved.

Parnell remained a powerful political figure until he became involved in a sensational divorce case. Gladstone and public opinion swung against him immediately and he lost his hold on the Irish party.

1881

James's *Portrait of a Lady*

The American novelist, Henry James (1843–1916) is regarded as the master of the psychological novel, and one of the great influences on twentieth century literature. *Portrait of a Lady* is largely concerned with the impact of American life on the older European civilization.

1882

Koch isolates TB bacillus

Tuberculosis is a serious disease that occurs throughout the world. The most common form is tuberculosis of the lungs, sometimes called 'consumption'. For years it was believed that the disease might be contagious , but the infecting agent was not discovered until 1882, when the German bacteriologist Robert Koch (1843–1910) isolated the tubercle bacillus.

He discovered that the lungs are invaded by the bacilli and that the infected person expels them into the atmosphere when he coughs or talks. The bacilli are tough and resist disinfectants, but can be killed quickly by sunlight or ultra-violet light.

'Consumption' used to be called the 'white plague' and was incurable, but thanks to Koch's work and modern treatment, patients can now be completely restored to normal health.

1882

Australia wins the Ashes

When an Australian cricket team visited England in 1882 the Australians won the match by seven runs; a stump was 'cremated' in celebration and the ashes placed in an urn. The shattering

English defeat was given an obituary notice in the *Sporting Times* and since then in test matches between England and Australia the two teams have played for the 'Ashes'.

1883

Treasure Island is published

Robert Louis Stevenson (1850–94) was born in Scotland but died far away on the Pacific island of Samoa, where he had gone for the sake of his health. *Treasure Island* was his first popular adventure thriller and is read by both adults and children all over the world. Other well-known works include *Kidnapped* (an adventure story of the Scottish highlands) and *The Strange Case of Dr Jekyll and Mr Hyde*.

1883

Founding of the Fabian Society

In the winter of 1883 a Socialist group calling itself the Fabian Society was formed by a small gathering in London. Its aim was to spread socialism by peaceful means and so gradually to reconstruct society in accordance with the highest moral principles.

The Fabians, who were joined and later led by George Bernard Shaw and Sidney Webb, were influenced by Marxism, but they based their economic philosophy not on Marx but on John Stuart Mill (*see 1859 On Liberty is published*). Unlike the Marxists, who believed that the state should be overthrown, the Fabians regarded the state as a social machine which should be used to develop social welfare.

Beatrice Webb, Sidney's wife, later joined the society and together in 1894 they published their classic *History of Trade Unionism* and started the journal *The New Statesman* in 1913.

The society was and is largely a body of intellectuals and many leading trade unionists have been members.

A scene from Stevenson's *Treasure Island*.

1883
Krakatoa erupts

The volcano of Krakatoa (between Java and Sumatra) had been dormant for two hundred years when in 1883 it burst into violent eruptions that could be heard as far away as west Australia. Dense, volcanic clouds and ash were hurled into the air as huge waves, over thirty-six metres high, swamped the coasts of Java and Sumatra, drowning thirty-six thousand people.

1883
Thus spake Zarathustra is published

Friedrich Wilhelm Nietzsche (1844–1900) was a German philosopher and critic who was strongly anti-Christian. He believed that mankind was divided into two: a large herd, which he despised and a small, aristocratic master-class. His idea of a 'superman', developed in *Also sprach Zarathustra* ('Thus spake Zarathustra'), appealed particularly to the racist Nazis, although they often misinterpreted his philosophy.

1884
First steam turbo-generator

Sir Charles Algernon Parsons (1854–1931) was an English engineer, famous for his work on the steam turbine engine which he first constructed as a turbo-generator in 1884. In 1894 Parsons took out a patent to use the generator in ship propulsion; the first ship to be driven in this way was the *Turbinia* (1897) which created a sensation when it outpaced all other vessels at the Spithead Review of that year.

1884
First gramophone record is made

The oldest existing record is a cylinder record made in 1884. It was made by a man called Emile Berliner and was a recording of him reciting the Lord's Prayer. The first practical foil cylinder phonograph was manufactured in the USA in 1886 (*see 1878 Edison patents the phonograph*). In 1888 Berliner invented the flat disc to replace the cylinder. After 1948, the flat shellac disc was replaced by the long-playing record. More recently, this in its turn is being replaced by the compact disc, in which qualities of sound have proved excellent.

1884
Toulouse-Lautrec settles in Montmartre

Henri de Toulouse-Lautrec (1864–1901) was a French painter permanently crippled after an accident. In 1884 he settled in Montmartre which his paintings and posters were to make famous. Lautrec's studies of prostitutes, barmaids, clowns, actors and cabaret stars leave us with a vivid picture of the café and night-club life of Paris in *la belle époque*.

1884
William Morris forms Socialist League

William Morris (1834–96) was an English poet, artist and socialist and possibly one of the most talented of Britain's Victorians. He and a group of friends known as the 'brotherhood', used to meet and together read theology, ecclesiastical history, and medieval poetry. Morris adored the Middle Ages for their beauty and good craftsmanship and devoted his life to work which would rid society of the uglier aspects of a modernized, industrial civilization.

Morris set up a business which included the artists D. G. Rossetti (1828–82) and Burne-Jones (1833–98) to undertake church decor, carving, stained glass, chintzes and paper-hangings, always using pure colour and handwork.

In 1884 he helped set up the Socialist League and was arrested several times for his public speaking. However, he became less prominent when the Anarchist section took over. It was said by friends that his socialism was tinged with an inaccessible idealism, but his influence both on art and politics still lives on.

finally completing his first car in 1885. This was one of the earliest petrol-driven vehicles. He sold this car, which could do between 10 and 16km/h, and then joined the firm of Panhard and Lavasseur.

Meanwhile Gottlieb Daimler (1834–1900) was involved in similar work, making his first motor bicycle in 1885 and his first four-wheeled vehicle in 1886. In 1890 he founded the Daimler *Motoren-Gesellschaft*. In 1926 Benz's firm merged with Daimler's.

General Gordon, killed in Khartoum by rebels of the Mahdi.

1885

Benz's first motor car

Karl Benz (1844–1929) was a German engineer. In 1879 he founded an engine factory of his own, having constructed a two-stroke engine model, but he left the firm when his backers refused to finance a mobile engine.

Benz then set up another firm, Benz and Co., *Rheinische Gasmotorenfabrik*, where he developed a light high-speed four-stroke engine,

1885

Death of General Gordon

Charles George Gordon (1833–85) was a British soldier and a colonial administrator. He had served in the Crimean War, and had taken part in the capture of Peking when in 1863 the Chinese asked for his help in suppressing a number of rebellions. His success in crushing the rebels earned him the name of 'Chinese Gordon'.

In 1877 Gordon was appointed governor of the Sudan where his feats of government astounded the world. He returned a few years later having brought peace and order to the land.

Early in 1884 he was sent back to the Sudan to deal with an armed revolt led by the Mahdi. Instead of evacuating Khartoum as ordered, Gordon was determined to quash the Mahdi, whose troops surrounded Khartoum. The siege lasted for five months, but a relief expedition sent by Britain arrived too late. Khartoum had fallen and Gordon had been killed on the palace steps.

1886

Lawn Tennis Association founded

In about 1874 the All England Croquet Club, at Wimbledon, a suburb of London, discovered that it was short of money. In an attempt to boost the funds it added 'Lawn Tennis' to its title and several grass courts to its facilities. The first championships were held there in June 1877. In 1886 the English Lawn Tennis Association was founded.

For the first ninety years of the Wimbledon tennis championships, the contestants had to be amateurs. In 1968, however, the rules were changed to allow professional tennis players to compete and today, the championships are the most prestigious in the world.

1886

Canadian Pacific Railway completed

In 1869, the United States was linked, coast to coast, by railway, and a golden spike was hammered into the ground at the meeting point of lines built from the east coast and west coast.

In 1886 the Canadian Pacific Railway was completed, linking the Pacific to the Atlantic. Until then Canada had been no more than a loose association of provinces which were beginning to feel acutely their isolation from one another. On May 23, 1887 the first train ran from the east to Vancouver, a distance of about 5,380 kilometres.

1887

Sherlock Holmes's first case

Sherlock Holmes, the super-observant amateur detective, was the creation of English novelist Sir Arthur Conan Doyle (1859–1930). *A Study in Scarlet*, which appeared in 1887, introduced Holmes and Dr Watson, his good-natured, questioning friend and partner in crime detection. Holmes' methods of observation and deduction eventually influenced the ways in which the police dealt with real-life crimes.

1887

Strindberg's *The Father* is published

Johan August Strindberg (1849–1912) was a Swedish dramatist, novelist and poet, born in Stockholm. His plays *Fadren* ('The Father') and *Fröken Julie* ('Miss Julie', 1888), form an important landmark in the history of naturalism in the European theatre. Other similar plays followed, most of which were concerned with Strindberg's attack on marriage, a result of his own marital tragedy.

1888

Van Gogh paints *Sunflowers*

Vincent van Gogh (1853–90) was a Dutch post-Impressionist painter whose strong brush strokes and vigorous use of colour make his paintings unmistakable. In 1888 he moved alone and in poverty to Arles, France, where the sunbaked, violent landscape was to influence him in paintings such as *Sunflowers*. In 1889 he entered an asylum after cutting off his ear, and in 1890 he shot himself.

Sunflowers, perhaps Van Gogh's most famous painting.

1888

Pasteur Institute founded

Louis Pasteur (1822–95), a French chemist, was responsible for revolutionizing medical science. His researches led him to discover that fermentation and mould in food was not caused by a chemical reaction, but by microscopic living organisms. These findings led to the modern study of bacteriology. They also led Pasteur to find that germs could be killed by moderate heat. This process, called 'pasteurization' could be used to prevent beer, wine and milk from deteriorating and made it free from germs and infections.

Pasteur is perhaps best remembered for his vaccination of sheep and cows against anthrax, when he discovered that to inject an animal with a weakened culture of a disease would prevent the animal from developing the disease itself.

His last triumph was the development of a rabies vaccination and in 1888 the Pasteur Institute was founded in Paris to produce this vaccine. There are now over sixty Pasteur Research Institutes in the world.

1888

Rimsky-Korsakov's *Scheherazade*

Nikolai Andreievich Rimsky-Korsakov (1844–1908), the Russian composer was a member of 'The Five' (*see 1874 Mussorgsky's Boris Godunov*). In 1877 he published a collection of Russian folk songs and from 1887 to 1888 he produced his three great orchestral masterpieces, *Capriccio Espagnol, Easter Festival* and *Scheherazade*. His operatic masterpiece was the pastoral *Snow Maiden* (1882).

1889

Mayerling tragedy

Rudolph of Hapsburg (1858–89), Crown Prince of Austria, was the only son of the emperor Francis Joseph I of Austria and his wife, Elizabeth.

Rudolph was an extremely talented boy, and his father had great hopes for his future, but while the emperor was chiefly intent on his son's military education, Rudolph was keenly interested in natural history and the arts. He had a wide knowledge of modern literature and philosophy and as his revolutionary views became more apparent, he drifted away from his father.

Rudolph was married but soon became involved in a passionate love affair with the young and beautiful Baroness Marie Vetsera. The emperor ordered him to break off this liaison and in January 1889 came the tragic news: in a fit of despair Rudolph had shot the Baroness and then committed suicide. The bodies of the two lovers had been found in Rudolph's hunting lodge in Mayerling, near Vienna.

1889

Eiffel Tower is built

The Eiffel Tower was erected between 1887–89 at the time of the great Paris Exhibition. The engineer responsible for it, Gustave Eiffel (1832–1923), had already designed several notable bridges and viaducts. The Tower was built on the Champ-de-Mars in Paris at a cost of £260,000 and was three hundred metres high on completion.

1889

Second Socialist International

The Second Socialist International set up in Paris in 1889 was a second attempt at the organization of International Socialism (*see 1864 First Socialist International*).

It was not a highly centralized association as its predecessor had been and did not establish a formal secretariat until 1900.

The movement was seriously weakened by internal conflict and in 1905 the International in Amsterdam condemned the participation of socialist parties in 'bourgeois coalitions'. The outbreak of World War I in 1914 totally shattered the association, for the International had approved resolutions demanding joint action by the workers to prevent war, but the various national parties failed to respond. (*See 1919 Comintern formed.*)

1890
Fall of Bismarck

After the peace of Frankfurt (*see 1870 Franco-Prussian War*) Bismarck's policy, both domestic and foreign, concentrated on consolidating and securing the young German empire.

His domestic policy was marked by universal suffrage, nationalization of the Prussian railways, codification of the law and many attempts to combat socialism. However, he distrusted movements with international affiliations and quarrelled bitterly with the Roman Catholics in the 1870s (Bismarck feared the political power of the Vatican) and with the Socialists in the 1880s.

In 1888, Kaiser Wilhelm II (1859–1941) came to the German throne as emperor. A wilful and stubborn personality, Wilhelm dismissed Bismarck two years later. The Chancellor now found himself out of step with the younger generation in Germany and quarrelled with Wilhelm over home and foreign policy.

Wilhelm sought a new course for Germany, asserting the country's claim to world leadership. A long spell of personal rule now followed for the emperor, helped out by political favourites such as Holstein and Van Bülow.

1891
Oscar Wilde writes *Dorian Gray*

Oscar Fingall O'Flahertie Wills Wilde (1854–1900) was an Irish writer and poet who achieved immortality with plays such as *Lady Windermere's Fan* (1893) and *The Importance of Being Ernest* (1899), which are masterpieces of humour. Wilde became a notorious figure in London society, for his witty epigrams and unconventional behaviour.

Oscar Wilde, (second from left) surrounded by figures of London Society.

His concept of 'art for art's sake', the idea that aesthetic pleasure was an end in itself, found an echo with many European intellectuals at a time when the mainstream of European literature was concerned with naturalism and social issues. The aesthetic approach of Wilde's novel *The Picture of Dorian Gray* (1891) is also to be found in an extreme expression in the French novel *A Rebours* ('Against Nature', 1884) by J. K. Huysmans (1848–1907), and the illustrations of Aubrey Beardsley (1872–98). The figure of the aesthetic poet, striking a pose, became a favourite target of cartoonists in *Punch* and other humorous magazines.

1891
Gaugin starts Tahiti paintings

Paul Gauguin (1848–1903) was a French post-Impressionist painter. He had a deep-rooted hatred of civilization which led him to abandon his wife and family in favour of a primitive life. He spent some time in Martinique and then in Tahiti, which inspired his tapestry-like paintings in distinctive purples, greens, reds and browns.

1892
Diesel invents engine

The first practical diesel engine was invented in 1892 and demonstrated in 1898 by the German inventor Rudolf Diesel (1858–1913). The engine uses oil as a fuel; the air is compressed and heated before the fuel is let in and then the oil is sprayed into the cylinder so that tiny drops are ignited in the hot air. Today diesel engines are commonly used for buses, taxis, lorries and railway locomotives.

1893
Lilienthal successfully flies a glider

Otto Lilienthal (1849–96) was a German aeronautical inventor. He studied birds in flight with the idea of building a heavier-than-air flying machine like the birdman designs of Leonardo da Vinci. Lilienthal made over two thousand short glides, but in 1896 he crashed to his death.

Pioneer aviator Otto Lilienthal and his glider.

1893

Dvorák's *From the New World*

Antonin Dvorák (1841–1904) was a Czech composer born near Prague; his close friend was Brahms. His most famous work is his ninth symphony which he wrote in 1893 in New York, calling it a symphony *From the New World*. It contains some American folk themes, and the beautiful solo of the cor anglais is particularly noteworthy.

1893

Nansen sets sail in the *Fram*

Fridtjof Nansen (1861–1930) was a Norwegian explorer, whose most spectacular achievement began in 1893, when he set out on his voyage to the North Pole. Nansen decided to let his ship get frozen into the ice north of Siberia and drift with the current towards Greenland; the *Fram* had been specially built to survive the ordeal.

By September 1893 the *Fram* had reached the most northerly point of Siberia, where the ice was ten metres thick. The ship made fast to an ice-floe and began to drift northward, and in 1895 Nansen and a companion set off on foot across the ice. They came to within three hundred and twenty kilometres of the North Pole, farther north than any previous explorers, but turned back, exhausted by the extreme cold.

The *Fram* turned up a week after they had returned to Norway. As Nansen had hoped, it had drifted round the North Pole.

1894

The Dreyfus scandal

In October 1894 Alfred Dreyfus (1859–1935), a Jewish officer from Alsace on the French General Staff, was court-martialled for treason and sentenced to life imprisonment on Devil's Island, French Guiana. The evidence consisted of military letters, apparently in Dreyfus's handwriting, that were betraying France.

Dreyfus's family never ceased to believe in his innocence. When in 1896 the new Chief of Intelligence tried to re-open the case, he was silenced and transferred to Tunisia. He had named the real traitor as Major Esterhazy, who was tried but acquitted by a court-martial.

The French Radicals were soon aroused, believing that the General Staff had acted out of anti-semitic prejudice. The author, Emil Zola and the politician, Georges Clemenceau took up the case and eventually it was discovered that false evidence had been used against Dreyfus. The Dreyfusards pressed for acquittal and in July 1906 the court-martial verdict was quashed. Dreyfus was finally re-admitted to the army and given the Legion of Honour.

1894

Kipling's *Jungle Books* published

Rudyard Kipling (1865–1936) was an English writer born in India who wrote both for adults and for children. His best-loved works are his two *Jungle Books* (1894–95). The stories of Mowgli, the man-child brought up in the jungle by the wolf family are still read by children all over the world. *Kim* (1901) and *The Just-So Stories* (1902) are also much enjoyed.

India is the setting of Kipling's famous story *Kim*, about a child spy.

1895

Marconi's first wireless message

Guglielmo Marconi (1874–1937) was an Italian physicist and the inventor of the first practical system of wireless telegraphy. In 1895 he succeeded in transmitting wireless signals between sending and receiving points without the use of connecting wires, to a distance just over two kilometres.

In 1896 Marconi went to London where he met William Preece, engineer-in-chief of the post office. Preece offered him help and encouragement and Marconi took out his first patent in England in June. During that year he gave a series of demonstrations using balloons and kites to obtain greater height for his aerials. In 1898 Marconi managed to arrange wireless communication between ships and the shore and in 1899 he set up the first wireless communication between Britain and Europe.

Marconi's greatest triumph was to come in 1901, when he successfully transmitted wireless signals across the Atlantic ocean between England and Newfoundland.

Guglielmo Marconi

1895

Röntgen discovers X-rays

It was in 1895 that the German physicist Wilhelm Konrad von Röntgen (1845–1923) made his most important discovery. He noticed that when electrons travelling at high speed hit an aluminium anode at one end of a cathode ray tube curious rays escaped from the tube. This new radiation was called X-rays.

The discovery of X-rays started a new era in physics and medicine. In physics they can be used to find out how atoms and molecules are grouped in crystals and how they are arranged together in some of the major chemicals found in the body.

In medicine X-rays can be used to check broken or badly-formed bones (the first X-ray picture taken by Röntgen in 1898 showed the bone structure of his wife's hand) and higher energy rays can be used to treat cancer.

For his work on X-rays Röntgen was awarded the Rumford medal in 1896 and in 1901 the Nobel prize for physics.

Röntgen's invention was to have many uses. X-rays can be used by engineers to show up metal defects.

1895

The Lumière cinematograph

August Lumière (1862–1954) and his brother Louis (1864–1948) were French pioneer film-makers.

In 1889 Thomas Edison (*see 1878 Edison patents the phonograph*) patented a form of peep-show machine for showing photographic moving pictures to one viewer at a time. The Lumière brothers then began to manufacture films for the Edison peep-show and by 1895 they had patented a device which would both photograph and project films.

Throughout the year the Lumière brothers gave demonstrations of their cinematograph to photographic societies, and in the winter they rented a room in a café for their first public shows. It was the first time that films had been shown to a paying audience.

The audience found the films so realistic that when they saw a train coming towards them on the screen, many jumped up and rushed out of the cinema.

1895

Freud starts psycho-analysis

The founder of modern psychology was Sigmund Freud (1856–1939). Born at Freiburg, Moravia, he did much research, as a young man, into the physiology of the nervous system and then set up as a specialist in nervous diseases.

Freud soon found that he was able to cure one patient of hysteria by allowing her to talk freely while under hypnosis. Finding hypnosis inadequate Freud then encouraged patients to ramble on with their thoughts while in a state of relaxed consciousness. This method of drawing memories from the unconscious to the conscious mind became known as 'psycho-analysis'.

Freud had many great followers including Carl Jung (1875–1961) and Alfred Adler (1870–1937). Their pioneer work into the subconscious processes of the mind has had a far-reaching effect on people's attitude to the mentally ill.

1895

Maison de l'Art Nouveau opens

The *Maison de l'Art Nouveau* was a shop specializing in modern design which opened in Paris. The Art Nouveau movement was a series of decorative styles linked by a desire to be new and to keep up with the demands of the new age of technology. The style was used particularly in illustration and achieved its most dramatic effects in the work of Aubrey Beardsley (1872–98). Other artists involved in the movement include Mucha, Klimt and Schiele.

1895

Michelin's first car tyre

The first pneumatic tyres (patented by civil engineer R. W. Thompson in 1845) were demonstrated publicly for the first time in 1846. Pneumatic tyres are inflated with air. In 1895 the Paris cycle-tyre manufacturer, Edouard Michelin, fitted the first pneumatic motor-car tyres to a 4-horsepower Daimler, which he drove in the Paris–Bordeaux Race on June 11. Michelin had to change the tyres twenty-two times over the 1,200 kilometres long route.

The WAR *of the* WORLDS
By H. G. Wells

Author of "Under the Knife," "The Time Machine," etc.

(Left) From *The War of the Worlds*, Wells's classic science-fiction story of Martian invaders – malevolent creatures, 'unspeakably terrible'.

1895
H. G. Wells: *The Time Machine*

Herbert George Wells (1866–1946) the English novelist, was writing at a time when science and engineering were changing the face of the world. His scientific stories are highly imaginative; *The Time Machine* (which tells of a machine which could travel into the future) and other stories including *The Invisible Man* (in which a drug could make a man invisible) and *War of the Worlds* are fantastic adventures.

1895
Kiel Canal opened

The Kiel canal connects the North Sea and the Baltic and is the safest, most convenient, shortest and cheapest route for ships going from the one to the other. It is over one hundred kilometres long and fourteen metres deep and runs from the mouth of the Elbe to Hortenau, near Kiel.

Construction of the canal was started in 1887 and took eight years, and at one point over eighty thousand men were working on the canal. One of the main reasons for building it was to provide the German navy with means of communication between the naval stations at Wilhelmshaven and Kiel; since then it has been used for merchant vessels.

Occasionally ice-breakers have to be used in winter, but the canal is never closed and ships may pass through under their own power or may be towed, providing they keep to a speed limit between 5.4 and 8.1 knots.

1896
Nobel establishes prizes

Alfred Bernhard Nobel (1833–96), the Swedish inventor, was the son of an explosives manufacturer. In 1867 Nobel was assisting his father when he discovered how to make a safe and

Alfred Nobel

manageable explosive – dynamite. Nobel was disturbed by the destructive war potential of his discovery, however. So, at his death he left a fortune of over £2,000,000, most of which he left for annual prizes in the fields of physics, chemistry, medicine, physiology, literature and peace.

1896
Tchekov: *The Seagull*

The work of Anton Pavlovitch Tchekov (1860–1904) possesses a timeless quality, although it also reflects perfectly the life of middle-class Russian families. Tchekov was a great humanist who above all wanted to point out to his fellow countrymen the futility and falsity of their lives. *The Seagull, The Three Sisters* and *The Cherry Orchard* contain a delicate irony and humour that have made Tchekov one of the best-loved Russian authors.

1896
Olympic Games re-introduced

The Olympic Games (*see c.776 BC The first Olympic Games*) had not been held since AD394. It was through the efforts of Baron Pierre de Courbetin (1863–1937), a brilliant French scholar, that the Olympic Games were revived. Courbetin felt that new international understanding could result if amateur athletes from throughout the world were to meet once every four years. A new marble stadium was constructed in Athens for the first cycle of the games.

1896

Puccini's *La Bohème*

Giacomo Puccini (1858–1924) was the son of an Italian family of musicians. *Manon Lescaut* (1893) was his first great success and three years later followed his masterpiece, *La Bohème*, the story of which is the touching, but over-romanticized picture of student life. These, as well as *Madame Butterfly* and *Tosca*, have remained popular favourites.

A scene from *La Bohème*, Act III.

1897

Discovery of the electron

Sir Joseph John Thomson (1856–1940) the British mathematical physicist, was one of the outstanding pioneers of nuclear physics. His early work involved the application of dynamics to physics and chemistry.

In 1897 Thomson discovered that cathode rays consisted of negatively charged particles (electrons). Thomson measured their speed and charge and came to the conclusion that these electrons must be nearly two thousand times smaller in mass than the lightest known atomic particle, the hydrogen ion.

It was Thomson's work that led to a much greater understanding of electric currents, for current is made up of a flow of electrons; when electrons in a metal wire move at random there is no current; when a current flows the electrons all move in the same direction.

1898

The Spanish-American War

Tension between the USA and her Latin-American neighbours flared into war in 1898. Annoyed by Spain's harsh treatment of her colony of Cuba, disturbed by the effect of Cuban unrest on American investment, and provoked by the blowing-up of USS *Maine* in Havana harbour, the USA declared war on Spain. Spain was forced to give up the Philippines, Guam, and

A contemporary illustration of the destruction of the American battleship *Maine* in Havana harbour on February 15, 1898.

Puerto Rico. Cuba became independent, but was held closely under US political and economic influence until the communist revolution led by Fidel Castro in 1959.

1898
Tsiolkovsky: principles of rocket propulsion

Five years before centuries of experiments in flying finally succeeded with the Wright Brothers' aircraft of 1903, one man was already looking ahead to the days of space flight. Russian school teacher Konstantin Tsiolkovsky (1857–1935) was one of the first to take the idea of space travel seriously.

As early as 1898 Tsiolkovsky stated the principles of rocket reaction propulsion, and in 1903 he published a paper in which he pointed out that the rocket engine alone would work in the vacuum of space.

Further development of rocket theory came in the 1920s from German Hermann Oberth, and also from American Robert Hutchings Goddard, who fired the first liquid-fuelled rocket (primitive solid-fuelled rockets having been used by the Chinese as early as 1232). In the Second World War the Germans developed the V-2 rocket, used to bomb London, and after the war both the USA and the USSR used German scientists and technology to found their space programmes of the 1950s.

1898
The discovery of radium

A major discovery was made in 1898, which was to change the course of science and transform medicine. The French physicist Pierre Curie (1859–1906) and his Polish wife Marie (1867–1934) discovered, in the course of their experiments, the radioactive elements radium and polonium.

(Left) Pierre and Marie Curie in their laboratory.

Their discovery of these elements was the birth of modern nuclear physics and led to the whole science of radiotherapy. The couple were awarded the Nobel Prize in 1903, which they shared with French physicist Antoine Henri Becquerel (1852–1908) who had first discovered the rays emitted by uranium salts.

Pierre Curie was killed in an accident in 1906, but Marie became Professor of Physics at the Sorbonne in his place. She went on to isolate the new elements in 1910 and afterwards worked to develop the medical and other uses of radium. Her achievements were recognized by a further Nobel Prize and an honorary professorship in radiology at Warsaw.

1899
The Second South African War

The struggle between British and Dutch settlers (or Boers) in South Africa continued. The Jameson Raid of 1895 (see 1881 The First South African War) had cleared the way for a major war, and in 1899 it broke out in earnest.

In the first months the Boers had the upper hand, besieging the British garrisons at Ladysmith, Mafeking and Kimberley.

Lord Roberts (1832–1914) and Lord Kitchener (1850–1916) launched the counter-attack; the garrisons were relieved, amidst rejoicing in England. Kruger fled, and in June 1900 the British took Pretoria. With their capital in enemy hands, the Boers took to a guerrilla campaign, harassing British units. Kitchener set up block-houses and moved civilians who supported the Boers into concentration camps.

Peace finally came with the Treaty of Vereeniging in 1902; Transvaal and the Orange Free State became part of the British Empire, and by 1910 the two sides had sufficiently settled their differences to form the Union of South Africa.

1899
Sibelius composes *Finlandia*

In 1899 Finnish composer Jean Sibelius (1865–1957) wrote a symphonic poem, *Finlandia*, that reflected his passionate love of his native country. His symphonic poems, symphonies and violin concerto all showed an originality that won him international renown. His last published work, *Tapiola* appeared in 1926.

1899
Sarah Bernhardt founds theatre

In 1899 a theatre was founded in Paris by the most remarkable actress of the day. French *tragédienne* Sarah Bernhardt (1844–1923) had made her début with the Théatre Français in 1862, and within a few years was appearing throughout Europe and America. In 1915 she had a leg amputated, but continued her acting career, a legend in her own time.

1900
The Boxer Rebellion

At the turn of the twentieth century, foreign influence in China had grown to such proportions that some Chinese felt their own way of life was threatened. In 1895, China had lost Korea to Japan, and the Japanese, Germans, Russians, British, French and Americans had many trading rights and privileges which had been wrung from successive Chinese Emperors. In 1900 a young nationalist movement known as the 'Society of Harmonious Fists' or the 'Boxers' rose against the foreigners.

Christians and missionaries were killed, and foreign-owned railways attacked. A riot occurred in Peking, supported by the Dowager Empress Tzu Hsi (1834–1908). The German minister was killed, and foreign embassies besieged.

A six-nation force (from Japan, Britain, Russia,

The Boxer Rebellion in Peking.

France, Germany and the USA) relieved the embassies, and then looted the city. The indemnities demanded from China for the revolt fostered further bitterness. Anti-foreign feeling grew, culminating in the nationalist movement of Sun Yat-Sen (*see 1911 China declared a republic*)

1900
Elgar's *The Dream of Gerontius*

In 1900 the English composer Edward Elgar (1857–1934) wrote his oratorio *The Dream of Gerontius*. Although it was not successful at its first performance, together with the *Enigma Variations* (1899) it established his position as a great figure in English music. Other works by Elgar include two symphonies, concertos for violin and cello, and the popular *Pomp and Circumstance* marches.

1900
Max Planck's Quantum Theory

In 1900 a German scientist, Max Planck (1858–1947), who was professor of physics at Berlin University, published his Quantum Theory. Put simply, this stated that energy is emitted in small units called quanta. It successfully explained certain scientific phenomena which Sir Isaac Newton's laws on physics had been unable to account for.

Planck's new theory was to influence almost every development in modern physics. Albert Einstein successfully applied the Quantum Theory to light and was thus able to formulate his theory of relativity. The Danish scientist Niels Bohr (1885–1962) made use of Planck's ideas in his research into atomic structure, which eventually led to the development of nuclear energy. In 1918 Max Planck was awarded the Nobel prize for physics for his work and in 1926 he was elected a member of the Royal Society.

1900

Conrad's *Lord Jim*

In 1900 the Polish-born naturalized British novelist Joseph Conrad (1857–1924) published *Lord Jim*, the story of a man who tries to redeem himself after an act of cowardice. Like many of Conrad's other novels, including *An Outcast of the Islands* (1896) and *Mirror of the Sea* (1906), it is concerned with life at sea in faraway places.

1901

Accession of Edward VII

In 1901 Queen Victoria died at the age of eighty-one; she had reigned over Britain for sixty-three years. The Victorian era had seen the peak of British imperialism and industrial advance; a quarter of the globe had come under the British flag. The queen had set strict standards of morality, and expected others to conform to them.

The Prince of Wales (1841–1910) who acceded to the throne as Edward VII on his mother's death, was a very different character: known throughout Europe for his life of idle pleasure and love of pageantry, he was nevertheless a popular figure and proved an able king in his short reign of nine years. He established the *Entente Cordiale* with France, and improved relations with Japan and Russia. Fortunately, the king did not live to see the failure of his efforts at increasing international understanding. That failure became clear with the outbreak of the First World War in 1914, by which time Edward had been succeeded by his son as King George V (1865–1936).

1901

Opening of the Trans-Siberian Railway

In 1891 work began on the Trans-Siberian Railway which was to link European Russia with the Pacific Coast. The railway was officially opened in 1901 although the final section was not completed until 1917. The longest continuous stretch of railway in the world (9,300 kilometres), it made possible the large-scale industrial development of Siberia.

1901

Theodore Roosevelt becomes president

In September 1901 William McKinley, the twenty-fifth president of the United States, was assassinated by an anarchist. He was succeeded in office by the vice-president, Theodore Roosevelt (1858–1919), who became the youngest president in the history of the country. McKinley had supported expansionist policies, and during his term of office the United States acquired the Philippines and Puerto Rico.

Roosevelt was an energetic and ambitious man, who had become famous during the Spanish–American War of 1898, when he commanded a volunteer force of 'rough riders' in Cuba. His aggressive foreign policy was designed to secure US dominance over South America and in 1903 he obtained control of the Panama Canal Zone.

At home Roosevelt expanded the powers of the presidency and took action to restrict the growth of big business organizations. Re-elected president in 1904, he retired in 1909, and was defeated when he stood again for office in 1912.

1902

W. B. Yeats' *Kathleen ni Houlihan*

In 1902 the play *Kathleen ni Houlihan* by the Irish poet and dramatist William Butler Yeats (1865–1939) was first performed. Yeats, who was a leading figure in the Irish literary revival, and already achieved success with *The Land of Heart's Desire* (1894). He is chiefly remembered for his fine volumes of lyric poetry, including *The Wild Swans at Coole* (1917) and *The Winding Stair* (1929).

1903

The Wright brothers' first flight

In the United States two brothers Orville (1871–1948) and Wilbur Wright (1867–1912) became interested in aviation when they read

The Wright brothers' *Flyer*.

about the gliding experiments of Otto Lilienthal in Germany (*see 1893 Lilienthal successfully flies a glider*). While running a cycle manufacturing and repair business they began building and flying gliders.

In 1903 they constructed an aeroplane fitted with a 12-horsepower petrol engine, which was successfully flown by Orville later that year near Kittyhawk, North Carolina – the first controlled flight made by man in a heavier-than-air machine. They went on to build other aeroplanes and in 1905 had a machine which could stay airborne for more than thirty minutes.

Wilbur Wright toured Europe where he made pioneering flights with their aeroplanes in Britain, France and Italy, and in 1909 the brothers formed their own aircraft production company. After Wilbur's death, Orville devoted most of his life to research.

1903
First Tour de France

By the 1890s cycling racing had become a popular sport in many countries. In 1903 a French cyclist Henri Degrange (1865–1940) established the Tour de France which has remained the most famous international cycling race. The contestants cover some 4,000 kilometres in about twenty-one daily stages in flat and hilly country, mainly in France and Belgium.

1903
Women's Political and Social Union formed

As early as 1792 English writer Mary Wollstonecraft had been campaigning for women's rights, and parliamentary lobbying had gone on throughout the nineteenth century with little progress except for an entitlement to vote in local elections (1894).

Foremost amongst the 'suffragettes' as the campaigners for women's suffrage were called, were Emmeline Pankhurst (1857–1928) and her daughters Christabel (1880–1958) and Sylvia (1882–1960). As all women's suffrage bills were rejected, the Women's Social and Political Union (founded in 1903) resorted to increasing militancy, cutting telephone lines, damaging property, chaining themselves to railings; in 1913 Emily Davidson even gave her life by throwing herself under the King's horse at the Derby.

All protests were met with brutal suppression; militants were sent to prison, where their hunger-strikes were dealt with by crude forced feeding that nearly killed some of them.

The First World War involved women for the first time in traditionally male areas of work. Public attitudes changed and the end of the war saw votes for certain categories of women (*see 1928 Votes for all women in UK*).

1904
J. M. Barrie's *Peter Pan*

In 1904 *Peter Pan*, a play by the Scottish novelist and dramatist James Barrie (1860–1937) was first performed. The story of a little boy who does not want to grow up, it has remained a great favourite with children. Other popular plays by Barrie include *The Admirable Crichton* (1902) and *Dear Brutus* (1917), and his best-known novel is *The Little Minister* (1891).

1904
Rodin's *The Thinker*

In 1904 the French sculptor Auguste Rodin (1840–1917) completed his statue *The Thinker*. Rodin had already established his reputation with such works as *The Burghers of Calais* (1886–95), *Balzac* (1891), and *The Kiss* (1898). He was influenced by the great sculptors of the Italian Renaissance and by sculpture of the Gothic period.

A demonstration in the campaign to gain the vote for women.

1904
Russo-Japanese War

During the nineteenth century Russia was continually trying to expand its eastern frontiers at the expense of a weakened Chinese Empire. However, Japan, which was rapidly transforming itself from a backward feudal state into a modern industrial power, also began to make demands on China. A clash between Russia and Japan became inevitable when both countries attempted to extend their influence in Manchuria and Korea.

In February 1904 without warning the Japanese navy attacked the Russian fleet at Port Arthur, a Chinese seaport which had been leased to Russia as a naval base. The Japanese army subsequently defeated the Russians at the Yalu river between Korea and Manchuria – the first time the Japanese had won a victory over a Western nation.

In May 1905 a Russian fleet which had sailed all the way from the Baltic was almost completely destroyed by Japanese warships off the island of Tsushima. A humiliated Russia made peace with Japan in September 1905.

帝國艦隊旅順攻擊手

Previous pages: the Japanese navy bombs Port Arthur during the Russo–Japanese War.

1905
Unrest in Russia

At the beginning of the twentieth century there was considerable unrest among the Russian people, because Czar Nicholas II (1868–1918) refused to establish a constitutional government. Opposition to his autocratic rule came to a head when Russia suffered humiliating defeats at the hands of the Japanese in the war of 1904–05.

On January 20, 1905, troops opened fire on demonstrators in St Petersburg (now Leningrad) and hundreds of people were killed or injured. This incident, known as 'Bloody Sunday', led to strikes and other disturbances in many parts of the country, and mutinies in the army and navy. In October 1905 Russia was paralyzed by a general strike and it seemed possible that revolutionaries might seize power.

With great reluctance Nicholas II issued the so-called 'October Manifesto' which promised to set up an elected parliament and to grant the Russian people full civil liberties.

1905
Einstein's Special Theory of Relativity

In 1905 the German physicist Albert Einstein (1879–1955) published his Special Theory of Relativity. This was one of the most important developments in the history of science, because it completely changed man's ideas about the nature of the universe and upset traditional notions about the measurement of time and space.

Einstein showed that there is no such thing as absolute motion, but that all motion is relative. Time, like motion, is not absolute, so that it is impossible to speak of two events occurring in different places as happening at the same time. Einstein also showed that there is no real difference between matter and energy, and that the mass of an object increases with the speed at which it travels.

In 1915 Einstein put forward his General Theory of Relativity which made fundamental changes to ideas about gravitation which had been held since the time of Sir Isaac Newton. Einstein was awarded the Nobel Prize for physics in 1921.

1905
Norway achieves independence

Norway, which had long been a dependency of Denmark, was united to Sweden in 1814. The Swedish king also became King of Norway, although the Norwegians kept their own parliament – the *Storting*.

The Norwegians grew increasingly discontented with their subordinate position and in 1905 the union with Sweden was ended. A Danish prince became king of an independent Norway as Haakon VII.

1905
Debussy's *La Mer*

In 1905 the French composer Claude Debussy (1862–1918) wrote his orchestral piece *La Mer*, a striking impression of the sea. It showed the same originality of musical expression which had already made his piano music famous. Debussy was the founder of the 'Impressionist School' in music, in which tone was all important. Other works by Debussy include *L'Après-Midi d'un Faune* (1894), *Pelléas et Mélisande* (1902), numerous pieces for piano, and chamber music.

1906
First Grand Prix

Motor racing had begun in 1894 between Paris and Rouen. In 1906 the French car manufacturing industry established at Le Mans a new kind of event, the Grand Prix, with no limitations on the number of cars entered by any country. In Britain the first track especially built for motor racing was opened at Brooklands, Surrey, in 1907.

1906
The Fauve movement

Fauvism was a style of painting which flourished in France in the early 1900s. When an exhibition by painters of this group was shown in Paris in 1905, one art critic, shocked by the violence of their work, referred to them as *fauves* ('wild beasts'), and this name remained attached.

By 1906 Fauvism had become established as an important art movement, with Henri Matisse (1869–1954) as its leader and most talented exponent. Paintings by the Fauves were characterized by the use of brilliant, intense colours, applied straight to the canvas in an apparently indiscriminate manner, with forceful brushstrokes, in order to create an explosive effect. Other notable Fauvist painters were André Dérain (1880–1954), Georges Rouault (1871–1958) and Maurice de Vlaminck (1876–1958).

By 1908 the Fauvist movement had come to an end but it had been a significant development in modern painting, which prepared the way for even more fundamental changes.

1906
The first Cubist painting

The most outstanding painter of his time was Spanish-born Pablo Picasso (1881–1973). Having quickly mastered both traditional and impressionist forms of painting, he sought an entirely new artistic expression. In 1906–07 he painted *Les Demoiselles d'Avignon*, which initiated the Cubist movement. The influence of Cubism spread among a number of young French painters, notably Georges Braque (1882–1963) and Fernand Léger (1881–1955), and the first Cubist paintings caused a storm. These artists explored geometrical forms, distorting and abstracting the conventional representation of the subject.

Picasso produced a vast amount of very diverse work during his life, constantly developing, and modifying his style. In 1917 he designed for the Diaghilev ballet and in his later years he designed ceramics. His greatest masterpiece is *Guernica* (1937) a large canvas expressing his horror of fascism and the bombing of this town in the Spanish Civil War.

1906
The San Francisco earthquake

San Francisco had already experienced earth tremors on three occasions in the past fifty years when on April 18, 1906, it suffered a severe

Following pages: Grand Prix racing really began in 1906 in France, on a circuit near Le Mans. Here, the artist Gordon Crosby (one of the most famous automotive artists ever) shows Szisz in the winning Renault overtaking Duray's De Dietrich. Szisz's average speed was 63 m.p.h.

earthquake. This caused widespread devastation and was followed by a fire in the centre of the town. Much of San Francisco was destroyed, hundreds of people died, and more than 200,000 were made homeless.

1906
First radio broadcast

In December 1906 an American physicist, R. A. Fessenden, broadcast the first-known radio programme from his experimental station at Brant Rock, Massachusetts, USA. The programme, which included some items of music and a talk, was heard by listeners with receiving equipment up to twenty-four kilometres away. However, proper sound broadcasting to large audiences did not begin until the 1920s.

1907
Rilke's *Poems*

In 1907–08 the Austrian poet Rainer Maria Rilke (1875–1926) published his *Poems*. He had already established his reputation with *Life and Songs* (1894) and *Poems from the Book of Hours* (1905). Rilke is one of the greatest lyric poets in the German language and his finest work is generally considered to be the *Duino Elegies* and *Sonnets to Orpheus*, both of which appeared in 1923.

1908
Revolt of the Young Turks

In the early 1900s there was much resentment in Turkey over the repressive regime of Sultan Abdul Hamid II (1876–1909). Many Turks who had fled abroad in order to escape his harsh rule

became influenced by Western political ideas. They wanted liberal reforms, including the restoration of the more democratic Constitution of 1876.

The exiles made contact with discontented Turkish army officers who rose in revolt in Macedonia in July 1908. The rebels were led by an organization known as the Committee of Union and Progress. Realizing he could not rely on other army units to put down the revolt, Abdul Hamid agreed to restore the Constitution and to summon a Parliament.

When in 1909 he attempted to stage a counter-revolution he was deposed and exiled. Turkey was now under the effective control of the 'Young Turk' army officers, who adopted a strongly nationalistic policy.

1908
Ravel's *Ma Mère l'Oye*

In 1908 the French composer Maurice Ravel (1875–1937) wrote his piano duet *Ma Mère l'Oye* ('Mother Goose). He had already achieved success with other piano pieces like *Pavane pour une Infante défunte* (1899), and *Sonatina* and *Miroirs* (both 1905). He went on to even greater fame with his music for the ballet *Daphnis et Chloé* (1912), his opera *L'Enfant et les Sortilèges* (1925) and his *Bolero* (1928).

1908
Belgium annexes the Congo Free State

The opening up of vast tracts of Africa in the late nineteenth century led to a race to found colonies there by the powerful nations of Europe. From 1885 the Congo Free State, the country now known as Zaïre, was ruled by an international association under King Leopold II of Belgium. He opened up trade and communication, subdued the Arab slave traders, and settled territorial claims by France and Portugal. Charges of corrupt administration and atrocities led the Belgian government to take over the state in 1908. Their rule was to last fifty-two years. (*See 1960 Fighting in the Congo (Zaïre).*)

1908
Boy Scout movement founded

In 1908 Robert Baden-Powell (1857–1941), a British army officer, founded the Boy Scout movement, an organization which taught boys to be good citizens and to become skilful in various outdoor activities. So great was its popularity that Boy Scout movements quickly grew up in other countries. In 1910 a similar organization for girls – the Girl Guides – was also established.

1909
Ford produces the Model T

In its early days motoring was the preserve of the rich man or the specialist. When Henry Ford

Model T Ford

(1863–1947) set up the Ford Motor Company in Detroit (USA) in 1903, he planned to bring motoring within the reach of all. By introducing mass production techniques, such as the continuously moving assembly line, he hoped to produce a cheap standardized car that required little maintenance.

Ford's solution was the Model T, a small family car that was to make his fortune. 'Any customer can have a car painted any colour that he wants, so long as it is black', announced Ford.

For eighteen years Ford produced nothing but the Model T, selling in this period nearly sixteen million cars. The 1909 price for a Model T was $950; by 1922 it was $295, and a new car was leaving the production line every fifteen seconds. The age of popular motoring had arrived.

1909
Peary reaches the North Pole

On April 6, 1909 Robert Peary, a commander in the US Navy, became the first man to stand at the North Pole. Peary (1856–1920) was the veteran of several Arctic expeditions in which he and his men had experienced extreme hardship and bitter cold. In 1908 he set out on the expedition which was to bring success, in the polar exploration ship *Roosevelt*.

Wintering in Grant Land, he set out across the ice from Cape Columbia in March 1909. As supplies ran low Peary sent his men back, until only Matt Henson, who was a Negro, and four Eskimos remained with him. They pressed forward, and on reaching the Pole spent thirty-six hours taking observations and soundings. Peary made the return journey in safety, but lost one member of his team; in 1911 he was made a Rear-admiral.

1909
Blériot flies the English Channel

In the early days of aviation bi-planes (two-winged) and tri-planes (three-winged) were much in favour. Louis Blériot (1872–1936) was a French engineer and aviator who was an early advocate of the monoplane which had only one wing. Having founded the first aircraft factory in

France in 1906, Blériot made several pioneering flights within France. On July 25, 1909 he left Calais in a small 25 hp monoplane, and landed successfully at Dover having made the first international flight. He was awarded a prize of £1,000 by the *London Daily Mail*.

1909
Diaghilev brings Nijinsky to Paris

Sergei Diaghilev (1872–1929) was a Russian impresario who brought Russian opera and ballet to Europe. The originality of his productions such as Mussorgsky's *Boris Godunov* inspired a vitality long absent from the Western

Nijinsky dances with Tamara Karsavina.

European stage. In 1909 he brought Vaslav Nijinsky to Paris as his leading dancer. Nijinsky (1890–1950) became an extremely popular dancer, though his choreography was less successful; tragically he became insane in 1917.

1910
The arrest of Crippen

In 1910 the British public was scandalized by news of a brutal murder. Dr Crippen was an American who settled in London, and was suspected of murdering his second wife for love of his secretary. Fleeing to Antwerp, he boarded an Atlantic liner with his secretary disguised as a boy. The captain was suspicious and telegraphed Scotland Yard – the first time radio had been used for police work. The arrest was dramatic: a detective disguised as a pilot boarded the liner and took them into custody. Crippen was tried and though he claimed he was innocent, he was found guilty and executed.

1911

Richard Strauss: *Der Rosenkavalier*

Richard Strauss (1864–1949) was a German composer who in works such as *Also Sprach Zarathustra* ('Thus spake Zarathustra', 1896) proved himself to be master of symphonic form. Turning to opera, he again achieved success: *Der Rosenkavalier*, with a libretto by the Austrian writer Hugo von Hofmannsthal (1874–1929), is a sensitive work, set in eighteenth-century Vienna. It was first produced in Dresden in 1911.

1911

Jung's *The Psychology of the Unconscious*

Until the publication of this work in 1911 the Swiss psychiatrist Carl Jung (1875–1961) was the leading collaborator of Sigmund Freud. His research into psychoanalysis led him to disagree with Freud's interpretations, and his life's work transformed the study of psychology. Much of this work was concerned with the symbolism of dreams, myths and religions. (*See 1895 Freud starts psychoanalysis*).

1911

Alexander's Ragtime Band

The most popular song of 1911 was an early tune by the American composer Irving Berlin: *Alexander's Ragtime Band*. The invention of the gramophone and the mass production of records led to a revolution in popular musical taste. In Britain the music halls provided a wealth of popular songs, but for some years the influence of American folk music and minstrel shows had been growing.

Negro work songs and spirituals led to the musical style known as 'blues', songs reflecting the hard life of the American negro. In New Orleans military band instruments accompanied parades, and negro pianists developed a style of playing known as 'ragtime' using syncopation, i.e. the stressing of normally unaccented beats.

From all these sources there evolved 'jazz', a highly rhythmic music relying on improvisation. This unconventional music soon became 'respectable' and very popular in both Europe and the USA.

1911

China declared a republic

In the unstable years after the 1900 Boxer rebellion, China was oppressed by foreign powers and seethed with internal discontent. In 1911 a revolution under Sun Yat-Sen (1866–1925) finally swept away the Manchu dynasty, and a republic was declared. Yuan Shih-k'ai (1859–1916) became president, but soon China reverted to political chaos and civil war.

1911

The Expressionist Exhibition

In December 1911 a first exhibition of paintings was held in Munich, Germany, by artists calling themselves the *Blauer Reiter* ('Blue Rider') Group. This group, including Wasilly Kandinsky (1866–1944) and Franz Marc (1880–1916), were part of a literary and artistic movement known as Expressionism, whose influence was to spread to drama, film, music and architecture.

Expressionism was a youthful reaction against the conventions of its day. Inspired by Marx and Nietzsche, the Expressionists wanted to involve the artist in the creation of a new age. They rejected the Impressionists' idea of recording light and atmosphere in order to reproduce the appearance of nature, preferring the powerful, tragic paintings of the Norwegian Edvard Munch (1863–1944). Other painters influenced by Expressionism were Paul Klee (1879–1940) and Oscar Kokoschka (1886–1980).

The Expressionist viewpoint appeared in the extremely emotional, fragmented literature of Germany at this time, and was later reflected in films such as Lang's *Dr Caligari*. The musician

Scott (centre) and his party at the South Pole – one month after Amundsen.

Arnold Schönberg was a member of the *Blauer Reiter* group (*see 1921 Schönberg: Twelve-note System of Composition*).

Amundsen's expedition reaches the South Pole.

1911

Amundsen and Scott reach the South Pole

In 1911 two expeditions were battling through the hostile and unknown landscape of Antarctica. Roald Amundsen (1872–1928) was a Norwegian experienced in polar exploration, whose expedition had set out the previous year. In December Amundsen became the first person to reach the South Pole.

The second expedition was headed by Robert Falcon Scott (1868–1912) a captain in the Royal Navy. His sledge team, including Wilson, Oates, Bowers and Evans, finally reached the Pole on January 17, 1912, only to find that Amundsen had beaten them by a month.

Disaster struck the return journey. Ferocious blizzards hindered their progress, and Evans died. A month later Captain Oates became too ill to continue. Rather than endanger his friends further, he walked out of his tent into a blizzard. The weather became worse and the situation hopeless; the remaining three perished at the end of March 1912. Their bodies, together with their diaries and records, were found by a search party eight months later.

1911
Revolution in Mexico

In 1911, the dictator Porfirio Diaz had been president of Mexico for thirty-five years. There was much discontent with Diaz' corrupt and despotic rule which gave foreigners many privileges in Mexico, and left ordinary people poor and starving while a few landowners and others became very rich. In 1911, however, a revolution headed by the democrat Francisco Madero overthrew Diaz. Madero became president, but his hopes for a better Mexico did not materialize immediately.

Madero was himself overthrown and murdered in 1913 and years of civil war followed before a new Mexico emerged with the Constitution of 1917. Under this Constitution, all Mexicans were given the vote, the power and property of foreigners and the rich were limited and a redistribution of land gave poorer Mexicans a chance to make a better life for themselves. These reforms were the first moves towards democracy ever made in Latin America.

1912
Shaw writes *Pygmalion*

Pygmalion is the story of a professor of phonetics who transforms a cockney flower girl into a lady of high society. Shaw named his play after a legendary king of Cyprus who fell in love with a statue and caused it to come to life. This play proved very popular, being filmed in 1938, and adapted into the musical *My Fair Lady* in 1956.

George Bernard Shaw (1856–1950) was born in Ireland; settling in London he soon became renowned as a fiery critic and pamphleteer. An energetic socialist involved in the Fabian Society, Shaw wrote plays with a message for his age, including *Arms and the Man*, *The Devil's Disciple*, *Candida*, *Caesar and Cleopatra*, *The Apple Cart* and *St Joan*.

1912
Sinking of the *Titanic*

The British ocean liner *Titanic* was intended to be the pride of the Atlantic crossing. At 46,300 tonnes she was the largest ship afloat and was widely regarded as unsinkable, so there was no shortage of passengers for her prestigious maiden voyage. The captain was eager to reach New York in daylight, but he underestimated the danger of icebergs. At 2.20a.m. on April 15, 1912, disaster struck: the *Titanic* ran into an iceberg at full speed and quickly sank. Of 2,224 passengers there were only 711 survivors. The disaster shocked the world, and led to a greater concern for maritime safety procedures especially the provision of radio on more ships.

1913
Alain-Fournier: *Le Grand Meaulnes*

Henri-Alban Fournier (1866–1914), better known by his pen name of Alain-Fournier, was killed in the First World War, having produced one of the outstanding French novels of this century. *Le Grand Meaulnes* ('The Wanderer', 1913) deals with a young man's awakening to love, and his yearning for the lost world of childhood.

1913
Robert Frost: *A Boy's Will*

Robert Frost (1874–1963) is recognized as one of the foremost American poets of the century. Born in San Francisco, he studied at Harvard; his poetry portrays the countryside and everyday life of New England. Frost spent three years in Britain, 1912–15, where he was encouraged to publish *A Boy's Will* which gained him an international reputation.

1913
Stravinsky: *The Rite of Spring*

Igor Stravinsky (1882–1971), an outstanding musical genius of the century, found fame with the Diaghilev Ballet's production of *The Firebird* and *Petrushka* (*see 1909 Diaghilev brings Nijinsky to Paris*). Primitive rituals of his native Russia form the basis of *The Rite of Spring*; its harsh dissonance and strange rhythms caused an outrage at its première. Stravinsky's interest extended to opera, choral and instrumental work, and eventually to twelve-note composition.

1913
Invention of the geiger counter

When a material is suspected of being radioactive, or a radiation leak is thought to be occurring, a geiger counter is used to detect the radiation. The device was invented by the German physicist Hans Geiger (1882–1945) as part of his investigations with Rutherford into beta-ray radioactivity in 1913.

Further developed with the help of Müller the counter, across which a high voltage is applied, contains a gas held at low pressure, which surrounds a metal cathode cylinder. This has a thin wire anode running down the centre. If any particles of ionizing radiation enter, the gas is ionized, and a momentary current runs through the tube. The change in voltage is amplified electronically to give a reading.

Radio-isotopes are widely used in medicine, and radiation can also be a dangerous hazard in much scientific and industrial work. Instruments measuring radioactivity are vital to health and safety.

A geiger counter.

1913
Albert Schweitzer founds his hospital

In 1913 a remarkable man appeared at the Lambaréné mission station on the Ogowe river in French Equatorial Africa (Gabon). Alsace-born Albert Schweitzer (1875–1965) had already become internationally famous as a musician and theologian when he decided to devote the rest

of his life to humanitarian work. He studied medicine, and with the help of his new wife set up a hospital at Lambaréné to fight sleeping sickness and leprosy.

For the rest of his life he worked at his hospital village, for which he raised funds by giving organ recitals in Europe.

Although paternalistic towards the local people, Schweitzer devoted himself to their welfare with vigour and application, developing an ethical code based on the principle of 'reverence for life'. His achievements were recognized by the award of a Nobel Peace Prize in 1952. Despite his tireless activities he found time to write a number of works on ethics and accounts of his experiences in Africa.

1913
Proust writes *Du Côté de Chez Swann*

Du Côté de Chez Swann ('Swann's Way') was the first of the thirteen volumes that make up the great work of French novelist Marcel Proust (1871–1922): *A la Recherche du Temps Perdu* ('Remembrance of Time Past').

Proust delves into the inner emotions of his characters; he is concerned with the role of memory in the subconscious, and with the passing of time.

1914
Charlie Chaplin goes to Hollywood

In the years before the First World War the film business was in its infancy. One of the best known stars of the early silent films was Charlie Chaplin, whose trademark of bowler hat and cane won international renown. Charlie Chaplin was born in poverty in London, in 1889, and his early stage experience was in vaudeville. He came to Hollywood in 1914, and in his portrayal of the down-and-out splay-footed tramp in films such as *The Gold Rush* is still popular today. He later turned to directing films.

The film industry grew in the USA as nowhere else. Giants such as directors Sam Goldwyn (1882–1974) and Cecil B. de Mille (1881–1959) laid the foundations, and in the post-

Images of Hollywood: Charlie Chaplin; *The Great Train Robbery* (the first western); Greta Garbo, star of the 1930s.

war years stars such as Mary Pickford, Rudolph Valentino, Laurel and Hardy and Buster Keaton became household names.

1914
Holst composes *The Planets*

The Planets, composed by English composer Gustav Holst between 1914 and 1917, is a seven-movement suite inspired by the astrological significance of each planet. This popular work was the first to show Holst (1874–1934) as a major composer. Other works include the *Hymn of Jesus* (1917) and the *Concerto for Two Violins* (1929).

1914
Outbreak of the First World War

The great European powers had long been suspicious of each other's motives, eager for power, and intent on arming themselves against the possibility of war. Tension between France and Germany had not relaxed since the Franco–Prussian war of 1871; Germany had the best army in Europe and was now rivalling Britain in naval power. Austria, Hungary and Russia were vying for power in the Balkans. In this mood of fear and aggression, both great and small powers were divided into two hostile camps: Europe was sitting on a keg of gunpowder.

The fatal spark that set it alight occurred on June 28, 1914. Archduke Franz Ferdinand, heir to the Austro-Hungarian throne, was driving through Sarajevo, a Bosnian town under Austrian rule. Gavrilo Princip, a young Bosnian in the crowd, shot him dead.

Austro-Hungary held Serbia responsible for the assassination. Russia mobilized to support Serbia, backed by her ally France. Germany mobilized, declaring war on Russia and France. Britain had a friendly agreement with France, known as the *entente cordiale*, and also stood to guarantee Belgian neutrality. So when Germany attacked France and invaded Belgium, the result was inevitable. On August 4, 1914 Britain entered the war.

Trench warfare: British troops advance to the German lines, under heavy artillery fire.

HISTORY OF AVIATION

1783 First flight of Montgolfier Brothers' balloon.

1799–1810 Experiments with gliders by Sir George Cayley, which laid the basis of modern aerodynamics.

1852 First airship flight by Henri Giffard.

1840 First steam-powered aircraft designed.

1890 Clement Ader claimed to be the first man to take off in a steam-powered aircraft.

1891–96 Otto Lilienthal experiments with man-carrying gliders.

1903 Secret of powered flight discovered by Wilbur and Orville Wright, whose Flyer I flew for 12 seconds at Devil Hill, Kittyhawk, USA on December 17, 1903. The Wrights made three other flights the same day, the final one lasting 59 seconds.

1909 Louis Bleriot makes the first international flight – across the English Channel from Calais to Dover, July 25.

1910 First successful take off of an aircraft from a ship.

1914–18 Aircraft used during the First World War, for bombing and reconnaissance.

1919 Two British officers, Alcock and Brown, make first non-stop transatlantic flight.

1919 First international airline service, between France and Belgium.

1923 First non-stop flight across the USA.

1924 First flight around the world, with various stops on the way, in 175 days.

1927 Charles Lindbergh makes first non-stop solo transatlantic flight.

1928 Charles Kingsford Smith makes first flight from Australia to California, across the Pacific Ocean.

1930 Wreck of the R-101 airship ends airship development in Britain. Later, similar disasters ended

development in Germany, the USA and elsewhere, by 1937.

1930–38 Several round the world flights and other long-distance flights. Amy Johnson (1903–41) becomes first woman to fly from England to Australia (1930). Amelia Earhart (1898–1938) becomes first person to fly solo from Hawaii to California (1935).

1936–37 First successful helicopters: Focke-Wulf (1936) and Sikorsky (1937).

1937 Frank Whittle develops first jet engine.

1939 First jet-powered aircraft flown in Germany.

1945 First jet-powered warplane, German Me-262 used in combat.

1969 Concorde, the first supersonic (faster than sound) airliner made first flight. Concorde went into service in 1976.

1914

The early battles

At the beginning of the war Britain and Germany were seized by patriotic fervour; enthusiastic crowds flocked to the recruiting stations. It was not thought that the war would last for long.

The Germans had planned a rapid sweep to Paris through Belgium, but were hindered by determined resistance. The British Expeditionary Force made a stand at Mons, but the Anglo-French forces under the French General Joffre (1852–1931) were pushed back to the Marne. Here the German advance was halted, and the armies dug in. By the end of the year the Western Front was a vast line of trenches, stretching from the North Sea to Switzerland.

In the East the Russians seized Galicia, but were defeated at Tannenberg in East Prussia by the German General von Hindenburg (1847–1934). The Russians received another setback when Turkey entered the war on the side of Germany.

It was clear that this war would be a long and bitter struggle.

1915

Gorky commences trilogy

In 1914 a writer returned to the political turmoil of Russia to engage in revolutionary propaganda. Alexei Peshkov (1868–1936), whose pen-name was Maxim Gorky, had had a hard and eventful life. Rejecting his earlier romanticism for realism, in 1915 he began his autobiographical trilogy: *Childhood, In the World* and *Reminiscences of Youth*. Gorky was an advocate of 'social realism' in Soviet art and literature.

1915
The sinking of the *Lusitania*

For the first time in history, civilians became totally involved in war, as air raids and submarine warfare took their toll. At times German submarines attacked merchant shipping and passenger liners indiscriminately. When the British liner *Lusitania* was torpedoed in 1915 off Ireland, 128 American citizens were killed. This hardened anti-German feeling in the USA, which was still neutral.

The battle of Jutland in May 1916. Britain was maintaining its blockade of Germany.

1915
Execution of Edith Cavell

On October 12, 1915 British nurse Edith Cavell faced a German firing squad. She was matron of a hospital in Brussels which had become a Red Cross hospital when Belgium was invaded. Although she had tended German and Allied patients impartially, she was found to be assisting in the escape of Allied prisoners. Her execution shocked the British public.

1915
The Dardanelles expedition

With the Western front in a stalemate, and Russia under pressure from the Turks, the Allies decided to attack the Dardanelles. These straits, a vital supply route to the Russians, had been closed when Turkey entered the war. The naval campaign (planned by Winston Churchill) and the army attempts to take the Gallipoli peninsula were costly failures.

1915

Somerset Maugham: *Of Human Bondage*

William Somerset Maugham (1874–1965) was a British writer who mastered the art of the short story and was a successful novelist. *Of Human Bondage*, published in 1915, is a great autobiographical novel. His early experience in medical practice and his later travels gave him an acute insight into human behaviour.

1916

The Easter Rising

On the outbreak of the First World War the British government had pledged limited Home Rule for Ireland, on the condition that it did not take effect until the war was over. Whilst many Irishmen volunteered to fight in the war, many could see the opportunity to revolt that they had been waiting for. With German and Irish-American money, the Sinn Fein party built up their rebel army.

Sir Roger Casement (1864–1916), a convinced Irish nationalist, visited the USA and Berlin to gain support for the Irish cause. On April 2, 1916 he returned to Ireland in a German submarine, accompanied by a boat full of arms, which was intercepted and sunk by a patrol.

Three days later Casement was captured by the British, who later hanged him as a traitor.

Despite this setback an armed rising did take place. On Easter Monday 1916 the rebels captured the general post office in Dublin and key points in the city. Padraig Pearse (1879–1916) commanded the rising, and he and his colleagues held out for a week under bombardment. On April 30 he surrendered.

The execution of the fifteen rebel leaders further embittered the Irish people, and whilst negotiations continued, the resistance movement was rebuilt (*see 1921 Formation of the Irish Free State*).

1916

Kafka writes *Metamorphosis*

'Metamorphosis' (*Die Verwandlung*) is the story of a man who wakes up to find himself transformed into an insect. Franz Kafka (1883–1924) was born in Prague of a Jewish family. His introspective, morbid personality resulted in a number of remarkable works, notably 'The Trial' (*Ein Prozess*) and 'The Castle' (*Das Schloss*), in which the individual is lost in a bewildering, seemingly pointless society.

1916

Assassination of Rasputin

In the last years of Czar Nicholas II an extraordinary figure became a favourite at the Russian court. Grigori Rasputin (c. 1871–1916) was a debauched monk who exerted a magnetic influence over his followers. These included the Czarina, Alexandra. She believed that Rasputin had saved the life of her son, who suffered from the blood disorder, haemophilia. His political influence became intolerable to many, and a group of noblemen attempted to poison, then shoot him. Finally, they threw his body into a river, where he drowned.

1916

The third year of war

The war had spread: Italy had joined the Allies; Bulgaria the Central Powers; Britain had occupied Palestine. In France the war dragged on in miserable conditions, the soldiers living and dying in a devastated area of mud and barbed wire. Horrific new weapons appeared: the Germans introduced poison-gas shells, the British introduced tanks as a counter-measure against another horror-weapon, the machine gun.

In the winter of 1916 the Germans launched a massive attack on the French at Verdun, but were held by the French under Pétain. In July 1916 the British counter-attacked fiercely along the Somme. Casualties were heavy: in one day 60,000 British soldiers were killed.

At sea Britain maintained a blockade of Germany, despite submarine losses and a running battle off Jutland in May 1916, where neither fleet gained advantage. In June 1916 Lord Kitchener, who had organized the British army for war, was lost when HMS *Hampshire* struck a mine off Orkney.

1916

The Dada movement is formed

Many artists and writers, having no sympathy with the climate of war, fled to neutral Switzerland. A Zurich group which included the Romanian poet Tristan Tzara and the Alsatian painter and sculptor Hans Arp (1888–1966)

(Right) Czar Nicholas II of Russia and his family, about 1900. Seated at the front are the Grand Duchesses Marie and Anastasia. Behind (left to right) the Grand Duchess Tatiana, the Czarina Alexandra with the Czarevitch Alexei, the Czar and the Grand Duchess Olga.

started producing satirical revues and engaging in artistic discussion. Sticking a pin into a French–German dictionary at random, they found the word *Dada*, and called their movement after it. They set out to attack all traditional aesthetic ideals, valuing the impact of shock, protest and change above all: 'art is nonsense' declared their manifesto of 1918.

French painters Francis Picabia (1879–1953) and Marcel Duchamp (1887–1968) exhibited every day objects as works of art; the latter scandalized artistic circles with his reproduction of the *Mona Lisa* with a moustache. The movement spread to France, Germany, Italy and the USA, greatly influencing twentieth century attitudes to art.

1917

USA enters the war

At the beginning of 1917 the outlook was bleak, and the weary armies seemed to be locked in a fight to the death. Few people at home in Britain and Germany grasped the realities of modern warfare. Battle followed battle and the carnage continued: Messines, Passchendaele, Vimy Ridge, Cambrai. There was mutiny in the French army, and the Russian troops were deserting in droves.

Two political events dominated 1917, which had a crucial effect on the war. Firstly, in March 1917 the Czar of Russia abdicated; in December the Bolshevik revolutionaries signed an armistice with Germany (see 1917 *Outbreak of the Russian Revolution*).

This setback for the Allies was balanced by the second important political development of the year: on April 6, the USA decided to enter the war. President Woodrow Wilson (1856–

1924) was finally forced to enter for a number of reasons: submarine warfare had killed innocent American civilians; Germany had been wooing Mexico with the promise of returning US territory to them, public opinion had rallied behind the Allied cause. A US expeditionary force was followed up by large numbers of fresh troops, to take on an exhausted enemy.

1917
Outbreak of the Russian Revolution

For some years Russia had been in a state of political unrest (see 1905 Unrest in Russia and 1916 Assassination of Rasputin). The terrible conditions of the war had demoralized the armed forces, and the masses were starving: strikes and hunger marches met with repression.

Czar Nicholas II (1868–1918) was an unimaginative ruler, lacking self-assurance and dangerously out of touch with modern times. Convinced of the absolute authority of his office his gestures towards democracy were too few and too late. When the Duma (parliament) pressed him for reforms in March 1917, he refused outright. The Duma formed a provisional government, and forced the abdication of the Czar, who could no longer find any military support. The Romanov dynasty had finally collapsed.

The government that came to power in the spring of 1917 was made up of liberals and social democrats, known as Mensheviks, under the inept leadership of Alexander Kerensky (1881–1970). He could not maintain order, and his decision to continue in the war was unpopular. In Petrograd (formerly St Petersburg) a Soviet of Workers' and Soldiers' Deputies was formed to oppose the government, made up of radical revolutionaries known as Bolsheviks.

Bolshevik leaders returned from long years of foreign exile to participate in the forthcoming revolution. Vladimir Ilyich Lenin (formerly Ulyanov, 1870–1924) returned from Germany, to address workers and organize the Bolsheviks. He was joined by Leon Trotsky (formerly Bronstein, 1879–1940) and Joseph Stalin (formerly Dzhugashvili, 1879–1953).

On November 7, 1917 (October 25 according to the Russian calendar then in use), the Bolsheviks rose against Kerensky's government, and the revolution quickly spread from Petrograd. Kerensky fled and Soviet power was established. Land was given over to the peasants, local councils ('Soviets') were set up, companies were nationalized, and the Orthodox Church penalized. The following years were a bitter struggle, but the communists maintained their powers (see 1918 The murder of the Russian royal family).

Lenin (left) with Stalin.

1917
The Balfour declaration

The origins of the modern Arab–Israeli conflict can be traced back to the year 1917, when a declaration was made by the British foreign secretary Lord Balfour (1848–1930) promising the Jews a national home in Palestine.

The Zionists, a Jewish nationalist group, were to be offered settlement in the hope that this would secure British interests in the Middle East and gain support for the allied war effort from world Jewry.

The declaration, supported by France, Italy and the USA, was open to a number of interpretations, and conflicted with promises made to the Arabs, whom the British had encouraged to revolt against the Turks.

In December 1917 Jerusalem was taken by the British General Allenby (1861–1936) and the fall of Damascus in 1918 secured the British position in the Middle East. Between the wars Jewish immigration grew amidst growing Arab discontent (see 1948 State of Israel proclaimed).

HISTORY OF RUSSIA

AD *860* Viking chieftain Rurik traditionally founded Russian royal dynasty.

to late 15th century Several small princely states formed in Russia.

1462 Ivan III, first national sovereign of Russia acceded to the throne.

1547 Ivan IV (the Terrible) crowned as the first Czar.

1613 Michael Romanov becomes Czar. The Romanov dynasty ruled Russia until 1917.

1637 Start of the development of Siberia.

1696 Peter I (the Great) becomes sole Czar and brings Russia into contact with foreign influence.

1762–96 Reign of Catherine II (the Great).

1853–56 Russian defeated in the Crimean War against Turkey, Britain and France.

1861 Edict liberating Russian serfs.

1870s Start of the industrialization of Russia.

1894 Nicholas II Romanov becomes Czar. His reign is marked by great social and political unrest.

1904–05 Russo–Japanese War. Russian fleet destroyed at Tsushima.

1914 Russia enters the First World War.

1917 Nicholas II overthrown by revolution and murdered (1918).

1917 Bolshevik Revolution: the Communists take power, under Lenin.

1933–38 Purge of Communist Party and the armed forces by Lenin's successor, Josef Stalin.

1941–45 USSR in the Second World War, after invasion by Nazi Germany (June 22, 1941).

1948–49 Formation of Communist 'satellite' states between USSR and Germany.

from 1947 'Cold War' of tension and rivalry between USSR and her Communist allies and the 'Western' bloc led by the USA.

1953 Death of Stalin. Khrushchev elected First Secretary. Three years later he condemns Stalin.

1957 USSR launches Sputnik I, the world's first spacecraft.

1964 Leonid Brezhnev becomes USSR leader, commencing nineteen years of hard-line rule by himself and his successors Andropov and Chernenko. Cold War deepens.

1985 Mikhail Gorbachev becomes USSR leader and inaugurates a new spirit of 'glasnost' (openness) and 'perestroika' (reconstruction) both in the USSR and in relations with the West.

1918

Death of Wilfred Owen

In 1918 a young English poet was killed in action on the Western Front. Wilfred Owen (1893–1918) had produced some remarkable verse expressing his horror at the bloodshed he had witnessed.

Many young writers had gone into the war optimistically. Rupert Brooke (1887–1915) produced some fresh lyrical verse before dying on Skyros on his way to the Dardanelles.

Siegfried Sassoon (1886–1967) survived the war. Initially sharing Brooke's optimism, his experience soon made him hate war with a ferocious bitterness, expressed in his *Counter-attack* (1918). Sassoon edited Owen's works and published Owen's *Collected Poems* in 1920.

The casualties of the First World War have been called the 'lost generation'. The work of the war poets is a monument to those who were killed, or who spent the rest of their lives crippled or suffering the effects of gas poisoning.

1918

The end of the First World War

By 1918 the Allied blockade was causing Germany extreme hardship, and many hoped for peace. The German General von Ludendorff decided to risk all in one final push, and smashed through British lines. He was finally halted at the Marne. The tide turned as the Allies broke through the German defences of the Hindenburg line.

Peace – but for how long? The Treaty of Versailles was signed in 1919 by Lloyd George, Woodrow Wilson and Clemenceau.

One by one the Central Powers surrendered. Kaiser Wilhelm II fled to neutral Holland after being forced to abdicate, and an armistice was signed with Germany on November 11, 1918. The First World War was not known as the Great War for nothing. Sixteen nations had mobilized sixty-five million men; well over eight million young men were killed, and countless more were maimed and injured for life. The war left a scar across the face of Europe that did not heal quickly. The map of the world was altered, and the structure of society changed.

The terms of peace were decided the next year. British Prime Minister Lloyd George, US President Woodrow Wilson and French Premier Clemenceau dominated the conference. The Treaty of Versailles was severe. Germany lost her colonies and Alsace-Lorraine, her military development was to be closely controlled, and she was to pay large sums of money (reparations) to the victors (see 1920 *The League of Nations established*).

1918
Czechoslovakia and Poland become independent

The Treaty of Versailles changed the map of Europe. In the East, the Central Powers were forced to recognize the independence of Poland and Czechoslovakia. The Polish nationalist movement under Josef Pilsudski (1867–1935) and the Czechoslovak under Thomas Masaryk (1850–1937) finally achieved their aim, although their political stability was at first uncertain.

1918
The *Bauhaus* founded

In 1918 a German architect, Walter Gropius (1883–1969) was made director of art schools in Weimar. He reorganized the schools into a centre of architecture, craft and design, known as the *Bauhaus*. Transferred to Dessau in 1925, the school was closed down with the rise of the Nazis after 1933.

At a time when industry and mass-production were spreading rapidly, and scientific progress was creating new technologies, the *Bauhaus* proved that function and beauty were compatible. Art and craft were to unite, and pupils were trained to think in terms of mass-production. The school had an enormous influence on international architecture, as well as industrial and graphic design, and art.

The *Bauhaus* attracted many of the great artists of the day as teachers. The Swiss artist Paul Klee taught there for twelve years, producing his *Pädagogisches Skizzenbuch* ('Educational Sketchbook'), and Wasilly Kandinsky, the Russian painter, was for a time director (*see 1911 The Expressionist Exhibition*).

1918
The murder of the Russian royal family

The Bolsheviks who had swept to power under Lenin in 1917 had more than their share of problems. Having moved the capital of Russia from Petrograd to Moscow, they now faced the task of organizing the economy of a vast and chaotic country.

In 1918 civil war broke out between the Reds (the Bolsheviks) and the Whites (their opponents). Although the Whites received military assistance from Allied units, the Red Army under Trotsky virtually crushed all opposition within two years.

The Czar, Nicholas II, was a liability to the Bolsheviks. Since his abdication, he and his family had become used to a life very different from the one they had known. In the turbulence of the civil war, the Czar and Czarina and their five children were moved to Eastern Russia. There, they fell under the power of hard-line revolutionaries, and were all shot dead at a house in Ekaterinburg in 1918 (*see 1919 Comintern formed*).

1918
The great influenza pandemic

Towards the end of 1918, a terrible form of influenza appeared first in Spain, then in the rest of Europe and finally spread all over the world. 'Spanish 'flu' as it was called from its origins continued into 1919 and it was a killer. There seemed to be no cure. Many people, however, consumed large quantities of onions and strangely, this appeared to have some effect.

Nevertheless, about 21 million people died worldwide and when the pandemic was at its height, there were many who feared the human race was going to be wiped out. Nothing like the influenza pandemic had been known since the Black Death (Plague) in the mid-fourteenth century (*see 1348 Black Death reaches Europe from the East*).

1919
Birth of the Weimar Republic

The new peace found Germany bitter, starving, and torn with political dissent. November 1918 saw a naval mutiny at Kiel, the signing of the armistice, and the formation of soviets on Russian lines in Berlin. With the Kaiser in Holland, the way was open for the formation of a republic, but its nature was only to be decided by fighting.

The communists, known as Spartacists, held the balance of power for a time, but in January 1919 were defeated by the counter-revolutionaries on the streets of Berlin. Spartacist leaders Karl Liebknecht and Rosa Luxemburg were murdered.

The new republic formed under the Weimar Constitution of 1919 allowed for a considerable degree of democracy, but in the long run was unable to stand up to economic disaster and manipulation by undemocratic elements. First president of the Weimar Republic was Friedrich Ebert (1871–1925) (*see 1925 Hindenburg becomes President of Germany*).

1919
Comintern formed

As the Civil War raged in Russia, the involvement of units from the Allied powers on the side of the Whites spurred on the communist party to call the Third Communist International, or *Comintern*. Foreign groups discussed how to spread the revolution abroad.

However, attempts to establish soviet systems elsewhere in Europe at this stage failed. The social democrats won the day in Germany, and in Hungary a communist government under revolutionary Béla Kun (1886–1937) collapsed after five months.

The Soviet Republic in Russia, from 1922 known as the Union of Soviet Socialist Republics, was bankrupt, and in 1921 Lenin was forced to moderate his economic policy. His New Economic Plan allowed a certain amount of private enterprise and the country became economically viable. The USSR gradually received official recognition by the West (*see 1924 Stalin succeeds Lenin*).

1919
Formation of fascist parties

The Europe of 1919 had all the seeds of new conflict. Disillusionment and fear of communism led some towards an extreme nationalism in which the authority of the state was thought to be supreme, and to justify any inhumanity. Fascism derived its name from the *fasces* of ancient Rome, a bundle of rods with an axe carried as a symbol of state authority.

Boastful and obsessed with power for its own sake, Benito Mussolini (1883–1945) formed his fascist group in Italy in 1919. Dropping his professed socialist ideals, he allied himself with industrialists and landowners while his thugs broke up communist and other opposition groups. In 1922 the black-shirted fascists marched on Rome, establishing Mussolini as dictator, although outnumbered ten to one in parliament.

The violent methods of Mussolini were soon to be duplicated by similar thugs in Germany. In 1919, a former corporal called Adolf Hitler (1889–1945) joined the small National Socialist German Workers' party to check it for possible communist influence. In time, Hitler took this party over, and transformed it into the most brutal fascist-type group of all: the Nazi Party.

1919
Alcock and Brown fly the Atlantic

On June 14, 1919, aviation history was made when a Vickers Vimy aircraft successfully crossed the Atlantic Ocean without stopping. The arduous crossing was carried out by Captain John Alcock (1892–1919), a famous air ace of World War I, and Lt. Arthur Whitten Brown (1886–1948). The aircraft took sixteen hours twelve minutes to cover the three thousand kilometres between St John's, Newfoundland, Canada and Clifden, Ireland. Their remarkable achievement was recognized when both men were knighted. However tragedy struck Alcock later in the year, when his amphibian (capable of landing on water or land) crashed in Normandy, on the way to Paris, and he was killed.

Alcock and Brown's achievement followed closely on that of Lt-Cdr. Albert C. Read of the US Navy, who with five crew in May 1919 had flown the Atlantic from Newfoundland to Lisbon in a Curtiss NC-4 flying boat – but not without stopping.

1919
Rutherford's atomic experiments

A brilliant scientist became Cavendish Professor of Physics at Cambridge in 1919. New Zealand-born Ernest Rutherford (1871–1937) was a pioneer in his field, and radically altered our understanding of atomic physics.

Rutherford had previously studied at Cambridge under Sir J. J. Thompson (1856–1940), the discoverer of the electron, and had researched into uranium radiation. Whilst Professor at McGill University, Canada, in 1898, Rutherford upset the laws of conservation of matter with his theory of atomic disintegration. Moving to Manchester in 1907 he worked with the Danish physicist Niels Bohr (1885–1962), and gave a new insight into the structure of the atom. The atom was revealed as a nucleus surrounded by electrons.

Rutherford's experiments of 1919 were remarkable, proving that atomic transformation took place in atmospheric nitrogen bombarded with alpha-rays, liberating hydrogen nuclei. In 1920 Rutherford foresaw the existence of the neutron, which was confirmed by Sir James Chadwick in 1932. In 1931 Rutherford was raised to the peerage.

Ernest Rutherford

1920

Pirandello writes *Six Characters in Search of an Author*

Italian writer Luigi Pirandello (1867–1936) had made his name as a novelist and short story writer when he turned to drama, producing his best known work in 1920. *Sei personaggi in cerca d'autore* ('Six Characters in Search of an Author') was performed throughout Europe.

Pirandello's constant theme is illusion and appearance. He received the Nobel Prize for Literature in 1934.

1920

The League of Nations established

An important part of the Treaty of Versailles in 1919 was the establishment of a League of Nations, which became the United Nations after 1945. It was the first real attempt at international co-operation and peace-making.

The Geneva-based league was made up of an Assembly of all member nations, a Council, consisting of the major powers and four other members, and a Secretariat. A world court would be set up to settle international disputes. On January 10, 1920 twenty-four members assembled for the first time.

The USA did not join the League. Opposing the personal wish of President Woodrow Wilson who had conceived the idea of the League, Congress decided to avoid all foreign involvements. The USSR joined in 1934.

Although there were eventually sixty members, the League never had the military support to be effective, and was so constituted that most important international action could be blocked by use of the veto. The League did, however, give much needed economic and technological aid to several countries.

1921

Formation of the Irish Free State

In Ireland the anti-British campaign had been continued since 1916. Whilst Sinn Fein leader Eamon de Valera (1882–1975) wanted a full republic, another leader, Michael Collins (1890–1922) was prepared to settle for the same status as Canada and Australia within the British empire.

Collins, a popular hero of the Easter Rising, managed to come to an agreement with the British, and headed a provisional government, but was shot dead in a Republican ambush. A bitter feud between the rival parties lasted for years, but the Irish Free State was agreed by both the British parliament and the *Dáil Éireann* (Irish assembly) in December 1921.

The new state did not include the six counties of Northern Ireland, where the largely Protestant population insisted on remaining part of the UK. This problem was to cause lasting bitterness and suffering, and when an independent republic, called Eire since 1936, was finally declared in 1949, Northern Ireland was not included.

Michael Collins

1921

Schönberg: *Twelve-note System of Composition*

Arnold Schönberg (1874–1951) was a self-taught Austrian composer, whose originality soon became apparent: the performance of his first *Chamber Symphony* in 1907 caused a riot. Involved in the Expressionist movement, he became a friend of the composer Mahler, and taught Berg and Webern. In these years he came to abandon the classical concept of tonality, and write in an 'atonal' style.

His theoretical work led him to publish in 1921 his *Twelve-note System of Composition*, in which he organized his atonal system into a structure based on a 'note row'. The composer arranges the twelve notes of the semitone scale in a sequence, each note appearing once but at any pitch. This sequence determines the relationship of the notes for the rest of the work. Schönberg's major twelve-note works included *Variations for Orchestra* (1928) and the unfinished opera *Moses and Aaron*.

Forced into exile by the Nazis, Schönberg settled in the USA; his system, also known as 'serial music', became a major influence on musicians such as Stravinsky. Berg and Webern developed the serial method of composition, however, to many people, the atonal harmony makes the music sound unpleasant.

1921
The first birth control clinic

In this century the rapid increase in world population has made measures to control the birth rate vital. One of the pioneers of birth control was a remarkable woman called Marie Stopes (1880–1958), a university science lecturer and suffragette. Her views caused a storm of controversy, but in 1921 she founded the first clinic for marital advice and birth control, in North London.

1921
The discovery of insulin

Many diseases which today can be cured or controlled were once fatal, and thousands died from diabetes before the discovery of insulin in 1921. In diabetes, there is a failure of the body to use sugars and other food properly.

In 1921, Sir Frederick Banting and Charles Best isolated the hormone insulin which in many cases can rectify this situation. They produced a solution of insulin from animal pancreases and injected it into a diabetic patient in Toronto, Canada. The patient recovered. A great breakthrough had been made and in 1923 Bantin received the Nobel Prize for medicine.

1922
Egypt becomes independent

In the First World War Britain had succeeded in bringing to an end the power of the Turks in the Middle East. In 1914 Egypt had been declared a British Protectorate. In 1922 the British granted Egypt independence, but were keen to protect their interests in the Suez Canal zone. They therefore retained some military bases and a degree of control which obliged the Egyptian king and government to act on British advice.

1922
T. S. Eliot publishes *The Waste Land*

Perhaps the most influential English-language poet of this century has been American-born T. S. Eliot (1888–1965), who took British nationality in 1927. *The Waste Land* (1922) was widely recognized for its quality and was followed by other outstanding poetry including *The Four Quarters* (1944). Eliot wrote a number of successful plays, including *Murder in the Cathedral* (1935) and *The Cocktail Party* (1950).

1922
BBC begins regular broadcasts

After the war the growth of interest in radio (or 'wireless telephony') was rapid. Many amateurs became interested in experimenting with crystal sets. From 1922 the privately run British Broadcasting Company started making regular broadcasts for entertainment and the primitive radio sets became more and more sophisticated.

A station was erected at Daventry in 1925 which made for easy reception all over Britain, and the broadcasts could be picked up on the continent as well. For the first time music of quality could be heard by all; the potential of this new medium was enormous – for education as well as for entertainment and information.

In 1927 the government established the British Broadcasting Corporation in place of the Company, an independent body responsible to the state. The age of the radio was here to stay.

1922

Tutankhamun's tomb is discovered

On November 4, 1922 a British archaeologist on Lord Carnarvon's expedition to Egypt, Howard Carter (1873–1939) uncovered steps leading to a royal tomb of ancient Egypt. When the tomb was opened it was revealed as a unique treasure house, which had not been disturbed for over three thousand years. Most of the splendid treasures were removed to the Cairo Museum, where they can still be seen today (*see 1362–56 BC The reign of Tutankhamun*).

This magnificent throne, over three thousand years old, was discovered in 1922 in the tomb of Tutankhamun.

1922

James Joyce publishes *Ulysses*

1922 saw the publication in Paris of a novel that was quite unlike any that had gone before it. In *Ulysses* Irish writer James Joyce (1882–1941) dispenses with the normal time sequence, to plunge the reader into the world of the subconscious. Joyce's minute observation of everyday life and interweaving of themes provides a brilliant if complex masterpiece. Joyce's other great work is *Finnegan's Wake* (1939).

1923

Atatürk founds modern Turkey

When the Ottoman empire broke up at the end of the First World War, nationalist groups pressed for an independent Turkish state free of all external commitments. This was set up in 1921, and in 1923 Turkey became a republic. The first president was national hero Mustafa Kemal Pasha (1881–1938), who later took the name of Atatürk (Father of the Turks).

Over the next fifteen years Atatürk introduced reforms to change centuries of tradition. For the first time the Islamic faith was no longer the State religion of the republic. Women were able to vote and participate in political life. Traditional dress, such as the fez, a brimless hat, was forbidden, and Western laws, coinage and alphabet introduced.

Turkey had become a modern republic with a democratic basis, although Atatürk wielded the power of a dictator. Achieving friendship with Britain and the West, as well as with the USSR, Turkey remained free to develop its new identity in the years between the wars.

Kemal Atatürk

1923
Hitler imprisoned

Continuing political unrest in Germany led the government to fear a left-wing Communist revolution might take place. The greatest threat to them however proved to be from extreme right-wing groups such as the Nazis. Political murder was the order of the day, and the leniency of the courts did little to deter right-wing terrorists.

In November 1923 an alliance of extreme right-wing groups attempted to seize power in Bavaria. The Nazis marched through Munich, much as the Italian fascists had marched on Rome the previous year. The police, however, gunned down the column, killing sixteen and seriously wounding Hermann Göring, who was to become Hitler's second in command.

Hitler narrowly escaped and was imprisoned for nine months. In jail he wrote his autobiography *Mein Kampf* ('My Struggle'), a work that reveals Hitler's peculiar psychological make-up, his ruthless ideas of politics and especially his hatred of the Jews. Released from prison, Hitler continued to push for power, attempting to gain support from the big industrialists.

1924
Ramsay Macdonald becomes first Labour prime minister

In 1874 the first trade union-sponsored MPs had entered parliament, and 1900 saw the formation of the Labour Party as we know it, by pioneers such as Keir Hardie (1856–1915). The long-standing domination of Parliament by the Conservatives and the Liberals finally ended in January 1924, when a minority Labour government came to power under James Ramsay Macdonald (1866–1937).

Dependent upon the Liberals for a majority in the House of Commons, Ramsay Macdonald introduced no radical changes, and his government fell to Conservative Stanley Baldwin (1867–1947) after only eleven months.

Despite this first showing by a Labour government, the future balance of power in British politics lay between the Conservative and Labour parties. Labour was returned again in

1929, but when in the economic depression of 1931 Ramsay Macdonald formed an all-party National Coalition, he was bitterly opposed by many of his own party who considered him a traitor.

1924
E. M. Forster writes *A Passage to India*

English novelist E. M. Forster (1879–1970) wrote a number of fine works (*A Room With a View*, 1908; *Howards End*, 1910) before he produced his masterpiece in 1924. *A Passage to India* is a gentle, ironical look at the uneasy co-existence of two civilizations in British India. This sensitive portrait was widely acclaimed both at the time and again in the 1980s when it was made into a film for the cinema.

1924
Stalin succeeds Lenin

Lenin was just succeeding in getting his economic plans for the USSR under way, when in 1924 he died (*see 1919 Comintern formed*). There followed a battle for power in the Communist party, and the victor was Joseph Stalin, an astute but totally ruthless politician. Within three years his main rival, Leon Trotsky, was expelled from the party and exiled; Stalin's position as leader was secured.

Stalin introduced a series of five-year economic plans to increase the number of collective farms, expand nationalized industry, and increase production.

Some economic successes, especially the rapid development of heavy industry, were striking, though only achieved by the brutal suppression of all opposition. Peasants, intellectuals and original revolutionaries who had devoted their lives to the cause of communism were exterminated or imprisoned: the country of revolution had become a brutal police state. Trotsky, exiled in Mexico, was murdered by a Soviet agent in 1940.

Stalin died in 1953 and was denounced three years later (*see 1956 Krushchev denounces Stalin*).

1925
Noël Coward produces *Hay Fever*

The English dramatist, actor and composer Noël Coward (1899–1973) was renowned for his witty dialogue and elegant satire. His plays, revues and musicals were extremely popular. *Hay Fever* was the success of 1925, and was followed by many others, including *Private Lives* (1930), *Cavalcade* (1931) and *Blithe Spirit* (1941). His operetta, *Bitter Sweet* (1929) had a long and successful run in London and New York.

Noël Coward received a knighthood in recognition of his work.

Noël Coward

1925
The Great Gatsby and the Jazz Age

The USA and Europe were on the road to economic disaster. But on the surface things were booming, and those who had the money spent it lavishly.

Freed from wartime austerity, the younger generation shocked their elders with fast cars, cocktail parties and dance crazes such as the Charleston. Women cut their hair short, smoked cigarettes and wore knee-length dresses.

This was the golden age of traditional jazz (*see 1911 Alexander's Ragtime Band*); the greatest artist of the day was a young trumpeter called Louis Armstrong (1900–71). The spirit of the twenties was captured by US writer F. Scott Fitzgerald (1896–1940) in works such as *The Great Gatsby* (1925).

The glitter of the Jazz Age concealed violence and corruption. Unpopular laws prohibiting alcohol in the USA led to 'bootlegging' (illicit trafficking in liquor), opening a market for gangsters such as Al Capone (1899–1947).

Gang warfare erupted in the streets, but the economic depression brought an end to the light-hearted life of the twenties (*see 1929 Wall Street Crash*).

1925
Hindenburg becomes President of Germany

The death in 1925 of Freidrich Ebert, the first president of the Weimar Republic, gave cause for concern in Germany and abroad: his successor, ageing war hero Paul von Hindenburg (1847–1934), who was to be president until his death, was an old-fashioned monarchist. However, Hindenburg proved to be a supporter of the republican constitution, and Germany became more stable.

Monetary reform was introduced, and the Treaty of Locarno signed, with the result that Germany confirmed its respect for the Belgian and French frontiers, and its renunciation of Alsace-Lorraine. Allied troops began to leave the occupied Rhineland.

Party politics, however, became increasingly bitter, and the strident chorus of the (still small) Nazi party made itself heard. Germany's economic recovery had depended largely on foreign credit, and when the worldwide depression set in, Germany was affected worse than most. In the 1932 election Hindenburg received 54 per cent of the vote to Hitler's 36 per cent, but Hitler was not easily deterred (*see 1933 Hitler comes to power*).

1926
The general strike

In 1926 there were about five million trade-union members in Britain, out of a wage-earning population of fifteen million. For the first time a direct confrontation arose between the Trades Union Congress and the Conservative government under Stanley Baldwin.

The general strike started off with a miners' strike against less pay for longer hours. The mine owners would not climb down, and the TUC sanctioned a general strike that spread throughout the country.

Strikers clash with police in the general strike.

Rail, transport, building, printing, iron and steel production all ground to a halt. The press closed down, and both government and TUC published their own newspapers. The government was determined not to give in. Baldwin called in troops and armed special constables. Hundreds of strikers were arrested.

After nine days a peace was negotiated, but it was bitterly resisted by the miners, who remained on strike for the whole summer, until economic conditions forced them to submit.

1926
Invention of television

Scottish inventor John Logie Baird (1888–1946) was forced to give up his business career by illness. Settling in Hastings, England, he set up a small attic workshop in which he experimented with light projection. In 1925 he managed to transmit the image of a face from one room to another, and in 1926 he gave the first demon-stration of a television image, to the Royal Institution of Great Britain, in London.

Baird at last received support for his research, and in 1929 his 240-line mechanically-scanned system was taken by the BBC. Other researchers were close behind him, in particular Russian-born American Vladimir Zworykin (b. 1889) whose 405-line electronically scanned system was adopted in 1937.

Baird also produced images in 3D, colour, and with stereophonic sound before his death in 1946.

1926
Virginia Woolf writes *To The Lighthouse*

One of the most original modern English novelists and essayists was Virginia Woolf (1882–1941), whose poetic, impressionistic

(Right) John Logie Baird.

style is combined with acute psychological perception. She committed suicide in 1941. Her novel *To the Lighthouse* (1926) was followed by *The Waves* (1931) and some excellent essays.

1926

T. E. Lawrence: *The Seven Pillars of Wisdom*

British soldier T. E. Lawrence (1888–1935) led the Arab revolt against Turkish rule in the First World War. A brilliant, unconventional man, he was unable to achieve all he had hoped for the Arab cause after the war, and retired from public life to join the RAF under an assumed name. Killed in a motorcycle accident, his marvellous account of his desert life appears in *The Seven Pillars of Wisdom* (1926).

The 'Spirit of St Louis' – the famous plane in which Lindbergh crossed the Atlantic.

1927

Lindbergh flies the Atlantic solo

In 1925 US aviator Charles Lindbergh (1902–74) decided to compete for a $25,000 prize offered for a New York to Paris flight. Having found the financial backing to build a special plane, which he called the 'Spirit of St Louis', by 1927 he was ready for the solo attempt.

Having made a record overland flight from San Diego to New York City, he left Long Island at 7.52 a.m. local time on May 20 and arrived at Le Bourget airfield 33 hours 29 minutes later. His achievement received international acclaim: the French cross of the Legion d'Honneur, the British Air Force Cross, the US Distinguished Flying Cross and Congressional medal.

An air tour of the States, Mexico, Central and South America and the West Indies was followed by a flight from the USA to Denmark. Lindbergh settled in England in 1935, and returned to the USA in 1939.

1927
The first 'talkie'

Until 1927 films were silent, normally accompanied in the cinema by a piano or organ. Warner Brothers' *The Jazz Singer* was the first talking picture. Film-star Al Jolson's voice was converted into an optical soundtrack. In projection this was scanned by a photoelectric cell. The variations in current were amplified and fed into a loudspeaker to reproduce the voice.

1928
Votes for all women in UK

The struggle of the women's movement in England had not been in vain. The fierce opposition to them (*see 1903 Women's Political and Social Union founded*) could not survive a war in which women had taken over many jobs traditionally done by men.

In 1918 the Representation of the People Act allowed married women, women householders, and women graduates over thirty to vote together with all men over the age of 21. A subsequent Act was passed allowing women to sit in the House of Commons: Nancy Astor (1879–1964) became the first female MP. Women were still not equal, however, and it was not until 1928 that the age of female voters was lowered to twenty-one, the age at which men could vote.

Women's position elsewhere in the world varied greatly. Victory for the US women's suffrage movement came in 1920. New Zealand enfranchized women as early as 1893, Australia in 1901, Denmark in 1915. The USSR offered political equality from the start. French women did not receive the vote until 1944, and Swiss women received the vote only in 1971.

1928
Fleming discovers penicillin

Twentieth-century medicine was revolutionized by the discovery of a powerful antibiotic. Scottish bacteriologist Alexander Fleming (1881–1955) had already been a pioneer in the use of anti-typhoid vaccines, when in 1928 he discovered penicillin by accident. In one of his tests he noticed a strange mould had formed. When he examined this *penicillium notatum*, one

Sir Alexander Fleming

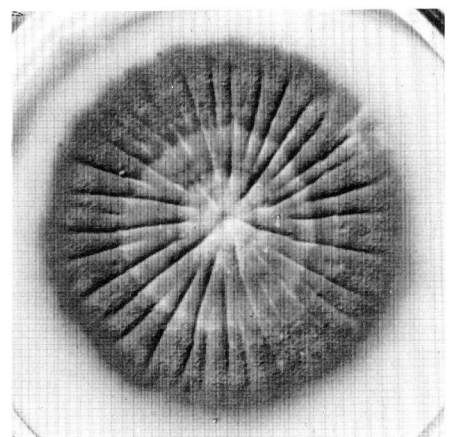

Penicillium notatum

of the same family of moulds that grow on blue cheese and jam, he found it to have extraordinary curing qualities.

It was another eleven years before a satisfactory method of producing penicillin as a practical medicine was found by two biochemists, Howard Florey and Ernest Chain. A formidable weapon had been added to man's warfare on harmful bacteria, and during the Second World War antibiotics became widely used. In 1945 all three men were awarded the Nobel prize.

1928

Evelyn Waugh writes *Decline and Fall*

Decline and Fall was the first of a number of novels by English writer Evelyn Waugh (1903–66) which form a witty commentary on the society of his day. Waugh's later work includes a number of masterpieces of sardonic humour, such as his popular trilogy, *Men at Arms* (1952), *Officers and Gentlemen* (1955) and *Unconditional Surrender* (1961).

1928

Chiang Kai-shek takes Peking

China was in a state of turmoil; as the traditional way of life crumbled in the face of twentieth-century values, political factions fought for influence. Sun Yat-Sen (*see 1911 China declared a republic*) accepted Communist supporters into his Kuomintang party. When he died in 1925 his successor Chiang Kai-shek (1887–1975) led Kuomintang armies northward from Canton.

In 1927, however, the Communists and their opponents within the Kuomintang party fell out. Chiang Kai-shek opposed the Communists, and they withdrew from the party to form their own headquarters at Hankow. The Kuomintang's base was at Nanking.

Chiang Kai-shek's armies swept north, and in 1928 took Peking. They soon controlled much of China, though the Communists held some areas, and warlords were still powerful. Fighting between Nationalists, under Chiang, and Communists under Mao Tse-tung (1893–1976) lasted up to 1949, although both factions agreed to a truce between them in order to concentrate on countering the Japanese invasion of China in 1937 (*see 1949 Mao Tse-tung proclaims Chinese People's Republic*).

1929

Wall Street Crash

On October 29, 1929, disaster hit the US stock exchange on Wall Street. The worst stock crash in history marked the start of a worldwide depression that was to bring misery and ruin to millions over the next decade.

World finance had never really recovered from the massive cost of the First World War and the industrial chaos it caused. Trading was made no easier by the high tariff barriers which individual countries had set up to protect their national interests.

The financial crash was caused by widespread panic. The USA and the European countries underwent great hardship. By 1932 thirteen million were unemployed in the USA, farmers were starving, and people were living in the streets. In England, France and Germany the story was similar (*see 1936 The Jarrow Hunger March*).

Political upheaval followed in the wake of the depression. US President Herbert Hoover (1874–1964), a Republican who had advocated waiting for big business to recover and revive the economy, lost the presidential election of 1932 to the Democrat Franklin Delano Roosevelt (1882–1945).

1929

Graf Zeppelin flies around the world

The early belief in the airship as a practical means of transport resulted in many models being manufactured during the First World War and post-war years. In 1929 the German *Graf Zeppelin* flew from New York to Friedrichshaven, Germany in $55\frac{1}{2}$ hours, and flew around the world in 21 days 7 hours.

Subsequent airship disasters – such as the British *R101* in 1930 and the German *Hindenburg* in 1937 – discouraged further development until the 1980s.

1930

Amy Johnson flies to Australia

On May 5, 1930 a young Englishwoman, Amy Johnson (1904–41), set off alone from London in a tiny plane to fly to Australia, completing the journey in nineteen days. She did not break the record, but her achievement as an inexperienced pilot made her famous. She later broke records in flights to Tokyo in 1931 and to Cape Town in 1932. She lost her life serving in the Air Transport Auxiliary in 1941.

1931
Gandhi attends London conference

Mohandas Karamchand (Mahatma) Gandhi (1896–1948) was a Hindu lawyer who gave up his career in order to devote himself to the achievement of Indian independence from British rule by peaceful means. In 1920 he led a campaign of civil disobedience and non-cooperation with the British government in India and was imprisoned during 1922–24.

In 1930 a conference was held in London to discuss the future constitution of India, but the Congress Movement, the main Indian nationalist party, which was led by Gandhi, refused to take part.

In 1931 he attended a London conference, but was unable to solve the important problem of the conflicts between the various communities in India.

Gandhi undertook long fasts in the continuing struggle, and was imprisoned for civil disobedience several times. His campaign of

Mahatma Gandhi

non-violence and his insistence on revitalizing the traditional culture of the Indian village were instrumental in achieving independence (*see 1947 India and Pakistan achieve independence*). He was assassinated in 1948.

1932
The splitting of the atom

Sir John Cockcroft (1897–1967) and Ernest Walton (*b*.1903) were two scientists engaged in research work at the Cavendish Laboratory in Cambridge under the supervision of Lord Rutherford (*see 1919 Rutherford's atomic experiments*). In April 1932 it was announced that they had succeeded in splitting the nucleus of a light metal called lithium by a process known as 'bombardment' by accelerated protons.

This was an important step forward in the search to extract and control the tremendous energy contained in the nucleus of atoms. It led eventually to the construction of the atomic bomb and the use of atomic power for industrial purposes. In 1951 Cockcroft and Walton were awarded the Nobel Prize for physics.

1932
Aldous Huxley's *Brave New World*

In 1932 Aldous Huxley (1894–1963), the English writer, published his most famous novel *Brave New World*, a gloomy picture of a future in which human beings are mass-produced in a laboratory. Among Huxley's other novels are *Antic Hay* (1923) and *Point Counter Point* (1928). He also wrote *The Doors of Perception* (1954), which studied the effects of drugs.

1932
Sir Malcolm Campbell breaks the land speed record

In 1932 the British racing motorist Sir Malcolm Campbell (1885–1948) reached a speed of nearly 409 km/h (254 mph) in his car *Bluebird*, beating his own previous record. In 1935 he

Campbell's *Bluebird*.

became the first motorist to exceed 483 km/h (300 mph). He also held the world water-speed record at the time of his death in 1948.

1932
De Valéra wins general election in Ireland

Although he had been one of the leading figures in his country's fight for independence from Britain, Eamon de Valéra (1882–1975) did not become head of the Irish government until 1932 when his party, *Fianna Fáil*, came to power. He held office for more than twenty years and during this time he made Ireland a completely sovereign state.

1933
Hitler comes to power

In January 1933 Adolf Hitler, the leader of the Nazis (*see 1919 Formation of fascist parties*), became chancellor or head of government in Germany. He at once called for a general election, since his party did not have a majority in parliament.

In February the *Reichstag*, the parliament building, was burnt down, probably by a Nazi gang. Blame was laid on the communists, and Hitler used the apparent Communist threat against the state to suspend the ordinary liberties of the people and to conduct a violent

election campaign. The Nazi Party won only a small majority but Hitler now took steps to make himself absolute ruler of Germany by suppressing all other political parties. In 1934, when President Hindenburg died, Hitler made himself both president and chancellor.

However, there were some Nazis, led by Ernst Röhm, who demanded sweeping changes in German society, including the abolition of capitalism. But Hitler did not wish to annoy the German industrialists and financiers, and in June 1934 Röhm and many of his supporters were executed without trial. In July 1934 a group of Nazis tried unsuccessfully to seize power in Austria and murdered the Austrian chancellor, Engelbert Dollfuss.

Adolf Hitler

1933
Roosevelt's Hundred Days

When Franklin Delano Roosevelt took power as US President on March 4, 1933, the United States was like a poor country, with millions out of work, homeless and destitute (*see 1929 Wall Street Crash*).

Roosevelt, however, planned to give Americans a 'New Deal' to solve these problems. The New Deal was a far-reaching programme of government action and was put into effect by means of many new laws, like the Farm Credit Act, which provided loans for farmers, and the Emergency Banking Relief Act which enabled the president to control the country's finances. This legal basis of the New Deal was laid during the Hundred Days, which began on March 9, 1933. Never before or since has the United States Congress passed so many new laws in so short a time.

1933

Jacob Epstein's *Ecce Homo*

Sir Jacob Epstein (1880–1959) was a sculptor born in New York of Russian–Polish parents, who spent most of his life in England. *Ecce Homo* was a symbolic religious work which expressed the artist's emotions and was very different from traditional sculpture. Epstein's other works included *Madonna and Child* (1927), *Genesis* (1931), and *Christ in Majesty* (1957).

1934

The Long March

In 1934, after six years of fighting Chiang Kai-shek's Kuomintang Nationalists, the Chinese Communists under Mao Tse Tung were facing defeat and extinction (*see 1928 Chiang Kai-shek takes Peking*). Mao therefore decided to escape with his army from Kiangsi province in south central China to Shensi, thousands of kilometres to the north-west.

The Long March, as this epic journey was later called, took 368 days, from October 1934 to October 1935. During this time Mao and the Communists crossed eighteen mountain ranges, twenty-four rivers and twelve provinces, fought hundreds of skirmishes with the Kuomintang and fifteen large-scale battles. The cost was very great. Of the hundred thousand who had set out with Mao from Kiangsi only five thousand survived to reach Shensi. The Communist forces were, however, preserved and ultimately de-

feated Chiang Kai-shek to take power in China fourteen years later (*see 1949 Mao Tse Tung proclaims Chinese People's Republic*).

1935

Watson-Watt develops radar

In 1935 a Scottish physicist, Robert Watson-Watt (1892–1973), working at the National Physical Laboratory at Teddington, near London, perfected a method for locating distant objects in space by the use of radio waves. This device, which was later to become known as radar (from *radio detecting and ranging*), provided early warning of an air attack, since enemy aircraft could be detected while they were still many miles away.

In 1936 a number of radar stations were set up in England. In 1938 the battleship HMS *Rodney* became the first ship successfully to detect approaching aircraft by using radar. By 1939 a chain of twenty radar stations had been installed along the east coast of England and they were to prove very important in the air defence of Britain during the Second World War.

Radar is now used for many purposes and is especially important in helping ships and aircraft to navigate in darkness and fog and in radar astronomy.

1935

Italy invades Ethiopia (Abyssinia)

In December 1934 there was fighting between Italian and Ethiopian soldiers on the frontier of the Italian Somaliland in an area which both Ethiopia and Italy claimed as their own. Mussolini, the fascist dictator of Italy, was determined to expand his country's empire in East Africa, and used this incident as an excuse to attack Ethiopia.

In October 1935 Italian forces, armed with modern military equipment, which included tanks, artillery, aircraft and poison gas, invaded Ethiopia. The poorly armed Ethiopian soldiers were no match for the Italians and by May 1936 they had been almost completely defeated.

The emperor of Ethiopia, Haile Selassie (1891–1975), was forced to leave his country,

Benito Mussolini

which became part of Italian East Africa. However, in 1941 British forces drove the Italians out of Ethiopia and Haile Selassie was restored to his throne. An unsuccessful attempt was made by his own people to overthrow him in 1960, but he was finally deposed in 1974.

1936

Civil War breaks out in Spain

In 1931, King Alfonso XIII of Spain was forced to abdicate because of his opposition to democracy, and Spain became a republic. In February 1936 the Popular Front, an alliance of left-wing parties, formed a government in Spain. It introduced a sweeping programme of social reform, including the redistribution of land. This aroused the opposition of the landowners, the Roman Catholic Church and the army.

In July 1936, led by General Francisco Franco (1892–1975) and other officers, many army units rose in revolt against the government. They quickly occupied large areas of the country, but failed to capture Madrid and Barcelona. Since most of the army was controlled by the rebels, or Nationalists as they were called, the government was forced to arm the workers in order to defend itself. It was also

Haile Selassie

helped by volunteers from many countries who formed International Brigades. The Nationalists received considerable support in the form of soldiers, aircraft and other military equipment from Fascist Italy and Nazi Germany.

Gradually the Nationalists captured more territory. In 1937 they took control of the Basque region in northern Spain after heavy bombing attacks, during which the town of Guernica was almost completely destroyed. In 1938 they began to occupy the eastern part of the country. The war ended with the surrender of Madrid in April 1939, and General Franco became head of state until his death in 1975 when, as nominated by General Franco, Prince Juan Carlos acceded to the throne.

(Right) Sketches by A. Kerner, of fighting men in the Spanish Civil War.

1936

Abdication of Edward VIII

In January 1936 Edward VIII (1894–1972) became King of Great Britain and Northern Ireland on the death of his father King George V. As Prince of Wales he had travelled widely while performing many official duties on behalf of his father and had achieved great popularity with the ordinary people.

The king wished to marry an American woman, Mrs Wallis Simpson, who had been divorced once and was about to divorce her second husband. Such a marriage would have caused a grave constitutional crisis, as the King of England is also head of the Church, and the Church does not approve of divorce. Edward wanted to remain king, but also wanted Mrs Simpson as his queen. Prime Minister Stanley Baldwin made it clear that this was impossible. Rather than give up Mrs Simpson, the king decided to abdicate.

The abdication was announced on December 12, 1936. Edward was succeeded by his younger brother, the Duke of York, who became King George VI. Edward, who married Mrs Simpson in June 1937 in France, received the title HRH (His Royal Highness) the Duke of Windsor. He died in 1972. His wife the Duchess of Windsor was not permitted to use the prefix 'Her Royal Highness'. She died in Paris in 1986.

1936

The Jarrow Hunger March

In 1929 the US Stock Market collapsed and caused a severe slump in the country's economy. This in turn had a serious effect upon international trade. There began a period called the Great Depression in which there was a general decline in prosperity in most European countries and a sharp rise in unemployment. By the early 1930s more than two million men were out of work in Britain.

The Jarrow Crusade or hunger march: unemployed men from North-East England march to London to demand work.

No. 10305   registered at the GPO as a newspaper   ONE PENNY

THE KING DECIDES: ABDICATION PLANS

DRAMATIC VISIT TO QUEEN MARY

THE KING HAS DECIDED.

His abdication—unless he makes an eleventh hour change in his decision—is regarded by the Cabinet as imminent.

His Majesty's decision will be announced by Mr. Baldwin in the House of Commons this afternoon. Lord Halifax will make a similar statement in the House of Lords.

Last night the Labour and Liberal Opposition leaders were informed by the Government of the latest moves in the crisis, and advised that there is little hope of a happy solution.

YESTERDAY AFTERNOON THE KING SLIPPED SECRETLY OUT OF FORT BELVEDERE—THE FIRST TIME HE HAD LEFT THE FORT FOR SIX DAYS—AND HE DROVE TO WINDSOR GREAT PARK, WHERE, IN ROYAL LODGE, HE HAD TEA WITH HIS MOTHER, QUEEN MARY.

This meeting was of the most moving character and had been arranged with the utmost privacy.

Elaborate precautions were taken to enable King Edward to leave the Fort unobserved.

Over Rough-Track Roads

To avoid being seen, the King left by one of the rough track roads seldom used by cars and was able to make the two-mile journey without being seen.

His car had only to traverse 200 yards of public roadway before it crossed from his estate into the long private drive through Windsor Great Park to the Lodge.

No one working in the grounds was allowed to see the King leave the house. Workmen were told to remain hidden in a garage.

After spending half an hour with his mother the King returned as secretly to the Fort.

Queen Mary was accompanied by the Princess Royal and the Earl of Athlone. Later she dined with the Duke and Duchess of Kent.

In Mr. Baldwin's private room at the House of Commons last night a special Cabinet meeting was called and Ministers were frankly told of all developments.

The King had a further consultation with his brothers, the Duke of York and the Duke of Kent at Fort Belvedere during the day. The Duke of York did not return to London till 9 p.m. He looked pale and worn. In the event of abdication he will automatically succeed to the Crown.

Throughout the day dispatch riders with important messages from London had arrived at the Fort. The King's car drove out at 8.30 and shortly before eleven o'clock the royal shooting brake which has been used for the transportation of luggage left Fort Belvedere, and also a dispatch rider.

The Duke of Kent drove to Marlborough House shortly after 8 o'clock and at 10.15 a large car entered the gates with the Duke of York as its only passenger.

M.P.s warned to be at the House to-day; Mrs. Simpson's drive.—Page 3.

KING EDWARD VIII

DIARY OF THE DAY'S EVENTS

Noon.—Mr. Walter Monckton, K.C., Attorney-General to the Duchy of Cornwall, and Sir E. Peacock back at No. 10.
1.15 p.m.—Cabinet meeting ended.
3.22 p.m.—Mr Baldwin made his statement in Commons
4.5 p.m.—Duke of York arrived at Fort Belvedere.
5.0 p.m.—Queen Mary meets the King at Royal Lodge, Windsor Great Park.
9.0 p.m.—Duke of York arrives back at 145.

Piccadilly. The Prime Minister, Sir John Simon and Mr. Monckton at No. 10. Succession of messengers with brief cases.
9.15 p.m.—Mr. Malcolm MacDonald at No. 10.
10.0 p.m.—Sir John Simon and Mr. Monckton again at No. 10.
10.30 p.m.—Mr. Ramsay MacDonald at Colonial Office
11.20 p.m.—Mr. Monckton left No 10 in the King's car.

On December 12, 1936 Edward VIII gave up the throne to marry the American divorcée Mrs Wallis Simpson.

In 1933 the shipbuilding yard at Jarrow in County Durham was forced to shut down. More than two-thirds of the town's entire labour force was thrown out of work. In 1936 Ellen Wilkinson (1891–1947), the MP for Jarrow, led a march of workers to London to seek help from the government. Attempts were made to bring new industries to Jarrow, but the town did not really recover until after the Second World War.

1936
The Olympic Games in Berlin

Adolf Hitler wanted the Olympic Games, held in 1936 in Berlin, to be a triumph for Nazi race theories that the Aryan or white race was superior to all others. Although Germans did, in fact, win most of the medals awarded at the Games, Hitler was enraged when a black American athlete Jesse Owens (1913–1980) proved to be the outstanding performer: Owens broke two existing Olympic records, equalled another and helped smash the world record for the relay.

1936
Prokofiev composes *Peter and the Wolf*

Peter and the Wolf was a piece of music written especially for children by the Russian composer Sergei Prokofiev (1891–1953). Prokofiev was a gifted composer and his best-known works include the opera *The Love for Three Oranges*, the ballet *Romeo and Juliet*, the *Classical Symphony*, piano and violin concertos, and film music.

1936
Germany builds the Siegfried line

In the previous three years, Hitler's government in Germany had shown it was not prepared to abide by the provisions of the Treaty of Versailles (*see 1918 The end of the First World War*) which were designed to prevent Germany

Hitler held massive Nazi rallies at Nuremberg.

becoming a great military power once again. The Germans, in fact, re-armed in secret. Then in 1936, they began work on the Siegfried line, a series of fortifications to protect Germany's western border in time of war. By 1939 it consisted of more than twelve thousand steel and concrete forts armed with heavy guns, stretching from the Dutch frontier in the north to Switzerland in the south.

1938
Germany annexes Austria

Adolf Hitler's plans for the expansion of Germany included the *Anschluss*, or the union of Austria with Germany, which had been expressly forbidden under the Treaty of Versailles. Nevertheless there was considerable support for this in Austria especially among Nazi sympathizers in that country, and in 1934 they had made an unsuccessful attempt to seize power in Vienna.

In February 1938 Hitler made his position in Germany even stronger by becoming supreme commander of the armed forces. Later the same month he summoned the Austrian chancellor, Kurt von Schuschnigg (1897–1977) to Germany and demanded that the Austrian Nazis be given important posts in Schuschnigg's government.

Schuschnigg wanted the Austrian people to decide by voting whether to accept union with Germany. However, threatened with a German invasion, he resigned. On March 12 German troops entered Austria and on the following day the union between the two countries was proclaimed. A government headed by the Austrian Nazi Arthur Seyss-Inquart (1892–1946) was established in Vienna.

In occupied Poland, Nazi troops transported thousands of Jews to brutal concentration camps, where they were murdered.

1938
The Munich Agreement

After his annexation of Austria earlier in 1938 Adolf Hitler was now determined to destroy Czechoslovakia. This country contained more than three million German-speaking people living in the Sudetenland region and many of them strongly supported the idea of union with Germany. In April 1938 their leader Konrad Henlein (1898–1945) demanded full self-government for the Sudetenland. This brought about a threat of war between Germany and Czechoslovakia, which might involve other countries.

The British prime minister, Neville Chamberlain (1869–1940), anxious to preserve peace at all costs, flew to Munich in September 1938 to attend a conference with Edouard Daladier, the French prime minister, Hitler and Mussolini. A settlement of the crisis was reached and the Sudetenland region and its population were transferred to Germany. On his return to England Chamberlain said, 'I believe it is peace in our time'. However, in March 1939 Germany annexed the rest of Czechoslovakia. Chamberlain realized he had been deceived.

1939
Outbreak of the Second World War

After Germany had annexed Austria and Czechoslovakia, Hitler began to threaten Poland. Britain and France realized that there was no limit to Hitler's ambitions and in March 1939 promised to help Poland if she should be attacked by Germany. In August 1939 Germany and the USSR signed a treaty in which they guaranteed not to attack each other and to remain neutral if either country was involved in a war.

On September 1 Germany invaded Poland and on September 3 Britain and France declared war on Germany. Despite heroic Polish resistance, German mechanized divisions supported by overwhelming air power overran the country in four weeks. Russian troops invaded Poland from the east and occupied a large area of Polish territory, leaving the rest in German hands.

In Britain there was a mass evacuation of children from London and other large towns, because of the fear of German air-raids, although very few air attacks on Britain took place early in the war.

At sea, in December 1939, there was a spectacular battle off the coast of South America between three British cruisers and a German battleship, the *Graf Spee*, which was badly damaged and later scuttled by its crew in the entrance of Montevideo harbour.

1939
Steinbeck publishes *The Grapes of Wrath*

In 1939 the American novelist John Steinbeck (1902–68) published *The Grapes of Wrath*, the story of a farming family from Oklahoma who migrated to California in search of a better life. Like his other well-known novels *Tortilla Flat* (1935), *Of Mice and Men* (1937) and *Cannery Row* (1952) it shows his concern for the sufferings of ordinary people.

1939
Henry Moore's *Reclining Figure*

In 1939 *Reclining Figure* established the reputation of Henry Moore (1898–1986) as one of the most original of modern English sculptors. Among his other works is the *Madonna and Child* (1943) and he created some notable sculptures for the UNESCO headquarters in Paris. During the Second World War, he produced a series of famous drawings of people in air-raid shelters.

1940
Germany invades Denmark, Norway, Belgium, the Netherlands and France

On April 9, 1940 Germany troops invaded Denmark which surrendered without fighting. On the same day German sea-borne forces landed in various parts of Norway. British and French forces were sent to help the Norwegian army, but had to be withdrawn later because they were needed in France which the Germans invaded on May 10, 1940. Norwegian resistance to the Germans did not cease until June 10.

On May 10, in addition to France, German armies invaded the Netherlands, Belgium, and Luxembourg. The Dutch port of Rotterdam was severely damaged by German air attacks before the Dutch army surrendered on May 15. The British Expeditionary Force, which had been in France since September 1939, was sent into Belgium to help the Belgian army, together with some French troops.

Using the method of *blitzkreig* (lightning war), strong German armoured forces broke through the French defences at Sedan, near the French border with Belgium, and moved swiftly towards the English Channel. In this way they cut off from the main French army those British and French soldiers who were fighting in Belgium. They were gradually being forced back

Henry Moore's *Reclining Figure.*

by the Germans and their position became extremely dangerous when the Belgian army surrendered on May 26.

1940
Ernest Hemingway: *For Whom the Bell Tolls*

Ernest Hemingway (1898–1961) was already a well-known American novelist when he published *For Whom the Bell Tolls*. It describes the heroism of an American fighting in the Spanish Civil War. Physical courage is a dominant theme in Hemingway's other novels which include *The Sun also Rises* (1926) and *A Farewell to Arms* (1929).

1940
Churchill becomes prime minister

In May 1940 Neville Chamberlain resigned as prime minister of Britain because many Members of Parliament were not satisfied with his leadership. He was succeeded by Winston Churchill (1874–1965) who had for a long time been a strong opponent of Chamberlain's policy of appeasement of Nazi Germany.

Churchill formed a coalition government of Conservatives, Labour and Liberal members, and the leader of the Parliamentary Labour Party, Clement Attlee (1883–1967), became his deputy prime minister. In his first speech to Parliament as prime minister on May 13, at a time of grave national crisis, Churchill declared, 'I have nothing to offer but blood, toil, tears and sweat'.

1940
Evacuation from Dunkirk

The surrender of the Belgian army and the arrival of German armoured forces at the Channel ports in France meant that by the end of May 1940 the British and French troops in Belgium were surrounded on all sides. The British government decided to evacuate these troops by sea from Dunkirk in northern France, just south of the Belgian border.

In order to carry such a large body of men nearly a thousand ships of all sizes were hastily sent, or volunteered to go, across the Channel from England many making repeated trips. Fortunately for the soldiers retreating towards Dunkirk, the German forces halted their offensive for a time.

Between May 26 and June 4 about 200,000 British and 120,000 French soldiers were taken away from the beach at Dunkirk by a fleet of small ships under very difficult conditions and heavy bombardment.

1940
The fall of France

On June 5, 1940 the German armies in France launched a big attack. After some resistance the French defence collapsed completely and the German forces moved rapidly southwards. On June 10 Italy declared war against France and Britain. Four days later the Germans entered Paris. The French military position was now hopeless and a new French government, led by Marshal Philippe Pétain (1856–1951) asked for an armistice.

Under the terms of the armistice (June 22, 1940) France was divided into two zones. One was to be under German military occupation and the other, with the town of Vichy as its capital, was to remain under French sovereignty. Pétain became head of state of Vichy France, and Pierre Laval (1883–1945) chief minister. Although Vichy France was occupied by the Germans in 1942 when the Allied forces invaded North Africa, its government remained in existence until 1944, when British, American and other Allied forces liberated France.

1940
The Battle of Britain

In July 1940 Adolf Hitler began to make plans for the invasion of Britain, his last unconquered opponent in Western Europe. Before this could take place it was necessary for the *Luftwaffe*, the German air force, to destroy British air power. The *Luftwaffe* launched a series of attacks, first against shipping and targets on the English coast, then against airfields, and finally against London and other towns.

The German planes greatly outnumbered the defending British aircraft. However, the use of radar (*see 1935 Watson-Watt develops radar*) gave the Royal Air Force advanced warning of attacks. On August 20, Winston Churchill said in the House of Commons, 'Never in the field of human conflict was so much owed by so many to so few'.

By the end of October 1940 the *Luftwaffe* had lost more than 1,700 aircraft in a vain attempt to destroy the Royal Air Force and Hitler was forced to give up the idea of invading Britain.

1941

Germany invades the USSR

On June 22, 1941, Germany, in alliance with Romania, Hungary and Finland, invaded the USSR. The first German attacks met with great success. The Russians were taken by surprise and their army suffered heavy losses. By December 1941 German forces were only a few kilometres from Moscow. Leningrad was cut off by the Germans and during a heroic siege which lasted nearly eighteen months large numbers of its inhabitants died of starvation.

However, the Germans had underestimated both the severity of the Russian winter and the almost limitless supplies of Russian manpower. A Russian attack in December forced the Germans to retreat almost everywhere.

In June 1942 the Germans launched a new offensive with the aim of gaining possession of the Caucasus region in the southern USSR. In August 1942 German armies began to attack the town of Stalingrad (now Volgograd), an important communications centre on the Volga river. But the Russian defenders resisted strongly for four months and the attacking German forces were themselves surrounded and captured.

This was the turning-point in the war. However, huge battles between the Russians and Germans involving hundreds of thousands of men and thousands of tanks were to be fought before the Germans were finally driven out of the USSR.

The Battle of Britain.

1941
Shostakovich's *Leningrad Symphony*

In 1941 the Russian composer Dmitri Shostakovich (1906–75) wrote his seventh symphony, the *Leningrad Symphony*, while Leningrad was besieged by the Germans. It enjoyed great popularity in the USSR and other countries. Although Shostakovich is best-known for his symphonies, he also wrote a violin concerto, piano concertos, ballets, operas and music for films.

1941
Whittle's jet engine

Frank Whittle (*b.* 1907), an officer in the Royal Air Force, invented a jet aeroplane engine in which the means of propulsion was provided by a stream of gas being forced out backwards at great speed. In May 1941 his new engine was fitted into a specially built aircraft which made a successful flight. By the end of the Second World War, the Gloster Meteor, the first British jet fighter aircraft, was being produced.

In Germany a jet engine similar to Whittle's was used in an aircraft which first flew in August 1939, and in 1944 a jet-powered German military aircraft was in service.

After the war there was a rapid development in the use of jet engines for combat aircraft. In 1952 the De Havilland Comet, the first commercial airliner to be fitted with jet engines, went into regular service. By 1970 most commercial and military aircraft were jet-powered.

1941
The Japanese attack Pearl Harbor

On December 7, 1941, Japanese planes, launched from aircraft carriers, carried out a surprise attack on Pearl Harbor, the main US naval base in Hawaii. Many American ships were sunk or damaged. However, the American aircraft carriers were not in Pearl Harbor at the time. These carriers were later to prove extremely important, for many of the sea battles in the Pacific War which followed were fought between aircraft that were carrier-based, and American carrier-power was far greater than the Japanese.

The purpose of the Pearl Harbor attack had been to stop the US Navy from interfering with Japanese plans to conquer south-east Asia, and for six months afterwards, Japanese forces were free to overrun almost all this area. They occupied Malaya, Singapore, the Dutch East Indies (now Indonesia) and the Philippines, and invaded Burma.

The United States, however, began to fight back. Their first successes were in naval battles in May and June 1942 when US aircraft inflicted heavy damage on the Japanese fleet. The Japanese were gradually driven out of many Pacific Island territories they had occupied. In October 1944 the reconquest of the Philippines began and by May 1945 the Japanese had been defeated in Burma by the Allies.

The Japanese fought with fanatical courage and in the later stages of the war *Kamikaze*

The Japanese attack Pearl Harbor.

airmen deliberately flew their aircraft, loaded with explosives, straight at enemy ships: the Japanese thought it shameful for soldiers to surrender. Because of this they treated their British, Australian and American prisoners of war with great brutality and many died in captivity.

1942
Battle of El Alamein

The war in the Middle East began in September 1940 when an Italian army from Libya invaded Egypt in order to attack the British forces stationed there. The British counter-attacked and drove them back into Libya. In March 1941 the Italians were reinforced by a mechanized German force, the Afrika Korps, commanded by General Erwin Rommel (1891–1944), who quickly compelled the British to retreat into Egypt. However, a British garrison in the Libyan port of Tobruk withstood a siege by the Germans and Italians for nine months.

In November 1941 the British army began another offensive. In May 1942 Rommel counter-attacked and pushed his forces deep into Egyptian territory until they were halted at El Alamein. It was from here in October 1942 that General Bernard Montgomery (1887–1976), commanding a force of British, Australian, New Zealand and Indian soldiers, launched a final offensive which was to lead to the expulsion of German and Italian troops from North Africa by 1943.

1943
The surrender of Italy

In November 1942 Allied forces landed along the North African coast, in Morocco, Algeria and Tunisia. In May 1943, together with the British army advancing from Egypt, they compelled the German and Italian armies in North Africa to surrender. Two months later Allied forces occupied Sicily and in September they invaded the mainland of Italy.

In July Benito Mussolini's Fascist regime had been overthrown. A new Italian government

Desert warfare: Montgomery's final offensive.

under Marshal Pietro Badoglio (1871–1956) surrendered to the Allies and later declared war on Germany. Mussolini was arrested and imprisoned, but rescued by German soldiers. He was, however, captured and executed by Italian partisans (resistance fighters) in 1945.

The Germans sent large forces into Italy and these put up a stubborn resistance. In an effort to speed up the advance, in January 1944 the Allies landed troops at the seaport of Anzio near Rome. But it was not until spring 1945, after much fierce fighting, that the Germans were finally driven out of Italy.

1943
Perón comes to power in Argentina

In June 1943 the government of President Ramón Castillo (1873–1944) of Argentina was overthrown by a group of army officers led by Juan Perón (1895–1974). Three years later Perón was elected president of Argentina and his supporters won a majority in parliament.

Perón at once began a five-year plan of economic reform and rapid industrialization. His programme of social welfare brought many benefits to the working classes and gained him great popularity with the mass of the people although he was in fact a dictator. Perón's wife Eva (1919–52) played an important part in her husband's career and became a legendary, much-loved figure in Argentina. She remained so after her early death.

Perón was deposed and exiled in 1955 after he had aroused the hostility of many powerful people. However, he still had numerous supporters and, following years of political unrest in Argentina, he returned there in 1973 to form a new government. He died the following year. Perón's third wife, Isabel, took over as president, but was herself overthrown by an army coup in 1976.

1944
The Allied invasion of France

On June 6, 1944 ('D-Day', as it was called) a huge force of American, British and Canadian soldiers landed on the Normandy coast of

France. They were commanded by the American General Dwight D. Eisenhower (1890–1969). Before the invasion took place railways and bridges in northern France had been heavily bombed, making it very difficult for the Germans to move their armies quickly.

After fierce fighting the Germans were forced to retreat. On August 15 Allied troops landed in the south of France and by the end of September most of the country had been freed from German occupation.

On September 3 British troops entered Belgium. Later the same month a large force of paratroops was dropped at Arnhem in the Netherlands in an unsuccessful attempt to obtain a bridgehead over the Rhine.

The Allied forces were halted at the German frontier by the Siegfried line. In December the commander of the German army, Field Marshal Gerd von Runstedt (1875–1953), launched a surprise counter-attack in the Ardennes region of Belgium which had some success. In February 1945 the Allies broke through the Siegfried line. In March they crossed the Rhine and began the invasion of Germany.

1944
The Liberation of Paris

By the end of July 1944 the Allied forces which had invaded Normandy in June were advancing rapidly through France. On August 17 American troops entered the town of Orléans only 113

Churchill, Roosevelt and Stalin meet at Yalta.

kilometres from Paris. Two days later the French resistance forces in Paris rose in revolt against the Germans. On August 25 a French armoured division under General Leclerc (1902–47) entered the city and received the surrender of the German garrison. Paris was finally liberated after four years of occupation.

On August 26 General Charles de Gaulle (1890–1970), who had led the Free French movement in London, took part in a triumphant procession along the Champs Elysées in Paris. Afterwards he attended a service of thanksgiving in Notre Dame Cathedral, bravely defying the bullets of hidden German snipers and French collaborators.

De Gaulle became head of a provisional government which maintained authority in France until a new constitution could be drawn up. However, in 1946, after political arguments, de Gaulle resigned from government and did not return until 1958, when he became president of France.

1945
The Yalta Conference

In February 1945 an important conference was held at Yalta in the Crimea, USSR. It was attended by President Franklin D. Roosevelt of the United States, the British prime minister, Winston Churchill, and the leader of the USSR, Joseph Stalin. They were accompanied by their foreign ministers and the chiefs of staff of their armed forces. The aim of the conference was to discuss a number of military and political problems.

The three leaders agreed upon plans for the final defeat of Germany. They also made arrangements for Germany to be divided into four zones after the end of the war, to be occupied by Britain, the United States, the USSR, and France, respectively.

The future frontiers of Poland were settled and the USSR agreed to enter the war against Japan after Germany had surrendered. Finally, the conference discussed plans for the setting up of the United Nations Organization.

1945

The surrender of Germany

In January 1945 Russian forces had reached the eastern frontier of Germany. In the west the British and American armies were preparing for the final offensive. Meanwhile the Allied air forces continued their bombing campaign and in February caused widespread destruction and many thousands of deaths when they raided the town of Dresden, Germany.

In March the American army crossed the Rhine and by the end of April had joined up with the Russians on the River Elbe. Russian troops entered Berlin on April 24 and captured the city after fierce street fighting. Adolf Hitler committed suicide in his underground bunker in Berlin on April 30. In May the German armies began surrendering and the war in Europe finally came to an end on May 8. The leaders of the victorious powers held their last wartime conference in Potsdam, on the outskirts of Berlin, during July and August 1945. The conference ended two weeks before the surrender of Japan.

1945

The concentration camps are discovered

As they began to overrun countries previously occupied by Germany and then Germany itself, the Allied forces were horrified to discover the concentration camps. These had originally been established in 1933 as places of detention for opponents of the Nazi regime. Later they were used to house Jews and other minority groups. By 1939 six camps had been established in Germany, containing more than 20,000 prisoners.

After the outbreak of the Second World War further concentration camps were built in Germany and Poland to take people from all over Nazi-occupied Europe. They were kept short of food in dreadful living conditions, and were also forced to undergo cruel medical experiments. The camps in Poland were extermination camps where millions of Jews and others were killed in gas chambers.

The mass murder of Jews, gypsies and Slavs from eastern Europe was part of Adolf Hitler's evil plan to exterminate peoples the Nazis considered inferior. Well over six million victims were killed in the camps, and many more died from disease.

1945

The surrender of Japan

Between 1942 and 1945 the Japanese armies were slowly driven from the territories they had overrun during the first six months of the war in the Pacific. In April 1945 the Americans invaded the island of Okinawa which they captured after much fierce fighting. They now had a base only 515 kilometres from the mainland of Japan.

In the following months American aircraft launched a series of heavy air raids on Japanese cities and industrial centres. After the collapse of Germany in May 1945 Japan had been left without allies. Her military position was now desperate and her navy had effectively been destroyed. Nevertheless, the suicidal fanaticism with which the Japanese had defended Okinawa, showed that if the mainland of Japan were invaded, American losses could be exceptionally heavy.

The US president Harry S. Truman (1884–1972) therefore decided to try and bring the war to a quick end by the use of the atomic bomb. This terrible new weapon, which had an explosive power far greater than any ordinary bomb, had been developed by scientists in the United States. On August 6 a bomb was dropped on Hiroshima and on August 9 a second on Nagasaki, killing more than 120,000 people and causing widespread devastation. On August 14 Japan surrendered.

Hiroshima, Japan, was devastated by the first atomic bomb.

1945

The United Nations formed

In April 1945 delegates from fifty countries met at San Francisco in the United States to draw up a charter for the United Nations Organization which was to be the successor to the League of Nations.

The charter, which was signed on June 26, 1945 declared that the organization was an association of states whose aim was to maintain international peace and encourage co-operation between nations.

The United Nations consists of six main bodies: the General Assembly, the Economic and Social Council, the Trusteeship Council, the International Court of Justice, the Security Council, and the Secretariat.

It also contains a number of special agencies, such as the Food and Agriculture Organization, and the UN Educational Scientific and Cultural Organization.

The Secretariat, which is the administrative body of the United Nations, is headed by a secretary-general chosen by the General Assembly on the advice of the Security Council.

The first secretary-general was a Norwegian, Trygve Lie (1896–1968), who held office 1946–53.

1945

Landslide Labour victory

The British general election of July 5, 1945, was won by the Labour Party with a huge majority over all other parties. The new government was

The General Assembly of the UN meets in New York.

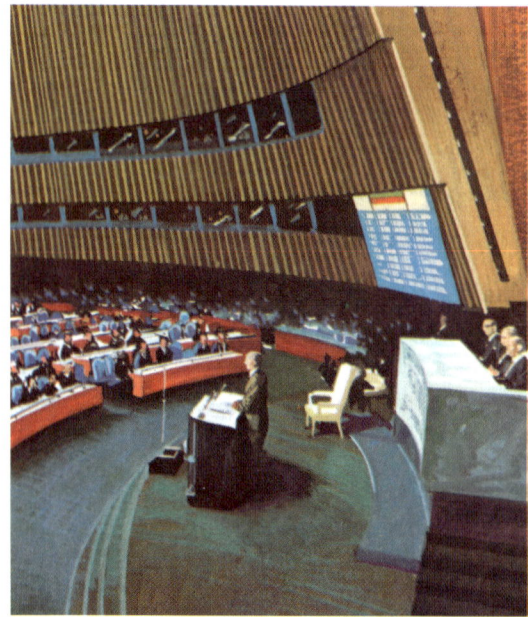

led by Clement Attlee (1883–1967) who had been Churchill's deputy 1942–45. It immediately began a sweeping programme of economic and social reforms, which were to transform Britain into the 'Welfare State'.

Among the most important measures were the nationalization of various industries including coal mining, the electricity supply industry, and the Bank of England. Another significant event was the establishment of the National Health Service which provided free medical care for everybody.

However, the war had left Britain's economy in a very serious condition and the country recovered its prosperity only very slowly, with the help of generous loans from the United States. It was a time of great hardship, and rationing of food, which had been introduced during the war, did not end until the early 1950s.

1945
France: the end of the Third Republic

In October 1945 elections were held in France for an Assembly which was to draw up the country's new constitution. The Assembly later proclaimed General Charles de Gaulle head of a provisional government, but de Gaulle resigned in January 1946.

The new constitution was finally adopted by a referendum in October 1946 and the Fourth French Republic came into existence. After elections in November the Communists became the largest party in the National Assembly. However, the Communists in the government quarrelled with their colleagues and were removed from office in May 1947. They now opposed the government as did the right-wing party formed by de Gaulle later the same year.

France's difficulties were increased by economic problems, strikes and a war in French Indo-China (South-east Asia). The next ten years were a period of political instability, during which there were frequent changes of government.

1945
Birth of modern jazz

In the 1940s some American jazz musicians tried new harmonic ideas and produced a kind of jazz known as bebop. Inspired by Charlie Parker, Dizzy Gillespie, Thelonius Monk and others,

modern jazz later developed in the 1950s and 60s a number of different styles, including the so-called 'cool' or relaxed jazz. The Modern Jazz Quartet found inspiration in the forms of classical music.

1945
George Orwell's *Animal Farm*

In 1945 the English writer George Orwell (1903–50) published his novel *Animal Farm*, the story of a group of animals who overthrow their human masters. A satire on communism, it created a great impression, as did his last novel, *Nineteen Eighty-Four* (1949). This is set in a nightmare world of the then future, in which the state has complete control over people's lives.

1946
Jackson Pollock: action painting

Jackson Pollock (1912–56) was a leading member of the US school of Abstract Expressionism in painting. He developed a new technique called action painting, of which *Untitled* (1946) is an example. The paint – and it was the qualities of the actual paint which delighted Pollock – was applied in a more or less random manner: dripped from the can, flicked or splashed on, or even cycled over. Pollock's large canvasses are impressive, but his work represents something of a dead end in painting. Though influential, he had no true followers.

1947
India and Pakistan achieve independence

Before 1947, India was part of the British Empire, ruled by a viceroy. There were also several 'princely' states with their own rulers, who recognized the British as their overlords. Of the numerous religions in India, the largest were Hinduism and Islam. Both communities wanted independence for India and there had, in fact, been

(Left) Mahatma Gandhi in August 1940, on his way in a rickshaw to a meeting with the Viceroy.

agitation for it since the 1880s. However, the Moslems, the smaller of the two communities, were afraid that their rights would be ignored by the Hindu majority.

The British government tried unsuccessfully to meet the wishes of both communities. However, the Moslem leader Mohammed Ali Jinnah demanded the creation of a separate state in those areas of India where Moslems were in the majority. This effectively meant areas in north-west and north-east Pakistan (now Bangladesh). With great reluctance and trepidation, Mahatma Gandhi and Jawaharlal Nehru, the Hindu leaders, agreed to the partition of India.

On August 15, 1947 India and Pakistan came into existence. The division of the Punjab and Bengal between them meant that millions of Hindus and Moslems had to be transferred from one country to another. During these mass migrations there was much fighting and many people were killed. Moreover, there was a dispute over Kashmir. It was claimed by India, but Pakistan objected on the grounds that the majority of the population was Moslem.

Gandhi travelled all over the country trying to keep the peace between the Hindus and Moslems, but he failed to stop the fighting and slaughter. A group of fanatical Hindus thought Gandhi showed too much favour to the Moslems and one of them assassinated him at a prayer meeting in Delhi on January 30, 1948.

Ceylon (now Sri Lanka) and Burma, formerly a part of Britain's Indian Empire both became independent in February 1948.

1947
The Marshall Plan

In 1947 the countries of Western Europe, which had suffered severely during the Second World War, were in some danger of economic collapse. In June of that year the US secretary of state, George C. Marshall (1880–1959), announced in a speech that the United States would be willing to help Europe in her efforts towards recovery. The Americans were particularly concerned at the rise of communism in post-war Europe, and intended to counteract this by giving aid.

In July 1947 seventeen Western European countries met in Paris to try and co-ordinate their plans for economic stability and to decide what assistance would be necessary from the United States. This was the European Recovery Programme, or Marshall Plan as it was popularly called.

The countries supporting the Programme subsequently set up a permanent body, known as the Organization for European Economic Co-operation, which was to administer aid given under the Marshall Plan. In 1948 the United States began to supply Europe with material and financial aid, which continued until 1952.

1947
The Dead Sea Scrolls

In 1947 some ancient manuscripts were discovered in a cave near the Dead Sea, about 12 kilometres south of Jericho. When the manuscripts were examined by experts it was found that they belonged to a community of Jews who lived around the time of Christ. They have provided much important information about Jewish history and the origins of Christianity.

1947
Tennessee Williams's *A Streetcar Named Desire*

A Streetcar Named Desire by the American playwright Tennessee Williams (1914–83), is about the disastrous consequences of a visit by a neurotic frustrated woman to her married sister. Like many of Williams's best-known plays including *The Glass Menagerie* (1945) and *Cat on a Hot Tin Roof* (1955) the scene is set in the 'Deep South' of the United States.

1947
Thor Heyerdahl's *Kon-Tiki* expedition

In 1947 a Norwegian scientist Thor Heyerdahl (b. 1914), with five companions, set off from Callao in Peru on the west coast of South America in a raft made of locally grown balsa wood. His object was to sail across the Pacific Ocean to Polynesia.

Heyerdahl had already noticed that certain aspects of Polynesian culture resembled that of the ancient inhabitants of Peru. He believed that the Polynesians were not Asiatic in origin and wanted to show the possibility that in ancient times people from South America could have crossed the ocean on primitive rafts and settled in Polynesia. After an epic voyage of three and a half months over 8,000 kilometres of ocean, Heyerdahl landed in Tuamotu Island in the South Pacific. His exploit made him world famous and he wrote about the voyage in *The Kon-Tiki Expedition* (1948).

1948
The Berlin Airlift

After the surrender of Germany in 1945 Berlin was divided into four sectors, each under the control of one of the Allies (*see 1945 The Yata Conference*). In 1948 the Western Allies (Britain, the United States and France) formed their zones of Germany into a single economic unit.

This was done in the face of opposition from the Russians, who began to blockade the city of Berlin, which lay right in the centre of their zone of occupation in Germany. All communications by rail and road with the west were cut off. The Russians moreover declared that the four-power administration of the city was no longer functioning and that the Western Allies had no right to be there. They went on to set up their own municipal government in the Russian sector of Berlin.

West Berlin was saved from starvation by a massive airlift of vital supplies by the British and Americans, which continued until the blockade was lifted in May 1949.

Stores being unloaded from a British plane at an airfield near Hanover, helping to beat the Russian blockade, July 1948.

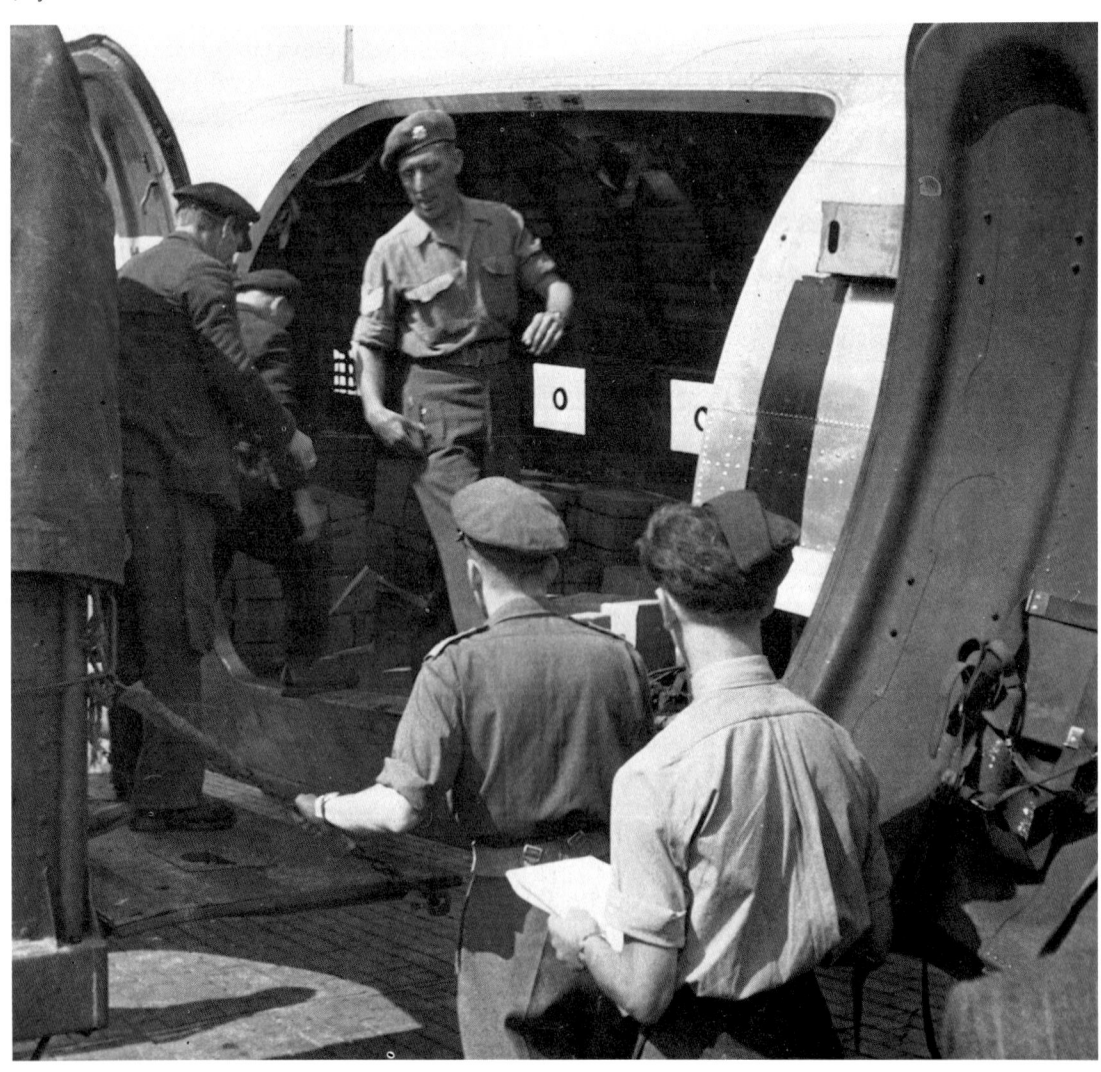

1948

State of Israel proclaimed

Many Jews settled in Palestine after the First World War (*see 1917 The Balfour declaration*) developing industry and agriculture. The Arabs living in Palestine strongly opposed the arrival of large numbers of Jews and there was frequent fighting between the two communities. The persecution of the Jews during the Second World War led to even greater immigration into Palestine. The British authorities tried to limit their numbers, but many entered illegally and Jewish terrorist organizations conducted a campaign of violence against the British.

The British controlled Palestine under a mandate given them by the League of Nations after the First World War. In 1947, the British asked the United Nations, the successor of the League, to decide the future of Palestine and in November, the UN voted in favour of partitioning Palestine between a Jewish state and an Arab state. The British withdrew in May 1948 and the same day, May 15, the Jewish state of Israel was proclaimed. The surrounding Arab states, however, had never accepted the partition of Palestine and a few hours after Israel was proclaimed, they invaded the country.

After nine months of fierce fighting, in which the Israeli forces were greatly outnumbered, the Arab armies were repulsed. Afterwards, the proposed Arab state of Palestine became part of Jordan and Jerusalem was divided between Israel and Jordan.

1948

Mount Palomar's reflecting telescope

In 1928 the California Institute of Technology received a grant from the Rockefeller Foundation for the construction of a reflecting telescope with a diameter of 200 inches (508 centimetres). It was to be housed in an observatory built at the height of nearly 1,800 metres on Mount Palomar in California.

The dome containing the gigantic telescope and the building supporting the dome were erected in 1938. The preparation of the disc for the telescope's mirror took nearly ten years and the finished mirror weighed about 15 tonnes. The telescope was finally completed and installed in 1948.

1949
Founding of NATO

After the Second World War, in face of the growing hostility of the USSR, the countries of western Europe decided to form a protective alliance with the United States and Canada. In April 1949 the North Atlantic Treaty Organization (NATO) was formed. The treaty was signed by delegates from twelve countries and provided for mutual assistance against aggression.

1949

The two Germanies

After the surrender of Germany in 1945 the country was divided into four occupation zones. Growing hostility between the USSR and the Western Allies made it impossible for Germany to be treated as a single political and economic unit as had been intended.

In order to deal with the desperate post-war plight of the Germans, which included near starvation and an enormous influx of refugees from the east, the British and Americans decided in 1946 to merge the economies of their two zones. They also began to hand over much responsibility for local administration to the Germans. In 1948 the three Western Allies went

The Mount Palomar telescope.

ahead with their plans for the creation of a centralized German government.

In April 1949 the German Federal Republic came into being as an independent sovereign state. Elections were held in August of that year and the Christian Democratic Party, led by Konrad Adenauer (1876–1967), took office in the parliament at Bonn. Theodor Heuss (1884–1973) became federal president.

Six months later, in October, the Russian zone became the communist German Democratic Republic, usually known as East Germany. Wilhelm Pieck became president and Otto Grotewohl, minister-president. The capital, Berlin, was divided between East Germany and West Germany. East Berlin became the former's capital, and Bonn, the latter's.

1949

Mao Tse-tung proclaims Chinese People's Republic

The struggle between the Chinese Nationalists and the Chinese Communists for the control of their country had begun in the 1920s (*see 1928 Chiang Kai-shek takes Peking*). Civil War between the opposing sides continued until the Japanese invasion of China in 1937. After the defeat of Japan the civil war was resumed.

The Chinese Communists, under the leadership of Mao Tse-tung (1893–1976) equipped themselves with enormous quantities of arms

Mao Tse-tung as a young man.

left behind by the Japanese. Their Nationalist opponents proved both incompetent and corrupt and gradually lost popular support. Although they received military assistance from the Americans, they were unable to win any significant victories over the Communists.

In 1948 the Nationalist armies suffered a series of defeats and began to disintegrate. In 1949 the remaining Nationalist forces, led by Chiang Kai-shek (1887–1975), were driven off mainland China and took refuge in the island of Formosa. On October 1 of that year Mao Tsetung proclaimed the establishment of the Chinese People's Republic. In 1950, Chiang Kaishek set up a Nationalist republic on Formosa, which later became known as Taiwan.

1950

Bertrand Russell receives Nobel Prize

In 1950 the English philosopher and writer Bertrand Russell (1872–1970) was awarded the Nobel Prize for literature. Russell began his long and distinguished career as a lecturer in mathematics at Cambridge University. His *Principles of*

Bertrand Russell

A helicopter evacuating United Nations wounded
during the Korean War.

Mathematics (1903) and *Principia Mathematica*
(1910–13) are, today, classics of mathematical
logic. He went on to make his reputation as an
outstanding philosopher with *The Analysis of
Mind* (1921) and *Human Knowledge, Its Scope and
Limits* (1948).

During the First World War he was sent to
prison for writing an article in a pacifist journal.
After the war he became a lecturer and journalist,
and wrote popular books on a variety of
subjects, including philosophy, marriage, education, and sociology.

Always, his outspoken views on morals and
politics brought him into conflict with authority.
In the 1950s he became associated first with the

Campaign for Nuclear Disarmament and subsequently with its more militant branch, the
Committee of 100, which advocated civil disobedience in support of its beliefs.

1950
The Korean War

After the surrender of Japan in 1945, Korea,
which had been controlled by Japan since 1895
and was annexed by that country in 1910, was
occupied by US and Russian troops. The Americans took the southern half and the Russians the
part north of the 38th parallel of latitude.

The conquest of Everest, the highest mountain in the world, by Hilary and Tenzing. News of the ascent was relayed to jubilant crowds at the coronation of Elizabeth II.

Although it had been agreed that a democratic government should be set up for the whole of Korea, in 1948 the Americans recognized South Korea as an independent state. The same year a Communist government was established in North Korea, and claimed authority over the entire country.

In June 1950 North Korean forces invaded South Korea. The United Nations asked member countries to stop the North Korean advance. By the end of 1950 a UN force, mainly composed of Americans, had pushed the North Koreans right back to the Chinese border. China now intervened on the side of North Korea, and after much fierce fighting an armistice was eventually signed in 1953. The frontier between the two Koreas was at the 38th parallel, exactly where it had been when the war began. Today, the Korean peninsula is still divided between North and South.

1950
McCarthy investigates 'Un-American' activities

In the early 1950s Americans became worried about Communist influence in the United States when several people were convicted of spying for the USSR. An American senator, Joseph McCarthy (1908–57), exploited their fears with wild accusations that Communists held important positions in government departments. He set up an investigation committee and many innocent people lost their jobs before McCarthy was finally discredited.

1953
Eisenhower becomes president

In 1952 Dwight D. Eisenhower (1890–1969), who had led the Allied armies in the invasion of Europe in 1944, was nominated as the Republican Party's candidate for the presidency of the United States. When the elections were held in November of that year Eisenhower won an impressive victory over the Democratic Party's candidate, Adlai E. Stevenson (1900–65), and took office as president in January 1953.

Eisenhower's first term as president was characterized by the growing prosperity of the United States. In his domestic politics he pursued a moderate policy. In foreign affairs he made great efforts to improve international relations, in the hope of lessening the tensions caused by the Cold War.

He was re-elected president in 1956 and during his second term of office he travelled widely, visiting other heads of state and received the Soviet prime minister, Nikita Khrushchev, on a visit to the United States.

1953
Discovery of DNA structure

One of the most important developments in biology has been the cracking of the 'genetic code'. The work started by Mendel (see 1865 Mendel announces heredity laws) and others had become a complex and advanced branch of science when Francis Crick and James Dewey Watson discovered the structure of the DNA (deoxyribose nucleic acid) molecule, so opening up for good or bad the possibilities for genetic 'engineering'.

1953
Conquest of Everest

Mount Everest, which lies in the Himalayan Range, on the border between Nepal and Tibet, is the highest mountain in the world, rising to a height of more than 8,800 metres. Many attempts had been made to climb it, and although some mountaineers had come very close to the summit, none were known to have reached it.

In 1953 the Royal Geographical Society of London and the Alpine Club sponsored a new expedition led by Colonel John Hunt. Elaborate preparations were made before the climb began, and the expedition followed a route which had not been tried before. By May 28 the mountaineers had reached a height of nearly 8,500 metres and on May 29 a New Zealand member of the expedition, Edmund Hillary, and a Sherpa guide, Tenzing, reached the summit. The news of this first successful ascent of Everest was greeted with enthusiasm everywhere.

1954
The fall of Dien Bien Phu

During the Second World War the French southeast Asian protectorates of Tonkin and Annam and colony of Cochin-China were occupied by the Japanese. After the defeat of the Japanese (*see 1945 The surrender of Japan*) Ho Chi-Minh (1892–1969) leader of a Communist-dominated nationalist party, the Viet Minh, proclaimed the independence of the three territories as the Democratic Republic of Vietnam.

The French attempted to re-establish their control in the country and in 1946 fighting broke out between their forces and the Viet Minh. Unable to secure a decisive victory, the French attempted to set up a rival non-Communist nationalist government.

However, by 1953 French forces were rapidly losing ground in the northern part of the country and in May 1954 the Viet Minh overran an important French military position at Dien Bien Phu. Following a conference held at Geneva the same year Vietnam was divided into Communist North Vietnam, and Nationalist South Vietnam.

1954
Dylan Thomas's *Under Milk Wood*

1954 saw the publication of the radio drama *Under Milk Wood* by Welsh poet Dylan Thomas (1914–53). This poetic evocation of a day in the life of a small Welsh town enjoyed an instant popular success. Thomas established his reputation as a poet with *Eighteen Poems* (1934); he was also well-known for his volume of short stories *Portrait of the Artist as a Young Dog* (1940).

1954
Hydrogen bomb exploded

In the early 1950s American scientists were working on the construction of the hydrogen bomb, whose destructive power was many times greater than the atomic bomb. One hydrogen bomb was tested in the Pacific in 1952. Another test took place on Bikini Atoll in the Pacific in

A nuclear test in the Pacific

March 1954, causing such a devastating explosion that there was worldwide protest against the continuation of such tests.

1954
Bannister's four-minute mile

On May 6, 1954 a young English athlete and medical student, Roger Bannister (*b.* 1929), competing in a race at Oxford, became the first man to run the mile (1.6 kilometres) in less than four minutes. His actual time was 3 minutes 59.4 seconds. Bannister also captured the European 1500 metres record the same year.

1955
Scientists appeal against nuclear weapons

After the United States had exploded a hydrogen bomb in the Pacific Ocean (*see 1954 Hydrogen bomb exploded*) there was growing alarm at the possible harmful effects of radioactivity if the tests continued. In July 1955 a group of world-famous people, including Albert Einstein and Bertrand Russell, appealed for the renunciation of warfare, and warned against the dangers resulting from thermonuclear explosions. (*See 1950 Bertrand Russell receives Nobel Prize*).

In 1958 the Campaign for Nuclear Disarmament (CND) was formed in England to press for the unilateral abolition of nuclear weapons by the British government. In 1960 Bertrand Russell, who had helped to found CND, broke away from the main body to found 'The Committee of 100', which proposed to use civil disobedience as a method of protest. Both groups were active in the early 1960s and a regular event was the Easter march by CND supporters from the Atomic Weapons Research Establishment at Aldermaston in Berkshire to Trafalgar Square in London.

The CND peace symbol.

1956
John Osborne's *Look Back in Anger*

In 1956 *Look Back in Anger* by the English playwright, John Osborne (*b.* 1929), had its first performance. It is the story of a young working-class man who protests against a society dominated by middle-class attitudes. This play was the beginning of a new kind of realistic drama.

Osborne and other young writers, including John Wain, Colin Wilson and Kingsley Amis, who were critical of contemporary social values, became known as the 'angry young men'.

1956
The rock'n'roll era

In the 1950s rock 'n roll quickly established itself as the dominant popular music in the United States. Made famous by such performers as Bill Haley and Elvis Presley, it is characterized by a heavily stressed, repetitive dance rhythm. It rapidly became popular with Britain's teenagers who were enjoying a new prosperity and dressing in the 'teddy boy' fashion, which resembled men's clothes of Edwardian times.

1956
Khrushchev denounces Stalin

Joseph Stalin died in 1953, after nearly thirty years of dictatorship. Power in the USSR passed to three men: Georgi Malenkov, Vyacheslav Molotov and Lavrenti Beria. But the man who was to dominate Soviet politics for the next decade was First Secretary of the Communist Party, Nikita Khrushchev (1894–1971), who by 1958 was also head of the government.

Nikita Khrushchev

A down-to-earth, obstinate figure, with a marked sense of humour, Khrushchev was to be a thorn in the flesh of Western politicians until 1964 (*see 1961 Kennedy becomes US President*).

The most remarkable feature of Khrushchev's internal politics was 'de-Stalinization'. In 1956, in secret session, he denounced Stalin, his brutal methods, and the cult of personality in politics.

Liberal reforms were introduced: thousands of prisoners were released from labour camps, and curbs on writers and artists were partially eased. The full extent of the misery created by Stalin became known to the world.

1956
The Cyprus crisis

The British took over Cyprus from Turkey in 1878, and by 1930 many of the predomiant Greek Cypriot population were pressing for *enosis*, or union with Greece, against the will of the Turkish Cypriot community.

After the Second World War, the *enosis* movement was led by Archbishop Makarios III (1913–77). It flared into violence with a campaign by Georgias Grivas (1898–1974) and his EOKA guerilla organization. In 1956 the British deported Makarios, and fighting broke out against the British and between the two communities. In trying to establish a constitution for an independent Cyprus, the British were unable to satisfy all parties, as the Turkish Cypriots demanded partition.

Independence in 1960 brought no long-term solution, although both sides were guaranteed representation under Makarios's presidency. UN forces were sent in, in the 1960s; in 1974 a National Guard coup temporarily ousted Makarios and Turkey invaded part of the island amidst bitter fighting.

1956
Beckett writes *Waiting for Godot*

En Attendant Godot ('Waiting for Godot') was originally written in French by Irish author Samuel Beckett (*b.* 1906); it was the theatrical success of 1956. Beckett, formerly secretary to James Joyce, portrays a stark, seemingly pointless world, in which characters are unable to communicate; the play is both amusing and tragic. It was followed by *Fin de Partie* ('Endgame') in 1957.

1956
The Suez Crisis

In 1952 an army revolt in Egypt forced the corrupt King Farouk (1920–65) to abdicate; Gamal Abdel Nasser (1918–70), who led the revolt, became president of the new republic in 1956. Nasser secured an arms deal with Czechoslovakia in 1955, and an Anglo-US offer of financial assistance for the building of the Aswan Dam. British troops withdrew from the Suez Canal Zone.

In July 1956 Britain and the USA became worried by Egypt's apparently pro-Communist sympathies and withdrew their Aswan Dam offer. Nasser replied by nationalizing the private Suez Canal Company, whose stockholders were mainly British and French.

In October Israeli troops invaded the Sinai. Britain and France demanded an end to hostilities between Israel and Egypt, but Egypt ignored them. Britain and France, anxious about the future of the Suez Canal, attacked Egypt. The UN ordered Britain, France and Israel to withdraw, and they were replaced by UN forces on the Egypt–Israeli border. Nasser turned to the USSR to finance the Aswan Dam.

1956
The Hungarian Revolution

The new Communist countries of Eastern Europe soon began to resent the extent of USSR control. June 1953 saw rioting in East Berlin, and in 1956 there were serious riots in Poznan, Poland after which Polish Communist leader Wladyslaw Gomulka (1905–82) managed to secure an increased measure of independence.

In October 1956 revolution broke out in Hungary. Students demonstrating against the degree of Soviet control were joined by workers and fought with Hungarian police. When the Hungarian Communist Party requested Soviet assistance, bitter fighting broke out with the troops sent in by the USSR.

Imre Nagy (1896–1958), a nationalistic communist, became Prime Minister and introduced sweeping reforms. Soviet troops were withdrawn from Budapest, political prisoners were released, the one-party system abolished. Hungary withdrew from the Warsaw Pact and appealed to the UN.

This was too much for the USSR. On November 4, 1956 they sent troops and tanks into Budapest and suppressed the revolution. A pro-USSR government was installed; Nagy was later captured and executed.

Crowds surround a captured Russian tank in Budapest, 1956.

1957
The EEC is formed

The 1950s saw the first attempt at economic union in Western Europe. It reflected the desire of France and Germany, who had been at war with each other three times in the previous eighty years or so, not to become enemies again. In 1952 France, West Germany, Italy, Belgium, the Netherlands and Luxembourg successfully formed the European Coal and Steel Community. In 1957 the experiment was extended and the same countries established the European Economic Community (EEC). Customs duties between member states were lowered, and a common market set up with a single tariff on imports. In 1958 a European parliament was formed.

In 1959 the rest of Europe formed a rival, less rigid economic union, which had none of the EEC's aspirations towards 'a united Europe'. The European Free Trade Association (EFTA) comprised Great Britain, Austria, Denmark, Norway, Sweden, Switzerland and Portugal.

Britain applied for EEC membership in 1963, but its application was vetoed by France. Only in 1973 did Britain finally enter the EEC, together with Ireland and Denmark; and Britain and Denmark withdrew from EFTA. Other European countries later applied for membership of the EEC.

1957
Sputnik I is launched

The exploration of space, mankind's greatest adventure, began on October 4, 1957, with the launching of the first man-made earth satellite by the USSR. Sputnik I, as it was called, was a sphere of about fifty-eight centimetres in diameter and weighing eighty-three kilograms. Orbiting the earth every 96.2 minutes and reaching a maximum altitude of 896 kilometres, Sputnik I sent out a steady stream of signals.

The USSR followed this success a month later with the launching of Sputnik II, a five-hundred kilogram satellite containing the first space traveller – a dog called 'Laika'. The USA launched Explorer I, on January 31, 1958, a small satellite of fourteen kilograms. In May, Explorer discovered an intense radiation belt in outer space, now known as the Van Allen belt.

1957
Pinter writes *The Birthday Party*

British dramatist Harold Pinter (*b*. 1930) caused a stir with his first plays: *The Birthday Party* (1957) and *The Caretaker* (1958) are full of the seemingly illogical, tortuous conversations that make up everyday talk, and this unusual dramatic language baffled critics of the day. Pinter has also written *The Homecoming* (1965) and a number of successful film-scripts.

1958
De Gaulle becomes President of France

In the post-war years France suffered from political chaos (*see 1945 France: the end of the Third Republic*). No party had a majority in the National Assembly, and shaky coalitions were unable to pass any effective legislation. France had been driven from its South-east Asian colonies, and in 1958 a report that France was to grant independence to the Algerians led to riots by French colonists in Algiers.

The government collapsed, and war-time leader of the Free French, General Charles de Gaulle (1890–1970), was called out of retirement. An election in November 1958 gave his party office, and in December de Gaulle became first President of the Fifth Republic, with sweeping personal powers. He successfully negotiated the French withdrawal from Algeria. His presidency brought France a period of stability and he was re-elected in 1965. He withdrew France from NATO and opposed British membership of the EEC.

An ardent nationalist, de Gaulle's aggressive foreign policy and great personal prestige kept him in power, but his position became weaker after the unrest of 1968 when students and workers rioted in the streets of Paris. He resigned after his government's defeat in a referendum on constitutional reform in 1969. He died in 1970 after completing only the first three volumes of his memoirs. (*See 1962 Algeria achieves independence*).

De Gaulle in 1944, leading the triumphal procession after the liberation of Paris. He became President of France in 1958.

1958
Dr Zhivago published

Boris Pasternak (1890–1960) had a longstanding reputation in the USSR as a poet and translator, but it was his first novel that caused a sensation. Pasternak misjudged the extent of post-Stalin liberalization, and it caused his expulsion from the Writers' Union. Despite his disenchantment he was a Marxist and a patriot, and was compelled to refuse the Nobel Prize awarded for his work.

1958
Nautilus crosses the North Pole

In 1958 the first US nuclear submarine *Nautilus*, under Commander William Anderson, performed an epic voyage by travelling 2,928 kilometres under the polar ice cap from Point Barrow, Alaska, to the Greenland Sea, crossing the North Pole on August 3. In 1960 the USS *Trident* completed the first submerged circumnavigation of the world.

1959
First passenger-carrying hovercraft flight

The first hovercraft flight took place at Cowes, Isle of Wight, in 1959. The four-tonne Saunders-Roe SR-N1 was soon able to reach sixty-eight knots. Invented by Briton Sir Christopher Cockerell (*b*.1910), the hovercraft soon proved its worth as a means of crossing water, marsh, or flat land, easily manoeuvrable on its cushion of air.

1959
Castro overthrows Batista

Cuba under the dictatorship of President Batista (1901–73) was corrupt and oppressed. A rising under former lawyer Fidel Castro (*b*. 1927) had failed in 1953, but returning to Cuba in 1956 Castro recovered from an initial setback to mount a guerrilla campaign.

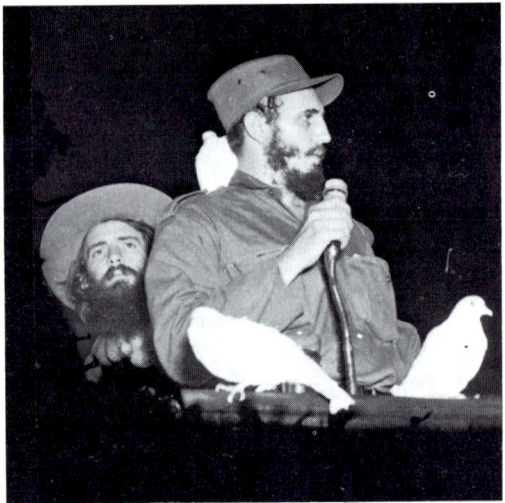

Fidel Castro, leader of the Cuban revolution.

In January 1959 Castro finally overthrew Batista, who fled to the Dominican Republic. On becoming prime minister Castro reformed Cuba on communist lines and seized American-owned plantations.

Cuba soon developed a close relationship with the USSR, and the USA became increasingly worried at the thought of having a pro-Soviet country only 150 kilometres off the coast of Florida.

In 1961 an unsuccessful attack on Cuba was made by US-trained Cuban exiles in the Bay of Pigs, and the next year saw the USA and the USSR on the brink of war, when US intelligence revealed Soviet missile sites in Cuba (*see 1961 Kennedy becomes US President*).

1959

Launching of NS *Savannah*

In 1959 the world's first nuclear-powered merchant ship was launched in the USA. Her name commemorated the first trans-Atlantic steam crossing by the *Savannah* (*see 1819 Voyage of the Savannah*). The NS *Savannah*, capable of carrying sixty passengers and 10,000 tonnes of cargo introduced a new era in shipping. Her nuclear reactor weighed 2,500 tonnes, but the amount of uranium oxide used was so small that she could travel fourteen times round the world without refuelling.

1960

Macmillan's 'Wind of Change' speech

In a speech on February 3, 1960 during a visit to Cape Town, the British prime minister, Harold Macmillan (1894–1986) said that '...the wind of

The age of nuclear power: *Nautilus*, and details of her reactor.

Fan propeller

Rudder

Engine room

Loading ramp

Car deck

Inner passenger cabin

Propulsion units (4)

Lifting fan intakes

Flexible skirt

Ventilators

Engine air intakes

Control cabin

Entrance to passenger cabins

Unloading ramp

Outer passenger cabin

Forward passenger cabin

The modern hovercraft, a descendant of Cockerell's prototype, can travel at speeds up to 90km/h and ferry cars across the English Channel.

change is blowing through the continent'. He referred to the rapid emergence of African countries towards independence as representing a major new development in the world.

During the 1950s no less than twenty-five African countries achieved independence, and the map of the continent was changed beyond recognition. New names appeared: Ghana, Tanzania, Malawi, Mali and many others. By 1961 eighty per cent of Africa was free from foreign control.

The new nations of Africa faced many crises during the 1960s; tribal loyalties often conflicted

with the new national interests, and different political factions fought for power. Whilst foreign control had largely gone, foreign powers such as China, the USSR, and the USA sought influence by providing aid and technology.

1960
Fighting in the Congo (Zaïre)

At a meeting of Belgian and Congolese representatives in Brussels from January 20 to February 20, 1960, it was agreed that the Congo (Zaïre) should be granted full independence on July 30 of that year.

Peace did not come easily: the rest of the year was marked by a series of tribal disputes in various parts of the country. In July many tribes were fighting, the *Offices des Transports du Congo* (Otraco) went on strike, and the army mutinied. Belgian forces in the country were put on immediate alert.

Katanga Province and Kasai Province broke away from the rest of the country and there were several serious disturbances in Leopoldville, the capital. An emergency United Nations force was sent to the Congo but it was not until early 1963 that the rebellion was suppressed.

Congolese affairs remained unstable for many years, but in 1970 Joseph Mobutu (*b*. 1930) was proclaimed President and the country was renamed Zaïre in 1971.

1960
First working laser

The principle of the laser (Light Amplification by the Stimulation of Radiation) was first propounded in 1958 by A. L. Schawlow and C. H. Townes. Two years later T. H. Maiman announced the building of the first working laser in the USA and since then it has been utilized in many different applications. These include welding, surgery, astronomy, communications and holography (a type of three-dimensional photography).

A laser beam cuts through metal.

1961
Kennedy becomes US President

After the most closely contested election in American history, Democrat John Fitzgerald Kennedy (1917–63) was inaugurated as President of the United States of America on January 20, 1961. He was the first Roman Catholic president and the second youngest man to hold this office.

Kennedy's first year in office was marked by

John F. Kennedy

an attempted invasion of Cuba by forces trained in America (*see 1959 Castro overthrows Batista*). On April 17, 1961 anti-Castro Cuban exiles mounted an abortive invasion in the Bay of Pigs.

The failure of this bid led the Soviet Premier, Nikita Khrushchev, to assume that Soviet ballistic missiles could be based in Cuba, but in October 1962 Kennedy imposed a naval 'quarantine' around the island to prevent Soviet ships delivering weapons. For a week it looked as if the USA and the USSR were on the brink of nuclear war; this eventuality was averted when Khrushchev halted work on the missile sites. In 1963 Kennedy secured a treaty with Russia partially banning nuclear tests.

Kennedy's home policy was marked by civil rights legislation; he was a keen supporter of a federal policy for the desegregation of schools and universities, also backed by his brother Robert Kennedy (1925–68), the Attorney-General. The promising careers of both were, however, doomed to tragedy (*see 1963 Assassination of President Kennedy*).

1961
First man in space

The world's first spaceman was the Russian Yuri Alekseyevich Gagarin (1934–68). On April 12, 1961, in the spacecraft *Vostok I*, he orbited the earth once, remaining in space for one hour 48 minutes, the actual orbit lasting 89.34 minutes.

Vostok I was launched from Tyuratam space base, Kazakhstan, at 9.07 a.m. Moscow Time (6.07 GMT). The capsule orbited the earth at a maximum speed of 28,090km/h at altitudes between 258 and 340 kilometres.

The return to earth was accomplished by the firing of retro-rockets after the craft had been turned round automatically. *Vostok I* entered the earth's atmosphere and Gagarin was ejected from the craft and carried earthwards by parachutes. He landed in a ploughed field near the village of Smelovaka, much to the amazement of two local farm-workers.

With his epic flight (as Gagarin himself said) 'the road to the stars had opened'. He was killed in an air crash in March 1968.

Yuri Gagarin

1961
Dag Hammarskjöld receives Nobel Prize

Dag Hammarskjöld (1905–61), Swedish economist and statesman, was second secretary-general of the United Nations from 1953 to 1961. His leadership improved the effectiveness and reputation of the UN.

Hammarskjöld died in an air crash whilst on a peace mission in Katanga (*see 1960 Fighting in the Congo (Zaïre)* and was posthumously awarded the Nobel Peace Prize later that year.

1961
Building of the Berlin Wall

The Berlin Wall, symbol of the Cold War.

Following a decree passed on August 12, 1961 by the East German *Volkskammer* (People's Chamber) a fence of barbed wire was erected around West Berlin to cut off communication with East Berlin and East Germany. At a later date the barbed wire was replaced by a fortified concrete wall manned by armed guards.

Berlin had been divided into four sectors, British, American, French, and Russian, at the end of the Second World War. During the 'Cold War', a war of words and economic weapons with little military involvement, the Russian sector (East Berlin) was separated from the other three.

From 1948 some 1,500,000 people had used Berlin to escape from communist domination to a freer life in the West. The East Germans built the wall to stem this flow but many people still attempt crossings in spite of the fact that they may well die in the attempt.

1962

First Beatles record

The British pop group 'The Beatles' (Paul McCartney, *b.* 1942, John Lennon, 1940–80, George Harrison, *b.* 1943, and Ringo Starr, *b.* 1940) revolutionized the world of popular music. They started making records in 1962 and within a short time had taken the world by storm. Their music inspired many other performers and marked the beginning of an era of youthful revolution in the arts.

The Beatles, the most successful pop group of all time, disbanded in 1971. John Lennon was murdered by one of his own fans, in New York, in 1980.

1962

Algeria achieves independence

In 1947 Algeria became unified politically with France, but the eighty-six per cent Moslem (Arab and Berber) population resented continuing domination by the French colonists, and in 1954 started the fight for independence. During the Algerian crisis the French were to employ half a million troops against the rebels.

In 1958 rumours that the French government was giving in to the rebels led to a riot of French colonists in Algiers. Instead of suppressing the riot, the French military joined it. It looked as if France itself could be torn by Civil War, and de Gaulle was called upon to take over (*see 1958 De Gaulle becomes President of France*).

Despite terrorist acts by the OAS (the Secret Army Organization, dedicated to keeping Algeria French) de Gaulle pursued his plans for Algerian independence, which was finally achieved in July 1962.

Charles de Gaulle

1962

Launch of *Telstar*

Telstar I, launched on July 10, 1962 was the first communications satellite to receive and transmit live television pictures across the Atlantic.

The first trans-Atlantic transmission via *Telstar*, from Andover, Maine, USA to Pleumeur Bodou, France, was made on July 11.

Telstar opened up a new era in world communications and paved the way for modern multi-channel satellites.

1963

Assassination of President Kennedy

John F. Kennedy, President of the United States of America, was assassinated in Dallas, Texas on November 22, 1963 whilst driving through the city on an official visit.

As the motorcade proceeded through the city three shots were fired from the sixth storey of a warehouse. Kennedy immediately slumped forward in the car, shot in the head and the neck.

Kennedy and Governor Connally, who had been injured in the shooting, were rushed to Parkland Hospital but the president died half an hour after admission.

A twenty-four-year-old ex-marine, Lee Harvey Oswald, was arrested and charged with the murder but he was never tried. On November 24 Oswald was shot and killed by Jack Leon Ruby, a night-club proprietor, who was a great admirer of Kennedy.

Upon the death of John F. Kennedy, vice-president Lyndon Baines Johnson (1908–73) was sworn in as President.

On June 5, 1968 Kennedy's brother Robert was shot and killed while campaigning for the presidency.

WHAAM! by Roy Lichtenstein.

Lichtenstein paints *WHAAM!*

The 'pop art' movement grew up in the late 1950s and 1960s. It was concerned with the trivia of modern materialistic society, such as comic strips and advertisements, and revelled in the 'bad taste' of its subjects. Principal pop artists in America include Roy Lichtenstein (*b*. 1923), Andy Warhol (1929–87) and Claes Oldenburg (*b*. 1929); in Britain, Richard Hamilton (*b*. 1922) and Peter Blake (*b*. 1932).

1964

The Vietnam War intensifies

The Geneva Agreement of 1954 (*see 1954 The fall of Dien Bien Phu*) confined the Communist Viet Minh, under Ho Chi Minh, to North Vietnam, with their capital at Hanoi; South Vietnam and its capital Saigon was held by anti-communists supported by France and the USA, who feared the spread of communism in Asia. The Agreement intended that elections for a unified government should he held, but these did not take place.

US military advisors were sent to South Vietnam, and in 1963 President Kennedy increased their number to sixteen thousand. In 1964 incidents involving American and North Viet-namese ships in the Tonkin Gulf led to total US involvement and the most horrific war of recent years.

From 1965 President Johnson ordered the sustained bombing of North Vietnam. The number of US military personnel was raised to over half a million. Australia and South Korea sent units to support the USA, and money and weapons from the Communist world poured into Hanoi. First Laos and then Cambodia were drawn into the battle arena.

The growing outcry in America and abroad and the US failure to achieve a military success led to President Johnson's retirement from politics. Although he was eligible, he did not stand for office at the presidential election of 1968. Instead, the president who brought the USA out of the Vietnam War was Richard Nixon.

Peace talks held in Paris achieved little but by 1973 the USA was ready to wind down its war effort, and withdraw. In 1975 Southern Vietnamese communists (Viet Cong) took Saigon, renaming it Ho Chi-Minh City.

Martin Luther King receives Nobel Prize

The Rev. Dr Martin Luther King (1929–68), a black American clergyman, was awarded the Nobel Peace Prize on November 14, 1964 for his work in promoting peaceful solutions to American racial problems.

King first came to prominence in the American civil rights movement in 1954 when he led a boycott of transport in Montgomery, Alabama to force desegregation on the city's buses. Six

Martin Luther King

years later he resigned his Baptist Ministry to devote his full attention to the cause of his people.

Although King was acknowledged to be a great leader of men, his non-violent policies to promote the cause of civil rights were not always popular. Militant members of the 'Black Power' movement attacked his ideas; white segregationists abhorred his aims. On April 4, 1968 he was assassinated by a sniper in Memphis, Tennessee.

1965
Death of Winston Churchill

The whole of Britain mourned when statesman Sir Winston Churchill (1874–1965) died on January 24, 1965.

Winston Churchill, wartime leader.

A great war leader, member of the House of Commons for over sixty years, eminent historian, brilliant orator, and gifted artist, he will be remembered by many as 'the greatest Englishman of his time'.

1965
Rhodesia declares UDI

(*See also 1980 Rhodesia becomes Zimbabwe.*)

In November 1965 the Rhodesian government, under the leadership of Ian Smith (*b.* 1919) made a unilateral declaration of independence.

The Rhodesians took this action as Britain would not consider granting independence to the country because it considered the administration, controlled by a white minority, to be unrepresentative of the people.

In March 1970 the Rhodesian government renounced its allegiance to the British throne and declared Rhodesia to be a republic, in the face of continuing economic sanctions.

1965
First space walk

On March 18, 1965 the Russian cosmonaut Aleksei Arkhipovich Leonov (*b.* 1934) became the first man to leave a space vehicle and to 'walk' in space.

Leonov was connected to the space vehicle *Voskhod II* by a cable in this experiment essential to the furtherance of space exploration. He floated in space, for twenty minutes.

1965
Indo-Pakistan War

In April 1965 forces of India and Pakistan fought in a recurrence of the border troubles that had led to the Sino–Indian War of 1962 when China sided with Pakistan on the Kashmir problem. Further clashes occurred in May and September 1965 until a UN resolution brought agreement from both sides.

Leonov floats in space, connected to his spacecraft by a cable.

1966

Cultural Revolution in China

The Great Proletarian Cultural Revolution in China from 1966 to 1969 was organized by the Communist Party Chairman Mao Tse-tung (1893–1976).

Mao's objective was to bring into line those elements of political and cultural life that appeared to be moving away from the strict ideological lines that he advocated. It was felt that if these 'backsliders' were allowed to continue they would ultimately damage Mao's system of Marxist–Leninist ideology which formed the basis of the Chinese communist state.

The people, and in particular the specially formed youth movement 'The Red Guard', were invited to question the ideological correctness of those in authority. They were encouraged to criticize any administrator who did not conform to Maoist thought.

Although the political scene was purged during the cultural revolution it caused enormous disruption in industry and agriculture and almost brought civil war to many areas of China.

1966

Assassination of Dr Verwoerd

Dr Hendrik F. Verwoerd (1901–66), South African Prime Minister and an exponent of the policy of apartheid, was stabbed to death by a parliamentary messenger, Dimitri Tsafendas on September 6, 1966.

At his trial in October Tsafendas was deemed to be mentally disorientated and unfit to plead. He was committed to prison.

1967

Military coup in Greece

After a long period of political instability the Greek army overthrew the constitutional government of Greece on April 21, 1967 to form a 'National Government'. The king, Constantine II, fled with his wife and family to England.

On May 9 the new government passed two new Acts: one to provide for the creation of a new constitution and the second to empower the government to rule by decree until the first had been ratified. The rule of the military junta was rigid and all opposition was ruthlessly suppressed.

Six years later, on June 1, 1973 Greece was proclaimed a republic under the presidency of George Papadopoulos and the monarchy was abolished two months after.

By the end of the year Papadopoulos himself had been overthrown, by a fast and bloodless *coup d'état* on November 25. Lieut-General Phaedon Ghizikis was made President on the same day and a new cabinet was formed.

The military dictatorship ended in July 1974 when the armed forces called upon nine former leading politicians to form a new government.

1967

The Six-Day War

One of the shortest wars in history started on June 5, 1967. Six days later the battle, between Israel and Egypt, was over.

Following pages: Astronaut Edward H. White II, the first American to walk in space, June 3 1965.

Tension had started mounting on May 18 when Egypt demanded the withdrawal of the UN peace-keeping force stationed along the Israeli–Egyptian border since 1956.

During the ensuing weeks the tension built up and eventually erupted into full-scale war. Israel gained the upper hand on the first day of fighting when its air force delivered devastating attacks on air bases in Egypt, Jordan, Syria, and Iraq. The United Nations called for a ceasefire but this was not accepted by all the countries concerned until June 10. By this time Israel had achieved substantial territorial gains.

1967

First heart transplant

On December 3, 1967, at the Groote Schuur Hospital in Cape Town, South Africa, Professor Christian Barnard (b. 1922) performed the world's first successful human heart transplant. The recipient was a fifty-six-year-old man Louis Washkansky and the donor a twenty-five-year-old woman, Denise Darval, who had been killed in a car crash.

Unfortunately Washkansky died on December 21, 1967. His death was caused, not by heart failure, but by the failure of his lungs following double pneumonia.

The rapid advance in modern surgery made a heart transplant operation possible.

1968

Invasion of Czechoslovakia

In February 1948 the Communists had seized control of Czechoslovakia by force and Jan Masaryk, the foreign minister was found dead. His enemies, it was suspected, had thrown him out of a window of a house in Prague, the Czech capital. Between 1945 and 1948 all the countries of eastern and south-eastern Europe, with the exception of Greece and Turkey, came under Communist domination. Only Yugoslavia, under the leadership of Marshal Tito (1892–1980), remained independent of the USSR although the government was communist.

Communist Party leader, Alexander Dubček (b. 1921), was the principal instigator of liberalism in Czechoslovakia in 1968. His influence led to the relaxation of press censorship and the importation of foreign literature. But as the spirit of freedom increased within Czechoslovakia the deep anxiety felt by other Warsaw-pact countries increased also.

A letter of protest to the Czech leaders, an anti-Dubček campaign in the Soviet press, an ominous build-up of Soviet troops along the border, and talks between Czech and Soviet leaders did little to deter Dubček and his followers from their chosen course.

During the night of August 20–21 sixty thousand troops of the USSR, East Germany, Poland, Hungary and Bulgaria invaded Czechoslovakia. The Czechs openly expressed hostility to the invaders but gradually censorship was reintroduced, the liberalization programmes were phased out, and all leaders associated with such policies were removed from office to be replaced by pro-Soviet leaders.

1969

Violence in Northern Ireland

A civil rights campaign on behalf of the Catholic minority in the province during the 1960s provoked vigorous response from the largely Protestant authorities. The conflict degenerated into sporadic acts of terrorism organized by extreme groups on both sides. The troops were brought in to protect the poor, Catholic areas in

THE SPACE AGE

1957 Sputnik I, the first earth satellite, launched by the USSR.

1959 The USSR launches the space probe Luna 1 and the USA launches the space probe Pioneer 4.

1960 The USA launches the weather satellite Tiros 1 and the communications satellite Echo 1.

1961 The Soviet Yuri Gagarin becomes the first human to travel in space, when his spacecraft Vostok 1 is launched.

1962 First Americans in orbit: John Glenn in February and M. Scott Carpenter in May.

1962 The US satellite Telstar launched from Cape Canaveral, Florida, enables transatlantic televison to be transmitted.

1962 The USA launches the rocket Mariner to explore the planet Venus and the USSR launches Mars 1 to explore Mars. Mariner sends back its first readings in December, after four months.

1963 The Soviet Valentina Tereshkova makes a three-day space flight. She is the first woman to travel in space.

1963 US astronaut Gordon Cooper orbits earth 22 times, and USA launches a belt of copper needles as test for a secure system of worldwide radio communication.

1964 Ranger VII takes close-up pictures of the moon's surface.

1965 USA launches Mariner IV and USSR launches Zond II with equipment for taking pictures of Mars.

1965 Soviet cosmonaut Alexei Leonov takes the first space walk (March). First American space walk by Edward White (June). Early Bird I, the first communications satellite launched by the USA. The French launch their first satellite.

1966 First successful docking in space by the American Gemini 8. Soviet Lunik IX makes the first unmanned landing on the moon and sends back pictures of the surface.

1967 First space fatalities: three US astronauts die in fire on Apollo I while still on the launch pad. Mariner V launched to Mars by USA. Soviet capsule lands on Venus.

1968 Apollo 7, first manned vehicle to orbit the moon.

1969 First landing on the moon by astronauts from American Apollo 11, July 21.

1970 China launches its first satellite.

1971 Soviets launch first space station, Salyut I.

1973 Americans launch space station, Skylab.

1974 Soviets launch Salyut 3 and 4.

1975 Link up in space by Soviet Soyuz and American Apollo spacecraft.

1979 USA launches Voyager I to the planet Jupiter.

1981 First flight of the space shuttle Columbia.

1983 Second space shuttle, Challenger, launched by the USA.

1986 Challenger, with the first civilian passenger to fly in space on board, blows up after launch, killing all on board.

---

the towns, but were soon involved in a counter-guerrilla war with various secret, military-type rebel groups, of which the best known were the IRA (Irish Republican Army) and its offshoot, the Provisionals.

From 1972 Northern Ireland was ruled direct from London. Atrocities continued, and despite many efforts to find a peaceful solution, the violence was still going on some twenty years later.

1969

First moon landing

With the words 'That's one small step for a man; one giant leap for mankind', the American astronaut Neil Armstrong (b. 1930) stepped down from the lunar module of *Apollo 11* on July 21, 1969 to become the first man to set foot on the moon.

With Armstrong on that epic flight were Colonel Edwin Aldrin and Colonel Michael Collins.

Man walks on the moon: Armstrong's historic moment.

Apollo 11 was launched by a Saturn 5 rocket from Cape Kennedy (Cape Canaveral) on July 16. Twelve minutes after take-off the third stage of the rocket (the first two stages having been fired and jettisoned) put the ship into earth orbit before the start of its 328,000 kilometres journey to the moon.

The astronauts remained on the moon's surface for twenty-two hours, exploring, collecting soil samples, and setting up experiments. Then the lunar module *Eagle* took off, taking the astronauts back to the command ship *Columbia*. Armstrong and Aldrin clambered back into the command module to join Collins who had remained at the controls in lunar orbit.

After splashdown in the Pacific on July 24 the astronauts were received on the aircraft carrier *Hornet* by President Nixon who greeted them with the words: 'This has been the greatest week since the Creation'. This epic event was watched on television as it happened by millions of people round the world.

1970
War in Biafra

On May 30, 1968 the Eastern region of Nigeria broke away from the federation and declared independence as the Republic of Biafra. Colonel Yakubu Gowon (*b.* 1934), head of the Nigerian government, imposed economic sanctions against Biafra and mobilized his forces to effect a blockade of the breakaway state.

Fierce fighting throughout the rest of the year culminated in the fall of Enugu, the rebel capital, in October. Starvation was widespread and thousands perished. By December it looked as if Biafra's fight for independence was at an end. In June 1969 the two sides met for peace talks at Kampala and later at Addis Ababa, but they failed to reach agreement and the fighting continued. The Biafrans held out until January 1970 when General Odumegwu Ojukwu (*b.*1933), the Biafran leader, fled the country. Fighting ceased on January 12 and the country was once again united.

1970
Solzhenitsyn awarded Nobel Prize for literature

The great Russian novelist Aleksandr I. Solzhenitsyn (*b.* 1918) became world-famous after the publication in the West of his documentary novels of Stalin's labour camps in the Soviet Union, *One Day in the Life of Ivan Denisovich* (English translation 1963), *The First Circle* (1968) and *Cancer Ward* (1968). They were based on personal experience, his internment having resulted from his uncompromisingly honest views and powerful criticism of Stalin. Unwilling to keep a world-renowned writer in captivity, the Soviet authorities forced Solzhenitsyn into exile.

1971
Bangladesh declares independence

The first one-man-one-vote election in Pakistan in December 1970 resulted in a wide split between the racial and linguistic groups that formed the populace – the Punjabis of West Pakistan and the Bengalis of East Pakistan. By March 1971 the split had widened so much that the first meeting of the Pakistan Constituent Assembly was postponed indefinitely. Sheikh Mujibur Rahman (1920–75) of East Pakistan and his separatist party the Awamī League called for a campaign of civil disobedience amid increasing demands for independence.

On March 23, Pakistan's Republic Day, people in the eastern state hauled down the national flag and replaced it with the flag of Bangladesh. Fighting broke out and Sheikh Mujibur was arrested and charged with treason, but the state formally declared its independence on April 17, although bitter fighting continued until the end of the year, with the secessionists supported by the Indian army.

Sheikh Mujibur, who was elected President during his imprisonment, received a tumultuous welcome when he returned to Bangladesh in January 1972, but his problems were not over. Natural disasters and famine compounded the political problems of corruption and fighting between factions. Sheikh Mujibur was assassinated in 1975.

1971
China admitted to the UN

Although the Communist regime of Mao Tse-tung had ruled mainland China since 1949, the country had been denied representation in the United Nations, chiefly because of the opposition of the USA, which remained loyal to the nationalist Chinese government of Chiang Kai-shek in Taiwan (Formosa). Under pressure from its allies, and with signs of improvement in US–China relations, the United States finally agreed to withdraw its veto as one of the five permanent members of the Security Council, (*see 1945 The United Nations formed*) against the Chinese People's Republic.

1973
The Watergate affair

The subject uppermost in the minds of Americans and much of the rest of the world in 1973 was the 'Watergate' scandal. During the year the increasing disclosures revealed a tangled web of political intrigue that eventually enveloped even the office of the president.

On January 10, 1973 the trial of five men involved in the break-in and 'bugging' of the Democrat headquarters in the Watergate apartments, Washington on June 17, 1972 was opened. The men, members of the Republican organization CREEP (Committee for the Re-Election of the President), pleaded guilty to the burglary. It appeared to be a straightforward affair until two reporters on the *Washington Post* followed up some of the loose ends to discover that the corruption was not minor. It involved White House officials, and even President Nixon (*b*.1913) appeared to be implicated. Many called for his impeachment and impeachment hearings were televised, live, in July 1974.

On August 8, 1974 Nixon became the first American president in history to resign from office and his vice-president, Gerald Ford, was sworn in on the next day.

Richard Nixon

1973
Skylab launched

Skylab was launched on May 14, 1973 and was the first American manned orbiting space station. The first mission involved astronauts, Charles

Skylab

Conrad, Dr Joseph Kerwin, and Paul Weitz, carrying out important experiments. These researches were largely concerned with human adaptation to long periods of weightlessness.

Initially it appeared that the mission would have to be abandoned as a set of solar energy panels failed to open and the craft's meteor shield had broken off soon after launch. The launch of the astronauts was postponed until May 25. They docked successfully and the following day they affixed an umbrella-like 'sunshade' over *Skylab* to provide shelter from the intense sunlight. This enabled them to continue with their scheduled mission for 28 days, after which *Skylab* was left in orbit ready to be used by two subsequent missions.

1973
The October War

The hostility of the Arab nations towards Israel once more exploded into open war when Egyptian forces attacked the Israelis across the Suez Canal and the Syrians attacked in the Golan Heights. It was Yom Kippur the Jews' day of atonement and fasting and the Israelis were taken by surprise. They retaliated effectively but suffered high casualties (about 3,000) in driving back the Arab forces.

1973
Counter-revolution in Chile

In 1970 President Salvador Allende of Chile (1908–73) became the first Marxist to be democratially elected as head of state. He introduced controversial socialist reforms, including nationalization of foreign-owned property, but by 1973 he had lost control of the country. Guerrilla fighting between extremists of Right and Left was taking place, and a military coup resulted in the overthrow of the government on September 11. Allende died (probably assassinated) and a harsh military government took over.

1974
World oil crisis

As a result of a decision by OPEC (Oil Producing and Exporting Countries), led by Libya, to raise their prices, the world price of oil quadrupled. The consequences in industrial countries included severe inflation coupled with a recession in manufacturing industries. Even worse hit were poor, non-industrialized countries with no oil reserves of their own. By 1981 the price of crude oil was twenty times the level it had been ten years earlier, but as a result of new discoveries (like the North Sea reserves) and lower consumption, combined with a more realistic approach to pricing by OPEC, fears of a serious world shortage of oil faded and prices levelled off.

1975
US and Russia link up in space

Despite the intense rivalry in space exploration between the United States of America and the Soviet Union, there was also some co-operation, which culminated in July 1975, with the first international manned space mission.

On July 15 *Soyuz 19* was launched from the Baikonur Cosmodrome, Kazakhstan, USSR. On the other side of the world, seven and a half hours later, *Apollo 18* was launched from Cape Kennedy (Canaveral) Florida, USA.

On the following day both craft adopted a circular orbit 225 kilometres above the earth and the two were linked together at 16.12 GMT on July 17. They remained docked together for two days and the two crews moved from spacecraft to spacecraft, conducting experiments and sharing meals.

1975
Europe's last colonies

The liberal government in Portugal which followed the overthrow of the dictatorial government of Dr Caetano in Portugal in 1974 had promised freedom to Portugal's 'overseas provinces' in southern Africa. First colonized by the Portuguese in the early 16th century both Mozambique and Angola had suffered civil war for some years as nationalist groups struggled against the Portuguese authorities. The Republic of Mozambique, founded in 1974, became fully independent in June 1975 under President Samora Machel; the People's Republic of Angola followed in October.

President Machel was killed in an aircraft crash in 1987 and some believed that neighbouring South Africa, which opposed the Machel regime, was involved.

1975
Death of Franco

General Francisco Franco, who had been head of state in Spain since the end of the Civil War in 1939 (*see 1936 Civil War breaks out in Spain*), died in November 1975. His death was followed by the restoration of a constitutional monarchy under Juan Carlos I, grandson of Alfonso XIII, the previous king of Spain. Juan Carlos had been groomed by Franco to succeed him, and in the last weeks of Franco's life, he acted as head of state. Political parties were legalized and in 1977 the first general election since 1936 was held. The failure of an attempted military coup in 1981 served to reinforce democracy in Spain.

1976
Concorde goes into service

Concorde, the world's first supersonic airliner went into regular passenger service on January 21, 1976. Concorde was designed and built jointly by the British Aircraft Corporation and Aerospatiale of France. It is a delta wing aircraft which can carry 100 passengers and, from the first, has been operated by Air France and British Airways.

Concorde cruises at 2,200km/h (more than twice the speed of sound) at a height of 16 kilometres.

1976
Raid on Entebbe

On June 27, 1976, an Air France aircraft flying from Tel Aviv in Israel to Paris was hijacked by the Popular Front for the Liberation of Palestine. The pilot was ordered to fly the aircraft to Entebbe in Uganda, and a demand was made for the release of 53 Arab terrorists. In Entebbe, half the passengers were released, but another 106, mostly Jewish, were kept prisoner at the airport. The Israeli government at first pretended that it would negotiate with the hijackers, but in secret prepared a commando raid on Entebbe. On July 3, the commandos made the 1,398 kilometre flight to Entebbe from Israel and landed on the airport runway. In a battle lasting thirty minutes,

Concorde, the world's first supersonic airliner, was developed jointly by Air France and British Airways. This is the Concorde producion line at Toulouse, France, the other line was at Filton, England.

seven hijackers were killed, as well as twenty Ugandan guards.

Three hostages and an Israeli officer also died, but the remaining hostages were freed and flew back to Israel. The Entebbe raid was much admired for its daring.

1977
Egypt and Israel make friends

On November 19, 1977, President Anwár Sadat of Egypt (1918–81) made history when he went to Jerusalem, met the Israeli prime minister Menachem Begin (b. 1913) and addressed the Knesset (parliament). Egypt and Israel had been enemies since Israel was created in 1948 and had fought many fierce wars and battles. Sadat, however, was anxious for peace so that he could concentrate on improving the lives of his people. So, he accepted Begin's invitation to come to Israel and later, a peace was signed between the two countries (see 1978 Camp David agreement). Sadat's action greatly angered most other Arab nations, who broke off relations with Egypt.

Sadat, who won the Nobel Peace Prize (1978) was murdered by Moslem fundamentalists in 1981. However, his successor, Hosni Mubarak, maintained the peace treaty with Israel and in 1987, some Arab states showed signs of greater friendliness towards Egypt.

1977
Queen Elizabeth's Silver Jubilee

On February 6, 1977, Queen Elizabeth II celebrated the twenty-fifth anniversary of her accession to the throne of Great Britain and Northern Ireland in 1952. The Silver Jubilee, the first in the country since 1935, was celebrated all over Britain and also throughout the British Commonwealth, of which the Queen is Head. She is also Queen of some Commonwealth countries, such as Canada and Australia. A special Omnibus edition of postage stamps (a matching set from several countries) was issued, as well as special coins and other souvenirs. On a personal level, 1977 was also an important year for the Queen for it saw the birth of her first grandchild, Peter Phillips, son of her daughter, Princess Anne.

1978
Camp David agreement

Following their historic meeting in Jerusalem (see 1977 Egypt and Israel make friends), Egyptian President Sadat and Israeli Prime Minister Begin conferred with the US President, Jimmy Carter (b. 1924), at Camp David in the United States in 1978.

The peace treaty signed by Egypt and Israel as a result was, however, rejected by other Arab governments and by the PLO (Palestine Liberation Organization), and Egypt lost its traditional role as the leader of the Arab world. Despite the assassination of President Sadat in 1981, peace – though not friendship – was assured. Egypt, however, incurred the displeasure of other Arab states over the treaty with Israel and it was not until 1987 that other Arabs were willing to renew friendship with Egypt.

1978
Election of a Polish pope

This was the year of three popes. After Pope Paul VI died on August 6, Cardinal Albino Luciani was elected as Pope Paul I. However, he died only thirty-three days after his election, and another pope, Karol Wojtyla, was elected, as John Paul II. He was invested as pope on October 22. John Paul II (b. 1920) was the 264th pope since St Peter, and the first non-Italian since Adrian VI, a Dutchman, became pope in 1522. John Paul II, formerly Archbishop of Cracow became the first Polish pope. Like his immediate predecessors, he undertook foreign visits and was rapturously received, especially in his native country which he visited in 1979 and 1983.

1979

Margaret Thatcher becomes British prime minister

Mrs Thatcher (b. 1925), a trained chemist and barrister, entered Parliament in 1959 and was minister for education from 1970 to 1974. Next year, to the surprise of many people, she was elected leader of the Conservative party, and following the general election of 1979 she became Britain's first woman prime minister. She proved a strong leader, steadfastly pursuing a deflationary policy despite industrial recession and rising unemployment. In 1983 her government was re-elected with a larger majority. Mrs Thatcher also won a third election in 1987, the first time a prime minister has achieved three consecutive successes since the advent of universal suffrage in Britain, in 1928.

1979

Islamic Revolution in Iran

After widespread and growing opposition to his regime, in which the secret police played a sinister part, the Shah of Iran left the country in January 1979. Ayatollah (a priestly title) Khomeini (b. 1902), the main spiritual leader of Shi'ite Moslems (the majority in Iran) returned from exile and, following a referendum, he declared the country an 'Islamic republic'. The government – in which Khomeini remained a 'grey eminence', undoubtedly very powerful through holding no official political post – was at first moderate, but was swiftly taken over by Moslem extremists, with bombings, shootings and trials of doubtful legality. Both Communist influence and the influence of the United States (whose embassy staff were held prisoner for many months) attracted ferocious hostility from the regime.

1979

Soviet invasion of Afghanistan

Soviet efforts to control Afghanistan have a long history. In 1973 the Afghan government, a constitutional monarchy, was overthrown and a

Left-wing republic established. Power changed hands rapidly in the next few years and the Soviet Union, which had supported the coup and hoped to profit from the installation of a Communist state, invaded the country in December 1979 to replace the current Afghan leader with a man of their own choice.

The invasion caused an international outcry, while the Soviet forces found themselves involved in a civil war against Afghan rebels in the inhospitable mountains. It was not until 1988 that the Soviet government began considering the withdrawl of its troops from Afghanistan.

1980

Rhodesia becomes Zimbabwe

The white-dominated government of Rhodesia, having rejected British sovereignty (see 1965 Rhodesia declares UDI), was confronted by increasingly violent opposition from various groups representing the African majority. In 1979 the strains of the guerrilla war became too much and the government submitted. Following democratic elections in 1980 the country became the independent republic of Zimbabwe, remaining within the Commonwealth. The election was won by Robert Mugabe, who thus established his superiority over several rival leaders and became the first president of the republic.

1980

Outbreak of the Gulf War

Iraq and Iran, Moslem neighbours in the Near East were on poor terms after the Islamic revolution in Iran. The severe disturbances which followed, encouraged Iraq to invade Iranian territory in 1980. The Iraqi forces were soon checked, but the war continued, periods of stalemate alternating with bouts of aggression. Both sides needed – and received – arms and supplies from other countries to keep the fighting going.

Other states in the Gulf of Iran were affected. In 1987, some states, such as Kuwait, resorted to having their ships 'reflagged' by the United States and Britain so that they could sail under the protection of these more powerful and influential nations. This, however, did not stop Iranian attacks on their shipping, nor did it halt the mining of the Gulf waters by Iranian vessels.

1981
Flight of the Space Shuttle

On 12 April, 1981, the US space shuttle, *Columbia*, crewed by two men, made its first flight into space – and back. This project had been in progress since 1972 and at this date had cost about ten billion dollars. The craft took off vertically like a conventional rocket and, after two days in orbit around the Earth, glided down to land at a base in California like an ordinary aircraft. It thus became the first reusable spaceship and made a number of subsequent flights, carrying out a variety of scientific experiments (including some proposed by schoolchildren). A second shuttle vehicle *Challenger*, was launched in 1983. In 1986, *Challenger* met with disaster when it blew up after launch, killing all on board.

1982
End of Brezhnev era

The Soviet leader, Leonid Brezhnev (1906–82) had been in poor health for years before he died on 10 November. His death was not announced until some days later, and on 16 November his successor was named as Yuri Andropov (1914–84), an elderly member of the Politburo (roughly equivalent to the British Cabinet) who was himself in less than perfect health. His background included a long spell as chief of the KGB, the Soviet security organization, or secret police. No major changes in policy, foreign or domestic, were promised, and none occurred. Andropov died on 9 February 1984.

1982
Battle for the Falklands

The Falkland Islands are a group of small, cold, barren islands in the South Atlantic. The population, mainly British, is very small (under 2,000 in 1982) and the land is good for little except sheep. Though under British rule since 1833, the islands are also claimed by Argentina, a claim inherited from Spain when Argentina became independent in the early 19th century. Anglo-Argentine discussions had been held at intervals, but agreement foundered on the determination of the islanders to remain British.

In April 1982 Argentina took the islands by a surprise attack. Though condemned by the UN, the military government of Argentina refused to withdraw unless Argentine sovereignty was acknowledged by Britain. The British, having made no progress by negotiation, sent a powerful force which, after a short, sharp campaign, forced the occupying Argentines to surrender. Besides men killed – about 300 on the Argentine cruiser *General Belgrano*, (sunk by a British submarine), alone – Argentina lost many aircraft and Britain several ships, which proved vulnerable to airborne missiles.

1982
War in Lebanon

For many years Lebanon had led a fragile existence, torn by warring Christian and Moslem factions and threatened with partition between Syria and Israel. After the Six-Day War (*see 1967 The Six-Day War*) Lebanon became the main base for the PLO (Palestine Liberation Organization) and other Palestine guerrilla groups opposed to the state of Israel. Bitter civil war in 1975–76, in which the once-prosperous capital, Beirut, was virtually ruined, faded into more sporadic violence. The Israelis temporarily took over the south in 1978, later handing it over to a friendly Lebanese Christian group. However, they were increasingly concerned by the build-up of PLO forces, and in 1982 they invaded the country and advanced on Beirut, where they encircled the PLO strongholds. The PLO, trapped, were forced to agree to withdraw to other Arab lands, farther from Israel's borders. After the soldiers had left, a large number of Palestinian civilians in the Beirut camps were massacred by Christian Lebanese groups in revenge for the assassination of the (Christian) Lebanese president. This outrage was especially shocking because the area was under Israeli military control at the time.

Following pages: the world's worst nuclear disaster at Chernobyl in the Ukraine, April 26 1986. This had at least the effect of awakening international consciousness to the horrors of nuclear accidents. The picture shows the damaged reactor from the air.

1983
Martial Law ends in Poland

Poland is one of those unfortunate countries with a system of government that is disliked by a majority of the people. It is a Communist state, but most Poles are devout Roman Catholics; it is under the domination of the Soviet Union, but the Russians are the traditional enemies of the Poles.

A movement for a free trade union (i.e. one not controlled by Communist party officials), known as Solidarity, had achieved widespread popularity and some power by 1981. Regarded as dangerously liberal, it was suppressed by the Polish government, and martial law was declared in December 1981. Following the visit of the Pope in 1983, martial law was lifted, though restrictive laws were introduced and Solidarity remained a banned organization.

1984
Assassination of Indian prime minister

On October 30, 1984, Mrs Indira Gandhi (1917–84), the Indian prime minister was killed in New Delhi by two members of her own bodyguard. The assassins were Sikhs, members of a religious group in India which had long been discontented with Mrs Gandhi's government. Earlier in 1984, Indian army forces had attacked the Sikhs' Golden Temple at Amritsar and important Sikh leaders had been killed. Mrs Gandhi's murder was revenge for this attack, but in India and elsewhere her violent death provoked sympathy and anger. She was succeeded as prime minister by her son, Rajiv (b. 1944).

1985
Football match tragedy

On May 29, 1985, violent crowd disturbances caused tragedy at the Heysel Stadium in Brussels, during the final of the European Cup football competition, between Juventus of Turin and Liverpool Football Club. Over four hundred people were injured and thirty-nine killed when a side wall collapsed as Juventus fans were chased by Liverpool supporters. Afterwards, the European Union of Football Associations (UEFA) placed a complete ban on English clubs playing matches in Europe, and several Liverpool supporters were arrested for trial in Brussels for their part in the violence.

1986
The world's worst nuclear accident

On April 26, 1986, explosions and fire occurred in one of the four nuclear reactors at Chernobyl near Kiev in the Ukraine (south-western USSR). Very high amounts of radiation were thrown into the atmosphere and during the two weeks it took to bring the fire under control, it was feared that there would be a 'meltdown' of the reactor's radioactive core. Although this did not happen, the accident at Chernobyl still had very serious effects. Nearly three hundred people were injured and twenty-four killed and one hundred thousand people within a 30 kilometre radius of Chernobyl had to leave their homes. An unknown, but probably very high, number of others were contaminated by radiation.

Radiation particles carried by the wind and rain drifted over into other countries, such as Poland, Romania, Britain, Israel and even Japan and the United States of America. Here, grassland and earth were 'poisoned'.

The manager of the nuclear plant and some of his assistants were blamed for the accident and at their trial were punished with heavy prison sentences.

1986
Revolution in the Philippines

In 1986, President Ferdinand Marcos had ruled the Philippines for twenty-one years and his government was much disliked for its corruption and inefficiency. Marcos and his wife Imelda were suspected of sending large sums of money overseas, buying expensive properties abroad and living a life of luxury while the people of the Philippines suffered unemployment and poverty.

When elections were held on February 7, 1986, Marcos was opposed by Mrs Cory Aquino whose husband, Benigno had been Marcos's fiercest opponent. Benigno Aquino had been murdered at Manila Airport in 1983 and Marcos, it was suspected, had been involved. Marcos won the election, but Mrs Aquino's supporters protested that he had 'rigged' the vote in his own favour. Protests and demonstrations became violent, some of Marcos's own ministers turned against him and the United States, to whom he appealed for help, refused to support him.

Marcos and his wife were forced to leave the Philippines and go into exile, and Mrs Aquino then became president in his place.

1987
Death of Rudolf Hess

On August 17, 1987, Rudolf Hess, formerly Deputy Leader of the Nazi party in Germany, died at Spandau Prison in Berlin, where he had been detained since the Nuremberg Trials of Nazi leaders (1945–47). Hess was ninety-three and had been the only prisoner in Spandau since 1966. Afterwards it was revealed that he had committed suicide by strangling himself with an electrical cord.

Hess's death aroused great feelings, especially among neo-Nazi groups and there were several clashes between demonstrators and police. Because of the risk of further unrest, plans to bury Hess in the family grave at Wundsiedel, Bavaria, had to be changed. Instead, Hess's body was buried in a secret location on or around August 24.

Now that Spandau was empty, it was announced that it would be totally destroyed to prevent it becoming a Nazi shrine and a supermarket for servicemen and their families would be built on the site.

1987
Nuclear weapons banned

On December 8, 1987, the most important international treaty ever made was signed in Washington, the US capital between the American President, Ronald Reagan and the Russian leader Mikhail Gorbachev. For over forty years, the great world power rivals, the USA and Russia, had possessed nuclear weapons which were capable of destroying the world. In the 1987 treaty, nuclear weapons were not completely banned, something which many people had long desired, but the two sides made a start by agreeing to give up their shorter and medium range nuclear missiles. This was the first time in history that two rival nations had come together to get rid of an entire class of armaments. Plans were also made for a further disarmament treaty in 1988. According to British prime minister, Margaret Thatcher, the treaty was 'A wonderful Christmas present for the world'.

Mikhail Gorbachev speaks at the meeting ceremony with President Reagan at the White House.

Index

Photographic Acknowledgements

Alte Pinakothek Munich 75; Bell Helicopter Textron 311; BBC Hulton Picture Library, London 308, 317; British Aerospace, Bristol 336; Chicago Historical Society 244–5; Mary Evans Picture Library, London 211, 219; Glaxo Laboratories Ltd 283 bottom; The Keystone Collection, London 270, 306, 340–1; The Mansell Collection, London 228; reproduced by courtesy of the Trustees, NASA Washington DC 328–9, 332; The National Gallery, London 128, 179, 235; The National Maritime Museum, London 154; The National Museums of Scotland, Edinburgh 140; Novosti Press Agency, London 343; Octopus Publishing Group, London 58, 176, 191, 223, 242, 281, 294 (photographed at the Tate Gallery, London); Octopus/Hawkley Studio Associates 116–17 (by courtesy of the Worshipful Society of Apothecaries, London); Octopus/Raymond Laniepce 186–7 (photographed at the Louvre, Paris); Octopus/Constantino Reyes-Valerio 53; Prensa Latina Servicia Fotografica 320; Reed Business Publishing, Sutton 256–7; Roger-Viollet, Paris 246; Gustav Schwarz, Mannheim 214–15 (photographed at the Städtische Kunsthalle Mannheim): Spanish Army Ministry, Madrid 289; The Tate Gallery, London 164; Judy Todd, London 34; US Navy, Washington 298–9.